CAVIAR AND SAUSAGES

ARSENAL IN THE TIME OF WENGER

TONY KOKKINOS

ANGEL INK

Dedicated to my Dad for taking me to my first Arsenal games at Highbury, the 1979 FA Cup Final, and hundreds of games from Highbury to Hackney Marshes.

Published by Angel Ink. The Angel logo is a trademark of Angel Ink.

FIRST EDITION

First published in Great Britain 2021

A catalogue record for this book is available from the British Library.

ISBN: 978-1-8384127-0-8 (printed); 978-1-8384127-1-5 (ebook)

Acknowledgements

Cover design by Ken Leeder (www.kenleederdesign.co.uk). Thanks Ken for a great Wenger drawing and a cool-looking cover.

Edited by Ryan Wells. Thanks to Ryan Wells for invaluable editing insights and feedback, encouragement to keep writing and publish my first book, and learning far more about Arsenal than he ever wanted to know.

Special thanks to Erika De Mello for extra graphic design help, and Brendan Donaghy for an incredibly-thorough proofreading job and offering excellent advice and suggestions.

1996 — 2018

CONTENTS

GRAPHICS

ICONS

	WITTY			GREAT FOOTBALL
	VEGETABLES			INVESTIGATIONS, FINES, BANS
	BOASTFUL			RED CARD
	INTELLIGENT			CLASSIC GOAL
	PHILOSOPHICAL			DIVE
	FIGHTING TALK/AGGRO			PIZZA
	LET'S BE FRIENDS/DEAL			WIND-UP
	MIC DROP			STUPID
	DIRTY			ANGRY

The Wenger Era in Three Stages

Arsène Wenger's 22 years at Arsenal are often split into the trophy-laden years up to 2005 and the barren years after. In Stage One, his innovative methods, in terms of both coaching and lifestyle, unsurpassed knowledge of footballers around the world and eye for talent quickly turned Arsenal into serial Premier League and FA Cup winners while playing breath-taking attacking football.

The post-2005 years are more accurately divided into two parts – Stage Two in 2005-2013 and Stage Three in 2013-2018. In Stage Two, there is some context to the lack of trophies as Arsenal had to fund the new stadium and oil-rich rivals came in the shape of Chelsea and then Man City. During this time, the media constantly reminded everyone of the number of years since Arsenal had won a trophy (something other 'big clubs' like Spurs and Everton never faced despite their much longer dry spells), enthusiastically adding another year when Arsenal's season faltered, often around February or March.

Wenger had raised expectations in Stage One to his detriment in Stage Two. He was managing under financial constraints and Arsenal could not pay top dollar for established players like their rivals could. They played the long game, paying off the new stadium debt while – with the benefit of hindsight mistakenly – putting their faith in the UEFA Financial Fair Play Regulations. At times, most notably in 2007/08, the Wengerball was as good as it was during Stage One. Later, given some of the sides Arsenal fielded, getting into the Champions League every year was actually an impressive achievement.

However, the strategy to prioritise a top-four finish (Wenger's 2012 statement that "The first trophy is to finish in the top four" was a sign of the lowered expectations) often meant Arsenal missed opportunities in the cups to get the trophy monkey off their back – for example, the mistake to bench Andrey Arshavin in the 2009 FA Cup semi-final versus Chelsea then see him fire four brilliant finishes in an ultimately meaningless league game at Anfield a few days later. On the other hand, the 2011 League Cup loss to relegated Birmingham was a choke with no excuses.

When the financial shackles came off in Stage Three (signified by the £42m signing of Mesut Özil in 2013), Arsenal still could not mount a serious league challenge and still got dumped out of the Champions League in the first knockout round. Despite the fun days out at Wembley, the three FA Cups in four years did not hide that Wenger had let things drift. His once-innovative methods had been overtaken, he had lost his touch in the transfer market and was now buying expensive misfits instead of unearthing gems, and he did not give his coaching staff more power to address obvious tactical faults, particularly defensively, as Alex Ferguson did throughout his Man Utd reign. Fifth and sixth place league finishes in the last two seasons confirmed the decline.

	Stage One: The Glory Years	Stage Two: The Austerity Years	Stage Three: The Stagnating Years
Years	1996-2005	2005-2013	2013-2018
In brief	Arsène Knows	In Arsène We Trust	More Money, More Problems
League position	1-2 (1.5 average)*	3-4 (3.5 average)	2-6 (3.5 average)
Trophy cabinet	98 02 04 98 02 03 05 / 98 99 02 04		14 15 17 / 14 15 17
Ones that got away	99 99 00 01 03 04	06 07 08 11	16 18
Wengerball	• Direct, electric one- and two-touch attacking football • High-speed passing and pacey ball-carriers enabled rapid transitions and clinical counter-attacks • Solid goalkeeper and defence meant Arsenal could grind out wins • Extended the careers of the Famous Back Four, then built a tough replacement back-line • Strong squads with a world-class spine and quality backups • Could take on all-comers	• Barcelona-lite *tiki taka* • Short quick passing, intricate triangles, intelligent movement, interchange of midfield and attacking positions • Sweeping counter-attacks • Often attractive football, but sometimes ineffective 'tippy-tappy' • Poor goalkeeper and weak defence meant opposition teams always had a chance • One or two world-class players, lightweight spine • Consistently dispatched lower-table teams, especially at home, but bad record against top teams	• Narrow possession-based passing game relying on surgical precision to cut through defences • Memorable moments, but often horseshoe-shaped passing patterns with little thrust or pace • Easily picked off on the counter-attack with full-backs high up the pitch and the midfield vacated • Poor goalkeeper and weak defence meant opposition teams always had a chance • One or two world-class players, lightweight spine • Usually dispatched lower-table teams, especially at home, but bad record against top teams
Formation	4-4-2	4-4-2 to 4-3-3 to 4-2-3-1	4-2-3-1
Typical player	• Fast, technical highly-conditioned athletes at their peak • Tall, strong centre-midfielders, pacey attacking full-backs and wide players • Strong characters with winning mentality; fight	• Nippy, technical, mobile, small, lightweight, young • Stockpiled short, tricky playmakers • Too few players with winning mentality; flight	• No clear pattern – usually technical, often lacked speed • Big one-paced man upfront • Too few players with winning mentality; flight

	Stage One: The Glory Years	Stage Two: The Austerity Years	Stage Three: The Stagnating Years
Transfer strategy	• Inside knowledge of a golden era for French talent • Bought unheralded players and turned them into stars or revived talented players' careers • Successfully converted players to different positions • Sold some stars at a big profit but easily found replacements and Arsenal generally saw their best years • Estimated net spend £50m	• Recruited quality players, often from France, but at a reduced success rate as every club was scouting the world for the best young players • Broke up the Invincibles too quickly • Could not keep the best players, who often won trophies elsewhere – Project Youth was born and Wenger kept having to rebuild • 'Socialist' wage structure rewarded underperforming players who outstayed their welcome • Estimated net income £30m	• The signings of Özil and Alexis Sánchez ended the austerity days and Arsenal spent big as transfer fees went crazy • Poor scouting and increasing reliance on *Moneyball*-style analytics produced some expensive flops and uninspiring squad fillers • Failed to achieve significant selling fees due to indecision, poor contract negotiations and high salaries • Bought no outfield player in summer 2015 then blew £90m on misfits the following year • Estimated net spend £190m
Legacy	• Three titles, four FA Cups, two Doubles and one Invincibles season • Arsenal's most successful era since the 1930s • Between 2001-04, Arsenal's best-ever team, winning four of the six main domestic trophies • Transformed the club from "boring boring Arsenal" to one known for playing attacking football, winning a generation of fans from France to Nigeria • Revolutionised English football • Some of Arsenal's, and English football's, best-ever players • Challenged Man Utd's status at the top of English football • No European trophy and no back-to-back titles	• Nine-year trophy drought • A new sold-out 60,000 stadium • Memorable run to Arsenal's first-ever Champions League Final, but left to rue being 14 minutes from glory • Entertaining football played by a vibrant young team • Perennially two or three quality players away from a winning squad as weak mentality, poor game management and lack of quality cover meant Arsenal could not prolong a league challenge and the season would often fade away around February-March • A series of third- and fourth-place finishes and Champions League football year after year	• Three FA Cup wins in four years • Three humiliating 5-1 defeats against Bayern Munich underlined Arsenal's second-tier status in Europe • An unbalanced squad with a huge wage bill and few sellable assets • Wenger's sad decline tarnished his legacy to some degree as Arsenal never mounted a serious league challenge, kept losing big games and became a Europa League club

*Excludes the outlier year of 1996-97 when Arsenal finished third as not a full Wenger season.

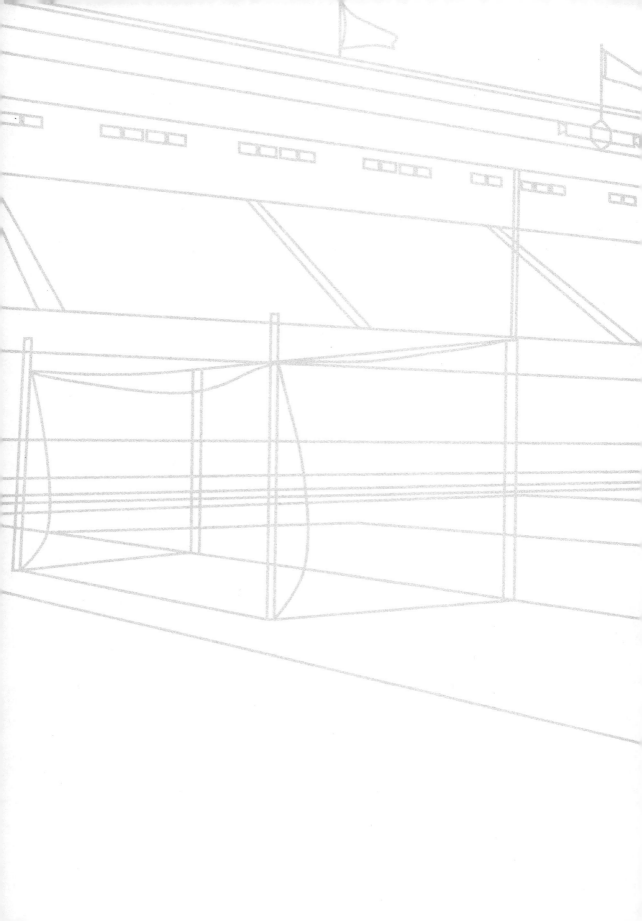

1996/97
ARSÈNE WHO?

Premier League	Third
FA Cup	Fourth round
UEFA Cup	First round
League Cup	Fourth round

PREMIER LEAGUE		PL	W	D	L	GF	GA	GD	PTS
1	MAN UTD	38	21	12	5	76	44	32	75
2	NEWCASTLE	38	19	11	8	73	40	33	68
3	ARSENAL	38	19	11	8	62	32	30	68
4	LIVERPOOL	38	19	11	8	62	37	25	68
5	ASTON VILLA	38	17	10	11	47	34	13	61
6	CHELSEA	38	16	11	11	58	55	3	59

Highlights: 3-1 win versus Spurs; Patrick Vieira immediately showing he was special on his debut against Sheffield Wednesday; ten-man win at Newcastle; introduction of Wengerball and renaissance of the Famous Back Four

Lowlights: Losing twice to champions Man Utd and poor record versus top teams; going out of UEFA Cup in the first round to Borussia Mönchengladbach

Player of the year: A rejuvenated Ian Wright guaranteed goals, energy and aggression, and was the main beneficiary of the transition to flowing football

Top scorers: Wright 30 (23 in PL), Dennis Bergkamp 14 (12)

Goal of the season: Bergkamp's classic left-foot control, right-foot finish versus Spurs, Highbury, Premier League

"Arsène Who?" ran the *Evening Standard's* infamous headline when Arsène Wenger was officially announced as Arsenal's 19th manager on 22 September 1996. Bruce Rioch had been sacked only five days before the start of the season after disagreements with the board (and a bad relationship in particular with vice-chairman David Dein) and there had been talk of Dutch legend Johann Cruyff or former England, Barcelona and Spurs manager Terry Venables taking over.

Instead, Arsenal announced that Wenger would officially take charge on 1 October once he was released from his current contract – the press, fans and English game in general were suspicious of foreigners and the manager of Nagoya Grampus Eight in Japan was met with derision by many. Chelsea manager Ruud Gullit was the only other non-British coach at the time and Aston Villa's Dr Josef Venglos (welcomed as "Dr Who?" in 1990) had left after one season, narrowly avoiding relegation.

Wenger was not an unknown in Europe having managed Monaco to the 1987/88 Ligue 1 title, 1990/91 Coupe de France and 1993/94 Champions League semi-final. He was highly spoken of by his ex-players such as Glenn Hoddle and 1995 World Player of the Year George Weah. However, no one expected him to make such an impact on the club or English football.

In a story fitting of the days when Arsenal were still known as the Bank of England club, Dein had met the then-Monaco manager in the cocktail lounge at Highbury in 1989 and invited him to dinner that night, where they played charades. Dein later recalled, "I thought 'This guy's something special, he's a bit different'." Dein remained in touch with Wenger and kept an eye on his career. He pushed for him to replace George Graham in 1995 but the board was too conservative. In 1996 he pushed harder.

Rioch had managed Arsenal to fifth place in his only year in charge, adding marquee signings Dennis Bergkamp and David Platt to goalscoring machine Ian Wright, quality but troubled Paul Merson, a legendary yet ageing defence and a host of squad fillers.

A seminal moment for the start of Wenger's reign came in a Monday night game on 16 September 1996 versus Sheffield Wednesday in front of Highbury's lowest attendance of the season. Wenger appeared on the Jumbotron big screen offering fans a message of reassurance, but what followed gave the unknown manager instant credibility. Patrick Vieira, signed the previous month along with fellow Frenchman Rémi Garde on Wenger's directive, came on after a low-quality 28 minutes with Arsenal 1-0 down. The crowd soon took note as Vieira made an immediate impact.

Tall (6'4"), strong, pacey with a long stride, the elegant 21-year-old could play and always looked to drive or pass forward. Like Bergkamp, he made his teammates better as he was always available for a pass and had the skill to take the ball in traffic and come away with it. He quickly became a crowd favourite with his famous song echoing around the ground: "He comes from Senegal, he plays for Arsenal." Wright was in heaven and scored a hat-trick as the game ended 4-1.

It wasn't just the fans that Wenger had to win over. "What does this Frenchman know about football?", club captain Tony Adams wrote in his autobiography. "He wears glasses and looks more like a schoolteacher. Does he even speak English properly?" Lee Dixon recalls Wenger's first training session: "The players filed in and in front of us stood this tall, slightly built man who gave no impression whatsoever of being a football manager." However, Wenger won over the players (who nicknamed him Inspector Clouseau due to his clumsy nature, while Adams said his sense of humour helped build team spirit: "Not only does Wenger love a good laugh, but he can laugh at himself.") and famously extended the careers of many of the ageing squad with his innovative approach to:

- Diet – out went Mars Bars, ketchup and sugar; in came steamed fish, boiled chicken, pasta and vegetables.

TYPICAL LINE-UP
(3-4-1-2 TO 4-4-2)

8 Wright / Hartson
10 Bergkamp

9 Merson

4 Vieira / Hughes / Morrow
7 Platt / Parlour / Garde

3 Winterburn
2 Dixon

5 Bould / Linighan
14 Keown / Marshall
6 Adams

1 Seaman / Lukic

Players in: Rémi Garde, Patrick Vieira, *Nicolas Anelka*

Players out: *Paul Dickov, Eddie McGoldrick, David Hillier, John Hartson, Andy Linighan, Steve Morrow*

NB: Players in italics moved during the season. See Notes & Glossary for more details.

- Alcohol – he ended the drinking culture and the Tuesday Drinking Club famous in the Graham years. He stuck by Adams in particular who, following a seven-week bender after England lost on penalties to Germany in Euro 96, told the team he was seeking help for a drinking problem and was attending Alcoholics Anonymous. Merson had admitted to alcohol, cocaine and gambling problems only two years earlier.

- Training – short sharp sessions timed to the second, always involving footballs and not hours of running like the English tradition.

- Conditioning – Wenger introduced plyometrics (exercises designed to strengthen muscles), implemented extensive stretches before and after matches, and brought in the French team's osteopath to realign the players' bodies each month.

- Teeth – he sent players for dental check-ups in the belief that the alignment of wisdom teeth caused Achilles tendon and muscle injuries.

- Until 2004, he encouraged his players to take Creatine for increased stamina, later stopping when he noticed side-effects.

RED MIST

Arsenal quickly got a reputation for ill-discipline and the media kept an ongoing tally of players sent off under Wenger – the final total was 118, half of which came in Stage One. It was a huge number for any side, but completely at odds with a team and manager that always tried to play football and campaigned against injury-threatening fouls. However, in Stage One, they also had players that could look after themselves or let their frustration get the better of them. In Stage Two and Three, the offences were usually last-man fouls or retaliation to more aggressive provocation.

When Wenger took charge of his first game against Blackburn Rovers, Arsenal had had a decent start under two caretaker managers – Stewart Houston (who became QPR manager after being rejected for the Arsenal job) and Pat Rice – leaving them in second place in the league but knocked out of the UEFA Cup in the first round by Borussia Mönchengladbach, losing both games 3-2. Wright buried two sublime finishes in a 2-0 win against Blackburn and made more headlines in the next game against Coventry, breaking Steve Ogrizovic's nose with his knee after the goalkeeper had held him back ("It was just a melee... Oggy's had a bit of cosmetic surgery which has improved his looks," Coventry manager Ron Atkinson joked). Arsenal ended October level on points at the top of the table with Newcastle after a 3-0 win versus Leeds in George Graham's first managerial return to Highbury.

Soon after joining, Wenger was also the subject of vicious and false rumours made up by a Spurs fan working in the City. The press knew they could not print them but sensed blood. On 7 November, Wenger showed he was not to be messed with and confronted them on the steps of Highbury: "If someone has something to say about me, they should come and say it. I don't know of any allegations but there are three things you should know. One is that I am very happy at Arsenal, two that we are doing very well, and three that there is nothing true I need fear. If anything is said about me that is not right, I will attack."

Back on the pitch, a Nigel Winterburn own-goal after David Seaman had made a mess of a bouncing back-pass meant a much-needed 1-0 win for Man Utd at Old Trafford. Peter Schmeichel was accused of racially abusing Wright, triggering a police investigation that resulted in no charges being pressed. Then came Spurs as Wenger began years of dominance of the North London rivals. Highbury was rocking late on after Adams scored an impressive left-footed volley off a

Bergkamp flick followed by a classic from the Dutchman – shaping to volley a high cross from Wright (who had just pulled off an outrageous dummy to make a fool of Spurs left-back Clive Wilson) with his left foot, he instead cushioned the ball perfectly and swept it home with his right. This was followed by a battling 2-1 win with ten men at title rivals Newcastle after Adams was sent off for a last-man foul on Alan Shearer, Wright setting up Dixon for a diving header before poaching the winner.

Arsenal were top of the league in early December before they went on a poor run. They drew three times and lost to Nottingham Forest without Seaman, Dixon, Adams and Vieira, again playing with ten men after Wright was dismissed. Bergkamp's sending off for a foul in a loss to Sunderland was Arsenal's fifth red in ten games, and the suspensions to key players started to tell. Reacting to criticism about the players' discipline, Wenger said, "The other strange fact is that three out of five dismissals have been strikers, when that sort of thing normally happens to defenders. To me, that shows our strikers must be taking their fair share of kicks. When teams play Arsenal, the games are physical and we have to defend ourselves."

After draws against Leeds and Spurs, the Arsenal-Man Utd rivalry from the

PLAYER, CAPTAIN, COACH, MANAGER

Pat Rice's 75% win rate as manager (three wins from four games) is the highest in Arsenal history. It is also the shortest tenure at two weeks, three days (13-30 September 1996). The Arsenal legend spent 13 years as an Arsenal player (three of which as captain), 12 as youth-team coach and 16 as assistant manager.

George Graham days was reignited. Wright and Schmeichel went in for a 50-50 that actually burst the ball and Wright later went in two-footed on the goalkeeper but got away with another red card. After the game, which Man Utd won 2-1, the police separated the pair and the FA got involved. In April, both clubs released statements to end the feud (a ceasefire that did not last long). After a home loss to Wimbledon and no wins in February, any title bid was over and Arsenal were playing for a European qualification spot.

In March, Arsenal suffered a 2-1 home defeat to Liverpool that was notable for Robbie Fowler winning a penalty and telling the referee Seaman had not touched him. Fowler guiltily took a weak penalty that Seaman saved but Jason McAteer had no such qualms and netted the rebound. However, victories against Chelsea (3-0) and Leicester (2-0) meant five wins in six.

The Blackburn game saw more controversy as their late equaliser came after Chris Sutton forced a corner after Vieira had kicked the ball out of play for an injury, instead of letting Arsenal have the ball from the restart. A 1-0 loss at Newcastle (meaning Arsenal lost five out of six games to their top-four rivals) and final day 3-1 win at Derby (again with ten men as Adams got his second red of the season but featuring a trademark Bergkamp chip) meant a third-place finish behind Newcastle on goal difference.

Just missing out on a Champions League place (in the days when only the top two qualified), adoption of a more exciting style of play under Wenger, and a strong spine in Seaman, Adams, Vieira and Bergkamp meant a transitional season ended with the fans optimistic.

1997/98
THE DOUBLE

Premier League	Winners
FA Cup	Winners
UEFA Cup	First round
League Cup	Semi-final

PREMIER LEAGUE		PL	W	D	L	GF	GA	GD	PTS
1	ARSENAL	38	23	9	6	68	33	35	78
2	MAN UTD	38	23	8	7	73	26	47	77
3	LIVERPOOL	38	18	11	9	68	42	26	65
4	CHELSEA	38	20	3	15	71	43	28	63
5	LEEDS	38	17	8	13	57	46	11	59
6	BLACKBURN ROVERS	38	16	10	12	57	52	5	58

Highlights: Tony Adams sealing the title in front of the North Bank; famous 1-0 win at Old Trafford; clinching the Double at Wembley; Dennis Bergkamp's hat-trick versus Leicester; Ian Wright breaking the club's goals record

Lowlights: November-December slump with defeats to Sheffield Wednesday, Liverpool and Blackburn; League Cup semi-final loss to Chelsea

Player of the year: Bergkamp was the best player in the league winning both the PFA Players' Player of the Year and FWA Footballer of the Year

Top scorers: Bergkamp 22 (16 in PL), Marc Overmars 16 (12), Wright 11 (10), Nicolas Anelka 9 (6)

Goal of the season: Bergkamp's third versus Leicester, Filbert Street, Premier League

Saturday, 14 March 1998, Old Trafford: 79 minutes in, Arsenal have been the better team but the game is goalless. Martin Keown has the ball right of centre inside his own half with nothing on. He hits a long diagonal punt, where Dennis Bergkamp and Nicolas Anelka surprisingly win successive headers. Marc Overmars puts on the afterburners, leaving Man Utd defenders in his slipstream as he had done all game, heads it on and sidefoots it left-footed through Peter Schmeichel's legs.

It was the first time Arsenal had scored at Old Trafford in the Premier League. It was also the moment that changed everything for Arsenal and Arsène Wenger – they had arrived and shown they would challenge Man Utd's dominance of English football. It put them six points behind Man Utd with three games in hand, but with difficult away games to come. Alex Ferguson said, "We'll see how they stand up to pressure now." See, he did.

But this was no smash and grab. Arsenal, without Ian Wright and David Seaman, went to the home of the Champions, who were missing Roy Keane and Ryan Giggs, and matched them physically while playing the attacking, passing football Wenger had instilled. Tony Adams and Martin Keown stood firm, Ray Parlour, Patrick Vieira and Emmanuel Petit were immense in midfield, and Alex Manninger saved one-on-ones from Teddy Sheringham and Andy Cole (the latter given a run-in on goal despite being clearly offside).

Man-of-the-match Overmars tormented right-back John Curtis, and neither of his second-half Neville brother replacements fared any better. The Flying Dutchman went close a few times and should have had a penalty as Curtis tripped him as he cut in on goal. He eventually had his moment, topping it off with a nonchalant stand-still celebration to allow everyone to take in the significance of the blow he had just landed.

Arsenal fans took pleasure in seeing Schmeichel limping back to his goal with a torn hamstring after coming up for a corner in the dying moments, even having a shot blocked. With no substitutions left, he had to carry on and was symbolically helped off the pitch at the end.

The celebrations at the final whistle showed that players and fans alike believed the title was on – none more so than a curly-haired Gooner in a black leather jacket going crazy. Barry Ferst became a celebrity among fans after Sky cameras zoomed in on his wild outpouring of elation, the *Gooner* fanzine's picture appropriately captioned, "This Is What It Meant".

While Arsenal were clearly on the rise under Wenger, no one expected their 100th season of competitive football to be so successful and end with the club's second Double, only the eighth in English football. During summer

1997, Wenger made eight signings (seven from abroad) as he continued to overhaul the squad. Two of these proved inspired – Petit and Overmars.

Petit was signed from Wenger's former club Monaco where he had converted him from a left-back to centre-midfielder. The French international had been in talks with Spurs and when they paid for his taxi afterwards, they did not know his destination was a meeting with Wenger and David Dein. He made an impression at the announcement of his signing in a light-blue *Miami Vice* suit and blonde ponytail. Petit formed a perfect left-foot, right-foot partnership with Vieira. Both were tall and strong tacklers. Vieira was more dynamic, covering more ground with or without the ball, and preferring to make shorter passes. Petit had a wider passing range, in particular lofting balls over or inside right-backs for Overmars to speed on to.

Overmars was already known across Europe as a quality Dutch international yet there were doubts whether he had recovered fully from a torn cruciate ligament. He officially played left-midfield in a 4-4-2 formation, but his defensive duties were limited and he was given free rein to launch counter-attacks or run on to Bergkamp or Petit passes covered by Vieira's athleticism as well as the energy and awareness of Petit and Parlour. He had roadrunner pace and was an efficient finisher – rarely trying to blast a shot, instead hitting it firmly and low. Like Petit,

TYPICAL LINE-UP (4-4-2)

8 Wright / Anelka
10 Bergkamp / Wreh
11 Overmars / Boa Morte
17 Petit / Hughes
4 Vieira / Platt
15 Parlour
3 Winterburn / Upson
6 Adams / Grimandi
14 Keown / Bould
2 Dixon / Grimandi Garde
1 Seaman / Manninger

Players in: Matthew Upson, Gilles Grimandi, Luís Boa Morte, Alberto Méndez, Marc Overmars, Emmanuel Petit, Alex Manninger, Christopher Wreh

Players out: Paul Merson, *Ian Selley, Glenn Helder*

he got better as the season went on, scoring crucial goals in big games such as at Old Trafford and in the FA Cup Final.

Surprisingly, fan favourite Paul Merson (stuck on 99 Arsenal goals in all competitions) went to relegated Middlesbrough for £4.5m, making him the most expensive player ever signed by a non-Premiership club. The 29-year-old subsequently said he accepted a longer contract than Arsenal offered, though Arsenal seemed happy with the transfer fee and incoming replacements. Middlesbrough also paid Merson's brother £400 a week to keep him company. "He was devastated when I left," Merson joked. No one begrudged him his goal when the two clubs met in the FA Cup fourth round, which Arsenal won 2-1.

Arsenal started the 1997/98 season in good form, going 12 games unbeaten in the league. Bergkamp and Wright in particular were on fire – the former winning Premier League Player of the Month for both August and September, the latter on a mission to beat Cliff Bastin's Arsenal record of 178 goals.

Wright scored in the opening 1-1 draw at Leeds and got both goals only two days later in a home win over Coventry. Bergkamp made his mark in the 3-1 win at Southampton – first running 40 yards with the ball before sidefooting

home, then hitting a piledriver from the edge of the area into the top corner after shrugging off defender Francis Benali's attempted wrestling move. Overmars had earlier got off the mark after beating two defenders.

At Leicester, Bergkamp produced one of the best hat-tricks ever seen: (1) the classic Bergkamp Curler, right-footed from just outside the box, left of centre, into the top-right corner; (2) after cushioning a Vieira pass brilliantly into his stride, leaving the defence flat-footed, he toed it over Kasey Keller's dive (the only imperfection in the three goals being that the goalkeeper got a touch that slowed its progress into the net); and (3) saving the best for last, he pulled a 40-yard David Platt ball out of the air, juggled it to beat defender Matt Elliott and, finally letting it hit the ground, shifted it on to his right and swept it home. However, Bergkamp's magic was marred by Arsenal only earning one point – they were 2-0 up after 84 minutes and, after conceding twice in nine minutes, went 3-2 up on 94; however, Steve Walsh headed an equaliser in the sixth minute of injury time for a 3-3 draw.

After a 0-0 draw at home to Spurs, where Overmars and Wright both hit the bar, Wright's moment came in a 4-1 win over Bolton in front of a jubilant Highbury crowd. He celebrated prematurely after his first goal equalled the record but a tap-in soon after gave him the chance to unveil his "179 Just done it" Nike shirt again, and a volley completed the hat-trick. Then came the first in a run of classic matches at Stamford Bridge where Arsenal always seemed to pull out something special late on. This time with the game tied at 2-2 (Bergkamp continuing his form with two well-taken goals), Nigel Winterburn strode forward and hit a 30-yard bullet into the top-right corner in the 89th minute – his first goal for over a year. 4-0 and 5-0 home demolitions of West Ham and Barnsley were notable for Bergkamp pulling the strings as well as scoring a classic Bergkamp Curler in the latter.

The only disappointment in this period was going out in the first round of the UEFA Cup to Greek club PAOK, losing 0-1 away and drawing 1-1 at home. Wenger did not seem too disappointed, later saying, "To be honest, the only European competition that really interests me is the Champions League."

October to December saw a slump with goalless draws against Crystal Palace and Aston Villa, as well as a 3-0 drubbing at Derby after Wright hit the bar with a penalty. Not good preparation for the impending arrival of Man Utd.

Anelka made his first start in the Derby game, replacing Bergkamp who began a three-game suspension for picking up five bookings. Wenger had used his insider knowledge of the French market to sign the 17-year-old prospect

HOT STUFF

Arsenal's 1998 FA Cup Final song was an inspired reworking of the Donna Summer hit *Hot Stuff* with the lyrics changed to tell the story of the season. It reached number nine in the UK charts whereas the 1979 original only made number 11. It has a five-star rating on Amazon (two reviews).

from Paris Saint-Germain in the latter half of the previous season.

The youngster announced himself with a well-struck 20-yard drive against Man Utd at Highbury which Vieira followed by drilling a cleared corner over Schmeichel and in off the bar. Ex-Spurs player Sheringham scored twice to level things in a breathless first half. Late on, Platt, who had been sidelined by the arrival of Petit, soared to head a corner over Phil Neville on the goalline for a crucial win over the Champions.

But Man Utd subsequently won six on the trot while Arsenal suffered three losses in four games to Sheffield Wednesday, Liverpool and Blackburn. This left them sixth at Christmas, 13 points back and seemingly out of title contention. The Blackburn game, when some fans strangely booed Wright because of his performance and he reacted by arguing with them from the dressing room window, was a turning point as the players had a clear-the-air meeting where Adams and company requested more protection from the midfield. Adams, who had been playing with injuries, felt he was not doing himself justice and told Wenger he needed to get his body fixed, leading to his absence for most of December and January.

At Wimbledon away, the floodlights failed and the game was abandoned one minute into the second half with the score 0-0, adding to the late-season fixture pile-up. Despite the embarrassment of Wimbledon officials and electricians, the truth was more surreal. There was a spate of floodlight failures around the time and four men linked to a Malaysian betting syndicate were later jailed for between 18 months and four years for planning to set off a circuit-breaker at a Charlton-Liverpool game using a remote control when the score was in their favour.

The 2-1 home win against Leicester on Boxing Day provided some comedy Christmas entertainment with a Steve Walsh own-goal – seemingly trying to outdo a Steve Bould hoof with an even bigger one of his own, Walsh instead volleyed it from outside his penalty box high into the air and over his goalkeeper. Seaman joined the fun by trying a mazy dribble, eventually losing

it outside his area, leaving Leicester to score into the empty net.

Importantly, this win was the start of a brilliant unbeaten run that led Arsenal to the Double. They had a great starting 11 but the unheralded squad players made critical contributions, especially in the second half of the season, as Adams, Bergkamp, Wright, Seaman and Vieira suffered long-term injuries and suspensions:

- Liberian Christopher Wreh scored crucial match-winning goals.

- 20-year-old Austrian Alex Manninger kept six successive clean sheets (and was rightly awarded a Premier League medal despite playing fewer than the ten games required at the time), figured prominently in the FA Cup and was unlucky to lose his place when Seaman was fit again.

- Gilles Grimandi filled in at centre-back, right-back, left-back and centre-midfield, notably volleying the winner versus Crystal Palace when only two of the first 11 were available.

- Stephen Hughes covered in centre-midfield, scoring both goals in the 2-0 victory over Chelsea.

- Anelka became the first-choice partner to Bergkamp in the second half of the season, with his explosive pace, strength belying his age and a thumping right foot which he employed to finish chances with early strikes.

A 2-1 win at home to Leeds in January was a confidence booster as Overmars scored two excellent finishes. A 2-2 draw at Coventry featured a Vieira red card for dissent (he was also sent off in the second leg of the League Cup semi-final versus Chelsea where Arsenal went out 4-3 on aggregate). Then came an amazing run of eight clean sheets – a then Premier League record – starting with home wins of 3-0 versus Southampton, 2-0 versus Chelsea and 1-0 versus Crystal Palace that still left Arsenal 12 points behind Man Utd at the end of February. Bookmaker Betfred called the title race over and paid out on Man Utd bets, subsequently losing £500,000. Arsenal had Manninger to thank for a goalless draw at West Ham, while Wreh's first goal, a nice sidefoot finish after an Overmars run, provided a 1-0 win at Wimbledon and set up the big showdown at Old Trafford.

After the 1-0 win in Manchester, Ferguson tried to ramp up the pressure on Arsenal who still had to win their games in hand to press home their advantage. But his attempted mind games were dealt with easily by Wenger off the pitch and the players on the pitch. "One-nil to the Arsenal" rang out again as the team got the job done in the next two games against Sheffield Wednesday (Bergkamp volleying the winner) and Bolton (with a Wreh bullet from outside the area his cousin George Weah would have been proud of). Manninger's performances were recognised as he won the Premier League Player of the Month for March.

Then Arsenal ran rampant as Stage One Wengerball clicked into place and "Boring boring Arsenal" was sung again, but this time by the Arsenal fans ironically. Wenger inherited George Graham's tough, organised but ageing defence and took their game up a level, as they became more comfortable on the ball and fitter. He added physical, fast and technical players, while Bergkamp's class, touch and vision brought it all together. His ability to receive the ball in tight situations gave confidence to the rest of the team, especially the old back four, and was key to Wenger's transformation to flowing passing football.

Anelka scored two as Arsenal beat Newcastle 3-1 at home, finally conceding after eight clean sheets. Vieira, who did not shoot from distance often, hit a 30-yard piledriver into the top corner, probably his best-ever Arsenal goal. Blackburn away in the snow was a potential banana skin but any signs of a choke were dispelled within 15 minutes as Arsenal were already 3-0 up. A brilliant performance made it 4-0 by half-time as Parlour, another Graham player that stepped up to show he was more than a hard-working battler, scored twice. Overmars, impressed with Parlour's ability to beat players on the right wing and quality on the ball, gave him the nickname the Romford Pelé. Bergkamp scored and assisted, while Anelka finished off a one-on-one in style with a dummy to sit down goalkeeper Alan Fettis.

GOAL OF THE MONTH

In August 1997, Bergkamp became the only player ever to occupy all three top spots in the BBC's Goal of the Month competition. His third at Leicester won, followed by his second in the same match, then his run and curled finish at Southampton.

This was followed by a 5-0 hammering of Wimbledon, with Petit finally scoring his first for the club, and a 2-0 win against Barnsley, who were again on the receiving end of a Bergkamp Curler. Derby at home was tense as the title got close. Arsenal won 1-0 as Petit scored a 20-yarder; however, Bergkamp went off with a hamstring injury and that was his season over, FA Cup Final included.

With three points needed from the last three games, Everton came to Highbury on a sunny day. As they were fighting to stay up, it was expected to be tricky. But an early Slaven Bilić-headed own-goal under pressure from Adams relaxed any nerves and two identical Overmars breakaways and left-foot finishes meant a tenth consecutive win was never in doubt. Unbelievably, the party got even better on 89 minutes with an iconic moment that symbolised Wenger's impact –

Bould picked up the ball on halfway, chipped over the defence, where Adams charged through, chested it down and hammered home a left-foot half-volley. The captain stood in front of the shaking North Bank with arms outstretched. He then collected the Premier League trophy, Arsenal's first title since 1991.

Arsenal lost their final two league matches as they took their foot off the pedal and rested players for the FA Cup Final, thereby misleadingly winning the league by only one point. From Christmas, Arsenal had won 48 out of 54 points from 18 games, surging to the title with ten wins in a row. A reserve team (eight changes) received a guard of honour at Anfield, while the Aston Villa game was notable for Dwight Yorke fooling Seaman with a Panenka penalty.

In the FA Cup, Arsenal, often fielding understrength teams, struggled through the early rounds. After two draws against First Division Port Vale, they won a penalty shootout with Vale's final attempt flying into orbit. Crystal Palace in the fifth round also required a replay, as did the next round against West Ham in March.

After a 1-1 draw at Highbury, Arsenal came through the replay on penalties with an excellent ten-man backs-to-the-wall performance only three days after the Old Trafford epic. Bergkamp was sent off after 33 minutes for elbowing Steve Lomas in the face. Anelka drilled a shot from outside the area but ex-Gunner John Hartson equalised on 84. Manninger was the hero making save after save, including one of the penalties. The shootout was level after five each as both Wreh's and Rémi Garde's penalties went wide. In sudden death, Adams showed them how it was done, bobbling his effort slowly down the middle as Bernard Lama dived out of the way, and Arsenal won 4-3. In the semi-final against Wolves, Wreh continued his purple patch with another neat sidefoot finish after a Vieira driving run.

In the Cup Final against Newcastle, Anelka missed a gaping goal with a header before Overmars continued his scoring run to latch on to a ball over the top from Petit and poke home. Newcastle had a spell of pressure in the second half as Alan Shearer drilled against the post after Keown stepped on the ball. But soon after, Anelka raced on to a Parlour pass and fired home hard and low. Man-of-the-match Parlour also hit the post after beating two defenders on the right wing, while fit-again Wright was frustrated not to make it onto the pitch.

The following day, 200,000 fans attended an open-top bus parade in Islington to celebrate Arsenal's second Double. In his first full season in English football, Wenger became the first non-British winner of the Premier League Manager of the Season.

Arsène Knows

"Arsenal is in a bad situation and needs a manager."

"I tried to watch the Tottenham match on television in my hotel yesterday, but I fell asleep."

September 1996

"I think in England you eat too much sugar and meat and not enough vegetables."

October 1996

"I told you last week that the race was not over when the bookmakers stopped betting. Surprise, surprise, they have started taking money again."

After beating Man Utd 1-0 at Old Trafford, March 1998

"When I first came to Arsenal, I realised the back four were all university graduates in the art of defending. As for Tony Adams, I consider him to be a doctor of defence. He is simply outstanding."

April 1999

"Nobody will finish above us in the league. It wouldn't surprise me if we were to go unbeaten for the whole of the season."

August 2002

"A football team is like a beautiful woman. When you do not tell her, she forgets she is beautiful."

December 2002

"We didn't think he would play on Sunday because he was suspended – that makes me think he has all the qualities to join Arsenal."

When signing José Antonio Reyes, January 2004

"My job is to give people who work hard all week something to enjoy on Saturdays and Wednesdays."

February 2004

"Somebody threw me a T-shirt after the trophy was presented which read 'Comical Wenger says we can go the whole season unbeaten.' I was just a season too early."

After the Invincibles celebrations at Highbury, May 2004

"I don't look at the passport of people. I look at their quality and their attitude."		After fielding a squad without an Englishman, February 2005
"They [Chelsea] are a financially doped club. They have enhancement of performances through financial resources which are unlimited. It puts pressure on the market that is not very healthy. They can go to Steven Gerrard or Rio Ferdinand and say, 'How much do you earn? We'll give you twice as much'. I don't know if there is anything we can do to stop it."		May 2005
"We do not buy superstars. We make them."		September 2007
"The biggest things in life have been achieved by people who, at the start, we would have judged crazy. And yet if they had not had these crazy ideas, the world would have been more stupid.		August 2009
"Sometimes I see it, but I say that I didn't see it to protect the players and because I could not find any rational explanation for what they did."		Wenger comes clean about his perennial "I didn't see it" defence, August 2009
"The penalty decision was Old Traffordish. We know how things work."		After losing 2-1 to Man Utd, August 2009
"You ask 100 people, 99 will say it's very bad and the 100th will be Mark Hughes."		After Emmanuel Adebayor stamped on Robin van Persie's head, September 2009
"If you have a child who is a good musician, what is your first reaction? It is to put them into a good music school, not in an average one. So why should that not happen in football?"		After FIFA president Sepp Blatter's "child slavery" comments, September 2009
"We live in a society where everybody knows everything and it looks like it is a shame to say, 'I don't know'."		December 2010

"What is unbelievable is that I am in a position where people reproach me for making a profit. The people who lose money – nobody says a word. Reproach the people who lose money."

September 2010

"When I arrive at the gates of Heaven, the Good Lord will ask 'what did you do in your life?' I will respond 'I tried to win football matches.' He will say: 'Are you certain that's all?' But, well, that's the story of my life."

October 2011

"The only moment of possible happiness is the present. The past gives regrets. And future uncertainties. Man quickly realised this and created religion. It forgives him what he has done wrong in the past and tells him not to worry about the future, as you will go to paradise."

November 2015

"It is well known the referees are protected very well like the lions in the zoo so we have to live with their decisions."

December 2016

"Have Tottenham closed the gap on Arsenal? Last time I checked, they were still four miles and 11 titles away."

On suggestions that Spurs are getting closer to Arsenal, 2015

"When you're dealing with someone who only has a pair of underpants on, if you take his underpants off, he has nothing left – he's naked. You're better off trying to find him a pair of trousers to complement him rather than change him."

On managing flair and not stifling creativity, February 2017

"After careful consideration and following discussions with the club, I feel it is the right time for me to step down at the end of the season. I am grateful for having had the privilege to serve the club for so many memorable years. I managed the club with full commitment and integrity. I want to thank the staff, the players, the directors and the fans who make this club so special. I urge our fans to stand behind the team to finish on a high. To all the Arsenal lovers, take care of the values of the club. My love and support forever."

20 April 2018

"I would like to finish in one simple sentence: I will miss you. Thank you all for having such an important part of my life, thank you all, well done."

After his last home game, 6 May 2018

1998/99
DOUBLE BYPASS

Premier League	Second
FA Cup	Semi-final
Champions League	Group stage
League Cup	Fourth round
Community Shield	Winners

PREMIER LEAGUE		PL	W	D	L	GF	GA	GD	PTS
1	MAN UTD	38	22	13	3	80	37	43	79
2	ARSENAL	38	22	12	4	59	17	42	78
3	CHELSEA	38	20	15	3	57	30	27	75
4	LEEDS	38	18	13	7	62	34	28	67
5	WEST HAM	38	16	9	13	46	53	-7	57
6	ASTON VILLA	38	15	10	13	51	46	5	55

Highlights: Consecutive 3-0 wins over Man Utd; Nwankwo Kanu's unworldly skills; the four-game reaction to the FA Cup semi-final loss that featured hammerings of Wimbledon and Middlesbrough and outclassing Spurs; Arsène Wenger offering a replay to Sheffield Utd

Lowlights: Losing epic FA Cup semi-final replay to Man Utd; losing the title at Leeds

Player of the year: Patrick Vieira dominated the midfield, tackling, driving forward and playing in the likes of Nicolas Anelka

Top scorers: Anelka 19 (17 in PL), Dennis Bergkamp 16 (12), Marc Overmars 12 (6)

Goal of the season: Kanu's flick over the defender and volley versus Spurs, White Hart Lane, Premier League

The 1998/99 team was one of Arsenal's best ever, yet they ended up with nothing to show for the brilliant football played, narrowly missing out on back-to-back Doubles. Playing Best Supporting Actor in a memorable season for English football was little consolation as arch-rivals Man Utd won a historic Treble. It was a classic season for the neutral – with the Premier League going to the final day of the season, three teams in the running for a long time (third-placed Chelsea only lost three games and finished four points off the top) and the Arsenal-Man Utd rivalry featuring in five mostly epic games.

After the brilliant Wengerball Double the previous season, Patrick Vieira and Emmanuel Petit on a high as World Cup winners with France (the former setting up his midfield partner for the third goal in the final against Brazil, sparking the *Daily Mirror* headline of "Arsenal Win the World Cup"), and a 3-0 win against Man Utd in the Community Shield (where Marc Overmars and Nicolas Anelka were again on the scoresheet at Wembley), Arsenal started the season optimistic they would defend their title.

There was concern, however, that Arsène Wenger had not reinforced the squad with established players. Only Argentine utility international Nelson Vivas came in alongside Wenger's usual gamble on young or unknown players, including Freddie Ljungberg fresh off a breakout performance for Sweden against England in their Euro 2000 qualifier win.

34-year-old Arsenal legend Ian Wright left to West Ham, finishing on 185 goals in 288 appearances despite joining just before his 28th birthday. David Platt retired. Man Utd did strengthen, buying Dwight Yorke, Jaap Stam and Jasper Blomqvist.

Arsenal's title defence got off to a lacklustre start. The Monday night opener against promoted Nottingham Forest ended in a 2-1 win as Marc Overmars raced 50 yards on a counter-attack to beat a naive high line. Dave Beasant saved the first effort but Overmars acrobatically volleyed the rebound back over him left-footed. However, this was followed by three goalless draws where neither team created many clear chances. Liverpool and Chelsea were tough places to visit but Charlton at home was points dropped. Arsenal finished the latter two with ten men, a feature of the season.

Then a 90th-minute Stephen Hughes swerving shot from 25 yards salvaged a point at Leicester in a 1-1 draw. Emile Heskey had a rampaging game and Wenger afterwards expressed his admiration: "We will still be buying a striker but unfortunately Leicester do not want to sell Heskey so we will have to go somewhere else." Things would have been very different if Heskey had been signed instead of Thierry Henry the following summer.

Like the previous season, Arsenal raised their game for the arrival of Man Utd, beating them for the fourth consecutive time and the second 3-0 in a row. Tony Adams opened the scoring with a header from a free-kick, outjumping Stam and Peter Schmeichel. David Beckham hit the post from 20 yards, then Anelka raced on to a Dennis Bergkamp ball over the top and finished the rebound after Schmeichel had saved the first effort. Early in the second half, Nicky Butt tripped Anelka as he headed towards goal and was sent off for the second time in five days. On 79 minutes, Ljungberg came on to make his debut and took only five minutes to show he would do Wright's number-eight shirt proud, lobbing the Man Utd goalkeeper.

The next game at Sheffield Wednesday was memorable for the shocking but comical Paolo Di Canio push on referee Paul Alcock. After skilfully turning two opponents in midfield, Vieira was pulled over by one of them, Wim Jonk. Vieira got up and shoved him over, which caused a melee. Di Canio and Martin Keown were prominent, with the Arsenal man unusually trying to act as peacemaker, yet getting a kick in the shin and hand in the face for his efforts.

Alcock showed Di Canio a red card, prompting the Italian to stun everyone by pushing Alcock in the chest. The

TYPICAL LINE-UP
(4-4-2)

9 Anelka

10 Bergkamp / Kanu

11 Overmars

17 Petit / Hughes

4 Vieira

15 Parlour / Ljungberg

3 Winterburn / Vivas

6 Adams

14 Keown / Bould

2 Dixon / Vivas

1 Seaman / Manninger

Players in: David Grondin, Nelson Vivas, *Freddie Ljungberg, Fabián Caballero (loan), Jermaine Pennant, Nwankwo Kanu, Kaba Diawara*

Players out: David Platt, Chris Kiwomya, Ian Wright, Scott Marshall

referee staggered back for five yards, desperately trying to regain balance like a 4am drunk before falling ungracefully. Nigel Winterburn gave Di Canio stick on his way off before recoiling when the Italian briefly threatened to turn his ire on him – a blow to the left-back's hard-man image but he quickly continued his tirade, admittedly with the linesman now in between the pair. Referee Alcock regained his composure to show Keown a red (which the FA subsequently reversed) and a smiling Vieira a yellow.

Di Canio, who got an 11-match ban in total, wrote in his autobiography: "I could push my eight-year-old daughter Ludovica that way and she wouldn't fall over. It certainly looked bizarre. My first reaction was that somebody must have been crouching behind him, like in one of those old slapstick comedies."

In terms of the football, Nigel Pressman made numerous excellent saves and was man of the match, while Manninger saved two close-range headers in the second half. However, after 89 minutes, Lee Briscoe scored a fine chip from the corner of the box to land Arsenal's first defeat of the season, and more crucial points dropped, leaving them down in tenth place at the end of September.

1998/99 was also Arsenal's first time in the Champions League and, with UEFA advertising rules lowering the Highbury capacity, the home games were held at Wembley. This meant crowds of 73,000 and the opportunity for those that could not get tickets to Highbury to go to games for as cheap as £10 – though they had to suffer long queues getting home via the inadequate public transport and late Tuesday/Wednesday nights more worthy of an away game. Arsenal took in over £1m each game and it was an early indication they could fill a larger stadium than Highbury. However, the historic stadium seemed to inspire visiting teams and the track around the bigger pitch meant Arsenal lost the Highbury intimidation factor. In most of the away fixtures, Arsenal were without Bergkamp, the Non-Flying Dutchman, due to his fear of flying.

They failed to qualify from their group, conceding crucial late goals in three games and winning only one of the three Wembley games. Coming behind Dynamo Kyiv was not a disgrace as the Ukrainian side were one of the best teams Arsenal had faced in years, going on to narrowly lose in the semi-final to Bayern Munich. Spearheaded by Andriy Shevchenko, Kyiv dominated both games. At Wembley however, Arsenal were ahead through a flying Bergkamp header from a rampaging Lee Dixon run and cross, but Oleh Luzhny cleared off the line from Overmars just before Serhiy Rebrov scored a 90th-minute equaliser. In Kyiv, the home side comfortably beat an understrength Arsenal 3-1.

However, only picking up one point from the two Lens games was disappointing as Arsenal looked good in the away match but conceded an injury-time equaliser from a poorly-defended corner. At Wembley, Arsenal strangely wore a shiny dark blue kit and, without Bergkamp, Vieira and Petit, lost 1-0, with Ray Parlour sent off late on for a frustrated kick at an opposing player.

Arsenal's league form picked up in October with a 3-0 win at home to Newcastle as Bergkamp finally got his first league goals of the season, but missed the chance of a hat-trick as his second penalty was saved. After a 1-1 draw with Southampton, there were wins against Blackburn, Coventry and Everton with Anelka scoring in five games in a row and Arsenal moved up to third behind Man Utd and leaders Aston Villa.

But then came the now-traditional November-December slump as they went out of the Champions League and League Cup. Wenger kept up his policy of playing young or fringe players in the League Cup but they suffered a record Highbury loss of 5-0 against a strong Chelsea team containing nine internationals. In the league, a 1-0 loss at Wimbledon was followed by an

THE FAMOUS BACK FIVE

Seaman, Dixon, Winterburn, Adams and Bould/Keown. Aged 32-36, the Famous Back Five were at their most resolute in 1998/99 conceding just 17 goals in 38 league games, including 23 clean sheets. Many thought they were on their last legs. However, under Wenger, they were fitter than ever and freed up to show their quality on the ball, but had not lost the organisation and thou-shall-not-pass mentality instilled under George Graham, delivering league titles to each manager seven years apart.

89th-minute Anelka finish salvaging a 1-1 draw with Middlesbrough at home. This was followed by a goalless draw at Derby. The lack of goals was a worry and surprising for a team that ran riot at the end of the previous season. Questioned about groans from the crowd, Wenger famously mused, "Perhaps we gave our fans too much by winning the Double. Once you've eaten caviar, it is difficult to go back to sausages."

In mid-December, Arsenal went to Aston Villa and order seemed to be restored. Bergkamp was back on form and gave a 2-0 lead. The half-time entertainment went badly wrong as a parachuting Santa hit the roof of the Trinity Stand and crashed to the ground. Nigel Rogoff later had his leg amputated. The delayed second half was another pivotal moment in the title battle as the league leaders came back to win 3-2 and push Arsenal down to sixth. It was the only time Arsenal conceded more than one goal all season in the league.

Just before Christmas, Arsenal beat Leeds 3-1 at home where Petit replicated his World Cup Final goal, this time from a Bergkamp through-ball. Vieira had earlier netted a fine left-footed strike. Substitute Gilles Grimandi only lasted 15 minutes as he was sent off for a 'footballer's headbutt' on Alan Smith. Two 1-0 wins in three days against West Ham and Charlton made it a successful holiday period, Overmars scoring both winners.

In the FA Cup, Arsenal survived a scare against Preston North End from the Second Division, coming back from 2-0 down at half-time, Luís Boa Morte making a rare impact and Petit adding a double. Arsenal's third goal was aided by on-loan Argentine Fabián Caballero, in his third and final appearance for the club, taking out defender Ryan Kidd with an elbow. The fourth round was also tough, as Arsenal beat Wolves

2-1 but lost Petit near the end with a second yellow card for abusing the linesman.

In the league, 1999 began with a goalless draw at home to Liverpool, followed by 1-0 wins over Nottingham Forest and Chelsea as the defence stood strong. At Forest, Big Ron Atkinson provided the pre-match entertainment as, on his first game as manager, he mistakenly sat in the Arsenal dugout to the bemusement of substitutes Caballero and Vivas. Title rivals Chelsea had gone 21 games unbeaten in the league but Bergkamp coolly finished a loose ball.

1996 African Footballer of the Year Nwankwo Kanu was signed in January from Inter Milan and had an immediate and controversial impact. Making his debut against First Division Sheffield Utd in the FA Cup fifth round, he could not believe it when he collected a throw-in from Parlour on the right wing in acres of space. He squared the ball for Overmars to tap in and was bemused when the opposition players went crazy. Their manager Steve Bruce even threatened to pull his players off the pitch. Kanu had not realised that Parlour was returning the ball to Sheffield Utd after they kicked it out of play for an injury. Overmars probably did, but got caught up in the excitement or was just plain ruthless. The goal ended up giving Arsenal a 2-1 win.

In an unprecedented move, Wenger offered a replay straight after the game. When Bruce suggested it be played at Bramall Lane, Wenger said, "We want to repair what happened. We want it here. We have a fair spirit but we're not stupid." The FA surprisingly accepted and the result was void. Arsenal won the replayed game and the hassle was almost justified by seeing Bergkamp score a sublime backspin clip over the goalkeeper as Arsenal again won 2-1, though more comfortably this time as the Sheffield goal came late on, and Arsenal fans sang to Bruce, "Do you want to start again?"

Football games are regularly settled by officials' mistakes, while players and managers constantly try to push the boundaries of fair play and deem it all part of the game. All managers have been on both sides of this, usually saying they deserved to win when they do and laying the blame when they do not. To Wenger's credit, it is hard to imagine many other managers offering a replay after an unjust win. Arsenal themselves had twice been the victim of similar situations in the previous two seasons and had to take it on the chin.

Kanu, however, proved an inspired signing, playing a major role in Arsenal's brilliant run in the second half of the season and much-needed back-up for Bergkamp and Anelka. Who knows what impact he would have had if he had been signed in the 1998 summer and added that extra quality in the first half of the season when

Bergkamp and Overmars were not consistently matching their world-class form of the previous season. He quickly became a crowd favourite as few had seen his languid style, outrageous close control and unique dummies before. He was not a typical Wenger signing. At 6'5", he was not fast, but he could dribble and manoeuvre his way out of tight spots; often when it looked like he had lost the ball, he would use his size 15 boots to toe it away from the defender. Unbelievably, he had heart surgery two years previously to replace an aortic valve.

Arsenal, and Bergkamp in particular, rediscovered their form of the previous season outclassing West Ham 4-0 at the start of February to set up another Old Trafford showdown. On a filthy Wednesday night and Sunday League quagmire pitch, the two teams produced another classic battle. Yorke put a penalty wide after Parlour had fouled Ronny Johnsen. Then came the UK premiere of the Kanu Dummy, which wrong-footed the entire Man Utd defence. Stam got back to block but Anelka buried the loose ball into the empty net. Thirteen minutes later, an unmarked Andy Cole headed the equaliser. David Seaman made some excellent saves and Arsenal had chances, but a draw was a fair result between the country's two best teams.

Back on the Highbury carpet, Arsenal were rampant against Leicester and their ragged offside trap, Bergkamp easily feeding Anelka for his first Arsenal hat-trick and Parlour for a double. The Iceman's four assists in one game set a Premier League record, since matched by six players including José Antonio Reyes, Cesc Fàbregas and Santi Cazorla. After a 1-1 draw at Newcastle, Arsenal looked like dropping more points in a Monday night game at home to Sheffield Wednesday, with the score 0-0 after 83 minutes. However, they finally got the breakthrough and won 3-0 with two Bergkamp finishes and a Kanu Dummy leaving defenders and goalkeeper scrambling and the Nigerian to finish easily.

Parlour came to the fore in the next two games against Everton and Coventry with well-struck finishes as well as winning a penalty. As Wenger said, "Parlour gets stronger when others get more tired." Arsenal ended March in second place, four points behind Man Utd. After a draw at Southampton, they won 1-0 against Blackburn, where Bergkamp scored a well-struck left-footed volley but then had another penalty saved, worryingly so in hindsight.

On 11 April 1999, the country's top two teams came head to head in the FA Cup semi-final at Villa Park. It was a tense game, with Roy Keane having a goal ruled out for offside against Yorke and card-magnet Vivas, replacing suspended Petit in midfield, sent off in extra time for a second yellow. Man Utd were the better team, but Arsenal held on. It was one of the ten red cards Arsenal received in 1998/99 led by Petit with three, all for two bookable offences, and Keown with two.

Three days later, the teams returned for the last-ever FA Cup semi-final replay as penalties were introduced the following year. It was also one of the best. On 17 minutes, Beckham curled a 25-yard shot past Seaman. On 69, Bergkamp turned and scored from almost exactly the same position, helped by a deflection off Stam. Anelka had a goal disallowed for offside, then on 75 Keane took out Overmars and received his second yellow card. Arsenal were in the ascendency and in injury time Parlour drove at Phil Neville, who tripped him and conceded a penalty. Bergkamp, who had seen three of his previous five penalties saved, went the same way as the Blackburn miss, to his right, but Schmeichel read it and saved.

Arsenal were on top in extra time but could not make the extra man count. Vieira played a loose pass across the halfway line where substitute Ryan Giggs picked up the ball, raced 50 yards past tired challenges of Vieira, Dixon and Keown, and smashed an amazing winner into the roof of the net.

The sight of Giggs celebrating, waving his shirt above his head and exposing his dark chest rug, will haunt Arsenal fans forever. Arsenal lost only one out of five games against Man Utd in 1998/99 but this one was massive. It was a huge psychological blow – Bergkamp never took another penalty – and most felt the winners would also go on to claim the league.

To Arsenal's credit, they bounced back, playing some of their best football in the next four games. They hammered Wimbledon at Highbury 5-1, which included a Vieira left-footed 20-yarder into the bottom corner.

On 24 April 1999, with the chance to go top for the first time all season and put the pressure on Man Utd, who played Leeds the following day, Arsenal produced an even better performance. They ran riot at Middlesbrough winning 6-1 and in two games and five days had wiped out nine-tenths of Man Utd's goal-difference advantage. Anelka ran in behind their defence time and again, fed by Vieira and others, scoring twice as well as winning a penalty, which Overmars converted despite scuffing down the middle. Kanu showcased his range of tricks, scoring twice – memorably celebrating the first with a one-kneed, big-grinned version of his famous two-fingered salute; while the second was an inspired volleyed flick through his legs from a Dixon cross.

After a 1-0 win at home to Derby, Arsenal went to White Hart Lane watched by their usual away

THE UNLUCKIEST PLAYER EVER?

Often included in lists of Wenger's worst signings, Diawara was centimetres from becoming an Arsenal hero. His *Sliding Doors* moment came in the crucial loss against Leeds where he came on with Arsenal chasing a win and had efforts saved, headed off the line and hit the crossbar. So close to being this season's Christopher Wreh, he just kept hitting the woodwork – including twice on his debut in the FA Cup game against Sheffield Utd (which would have avoided the Kanu replay fiasco). Bought in January 1999 from Bordeaux for £2.5m, he was sold six months later to Marseilles for a £0.5m profit after only three starts, 12 substitute appearances and no goals.

contingent as well as 13,000 fans back at Highbury on a big screen. Arsenal quickly dispelled Spurs' hopes of ruining their title chances as Petit and Anelka confidently finished slide-rule through-balls from Bergkamp. Seaman dived over a free-kick from Darren Anderton before Kanu sealed a 3-1 win in style. Receiving a Vieira free-kick on the edge of the area with his back to goal, he controlled, flicked it over defender Luke Young's despairing jump, ran around the other side and volleyed home. With Paul Ince scoring a late goal for Liverpool against Man Utd to make it 2-2, it seemed Arsenal had the momentum.

With two games left, Arsenal and Man Utd both had 75 points and a +42-goal difference, United ahead only on goals scored. Arsenal were first up on Tuesday night with a tough visit to Leeds, managed by Arsenal's record appearance-holder David O'Leary. Although Leeds had nothing to play for as they had secured fourth place and a European spot, they were certainly up for it. A frenetic game could have ended up 5-5. Leeds started strong. Ian Harte crashed a penalty off the bar after Keown had unnecessarily brought down Smith, and Seaman made a great save from Jimmy Floyd Hasselbaink's rebound. At the other end, Nigel Martyn made save after save.

In the second half, Arsenal threw everything at Leeds but somehow failed to score. When they did get past Martyn, a defender cleared off the line or the ball rebounded off the woodwork. Around 70 minutes, Wenger went for broke, sending on Kanu and then Kaba Diawara, who in a crazy cameo saw Martyn save a one-on-one, Jonathan Woodgate head his volley off the line and a header hit the crossbar.

Then came the sucker punch. With Winterburn off with a smashed nose, his replacement Vivas lost Hasselbaink who headed his customary goal against Arsenal at the back post. A deflating finish to a great game, made worse by O'Leary celebrating on the pitch and congratulating every Leeds player like they were on course to win the title themselves.

The following night Man Utd drew with Blackburn meaning there was still a chance on the final day of the season. Their opponents? Spurs, managed by George Graham. Arsenal had Aston Villa at home and knew they had to win, but not many expected their rivals to do them a favour at Old Trafford, a place where they rarely came away with anything. It briefly seemed possible when Les Ferdinand scored a fluke goal – and looked sheepish. There were brief chants of "Come on Tottenham" from the home crowd at Highbury for the first time ever. However, Man Utd were 2-1 up when Kanu scored Arsenal's winner from a corner in the second half and Arsenal finished runners-up, one point behind.

The lacklustre first half of the season, in particular the failure to put away lower-placed teams, proved crucial to Arsenal's title hopes as they again went on a brilliant run and were unbeaten for their next 19 games, winning 15, until the decisive defeat against Leeds in their penultimate fixture. However, this time Man Utd matched them, winning 14 and losing none of their final 20.

1999/00
PAYING THE PENALTY

Premier League	Second
FA Cup	Fourth round
CL / UEFA Cup	Group stage / Final
League Cup	Fourth round
Community Shield	Winners

PREMIER LEAGUE		PL	W	D	L	GF	GA	GD	PTS
1	MAN UTD	38	28	7	3	97	45	52	91
2	ARSENAL	38	22	7	9	73	43	30	73
3	LEEDS	38	21	6	11	58	43	15	69
4	LIVERPOOL	38	19	10	9	51	30	21	67
5	CHELSEA	38	18	11	9	53	34	19	65
6	ASTON VILLA	38	15	13	10	46	35	11	58

Highlights: Nwankwo Kanu's 15-minute hat-trick versus Chelsea; Thierry Henry on fire in the second half of the season; cruising to a 4-0 win at Leeds; high-scoring wins in the UEFA Cup against Deportivo de La Coruña and Werder Bremen followed by a professional semi-final defeat of Lens

Lowlights: Losing UEFA Cup Final on penalties to Galatasaray; disappointing Wembley nights in Champions League; lack of title challenge

Player of the year: Patrick Vieira – "Two players in one. He has tremendous physique, but also sophisticated technique." (Marcel Desailly)

Top scorers: Henry 26 (17 in PL), Kanu 17 (12), Marc Overmars 13 (7), Davor Šuker 11 (8), Dennis Bergkamp 10 (6)

Goal of the season: Kanu's third versus Chelsea, Stamford Bridge, Premier League

The 1999/00 season saw three landmark moments for the club: (1) after 18 years, Arsenal no longer wore the iconic JVC-sponsored shirts and sported SEGA Dreamcast (home kit) and SEGA (away kit) logos; (2) the decision was made to leave Highbury after 90 years and build a new stadium in the area; and (3) Arsenal signed their greatest goalscorer and their best player ever in Thierry Henry.

Nicolas Anelka, who was voted PFA Young Player of the Year the previous season and led the line well aged only 19, eventually joined Real Madrid after a summer of transfer speculation and expressions of frustration by him and his agent brother. Labelled Le Sulk due to his perceived moody demeanour (maybe he was just an introverted young man living in a foreign country) and criticism of the media ("The one thing I can tell you is that I can't stand the English press, who cause me enormous problems on a personal level."), his departure meant Arsenal lost a world-class talent. However, the £22.3m transfer fee was a massive profit on the £500,000 outlay and paid for struggling French winger Thierry Henry for £11m from Juventus as well as the club's state-of-the-art training ground in London Colney.

Arsenal also signed 1998 World Cup Golden Boot winner Davor Šuker for £3.5m as these were the days when Wenger stockpiled a battery of quality forwards, often putting all four on the pitch when chasing a win or equaliser. The transition from the Famous Back Four began as Steve Bould left for Sunderland and in came the industrious Oleh Luzhny, seen the year before marauding the right flank for Dynamo Kyiv against Arsenal, and the elegant left-back Sylvinho, the club's first Brazilian player.

Like the previous season, a Community Shield win over Man Utd offered hope Arsenal would challenge them for the title. After being 1-0 down, Kanu sidefooted a penalty in typically nonchalant style before playing Ray Parlour in on the right to drill home off the post.

The league opener against Leicester was won courtesy of a 90th-minute header by own-goal specialist Frank Sinclair, who inexplicably beat his own goalkeeper to the ball like he was at the other end of the pitch. Henry came on for a cameo and showed his lightning pace to get behind the defence on numerous occasions, but rushed his finish each time. At Derby a few days later, Emmanuel Petit curled a brilliant 25 yarder into the top corner, but this was cancelled out by Rory Delap's instinctive grasscutter volley from Martin Keown's clearance. Dennis Bergkamp sealed the points with a calm sidefoot finish.

After a goalless draw at Sunderland came the key home fixture against the Champions. Andy Cole, Ryan Giggs,

Dwight Yorke, Henry and Bergkamp all had chances, while Alex Manninger and Raimond van der Gouw both made good saves. Just before half-time, Bergkamp's pass found Freddie Ljungberg on a third-man run to fire the opener – a combination that would be seen over and over again. The second half remained end to end as Bergkamp's effort was saved at close range and Matthew Upson hit the post from a corner before Roy Keane scored a similar goal to Ljungberg's.

There was the usual melee as Keane kicked Vieira, who reacted by putting his head in Keane's face, leading to a shoving match between the two. Jaap Stam got involved, butting heads with Vieira and grabbing him in a chokehold. Amazingly, the only card waved was Šuker's imaginary one as referee Graham Poll told everyone off instead of dismissing the three aggressors. On 88 minutes, Giggs dispossessed Parlour in centre-midfield and his deflected shot fell into the path of Keane to score again and make it 2-1 to Man Utd. There was still time for der Gouw to save an Upson header on the line and Keown to steam in and send ball, goalkeeper and himself into the back of the net, but the goal was eventually disallowed for a foul. It was Arsenal's first home defeat in the Premier League for just under two years.

Following a comfortable 2-0 win over Bradford, thanks to a Vieira header and Kanu penalty, Arsenal lost again at Anfield as Robbie Fowler hit a laser

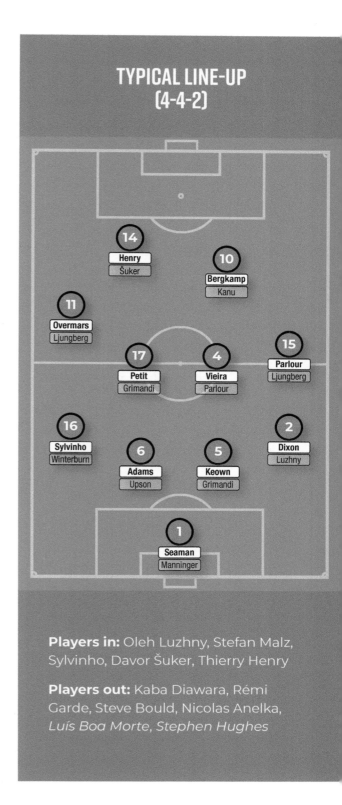

TYPICAL LINE-UP (4-4-2)

14 Henry / Šuker
10 Bergkamp / Kanu
11 Overmars / Ljungberg
17 Petit / Grimandi
4 Vieira / Parlour
15 Parlour / Ljungberg
16 Sylvinho / Winterburn
6 Adams / Upson
5 Keown / Grimandi
2 Dixon / Luzhny
1 Seaman / Manninger

Players in: Oleh Luzhny, Stefan Malz, Sylvinho, Davor Šuker, Thierry Henry

Players out: Kaba Diawara, Rémi Garde, Steve Bould, Nicolas Anelka, *Luís Boa Morte, Stephen Hughes*

into the top corner and Patrick Berger scored a deflected free-kick. At the end of August, Arsenal were already six points behind leaders Man Utd.

Performances picked up in September with three league wins. Šuker showed his left-foot finishing prowess twice against Aston Villa in a 3-1 comeback win. At Southampton, after eight goalless games, Henry's moment finally came. After 79 minutes, Tony Adams passed to substitute Henry, who had his back to goal and a defender in close attention. He held him off and curled the winner from 20 yards. Henry later admitted his drought was getting to him: "I have missed at least 14 or 15 chances for Arsenal and my confidence was low." Another 1-0 against Watford came from a Kanu goal after he had already hit the post twice, and Arsenal closed the gap to Man Utd to two points.

In the Champions League, the previous season's pattern of a tough group, failing to convert strong performances into wins and frustrating Wembley nights continued. Kanu had a late penalty saved at Fiorentina, the match ending 0-0, before late goals 'at home' saw off AIK Solna 3-1.

Kanu's shinned volley earnt a credible 1-1 draw in Camp Nou after Vieira had earlier been caught juggling the ball in his six-yard box. Arsenal played

the last ten minutes, and equalised, with ten men after Grimandi elbowed Pep Guardiola. Early in the Wembley fixture, a Barcelona team featuring the firepower of Rivaldo, Luís Figo, Patrick Kluivert and future managers Pep Guardiola and Luis Enrique sliced open Arsenal's unusually open defence twice in 60 seconds. The first came from a penalty after Phillip Cocu beat Adams to the ball and dived into the area; for the second, with Keown off the pitch getting treatment, Adams was exposed and slipped, Enrique doing the rest.

Arsenal made a game of it after Bergkamp brilliantly cushioned a drilled Kanu cross and finished left-footed, but Barcelona put on a counter-attacking masterclass and scored twice before a late Marc Overmars consolation. The 4-2 loss meant the Fiorentina game was crucial but Argentine Gabriel Batistuta, from a tight angle, knocked Arsenal out with one of the hardest strikes seen at Wembley into the roof of the net.

Back in the league, Paulo Di Canio, now playing for West Ham, produced two moments of skill to give his side a 2-1 win. Vieira was sent off for two bookable offences and lost the plot, spitting at wind-up merchant Neil Ruddock. With three losses already in October, the six-game total suspension to their midfield general was the last thing Arsenal needed. Two goals from

Šuker then aided an easy 4-1 win over Everton.

On a wet October Saturday at Stamford Bridge, Arsenal were down and out to two Chelsea headers before Kanu produced an incredible 15-minute hat-trick out of the puddles: (1) he stopped a weak Overmars shot, turned and toe-poked it home; (2) he controlled a low Overmars cross and fired it in at the near post; and (3) he blocked a clearance from right-back Albert Ferrer, collected the ball near the goalline and was surprisingly faced by goalkeeper Ed De Goey outside his area; unperturbed, Kanu dribbled around him and, from an almost impossible angle, curled it teasingly over the despairing jumps of Marcel Desailly and Frank Leboeuf on the line. Like Bergkamp at Leicester, the Nigerian had saved the best for last, inspiring Martin Tyler's classic "Kanu believe it" commentary. Chelsea, who had not conceded a goal at home this season, were again stunned by a late Arsenal winner.

In a feisty North London derby at White Hart Lane, Arsenal were again 2-0 down early on. A Vieira header suggested another comeback but chances faded when Ljungberg was sent off for 'headbutting' Justin Edinburgh after the Spurs defender followed through on him. Despite numerous others piling in and Edinburgh's head actually being hit by something thrown from the crowd, only Ljungberg saw red. Understandably wound up, the Swede gave the referee and crowd

NOT THE HOME OF FOOTBALL

Arsenal's Champions League record at Wembley in the two seasons they played there was a disappointing, and costly, won two, drew one and lost three (WDLWLL).

two fingers on the way off and booted a door in the tunnel. Arsenal ended up with nine men late on as there was no way Keown was going to let José Dominguez showboat and make a fool of him.

Overmars scored a hat-trick in a 5-1 win over Middlesbrough and Henry scored two well-taken goals against Derby, a watershed moment playing upfront alongside Bergkamp for the first time. This left Arsenal in touch with leaders Leeds and Man Utd at the end of November.

Next, Leicester were dealt with easily 3-0 as Gilles Grimandi and Lee Dixon continued their unusual goal-poaching form while Henry skinned pantomime villain Robbie Savage, not for the last time in their careers. However, Arsenal's title hopes took a hit with a 1-1 draw against Wimbledon and 3-2 Boxing Day loss at Coventry. In the latter, the defence was again vulnerable and Seaman flat-footed to admittedly good finishes from Hadji and Robbie Keane. Arsenal threatened a late comeback after Šuker scored a brilliant goal cutting in from the left, dummying two defenders and poking home with his favourite left foot.

Young title pretenders Leeds arrived at Highbury eight points ahead of Arsenal, but with Vieira back from suspension the Gunners dispatched them 2-0 with goals from Ljungberg and Henry. The second was a classic exhibition of Henry's pace, strength and calm sidefoot finishing that Arsenal fans were now getting used to. Wenger, who had managed Henry at Monaco as a 17-year-old, converted him back to striker from winger. Once Henry found his feet in the middle, though he was still usually found cutting in from the left, it proved an inspired move. The Frenchman had his own Goal of the Second Half of the Season competition, scored in ten consecutive games and netted 22 in 35 games – firing long-range tracer bullets, finishing off dribbles with composed finishes or using his pace playing off the last defender.

The new millennium opened with a frustrating draw against Sheffield Wednesday as Kanu left for the African Nations Cup. Sunderland, and poor 37-year-old Arsenal legend Bould, were given the runaround by a rampant Arsenal and Henry, who scored twice as did Šuker including a classic dipping volley.

At the end of January, Arsenal travelled to leaders Man Utd up against it with Adams, Bergkamp, Kanu, Šuker and Overmars injured or suspended. Playing five in midfield and Henry upfront on his own, Arsenal took the lead when Ljungberg outmuscled Stam and again scored against Man Utd. The home side, who had been playing in the World Club Championship and were controversially excused from the FA Cup, equalised in the second half through Teddy Sheringham and finished strongly. Wenger later complained about Man Utd's 'winter break' advantage. It was a battling performance but the 1-1 draw only left Arsenal level on points with Man Utd despite having played three games more.

Any title hopes went with losses in the next two games at Bradford (2-1) and home to Liverpool (1-0). The latter were Arsenal's bogey team around this time and Titi Camara was left in acres of space as he beat the offside trap and slotted home.

Down to fourth place in late February, Arsenal had a much-needed 3-1 win against Southampton, with Bergkamp back from injury and showing his class with a goal and an assist. More away-day disappointments came against Aston Villa and Middlesbrough, teams Arsenal expected to dispatch comfortably. At least fans could cheer a North London derby win as Henry converted a penalty after Chris Armstrong scored headers at both ends. The victory was the start of another strong run-in as Arsenal won eight league games in a row to secure second place and Champions League football. Players coming back from injury and suspension helped, as did Henry's brilliant form and the better spring pitches.

An easy 3-0 against Coventry saw Kanu finish a one-on-one in trademark style – taking his time, he dummied multiple times to leave Steve Ogrizovic flapping on the floor before passing into the empty net. Two Kanu goals and an Henry penalty saw off Wimbledon 3-1, and Leeds were given an Arsenal masterclass at Elland Road, the score 4-0.

Watford's high line was exposed as Henry buried Petit's long pass, then Parlour ran on to Henry's through-ball and rounded the goalkeeper. Henry continued to show his confidence and ability by collecting the ball well outside the penalty area, bursting past two midfielders, twisting and turning two backpedalling defenders, and curling inside the right-hand post.

Watford scored two consolation goals as Seaman again showed unexpected vulnerability but Arsenal won 3-2. A typical Overmars run and cool finish at Everton meant Arsenal's tricky run of four away games produced four wins.

Two 2-1 wins against London rivals West Ham and Chelsea guaranteed Champions League football. In the latter, Henry's second goal was notable for him going shoulder to shoulder with fellow World Cup winner Marcel Desailly and leaving the defender in a heap like few, if any, had done before. The league season finished with a 4-2 loss at Newcastle as Arsenal focused on the upcoming UEFA Cup Final.

After pushing Man Utd so close the previous season, Arsenal's failure to challenge for the 1999/00 title or progress in the Champions League was disappointing. Man Utd dominated and finished 18 points ahead. Inconsistent performances, particularly away from home, meant Arsenal never posed a serious threat, while injuries and suspensions did not help. Defensively, they were nowhere near as tight as the previous season. They did score 112 goals in all competitions and they came from all over the place – the four strikers, right-back Dixon got five, Grimandi had a run of three in three and Parlour got his first hat-trick.

PAYING THE PENALTY

Nine players (Kanu, Overmars, Dixon, Grimandi, Vivas, Upson, Sylvinho, Šuker and Vieira) missed from the spot during the 1999/00 season as Arsenal went out of the FA Cup and League Cup in fourth-round shootouts and lost the UEFA Cup Final on penalties. With Bergkamp no longer taking penalties, the baton was passed to Kanu (casual style with mixed results) then Overmars (unconvincing but usually scored) before Henry took over and provided relief.

Finishing third in their Champions League group meant Arsenal went into the UEFA Cup. Happily playing back at Highbury, Arsenal enjoyed some entertaining and high-scoring encounters. In the third round, Nantes were beaten 3-0 in the first leg as Nigel Winterburn fired a swerving drive. The French team scored first at home to threaten a comeback but Arsenal were 3-1 up by half-time to go through comfortably even though the game finished 3-3.

In the next round, Arsenal were 2-0 up against eventual Spanish champions Deportivo de La Coruña through a Dixon header and Henry finish from a flowing move. When Djalminha scored a dubiously-given Panenka penalty past Seaman early in the second half, the home crowd were tense but the Brazilian quickly unravelled with yellow cards for both a dive and reacting to a Grimandi foul by burying his head in the Frenchman's chest. Arsenal took advantage of the extra man as Henry scored a rare header and Kanu made another goalkeeper look foolish in a one-on-one, this time sitting Jacques Songo'o down and leaving an empty net without even touching the ball. The 5-1 win was more than enough as Deportivo won the second leg 2-1.

The quarter-final saw another strong Highbury performance as Werder Bremen were beaten 2-0 with Henry and Ljungberg goals. Arsenal won the away leg 4-2 on a poor pitch as Parlour scored an excellent hat-trick. The first was a swerving drive with the outside of his foot from the right corner of the penalty area, the second came after a strong run bouncing off defenders and the third a calm one-on-one finish. Parlour also laid one on a plate for Henry, who was wrongly sent off for a nothing foul.

Bergkamp settled the semi-final first leg against Lens after only two minutes, latching on to a Petit ball over the top and rounding goalkeeper Guillaume Warmuz who had needlessly come charging out of his area. In France, Henry was back from suspension and sealed the tie with a brilliant turn and hit from just inside the area. The game finished 2-1 to Arsenal as Kanu scored a second and Arsenal were on the way to Copenhagen to play Galatasaray, hoping for a repeat of the 1994 Cup Winners' Cup Final in the same city.

Sadly, the Battle of Copenhagen came off the pitch in the city centre as there were fights between both sets of supporters and others that had come for the expected trouble. Four people were stabbed. A month earlier, two Leeds fans were killed before the Leeds-Galatasaray semi-final in Istanbul.

Galatasaray were a strong side that had already secured a domestic double and featured many players from the Turkey team that later came third in the 2002 World Cup supplemented by Brazilian and Romanian internationals including 35-year-old Gheorghe Hagi, the Maradona of the Carpathians, but Arsenal were firm favourites.

Galatasaray started the better, although Overmars almost sneaked a low drive in at the near post. Arif Erdem beat the offside trap and had a great chance but drilled his shot wide. Early in the second half, both Hakan Şükür, courtesy of an excellent last-ditch tackle by Keown, and Parlour hit the post. Keown then missed Arsenal's best chance from five yards, sliding in but skying Henry's low cross after the Frenchman had ghosted past two defenders.

The game livened up in extra time as both teams had chances to score the decisive golden goal. Adams made a great tackle on Hagi, who held him back. Adams swung his arms to shrug him off and the Romanian thumped him on the back. Hagi was sent off and Adams yellow-carded giving Arsenal the initiative for the remaining 26 minutes. However, Brazil's Cláudio Taffarel made a brilliant save from a close-range Henry header and twice blocked efforts from Kanu cutting in from the right.

The Turkish team still looked dangerous but it went to penalties, which were taken at the vocal Galatasaray supporters' end, the referee making a unilateral decision instead of having the usual coin toss, according to Wenger. Šuker, who was brought on at the end of extra time partly for his penalty prowess, took Arsenal's first and hit the post, his last kick for the club. Parlour scored but Vieira cracked against the bar, while Galatasaray's penalties were assured, leaving former Spurs player Gica Popescu to win the shootout 4-1.

Either due to complacency, freezing or the toxic atmosphere, Arsenal failed to repeat their free-flowing performances of the previous rounds and missed a big opportunity to end the season on a high and claim a European trophy.

Signings – The Good

	Bought/ Sold	From/To	Paid/ Received (£m)	
Patrick Vieira	14-Aug-96	AC Milan	£3.5	A game-changing arrival for the club and the role of centre-midfield generally. Captain of the Invincibles, three league titles, four FA Cups. Sold too soon.
	14-Jul-05	Juventus	£13.7	
Nicolas Anelka	22-Feb-97	Paris St Germain	£0.5	Two excellent seasons, a great partnership with Dennis Bergkamp and key in the 1997/98 Double. Reluctantly sold, but at a huge profit that paid for Henry and a new training ground.
	4-Aug-99	Real Madrid	£23.0	
Marc Overmars	1-Jul-97	Ajax	£7.0	A brilliant 1997/98 Double season, Arsenal got the best out of the Flying Dutchman before he went to Barcelona with Petit.
	28-Jul-00	Barcelona	£25.0	
Freddie Ljungberg	12-Sep-98	Halmstad	£3.0	Tough, energetic, a man for the big occasion, making perfectly-timed runs to score crucial goals, in particular in the 2001/02 Double.
	23-Jul-07	West Ham	£2.0	
Thierry Henry	3-Aug-99	Juventus	£10.5	Converted from winger to central striker and one of the best players in the world; 228 goals in 377 games, two league titles, three FA Cups, four Golden Boots.
	25-Jun-07	Barcelona	£16.1	
Robert Pires	3-Jul-00	Marseille	£6.0	A brilliant replacement for Overmars. Six years of sublime touch, passing and finishes. A crucial part of Arsenal's devasting left-sided attacking focus.
	30-Jul-06	Villarreal	Free	
Kolo Touré	14-Feb-02	ASEC Mimosas	£0.2	Signed for almost nothing as a total unknown, was converted to centre-back to form an Invincible partnership with Campbell.
	29-Jul-09	Man City	£16.0	
Sol Campbell	3-Jul-01	Spurs	Free	Spurs' captain joined on a free transfer in a controversial and stunning transfer coup. The Invincible won two titles and three FA Cups.
	1-Jul-06	Portsmouth	Free	
Cesc Fàbregas	11-Sep-03	Barcelona	£2.8	Signed aged 16, played 303 games before returning to Barcelona at 70 times the price. A solitary FA Cup was a poor haul for a world-class player, but a symptom of the lack of quality around him.
	15-Aug-11	Barcelona	£25.4	
Robin van Persie	17-May-04	Feyenoord	£2.8	As he did with Henry, Wenger converted van Persie to a world-class central striker. Frustrated like Fàbregas, went to Man Utd and spearheaded them to the title.
	17-Aug-12	Man Utd	£22.5	

Honourable mentions: Emmanuel Petit, Nwankwo Kanu, Lauren, Gilberto Silva, Gaël Clichy, Alexander Hleb, Bacary Sagna, Laurent Koscielny, Santi Cazorla.

Signings – The Bad

	Bought/ Sold	From/ To	Paid/ Received (£m)	
Igors Stepanovs	4-Sep-00	Skonto Riga	£1.0	Never recovered from the 6-1 mauling at Old Trafford. Made 17 league appearances in four years but did win a Premier League and two FA Cup medals.
	1-Jul-04	Grasshopper	Free	
Francis Jeffers	14-Jun-01	Everton	£8.0	The 'fox in the box' scored eight times in 39 games. He won two FA Cup medals despite not playing in either final and was sent off in his last game, the 2003 Community Shield.
	10-Aug-04	Charlton	£2.6	
Richard Wright	5-Jul-01	Ipswich	£6.0	Signed as David Seaman's future replacement, Wright made just 22 appearances.
	24-Jul-02	Everton	£3.5	
Manuel Almunia	14-Jul-04	Celta Vigo	£2.5	Unbelievably he was at the club for eight years and first-choice goalkeeper for three. Not the elite number one a title-chasing team needed.
	31-Jul-12	Released	Released	
Mikaël Silvestre	20-Aug-08	Man Utd	£0.8	How Alex Ferguson must have laughed at offloading the 31-year-old Frenchman, who was well past his best, onto supposed rivals, even receiving a fee.
	30-Jun-10	Werder Bremen	Free	
Marouane Chamakh	21-May-10	Bordeaux	Free	Started well but lightweight, slow, and Arsenal did not play to his strengths and put crosses in. Out of the team once van Persie came back from injury. Only 14 goals in 67 appearances.
	10-Aug-13	Crystal Palace	Free	
André Santos	31-Aug-11	Fenerbahçe	£6.2	The left-back panic buy was decent going forward but did not have much interest in defending. Made only 25 league appearances in two years before being offloaded.
	18-Jul-13	Flamengo	Free	
Gervinho	12-Jul-11	Lille	£10.6	11 goals in 69 games sums up the winger's lack of end-product. Promising mazy dribbles usually ended with a scuffed shot or wasted cross.
	13-Aug-13	AS Roma	£6.9	
Shkodran Mustafi	30-Aug-16	Valencia	£34.3	The third-most-expensive defender in history; jockeying and staying on his feet were alien concepts for the 'anti-Maldini'.
	2-Feb-21	FC Schalke 04	Free	
Granit Xhaka	25-May-16	Mönchengladbach	£26.7	A high price to pay for a holding midfielder with a good left foot but who was a poor tackler, lacked mobility and did not track back.
	N/A	N/A	N/A	

Honourable mentions: Sébastien Squillaci, Mathieu Debuchy, Lucas Pérez, Alexandre Lacazette, Henrikh Mkhitaryan.

NB: Best and worst lists are not necessarily the best and worst footballers but are based on a combination of factors such as: the player's performances and success at the club; how much Arsenal paid relative to the market rate; and which other players were available at the time.

Signings – The Strange

	Bought/ Sold	From/ To	Paid/ Received (£m)	
Alberto Mendez	17-Jun-97	SC Feucht	Free	Signed from German non-league team SC Feucht and scored on League Cup debut; played 11 games in five years which included three loan spells away.
	1-Jul-02	Racing Ferrol	Free	
David Grondin	19-Jun-98	Saint-Étienne	£0.5	Arrived aged 18 but made only one league appearance in five years, during which time he was loaned out four times.
	1-Jan-03	Dunfermline	Free	
Stefan Malz	24-Jun-99	1860 München	£0.7	Made 14 appearances in two years, scoring twice. On the bench in the 2000 UEFA Cup Final loss.
	15-Jun-01	Kaiserslautern	£0.5	
Junichi Inamoto	20-Jul-01	Gamba Osaka	£3.5	Cynics said he was bought as a marketing ploy in Japan; never played in the league, but did get on once in the Champions League.
	20-Jun-02	Released	Released	
Amaury Bischoff	30-Jul-08	Werder Bremen	£0.3	Wenger called it a "gamble" due to his injury history; saw only 25 minutes in a solitary Premier League outing.
	30-Jun-09	Released	Released	
Ryo Miyaichi	1-Jan-11	Chukyodai Chuyko	Free	'Ryodinho' spent most of his four years out on loan or injured; played just 215 minutes for the first team.
	18-Jun-15	FC St Pauli	Free	
Park Chu-young	30-Aug-11	Monaco	£2.7	The South Korea international was having a medical at Lille when Arsenal pounced; the number nine curled an excellent finish in the League Cup but only played seven times in three years.
	30-Jun-14	Released	Released	
Yaya Sanogo	1-Jul-13	Auxerre	£0.4	The French youth striker was quick and tall but his touch was poor; scored once in 20 games over four years. Caused chaos and made an important impact as substitute in the 2014 FA Cup Final.
	30-Jun-17	Released	Released	
Kim Källström	31-Jan-14	Spartak Moscow	Loan	Signed on loan to solve an injury crisis despite the medical revealing a broken back. Made the pitch nearly two months later. Scored in the FA Cup semi-final penalty shootout and left with a medal.
	30-Jun-14	Spartak Moscow	N/A	
Takuma Asano	3-Jul-16	Sanfrecce Hiroshima	£0.8	The Japan striker did not receive a work permit and never played for Arsenal, scoring six goals in three years on loan in Germany.
	1-Aug-19	Partizan Belgrade	£1.0m	

Honourable mentions: Guy Demel, Tomas Danilevičius, Thomas Eisfeld, Wellington Silva.

2000/01
THE GREAT CUP FINAL ROBBERY

Premier League	Second
FA Cup	Final
Champions League	Quarter-final
League Cup	Third round

PREMIER LEAGUE		PL	W	D	L	GF	GA	GD	PTS
1	MAN UTD	38	24	8	6	79	31	48	80
2	ARSENAL	38	20	10	8	63	38	25	70
3	LIVERPOOL	38	20	9	9	71	39	32	69
4	LEEDS	38	20	8	10	64	43	21	68
5	IPSWICH TOWN	38	20	6	12	57	42	15	66
6	CHELSEA	38	17	10	11	68	45	23	61

Highlights: Thierry Henry's winning volley versus Man Utd; finally progressing to the knockout stages of the Champions League; beating Spurs in the FA Cup semi-final

Lowlights: Dominating but losing the FA Cup Final; 6-1 humiliation at Old Trafford; losing Champions League quarter-final to Valencia after outplaying them in the first leg

Player of the year: Patrick Vieira ran the midfield week after week, including against Steven Gerrard in the FA Cup Final, but finished with nothing to show for it

Top scorers: Henry 22 (17 in PL), Sylvain Wiltord 15 (8)

Goal of the season: Henry's brilliant improvised flick up and volley versus Man Utd, Highbury, Premier League

In July 2000, Marc Overmars and Emmanuel Petit moved to Barcelona for a total of £32m, broken down £25m for Overmars and £7m for Petit. Although they were not coming off their best seasons, losing half of a quality midfield was a blow. However, Arsenal made a big profit, on Overmars in particular, and neither player hit the same heights in Spain, partly due to injuries.

Wenger again spent the funds well, using his knowledge of French and world football to build his second team. Robert Pires replaced Overmars while Sylvain Wiltord was signed for an Arsenal record of £13m. The pair had recently made a defining impact as substitutes in France's Euro 2000 golden goal win over Italy.

Cameroon midfielder Lauren came in, though he was away in September winning a Gold Medal in the Sydney Olympics. Brazilian Edu was scheduled to join but embarrassingly he was refused entry at Heathrow Airport as he had a fake Portuguese passport, so the transfer was put on hold. He eventually joined in January 2001 after securing an EU passport through his father's Italian ancestry.

For every unknown gem Wenger made a star however, there was a gamble that did not pay off or made the Arsenal faithful wonder what the manager was thinking. According to Ray Parlour, Latvian Igors Stepanovs was signed after a trial game where the Arsenal players were bigging up

his contributions in Wenger's earshot just to wind up fellow centre-back Martin Keown.

Nigel Winterburn joined West Ham, as did Davor Šuker, to meet up with old friend Paolo Di Canio. The left-back had a hugely successful career as part of the Famous Back Five, winning seven major trophies in 13 years. With 584 appearances, he is number five on Arsenal's all-time list.

Pre-season optimism quickly gave way to worries that Patrick Vieira would leave after he was sent off in the first two games of the season. At Sunderland, he was the best player on the pitch before reacting to being held by throwing his arm back. Darren Williams made a meal of it, the home crowd erupted and the referee did the rest. The punishment was harsh as it was not an elbow or forearm smash. Arsenal lost 1-0 as former Gunner Niall Quinn outjumped David Seaman and Arsenal missed numerous chances including Parlour spooning over the bar with an open goal at his mercy.

Three nights later, an upset Vieira was walking again, and he was right to feel aggrieved. He received a second yellow, as well as Diettar Hamman's studs on his thigh, for a clean sliding tackle. Referee Graham Poll, who had already sent off Gary McAllister for a two-footed scissor-tackle on Vieira, saw things differently. To complete his poor showing, Poll later gave Hamman a second yellow for a nothing challenge. At least Arsenal finally beat Liverpool, the first time since 1994, winning 2-0 with goals from Lauren, on his first start, and Thierry Henry. It was the beginning of a 15-game unbeaten run that took Arsenal to the top of the league and into the second stage of the Champions League for the first time.

Vieira ended his Arsenal career tied with Duncan Ferguson and Richard Dunne for the most red cards in Premier League history at eight (he also picked up two in other competitions). This was an unfair blight on a player who was tough and could put his foot in but was neither dirty nor did he commit leg-breaker challenges; only two of the ten were straight reds. The softly-spoken Frenchman did however lose his temper often and get in trouble for arguing or retaliating. Once he had gained a reputation, referees were quick to punish any perceived offence, often given plenty of encouragement by opponents milking any contact. His frustration also cost him numerous FA charges for spitting, arguing with policemen and referees, and sticking two fingers up at the crowd.

The Arsenal midfielder reacted well to his back-to-back red cards and was named Premier League Player of the Season for 2000/01, a rare acknowledgement of his consistent midfield domination as individual honours usually went to attacking players or high-profile Brits. In the

TYPICAL LINE-UP
(4-4-2)

14 Henry (Wiltord)
10 Bergkamp (Kanu)

7 Pires (Ljungberg)
4 Vieira
18 Grimandi (Parlour)
8 Ljungberg (Pires / Lauren / Parlour)

16 Sylvinho (Cole)
6 Adams (Stepanovs)
5 Keown
2 Dixon (Luzhny)

1 Seaman (Manninger)

Players in: Lauren, Robert Pires, Guy Demel, Sylvain Wiltord, Igors Stepanovs, *Edu, Tomas Danilevičius*

Players out: Nigel Winterburn, Davor Šuker, Marc Overmars, Emmanuel Petit, *Paolo Vernazza, Christopher Wreh*

next game against Charlton, he signed off with two goals before his suspension. The away team twice took the lead as they exposed Arsenal's vulnerability to crosses but the Gunners won 5-3 and all five goals were quality. Vieira showed great skill when through one-on-one with a right-foot stepover and left-foot dink. Henry also scored two, the best where he flicked up a pass and volleyed from 20 yards, a trick he would repeat a few weeks later in even more spectacular style. Sylvinho sprinted through the defence and fired the fifth.

Like the previous season, Arsenal were 2-0 down at Chelsea with 15 minutes to go after good strikes from Jimmy Floyd Hasselbaink and Gianfranco Zola. Wenger went for broke with all four strikers on the pitch, Kanu playing deeper in a chaotic freestyle formation, and the tactic paid off. Henry finished from a Sylvinho through-ball. On 86 minutes, the Brazilian left-back followed in Winterburn's footsteps to silence the Stamford Bridge crowd with a brilliant swerving piledriver into the top corner to earn a 2-2 draw.

Two disappointing 1-1 draws came at Bradford (as 19-year-old Ashley Cole, in for the injured Sylvinho, got on the scoresheet) and Ipswich. In between, Arsenal dispatched Coventry 2-1 at Highbury with Sylvain Wiltord scoring his first for the club as did local prospect Paolo Vernazza, although it was also his last.

Arsenal finally made progress in the Champions League, helped by the end of the Wembley experiment. At Sparta Prague, Sylvinho again showed his attacking prowess with a mazy run and dink over the goalkeeper to give a 1-0 win. Back at Highbury, it was 'Keown Night' against Shakhtar Donetsk as Arsenal came from 2-0 down to win 3-2 with the centre-back poaching two goals in the last six minutes. Lazio were dealt with more comfortably at home as Freddie Ljungberg made two typical late runs to finish Dennis Bergkamp assists.

A few weeks later, on a wet night in Rome, Pavel Nedvěd put Lazio ahead with a freak goal, the ball looping over 39-year-old stand-in John Lukic after a Sylvinho tackle outside the area. Gilles Grimandi got away with smashing Diego Simeone in the face at a corner – what was it about the Frenchman and future top managers? Luckily he never played against José Mourinho. After 88 minutes, Robert Pires showed his trademark finish for the first time – cutting in from the right, one touch to cushion the ball perfectly into his stride, the second a casual sweep with his sidefoot that generated remarkable power into the far corner. A variation on the Henry Sidefoot Finish, which was usually rolled in, Pires' version was often taken from further out and lifted off the ground, using dip as well as curl to evade the goalkeeper.

An entertaining 4-2 win against Sparta Prague sealed top spot in the group as Arsenal, with five centre-backs out, fielded an entire defence of full-backs including a centre-back pairing of Nelson Vivas and Oleh Luzhny. It did not matter as Parlour thumped an early drive into the top corner. At half-time, Arsenal had to change their dark blue shirts to yellow because of a clash with Sparta's dark red kit, which was inspired by Arsenal's design in the early 1900s. Future fan favourite Tomáš Rosický scored an excellent late consolation for Sparta, beating two defenders and firing into the bottom corner.

Back at Highbury against Man Utd at the start of October, Henry, who had not scored in his previous six games, improvised an inspired piece of skill to score a famous goal. Receiving a quick free-kick outside the area with Denis Irwin in close attention behind him, he flicked the ball up, swivelled, and hit a swerving, looping volley over stunned goalkeeper Fabien Barthez. An all-time classic Arsenal goal, made even better given the opposition.

Aston Villa and West Ham were dealt with 1-0 and 2-1, the latter featuring a classic Pires sidefoot lob and a Rio Ferdinand own-goal. Man City were dispatched 5-0 as Cole drilled home a free-kick from outside the area, something he rarely tried (or was

OH ROCKY ROCKY

David Rocastle was a true Arsenal legend who came through the youth system. He could dribble, produce moments of brilliant flair and regularly foxed defenders with stepovers years before the likes of Ronaldinho and Cristiano Ronaldo. He could also tackle and was a warrior on the pitch, winning two league titles and one League Cup. That his famous quote – "Remember who you are, what you are, and who you represent." – is still cited regularly at Arsenal and the fans sing his song 20 years later says a lot about the player and the man.

allowed to) again in the subsequent five years. After that, the pace and rapid interplay of Arsenal was too much for Man City as Henry (twice), Bergkamp and Wiltord finished off flowing moves.

Having moved level at the top of the table with Man Utd, the traditional November slump arrived, dealing a blow to Arsenal's title bid. An Henry penalty secured a 1-0 win at Middlesbrough after their goalkeeper Mark Crossley had taken out Ljungberg and was sent off. However, Arsenal could only draw 0-0 at home to Derby and lost their next two league games away to Everton (2-0 with old-boy Kevin Campbell scoring the second) and Leeds (1-0), hitting the woodwork in both. Wenger called the Everton performance "not acceptable" and one point out of nine and no goals in three games was a poor return.

Arsenal were happier back at Highbury, beating Southampton 1-0 and smashing Newcastle 5-0. In the latter, Henry showed a great touch to take a Tony Adams long ball out of the air and set himself up for an Henry Sidefoot Finish. Parlour enjoyed himself in centre-midfield and scored another hat-trick, running late to finish through-balls twice and head an Henry cross once. At White Hart Lane, Vieira headed an 89th-minute equaliser to give a deserved 1-1 draw.

Just before Christmas, it was another bad away day at Anfield as Arsenal lost 4-0 with goals from Englishmen Steven Gerrard, Michael Owen, Nick Barmby and Robbie Fowler. Arsenal had still not scored there since 1996. Boxing Day was better as Arsenal, whose players had strangely been given a job lot of light grey gloves, thrashed Leicester 6-1. Henry scored a hat-trick, the best coming when he met a Pires corner on the half-volley outside the area. Adams finished the scoring, sliding to volley an Henry cross left-footed into the roof of the net and celebrate arms

outstretched in front of the North Bank in shades of Everton 1998.

Arsenal lost a two-goal lead and dropped two points against Sunderland as Vieira, who had earlier scored a header and then been unfairly punished with a penalty for handball, uncharacteristically lost the ball twice in succession, Gavin McCann curling the loose ball over Manninger.

2001 started with a New Year hangover at Charlton as a Jonatan Johansson header won the game. Vivas, surprisingly on penalty duties with Henry injured and Pires off the pitch, missed from 12 yards. Wenger afterwards explained, "Vivas takes them very well in training, but the keeper made a great save here." This was followed by draws against Chelsea and Leicester, and then a 2-0 win over Bradford where Parlour scored a 25-yard drive and Lauren a header. At the end of January, Arsenal were already 15 points behind Man Utd and the season rested on the cups and qualifying for the Champions League.

February opened with two 1-0 wins over Coventry and Ipswich, the first courtesy of a rare Bergkamp header from Wiltord's cross, the second a more expected Henry Sidefoot Finish from a Bergkamp through-ball.

With the Champions League going to a second group stage, Arsenal opened their account at Spartak Moscow in front of a 75,000 crowd. On a rough pitch and temperatures below zero, surprisingly it was the Brazilians on both sides that shone. Sylvinho finished well after only two minutes, but after Kanu missed a chance to make it two, Spartak dominated and won 4-1 as Marcao and Luis Robson gave Arsenal's defence a hard time. It was Arsenal's biggest away defeat in Europe.

Henry and Kanu scored one each to give Arsenal a 2-0 lead over Bayern Munich, but the German side fought back with goals from set-pieces. In the two games against Lyon, an Henry header secured the points away, but a Bergkamp Curler was only good enough for a draw at Highbury. Henry soared for another winning header against Spartak Moscow at Highbury; with his height and athleticism, he should have scored more with his head and it was the only weakness in his game. Arsenal lost the final game in Munich but were lucky to qualify with eight points as Lyon failed to beat Spartak Moscow.

In the FA Cup, Wiltord shone, scoring six goals in the first four rounds, including two in a 6-0 rout of QPR. More importantly, against Chelsea, he came on after 70 minutes with the game 1-1 and produced two key finishes. The first was a nice lob over Carlo Cudicini, the second a first-time finish from Lauren's cutback. It was a big win for an Arsenal team forced to play Luzhny and Stepanovs at centre-back. Wiltord, while not always clinical, proved strong back-up to the Henry-Bergkamp partnership; he was quick and could strike the ball well with both feet.

In the quarter-final against Blackburn, a Wiltord finish and Adams header put Arsenal two up after only five minutes. Pires finished it off with a classy touch and sweeping finish, this time coming in from the right.

At the end of February, Arsenal went to Old Trafford with hopes of making a statement. However, it only took Man Utd three minutes to expose the makeshift defence of Luzhny, Stepanovs, Grimandi and Cole. Henry equalised after a flowing move where Pires played one-twos with Luzhny and Wiltord. But then Man Utd, and an out-of-favour Dwight Yorke in particular, gave Arsenal's defence a roasting. Yorke's second came from a simple ball over the top with Stepanovs pushing up for offside and Grimandi sitting back.

Flat-footed Stepanovs was exposed again as he got under a Beckham long-ball and Yorke completed a 19-minute hat-trick. Then Yorke evaded Stepanovs' desperate attempt at a tackle/foul to tee up Roy Keane. Grimandi, who had often done a good job filling in

SQUAD GAME

Due to injuries and suspensions, Arsenal did not field the same side two games running in the Premier League in 2000/01. Thirty-five players represented the club in all competitions and there were 17 different goalscorers.

31 March 2001 was an emotional day at Highbury with the news that Arsenal legend David Rocastle had died that morning from non-Hodgkin's lymphoma at the age of 33. Promising 17-year-old Italian youth defender Niccolò Galli also lost his life a few weeks earlier, killed in an accident while riding his moped from Arsenal training. The game was the first of a North London double header with the FA Cup semi-final the following week. After a minute's silence, Arsenal dominated but Henry, Wiltord and Pires could not beat Neil Sullivan for 70 minutes until Pires, who wore Rocastle's number-seven shirt, cut in from the left and fired a low curler inside the far post. Henry finished it off as he was left one-on-one with defender Chris Perry, and twisted and turned him before passing home.

The first leg of Arsenal's first-ever Champions League quarter-final against previous season's finalists Valencia was sandwiched between the two Spurs games. Highbury was silenced just before half-time by a Roberto Ayala volley, but was rocking in the second half after two goals in three minutes. Henry finished after a Pires back-heel and Parlour hammered a shot into the top corner from 22 yards. The energetic midfielder was not a prolific scorer but when he did it was usually an excellent right-footed strike. Henry then raced on to a Vieira through-ball and unusually took it past the goalkeeper instead of his usual Henry Sidefoot Finish;

at centre-back alongside Adams or Keown, also had a shocker. He was regularly pulled out of position away from his centre-back partner, capping it off by inexplicably falling over for Man Utd's fifth goal.

It was 5-1 at half-time and Parlour recalled, "I think it was the only time I saw Arsène Wenger lose his rag in a half-time team-talk." Wenger said after the 6-1 humiliation, "We are not in March yet and the season is already over. I cannot be very proud of that. This hurts."

Arsenal tried to put it behind them as Wiltord scored a first-half hat-trick against West Ham, including a low left-foot curler and a Romario-style toe-poke one-on-one finish.

defender Jocelyn Angloma made a crucial recovery tackle. In the second leg in Spain, Arsenal were 15 minutes away from a very winnable semi-final against Leeds when John Carew scored a header to knock Arsenal out and punish them for failing to make their superiority at Highbury count.

In the FA Cup semi-final at Old Trafford, Spurs had a new manager in Glenn Hoddle, who replaced the sacked George Graham, but the pattern was the same as the week before – Arsenal dominated but missed chance after chance. This time they went behind as Gary Doherty diverted a wayward volley with his head before Vieira equalised with a towering header from a Lee Dixon free-kick. On 74 minutes, Vieira drove through the midfield and played in Wiltord on the right. He drove it across the box for Pires to tap home and again prove he was a specialist in goals against the North London rivals as well as ending Spurs' "when-the-year-ends-in-one" myth for another decade.

Back in the league, Man City were taken apart in a devasting first half at Maine Road as Ljungberg scored twice and Kanu and Wiltord got one each. Then came Arsenal's only home loss of the season in the major competitions, a strange game that confirmed Man Utd as Champions. Middlesbrough won 3-0 despite having one shot on target

as Brazilians Edu and Sylvinho both scored own-goals.

Edu's Arsenal career seemed jinxed. After the fake passport issue, he finally made his debut against Leicester as a substitute but had to be replaced with a hamstring injury 15 minutes later. Arsenal fans wondered if his signing was worth all of the hassle. In subsequent seasons, Edu proved it was as he was an assured centre-midfielder with good passing technique as well as a willingness to put his foot in. Arsenal then pushed for a Champions League place with consecutive wins over Everton, Derby and Leeds.

So the season again rested on a cup final as Arsenal took on Liverpool in Cardiff, the first FA Cup Final held outside England. While against tradition, it was a great stadium in a city centre location. It also kept some FA hangers-on away meaning a higher proportion than normal of the 72,000 fans were supporters of the two clubs.

The game itself summed up Arsenal's season – carve out openings through incisive passing and quick movement, but fail to finish them off. It also saw Liverpool centre-back Stéphane Henchoz play 'rush goalkeeper' and twice handle the ball in his area. The first came when Ljungberg played in Henry, who rounded Sander

Westerveld and slotted home – or so everyone thought, until Henchoz slid in and made a last-ditch save his goalkeeper would have been proud of. Unbelievably, the referee and linesman combined to give a goal-kick. What would have happened had Arsenal, on a hot day and big pitch, played 73 minutes against ten men and with a penalty to take?

While unlucky with those decisions, there were plenty of other spurned chances. Sami Hyypiä made three goalline clearances from Cole, Ljungberg and Henry, while Westerveld made close-range blocks from Henry in particular.

On 72 minutes, Pires slipped in Ljungberg, on a trademark late run, who took it past Westerveld and finally gave Arsenal the lead they deserved. However, 11 minutes later, Michael Owen hooked home a loose ball after Arsenal failed to clear a free-kick, and five minutes later he broke free, outpaced Dixon and Adams, and finished left-footed across Seaman. It was a stunning turnaround and Arsenal had somehow managed to lose one of the most one-sided cup finals in history. Liverpool went on to win a cup treble while Arsenal were again left empty-handed.

A 0-0 draw at Newcastle in the league three days later secured second place and automatic Champions League football before Arsenal played Southampton in the final match at their 103-year-old stadium, The Dell. Arsenal led twice but Saints legend Matthew Le Tissier scored an 89th-minute half-volley for a 3-2 win and fitting finale.

Almost every club would have been satisfied with three consecutive second-place finishes, going deep in cup competitions and competing in the Champions League, as well as regularly playing sublime attacking football. However, Wenger set a high bar with the Double in his first full season. With a spine as good as anyone's in Adams, Keown, Vieira, Henry and Bergkamp, and a supporting cast including the likes of Petit, Overmars, Pires, Ljungberg, Parlour and Kanu, three years without a trophy was a period of underachievement. Losing two finals they should have won showed a worrying lack of winner's mentality.

The problem in the league in 2000/01 was away from home, where Arsenal won only five games and lost seven. Surprisingly given their firepower, the main issue was a lack of clinical finishing. They kept 17 clean sheets in the league, the same as Man Utd. Wenger lamented in December 2000: "It has been our problem all season. We so very rarely score two in a match, and that makes life very difficult." Bergkamp and Kanu, who only started 50 games between them due to injuries and rotation, contributed just ten goals.

2001/02
DOUBLE DOUBLE

Premier League	Winners	
FA Cup	Winners	
Champions League	Second group	
League Cup	Quarter-final	

PREMIER LEAGUE		PL	W	D	L	GF	GA	GD	PTS
1	ARSENAL	38	26	9	3	79	36	43	87
2	LIVERPOOL	38	24	8	6	67	30	37	80
3	MAN UTD	38	24	5	9	87	45	42	77
4	NEWCASTLE	38	21	8	9	74	52	22	71
5	LEEDS	38	18	12	8	53	37	16	66
6	CHELSEA	38	17	13	8	66	38	28	64

Highlights: Winning the league at Old Trafford a few days after beating Chelsea in the FA Cup Final with two memorable goals; Dennis Bergkamp's brilliant improvised turn and finish at Newcastle; ten-man win at Anfield

Lowlights: Robert Pires tearing his anterior cruciate ligament while in the form of his life; lack of progress in the Champions League

Player of the year: Pires was the best player in the league and pivotal in Arsenal's favoured left-side interplay, scoring and setting up crucial goals

Top scorers: Thierry Henry 32 (24 in PL), Freddie Ljungberg 17 (12), Sylvain Wiltord 17 (10), Bergkamp 14 (9), Pires 13 (9)

Goal of the season: Bergkamp's never-seen-before spin versus Newcastle, St James Park, Premier League

Wednesday, 8 May 2002, Old Trafford: 55 minutes in, a tight game is goalless. Ray Parlour dispossesses Man Utd left-back Mikaël Silvestre just inside the Arsenal half and feeds Sylvain Wiltord. The Frenchman, playing upfront with Kanu in the absence of Thierry Henry and Dennis Bergkamp, drives forward and passes to the advancing Freddie Ljungberg. The tireless midfielder gets the better of Laurent Blanc and hits a low shot that Fabian Barthez saves but cannot hold. Wiltord follows up and sidefoots home left-footed, just like Marc Overmars did four years earlier from an almost identical spot. Wiltord stands in front of the Arsenal fans to celebrate and Kanu brilliantly hurdles him with a huge star jump. In 1998, Arsenal's 1-0 victory at Old Trafford was the de facto title winner; in 2002, it was the real thing, and the players and fans could fully celebrate in enemy territory.

Four days after winning the FA Cup, Arsenal needed a point at the home of their rivals to win the Double. Playing in classic gold Sega-sponsored away shirts, they did even better. Arsenal's 12th consecutive league win ensured there was no argument over who was the better team. They put in a brilliant controlled away performance led by the immense Patrick Vieira and refused to be intimidated by Man Utd's attempts to bully them, with Phil Neville and Paul Scholes making typically wild fouls. In a frantic atmosphere, neither side had created clear chances. Early in the second half, some Arsenal fans produced a banner saying "Old Trafford Champions Section" and their confidence was quickly justified as Wiltord cemented his reputation for scoring important goals.

After Michael Owen's smash and grab in the 2001 FA Cup Final, Henry and others said Arsenal needed a "fox in the box" to finish all the chances they created. Arsène Wenger answered the call by buying Francis Jeffers for £10m from Everton. However, the new number nine was not needed as he started only three games in 2001/02.

More significantly, Arsenal pulled off a huge transfer coup, shocking everyone by turning up at a press conference not with goalkeeper Richard Wright as expected, but unveiling Spurs captain Sol Campbell. Campbell's contract had expired and, available on a free transfer, he made the controversial, brave and soon-to-be vindicated decision to move to his North London rivals.

Vieira, speaking before the Campbell deal, was not impressed with Arsenal's dealings: "I need to leave because I want to win more trophies and I just cannot see that happening at Arsenal... I do not honestly see Arsenal finishing in the top five in the league – and you can forget the Champions League... Arsène Wenger has signed two 'hopeful' players [Jeffers and Giovanni van Bronckhorst] who haven't proved themselves in the Premiership yet. One of them is a boy of 20." Fortunately, he was persuaded to stay and made vice-captain.

Wenger's second team fully took shape with the addition of Campbell's toughness, Robert Pires stepping up from a promising first season to world-class, and old-school defenders Lee Dixon and Nigel Winterburn replaced with pacey full-backs that played as big a role in the attacking third as they did in defence. After a solid first season mostly as a utility midfielder, Lauren was converted into a tough ball-playing right-back. Sylvinho was sold despite being named in the 2001 PFA Team of the Year as Ashley Cole had replaced him as first-choice left-back. There were also reports of another passport issue, which both the player and club denied.

In the season opener at Middlesbrough, Henry chested down and hit a sweet volley to put Arsenal 1-0 up. Parlour got a second yellow card early in the second half but Arsenal were not troubled and, late on, Ugo Ehiogu made it ten aside as he was adjudged to have fouled Cole, although contact was minimal and the left-back took a dive. Pires converted the penalty before substitute Bergkamp scored two classy finishes playing off the last man – both times taking one touch to control and one to beat the goalkeeper.

Three days later, Leeds won a feisty encounter 2-1 at Highbury despite finishing with nine men. Harte stroked a free-kick in while David Seaman was still lining up the wall. Wiltord did well to divert a mis-hit Cole shot with his head. However, early in the second half, Mark Viduka sidestepped Tony Adams and fired into the bottom corner from the edge of the box. Late on, Lee Bowyer and Danny Mills got second

**TYPICAL LINE-UP
(4-4-2)**

14 Henry / Wiltord

10 Bergkamp / Kanu

7 Pires / van Bronckhorst

8 Ljungberg / Wiltord / Parlour

4 Vieira / van Bronckhorst

15 Parlour / Edu / Grimandi

3 Cole

5 Keown / Adams

23 Campbell / Upson / Stepanovs

12 Lauren / Luzhny / Dixon

1 Seaman / Wright / Taylor

Players in: Francis Jeffers, Giovanni van Bronckhorst, Sol Campbell, Junichi Inamoto, *Kolo Touré*

Players out: John Lukic, Nelson Vivas, Stefan Malz, Guy Demel, *Sylvinho*

yellow cards, the latter harshly given for playing a soft one-two off a prostrate Cole. The rivalry between the two teams attracted FA chief executive Adam Crozier's attention: "The Arsenal-Leeds game has developed an edge that isn't entirely desirable."

Leicester were given a masterclass with Pires instrumental and laying goals on a plate for Ljungberg and Wiltord. Predictably, Vieira and wind-up artist Dennis Wise clashed, and were both sent off, before Henry and Kanu completed another 4-0 win. At Stamford Bridge, Arsenal drew 1-1 with Chelsea, who fielded Arsenal old boy Emmanuel Petit after an unsuccessful season at Barcelona. There was another red card – this time for Jimmy Floyd Hasselbaink, who had earlier converted a one-step penalty to equalise Henry's opener.

Late goals at Fulham secured a 3-1 win as Ljungberg slipped in Henry and Wiltord cut the ball back for Bergkamp to sidefoot into the roof of the net. Against Bolton, quick passing and movement put Pires in, who, as he often did, unselfishly gave Jeffers a tap-in for his first Arsenal goal. However, Michael Ricketts equalised with a close-range volley nine minutes later to frustrate the home side, who again failed to capitalise on a one-man advantage after Ricardo Gardner had pulled back Bergkamp when in on goal. At the end of September, Derby were dispatched 2-0 as Henry curled a free-kick into the top corner and scored a penalty.

In the Champions League group stage, Arsenal were consistent – three home wins, three away losses. The campaign started on the night of the 9/11 attacks with a 1-0 loss to Real Mallorca. Arsenal, wearing a garish blue shirt, yellow shorts and socks combo, saw Cole sent off after 11 minutes and the resultant penalty converted. Schalke were then beaten 3-2 in an entertaining game with Henry scoring two.

The Panathinaikos double header saw a 1-0 loss and 2-1 win as Vieira won a trademark slide tackle on the halfway line, got up and played in Henry. Wright, whose Arsenal career had got off to an indifferent start when replacing the injured Seaman, justified his reputation as a penalty specialist with a save from 12 yards. The Greek team did equalise but Henry showed them how to take a penalty after Wiltord was sandwiched by two defenders.

Two goals in three minutes, including a soaring Bergkamp header, gave Arsenal a 2-1 lead over Mallorca. Crucially, on 93 minutes, a quick free-kick on the edge of his own area by van Bronckhorst set up an Henry Sidefoot Finish that guaranteed Arsenal qualified in second place, making the final game redundant.

At the start of October, Arsenal visited Southampton's new St Mary's Stadium. A quick transition led to Pires stroking home right-footed from his favourite inside-left position before a deflected Henry shot sealed a 2-0 win. Blackburn equalised twice at Highbury in a 3-3 draw, the last a David Dunn volley that rolled into an empty net from 25 yards after Wright had come out to block a one-on-one. More frustration came at Sunderland. Kanu was put through by a brilliant Wiltord ball and, after the goalkeeper's half-save and a couple of dummies, he finished. Former Arsenal player Stefan Schwarz scored an excellent dipping volley from the edge of the area before Vieira, with Henry and Pires rested on the bench, skied a penalty into the jubilant home crowd.

The next home game against Charlton was going to plan when Henry drilled a left-footed finish on six minutes. However, Arsenal's weakness from crosses was exposed twice, the second when Wright came for a cross but under pressure only succeeded in punching it slowly backwards into his net. Charlton were not done – first Claus Jensen scored a Bergkamp-esque chip, then Jason Euell finished a one-on-one. Henry converted a penalty on 60 minutes but Arsenal lost 4-2 despite having 27 shots on goal.

It was a worry that the previous season's habit of spurning chances due to taking too many touches or making one extra pass was still there. However, Arsenal proved they did not need a fox in the box to score scrappy goals. Instead, Henry got even better and more prolific, Bergkamp was back on

form, Wiltord regularly chipped in, and midfielders Pires and Ljungberg had standout seasons. All five hit double figures.

Highbury was a happier place 24 hours later as Arsenal and Man Utd were ridiculously forced to play in the League Cup the day after Premier League games. A first-half Wiltord hat-trick secured a 4-0 win as Arsenal showed the strength of their squad as both managers rotated heavily.

At White Hart Lane, on 81 minutes, Pires scored again in the North London derby, firing a curler from 25 yards. Campbell opened with a big tackle and kept his cool amid a vitriolic atmosphere and the home fans' Judas (and much worse) banners, balloons and chants. The Spurs fans ended up happy, however, as Wright could not keep out Gus Poyet's volley with almost the last kick of the game.

On a wet night in North London, Man Utd this time brought their first team. After 14 minutes, Silvestre beat Lauren on the left and crossed for Scholes to finish past 20-year-old Stuart Taylor, making his debut as both Seaman and Wright were injured. Just after half-time, Gary Neville inadvertently passed to Pires, who fed the advancing Ljungberg on the right and the Swede flicked an inspired chip over Barthez.

Arsenal were on top but the French goalkeeper, who had made numerous saves from Henry and Kanu, looked like he was going to earn his team a point – until 80 minutes when he scuffed a kick straight to Henry, who gratefully slid it back past him. Amazingly, five minutes later, he presented Henry with another gift as he fumbled a long ball and left his French teammate with an open goal. The home crowd jubilantly sang, "Give it to Barthez." It was a deserved win and crucial psychological blow over their title rivals.

At the start of December, Arsenal were third, three points behind Liverpool with Leeds second. Arsenal favoured building up play down the left, with Cole, Pires and Henry triangles prominent, and this proved a perfect combination with Ljungberg's well-timed diagonal runs from the right. Ipswich were one of many teams to be unpicked by a slide-rule pass and first-time Ljungberg finish without breaking stride. An Henry penalty sealed a 2-0 win.

At Highbury, the home crowd were silenced by Aston Villa, who were 2-0 up at half-time. The first was route one as Dion Dublin headed on a goal-kick and Paul Merson lobbed Taylor. Wenger sent Wiltord on to play three upfront and it worked as he initiated a memorable comeback with a left-foot volley. Vieira then dispossessed right-back Jlloyd Samuel and curled a ball across for Henry to control and finish calmly. With 91 minutes gone and the ball in the hands of Villa goalkeeper Peter Enckelman, a draw was on the cards. But ten seconds later, an Henry

SHOW ME A HERO

Ljungberg cemented his reputation as a man for the big occasion, scoring in five of the last eight league matches, including the crucial nerve-settling opener in four consecutive games, as well as a famous goal in the Cup Final. He was tenacious, quick and never stopped making runs into the box. With a habit of scoring against Man Utd and a red streak through his hair, it was no wonder he was a fan favourite.

Sidefoot Finish made it 3-2 and sent the home crowd wild; it was not a great kick by the goalkeeper, Pires unusually won the loose ball in midfield ahead of George Boateng, and not so unusually slipped in Henry.

After a 1-1 draw against West Ham, Arsenal lost their third home game of the season, this time to Newcastle, a win that sent the Geordies top of the table. Arsenal took the lead through Pires before referee Graeme Poll again made himself centre of attention. Just before half-time, he gave Parlour a second yellow despite the protests of Newcastle's Alan Shearer. In the second half, Andy O'Brien headed in a corner to equalise. Poll sent off Craig Bellamy for an 'elbow' on Cole that the FA later rescinded. On 86 minutes, Shearer converted a penalty Poll had given despite Campbell making a clean sliding tackle. Laurent Robert made it 3-1 at the end as Arsenal chased an equaliser. At the final whistle, Henry was furious and gave Poll a prolonged mouthful that subsequently earnt him a three-match ban.

Arsenal went to Anfield the following Monday night and again had to play a large part of the game with ten men. Referee Paul Durkin bizarrely gave van Bronckhorst, who was filling in for the suspended Vieira, a second yellow for a 'dive', even though the Dutchman simply fell over, got up and ran back with no attempt to claim a penalty. The remaining ten men produced an epic performance of grit and quality, one of the best in Wenger's entire 22-year reign.

Kanu moved back to centre-midfield, and gave a masterclass of close control and skill alongside Parlour, who was everywhere. Just before half-time, Kanu slipped in Ljungberg, who was taken out by goalkeeper Jerzy Dudek. Henry put the penalty past Dudek, who was not given a card of any colour, let alone the red that professional fouls earnt in those days. On 53 minutes, Pires waltzed past Steven Gerrard in the right-back position and fizzed across goal for Ljungberg to finish and celebrate with the ecstatic away fans. It ended up 2-1, Wenger's first win at Anfield, and was one of the defining moments of the season.

"Perhaps we had better start practising with ten men," suggested Wenger. Whether they did or not, they knew what to do – two banks of four, one upfront, usually Henry – and were so good at it, they won seven games with less than 11 men in 2001/02. They were defensively solid, had the technique to keep possession to avoid being under siege and could still hurt teams on the break.

On Boxing Day, Chelsea took the lead through Frank Lampard before Campbell got his first Arsenal goal with a towering header. Wiltord bounced in a volley from the edge of the area to win the game 2-1. Two days later against Middlesbrough, Campbell's failure to deal with a long clearance let in Noel Whelan to finish one-on-one and celebrate with a dubious dance. In the second half, Pires hit a swerving, dipping volley from 25 yards and Bergkamp picked out Cole to guide a header home. The 2-1 win meant Arsenal began 2002 top of the table with only three points separating first and fifth.

Title rivals Liverpool came to Highbury for the first home game of the year and Pires and Ljungberg combined for an almost carbon copy of their Anfield goal. Six minutes later, Steven Gerrard played in John Arne Riise to sidefoot past Taylor at the near post. The tricky fixtures continued with a visit to Elland Road and it ended in another 1-1 draw. Leeds took the lead early on with a Robbie Fowler header before an Henry dummy fooled the defence and left Pires in on goal to fire left-footed into the top corner.

Arsenal then notched two away wins. They won 3-1 at Leicester as van Bronckhorst headed his first Arsenal goal. At Blackburn, Bergkamp and Henry finishes gave Arsenal a 2-0 lead. This was cancelled out by half-time as Matt Jansen first beat Wright to a corner, then finished after Oleh Luzhny slipped with no one around him. The Horse was later sent off but Arsenal again showed their ability with ten men as Pires slipped in Bergkamp, who finished with his left foot.

Ominously, at the end of January, Man Utd were leaders. An 80th-minute Jo Tessem header for Southampton cancelled out Wiltord's first-half goal and frustrated the Highbury crowd, as did the club's new crest. A tacky new design was unveiled and met with the chant, "What a load of rubbish." It replaced the club's classic *Victoria Concordia Crescit* crest that had been used in some form since 1949 but could not be copyrighted and so commercialised.

Those were the last points Arsenal dropped all season as they went on a record 13-match winning run to hold off Liverpool (who won 13 of their last 15) and Man Utd (who won 18 of 21 going into the final week). Arsenal's run started with some luck in tough conditions at Everton as Wiltord sliced a volley that looped over Steve Simonsen in goal and went in off the post. The quick one- and two-touch interplay returned as Arsenal thrashed Fulham 4-1, though Henry's second came when Lauren's header rebounded off the post and back off his shins before he could react.

In the Champions League, Arsenal drew a tough second group and got off to a bad start as Deportivo de La Coruña's Roy Makaay scored a bouncing volley after eight minutes. Not long after, Diego Tristán hit a shot from 25 yards that Wright seemed to wave in at the near post.

But then came a memorable Highbury night, and a famous goal, against a Juventus team that featured Gianluigi Buffon, Lilian Thuram, Gianluca Zambrotta, Pavel Nedvěd, Alessandro Del Piero and David Trezeguet. Ljungberg followed up a Vieira shot that Buffon could not hold and Henry curled a free-kick into the top corner. Just after half-time, Taylor, who had made some good saves, was unlucky when Campbell's goalline block came off his back and set up a nervous second half. Arsenal sealed a 3-1 win near the end with a counter-attack and some Bergkamp magic. The ball reached the Iceman just outside the Juventus area, where he twisted, turned, did a stepover, then dragback before flicking the ball between two defenders for Ljungberg to lob over Buffon's dive. Unlike most players, Bergkamp took more pleasure providing a classy assist than scoring a run-of-the-mill goal himself.

In Germany, Bayer Leverkusen scored a crucial 90th-minute equaliser to capitalise on poor marking. Pires had earlier opened the scoring and Arsenal looked like hanging on despite Parlour seeing red for two bookable offences. At Highbury, Arsenal raced out of the blocks with Vieira making a big tackle in midfield on five minutes, Pires driving forward, cutting inside, and sidefooting inside the post from the edge of the area. Two minutes later, Pires had the ball in the left-back position under pressure. Instead of hoofing clear, he kept possession and passed to Bergkamp who laid it off first time to Vieira, back to Bergkamp, on to Wiltord, who crossed for Henry to finish – a classic Wengerball team goal that few sides in this era would even attempt, let alone carry off. A Vieira diving header and trademark Bergkamp chip sealed a 4-1 victory. That was as good as it got though as Arsenal lost 2-0 at home to the tricky Deportivo and 1-0 at Juventus, Henry having penalties saved in both games. Arsenal failed to keep a clean sheet in 12 Champions League matches in 2001/02.

In the league, Arsenal went to Newcastle without Henry but still sent a message to their title rivals as Bergkamp produced an iconic piece of improvisation and skill. After 11 minutes, Pires fizzed a pass into him on the edge of the area with his back to goal and Nikolaos Dabizas in close attention. Two touches later and the Dutchman had silenced the noisy home crowd. With his left foot, he stunned the ball to his right and behind the defender. He then spun the other way, shrugged off the bewildered Dabizas and sidefooted home. No one had seen it done before and many questioned whether he

meant it; this would be understandable for most players, but the Dutchman had an extensive portfolio of amazing moments of skill, touch and vision. Campbell powered in a diving header to seal a 2-0 win.

Arsenal eventually broke Derby's resistance with a Pires goal to win 1-0 before the Frenchman again produced his finger-wagging celebration at Aston Villa. First came an Edu goal and excellent Seaman one-handed penalty save from Gareth Barry. Ljungberg hit a diagonal ball to the left wing where Pires flicked it over Boateng, let the ball bounce twice and nonchalantly sidefooted over Peter Schmeichel. Dublin got one back with a header but Arsenal won 2-1.

Arsenal racked up six more points over the Easter weekend with easy 3-0 wins over Sunderland and Charlton, all the goals coming in the first 30 minutes of each game.

Arsenal began their FA Cup quest at a murky Vicarage Road, where Kanu trickery opened up the defence twice in the opening ten minutes. Watford got one back but a late Kanu header and Bergkamp tap-in from a classic Wengerball move helped a 4-2 win.

The fourth round was an eventful re-run of the previous year's final. Henry played a one-two with van Bronckhorst and crossed from the left for Bergkamp to head in. On 67 minutes, referee Mike Riley sent off Martin Keown for a professional foul on Owen. Minutes later, a wound-up Bergkamp went in on Jamie Carragher and, although his stamp missed, was also shown red. Luckily, there was no time for Liverpool to exploit the two-man advantage as Carragher followed him down the tunnel after picking up a £1 coin that someone in the crowd had thrown and returning fire. Arsenal's 4-3-1 formation held on in the rain against Liverpool's ten men.

In the fifth round, second-tier Gillingham equalised twice before Arsenal's class told. Parlour sealed a 5-2 win by crashing in an instinctive volley with the outside of his right foot. After a 1-1 draw at Newcastle, Arsenal got off to another fast start in the replay as Pires sidefooted a trademark curler from the inside-right position after only two minutes before crossing for Bergkamp to slide home. A Campbell header sealed a 3-0 win.

Sadly, that was Pires' last contribution of the season as he landed awkwardly after hurdling a tackle and ruptured his anterior cruciate ligament. It was a cruel blow for a player in the form of his life to miss the title run-in, FA Cup Final and the World Cup. He was deceptively quick despite his duck running style, a calm finisher, and consistently played cushioned through-balls for the likes of Henry and Ljungberg. He had already made 15 assists in the league to add to his 13 goals.

In the semi-final against Middlesbrough, Gianluca Festa shinned in Henry's corner, the own-goal enough to set up a final against Claudio Ranieri's Chelsea.

On a sunny Saturday in April, Arsenal's title charge was on course against Spurs when Bergkamp played in Ljungberg to finish left-footed. After 79 minutes, it became a story of two dodgy penalties. The ball was chipped to the left of the Arsenal goal, Seaman came out, and both he and Gus Poyet missed the ball and had seemingly innocuous contact. Mark Halsey gave a penalty which Teddy Sheringham gleefully dispatched. A few minutes later, Arsenal had the ball at the other end, Dean Richards and Henry went down, and Halsey again pointed to the spot. During a long delay while Henry received treatment, Arsenal fans were surprised, and some concerned, to see Lauren holding the ball. However, the Cameroon international had been successful in shootouts in the 2000 Olympics and 2002 African Cup of Nations finals, and he stroked the ball down the middle, fortunately evading the feet of the diving Kasey Keller, and Highbury erupted.

Arsenal hit the woodwork four times against Ipswich before Ljungberg again made the breakthrough, turning and sweeping home after Keown had headed down. He added another with his knee after his header was saved by Andy Marshall. The following Wednesday night was a similarly nervous occasion as West Ham kept it goalless for 80 minutes before Bergkamp drove forward and played a through-ball for Ljungberg to yet again time his run and finish to perfection. Kanu volleyed in a high

Ljungberg cross to make it 2-0. Arsenal had been lucky in the first half when Frédéric Kanouté rounded Seaman and Cole made a trademark goalline clearance – the ball appeared over the line but there was no technology then to prove it.

Ljungberg did not leave it so late at Bolton. In the absence of Pires, he made his run off the left wing and buried Bergkamp's flick between three defenders. It was the Swede's sixth goal in five games and the fourth match in a row that he had scored the crucial opener. Another Bergkamp through-ball put in Wiltord for a 2-0 win to set up the Old Trafford showdown.

First came the FA Cup Final, which was unusually played before the last week of the league season. A massive few days for Arsenal and a chance to prove their winner's mentality after disappointments in the previous three seasons.

It was another sunny day in Cardiff, although the rivalry between the two sets of supporters was less congenial than at the previous season's final. Thousands of Arsenal fans adopted the Ljungberg red streak through their hair. Wenger brought back Seaman in goal despite Wright playing the earlier rounds and paired Campbell and Adams in centre-defence. It was not a great game and there were few chances. Bergkamp headed Vieira's long ball over Carlo Cudicini but wide, while Lauren put a diving header

over the bar. Seaman tipped an Eidur Gudjohnsen curler over.

With 70 minutes gone, Wiltord played a good ball to Parlour bursting through the midfield, the Chelsea defence backtracked maybe thinking along the same lines as Chelsea's 'celebrity fan' Tim Lovejoy, who was doing the FanZone commentary on Sky Sports: "Ah, it's alright, it's only Ray Parlour." It was only Ray Parlour, and it was only Ray Parlour scoring one of the best Cup Final goals ever. The Romford Pelé curled a 25-yarder into the top corner. Ten minutes later, Ljungberg picked the ball up on the left in his own half. The Swede drove between three defenders and shrugged off John Terry to symbolically leave 'Mr Chelsea' in

AWAY DAY MASTERS

Arsenal became the first team to go an entire season undefeated away from home (unusually they lost three at home), banishing the inconsistent away form that cost the title in previous seasons. They conceded just 11 goals in 19 away games, winning 47 points away and just 40 at home. Campbell added toughness and steel, and the bigger pitches away from Highbury gave them more space for their rapid counter-attacks and to play in the likes of Henry behind defences.

a heap, before curling another classic into the same top-right corner to make it 2-0.

Adams and Vieira jointly lifted the trophy and Arsenal clinched part two of the Double a few days later in Manchester, their second in four years under Wenger – an impressive achievement given it has only been done 12 times in English football history.

That left a party atmosphere at Highbury for the final league game of the season against Everton, who gave the Champions a guard of honour onto the pitch. Arsenal won 4-3 and Taylor came on near the end for his tenth appearance, meaning all three goalkeepers won Premier League medals. Adams lifted the Premier League trophy, captaining the team to the title in three different decades, and

the respect for Pires was shown as the Arsenal players bowed in a 'we are not worthy' gesture when he collected his medal and lifted the trophy. Famous Back Five legends Adams and Dixon retired on a high after 22 and 14 years, 669 and 619 games, and ten and eight major trophies, respectively.

Arsenal broke all sorts of records and cleaned up in the end-of-season awards. They became the first team to go the entire season unbeaten away from home and to score in every game. All despite receiving a record 12 red cards in 60 games overall. Pires won the FWA Player of the Year despite missing the last two months of the season, Ljungberg Premier League Player of the Season, Wenger Manager of the Year, Henry Premier League Golden Boot and Bergkamp Goal of the Season.

Battle Royale

The Arsenal-Man Utd rivalry was an epic nine-year war between 1996 and 2005. It actually had its roots back in the George Graham era – the first Battle of Old Trafford was in 1990-91 when a 21-man melee caused points deductions that did not prevent Arsenal winning the league.

They were the two best teams in the country – no one else won the league from 1996 to 2004 – and the players, managers and fans hated each other. For Arsenal fans, the Spurs games were no longer the first dates to look for when the fixtures were released each year. Arsenal and Man Utd pushed each other to new heights. Each game was a Battle Royale that for once lived up to the media hype with brilliant football and unmatched intensity in between the hostilities. The 90 minutes on the pitch often proved insufficient as the clashes moved to the tunnel, both before and after the game, and provoked flying pizza and boots.

It was refreshing to see Arsène Wenger stand up to Alex Ferguson, who was the dominant character in English football as manager of the biggest club and was an intimidating figure for other managers, referees and journalists. The sides of many British Football Managers often rolled over at Old Trafford, but were fired up to put one over the Frenchman's team.

While they also played good football and had quality players, Man Utd resorted (sometimes successfully, most notably in the 2004 Battle of the Buffet) to roughing Arsenal up. "It's funny," Paul Scholes revealed years later, "In team talks against Arsenal, the ball was rarely mentioned." Phil Neville also admitted they took it in turns to kick José Antonio Reyes in that game. Unlike in Stage Two and Three Wenger, Arsenal had strong physical players that could stand up for themselves and give as good as they got.

Captains Patrick Vieira and Roy Keane led the way and regularly clashed, while there were numerous other classic individual battles such as Ian Wright-Peter Schmeichel, Marc Overmars-Gary Neville, Nicolas Anelka-Jaap Stam, Martin Keown-Ruud van Nistelrooy and Lauren/Ashley Cole-Cristiano Ronaldo.

The 2005 FA Cup Final was the natural endpoint to the intense rivalry between the two clubs. Both Vieira and Keane had left by the end of the year and Arsenal were no longer a serious title force with their expensive move to the Emirates and the arrival of big-spenders Chelsea. That allowed the relationship between the two managers to improve in later years when Ferguson was no longer threatened by Wenger – reinforced by Man Utd's easy Champions League semi-final win in 2009 and the 8-2 humiliation in 2011.

BATTLE ROYALE TIMELINE

Nov 1996, Old Trafford	MU 1 AFC 0	PL	A Nigel Winterburn own-goal gives Man Utd the win and Arsenal are still yet to score at Old Trafford in the Premier League. Schmeichel is accused of racially abusing Wright.
Feb 1997, Highbury	AFC 1 MU 2	PL	Man Utd win as Wright goes in two-footed on Schmeichel and the police keep them apart after the final whistle. The FA intervene and meet with both clubs.
Nov 1997, Highbury	AFC 3 MU 2	PL	Anelka announces himself with a fine strike but Man Utd come back from 2-0 down before a late David Platt header gives a 3-2 win and shows Arsenal are ready to challenge the Champions.
Mar 1998, Old Trafford	MU 0 AFC 1	PL	Famous 79th-minute Overmars winner puts Arsenal in the box seat for the title.
Aug 1998, Wembley	AFC 3 MU 0	CS	Overmars, Christopher Wreh and Anelka give Arsenal a comfortable Community Shield win.
Sep 1998, Highbury	AFC 3 MU 0	PL	Arsenal make it four wins in a row against Utd with another 3-0 victory as Nicky Butt is sent off. Sub Freddie Ljungberg lobs Schmeichel on his debut.
Feb 1999, Old Trafford	MU 1 AFC 1	PL	A forgotten classic on a wet Wednesday night and mudbath of a pitch. Dwight Yorke misses a penalty, Anelka gives Arsenal the lead but Andy Cole heads the equaliser.
April 1999, Villa Park	AFC 0 MU 0 (AET)	FA Cup semi-final	Arsenal survive with a 0-0 draw as a Keane goal is controversially disallowed for offside and Nelson Vivas is red-carded in extra time.

Apr 1999, Villa Park	AFC 1 MU 2 (AET)	FA Cup semi-final replay	Keane is sent off, but Schmeichel saves Dennis Bergkamp's late penalty and Ryan Giggs scores a famous solo goal in extra time, putting Man Utd on course for the Treble.
Aug 1999, Wembley	AFC 2 MU 1	CS	A Kanu penalty and Ray Parlour winner give Arsenal a 2-1 win after a David Beckham 30-yard free-kick. Keown and Butt start the usual melee.
Aug 1999, Highbury	AFC 1 MU 2	PL	Keane scores twice to give Man Utd a 2-1 comeback win in another end-to-end game. Vieira locks horns with both Keane and Stam; amazingly, all three avoid being sent off.
Jan 2000, Old Trafford	MU 1 AFC 1	PL	An understrength Arsenal take the lead with another Ljungberg goal against Man Utd but leave happy with a draw.
Oct 2000, Highbury	AFC 1 MU 0	PL	Thierry Henry scores an all-time classic to give Arsenal a 1-0 win, flicking the ball up with his back to goal outside the box, pivoting and hitting a dipping volley.
Feb 2001, Old Trafford	MU 6 AFC 1	PL	United smash Arsenal 6-1 with out-of-favour Yorke giving Igors Stepanovs the runaround and scoring a 19-minute hat-trick. Wenger, for once, loses it in the half-time team-talk.
Nov 2001, Highbury	AFC 4 MU 0	LC third round	A Sylvain Wiltord hat-trick secures a 4-0 League Cup win in the battle of the squad players, both teams having to play a day after Premier League losses. Arsenal substitute John Halls is sent off on his debut.
Nov 2001, Highbury	AFC 3 MU 1	PL	"Give it to Barthez" sing the crowd as Henry capitalises on two late errors by the French goalkeeper.

May 2002, Old Trafford	MU 0 AFC 1	PL	"We won the league in Manchester" sing the away fans. A brilliant Arsenal performance and Wiltord winner clinch the league title, and Double, at the home of their fierce rivals.
Dec 2002, Old Trafford	MU 2 AFC 0	PL	Man Utd win 2-0 with Phil Neville man of the match in centre-midfield.
Feb 2003, Old Trafford	MU 0 AFC 2	FA Cup fifth round	Vieira and Edu win the midfield battle this time. Tackles fly in, Giggs skies an open goal and Wiltord scores again at Old Trafford. Ferguson kicks a boot at Beckham in the dressing room, leaving him with a cut above the eye.
April 2003, Highbury	AFC 2 MU 2	PL	Ferguson celebrates on the Highbury pitch as a 2-2 draw keeps Man Utd on course for the title. Sol Campbell is sent off for 'elbowing' Ole Gunnar Solskjær and suspended for the run-in and FA Cup Final.
Aug 2003, Cardiff	AFC 1 MU 1 (MU win 4-3 on pens)	CS	Phil Neville sets the tone in the first minute with a foul (and booking) on Vieira. Francis Jeffers is sent off for kicking Neville and Campbell is later banned for reacting the same way to Eric Djemba-Djemba's kung-fu kick. Utd win 4-3 on penalties.
Sept 2003, Old Trafford	MU 0 AFC 0	PL	The Battle of Old Trafford. 31 fouls. Vieira is sent off for trying to kick van Nistelrooy, who smashes a 93rd-minute penalty (given after a Diego Forlán dive) against the crossbar. Keown jumps all over the Dutchman to rub it in, and it all kicks off with Lauren, Parlour and others backing him up. Arsenal come off fired up and don't mind the numerous bans and fines that follow.
March 2004, Highbury	AFC 1 MU 1	PL	Henry thumps a vicious swerving strike from 30 yards but Louis Saha equalises late on. A 1-1 draw stretches the Invincibles' streak.

April 2004, Villa Park	AFC 0 MU 1	FA Cup semi-final	A week later in the FA Cup semi-final, Edu and Vieira hit the woodwork but Scholes scores the winner, ending Arsenal's Treble chances. The Man Utd midfielder later makes a shocking foul on substitute Reyes, but only gets yellow.
Aug 2004, Cardiff	AFC 3 MU 1	CS	An Alan Smith volley cancels out Gilberto Silva's opener, but Reyes and a Mikaël Silvestre own-goal give Arsenal a 3-1 win.
Oct 2004, Old Trafford	MU 2 AFC 0	PL	The Battle of the Buffet. Man Utd end Arsenal's unbeaten run at 49 games as referee Mike Riley fails to send off Rio Ferdinand for a professional foul on Ljungberg, van Nistelrooy for planting his studs on Ashley Cole's knee or the Neville brothers for targeting Reyes' Achilles. The Dutchman later scores a cathartic penalty after a Wayne Rooney dive and it kicks off in the tunnel ending with Cesc Fàbregas landing a slice of pizza in Ferguson's face.
Dec 2004, Old Trafford	MU 1 AFC 0	LC quarter-final	Manuel Almunia fumbles David Bellion's shot after 19 seconds. The back-up players from both teams keep up tradition as Robin van Persie and Kieran Richardson clash and trigger a melee.
Feb 2005, Highbury	AFC 2 MU 4	PL	Vieira confronts Gary Neville in the tunnel before the game and a fired-up Keane intervenes. Vieira scores the first as Arsenal lead twice, but Man Utd come back as Almunia goes walkabout and is later chipped by John O'Shea. Silvestre is sent off for headbutting Ljungberg.
May 2005, Cardiff	AFC 0 MU 0 (AFC win 5-4 on pens)	FA Cup Final	Daylight robbery as Arsenal win the FA Cup on penalties after being dominated for 120 minutes with 36-year-old Bergkamp on his own upfront and Reyes sent off at the end. Jens Lehmann saves Scholes' penalty and Vieira seals the trophy with his last kick for the club.

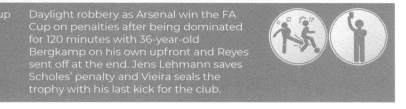

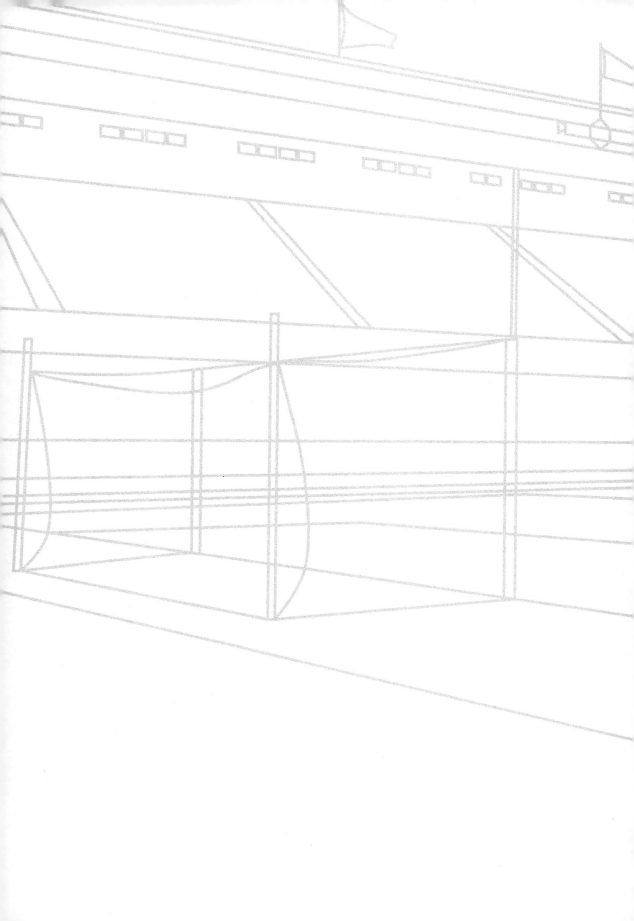

2002/03
FA CUP BUT TITLE COLLAPSE HURTS

Premier League	Second
FA Cup	Winners
Champions League	Second group
League Cup	Third round
Community Shield	Winners

PREMIER LEAGUE	PL	W	D	L	GF	GA	GD	PTS
1 MAN UTD	38	25	8	5	74	34	40	83
2 ARSENAL	38	23	9	6	85	42	43	78
3 NEWCASTLE	38	21	6	11	63	48	15	69
4 CHELSEA	38	19	10	9	68	38	30	67
5 LIVERPOOL	38	18	10	10	61	41	20	64
6 BLACKBURN ROVERS	38	16	12	10	52	43	9	60

Highlights: Winning back-to-back FA Cups; Thierry Henry's solo goal versus Spurs; sublime Wengerball in August-October

Lowlights: Blowing a five-point lead; drawing at Bolton after being 2-0 up was the worst of too many bad away days; going out of the Champions League in Valencia again

Player of the year: Henry took the 'va va voom' to another level with 32 goals and 23 assists

Top scorers: Henry 32 (24 in PL), Robert Pires 16 (14), Sylvain Wiltord 13 (10)

Goal of the season: Henry from his own half versus Spurs was Premier League Goal of the Season, Highbury, Premier League

Before the 2002/03 season, Arsène Wenger bragged, "Nobody will finish above us in the league. It wouldn't surprise me if we were to go unbeaten for the whole of the season." Similarly to after his first Double, the manager made minimal changes to the squad. Frenchman Pascal Cygan replaced Tony Adams for £2m (11 days later, Man Utd bought Rio Ferdinand for a British record fee of over £30m, a clear reflection of the contrasting financial clout and *modus operandi* of the two clubs) and defensive midfielder Gilberto Silva joined after impressing in Brazil's 2002 World Cup win. The aims were clear – defend the title and finally make an impact in the Champions League.

New captain Patrick Vieira lifted the Community Shield in Cardiff after a 1-0 win over Liverpool, substitute Gilberto drilling home Dennis Bergkamp's cutback on his debut. Unusually, Arsenal flew out of the blocks, winning seven of their first nine matches even though they were still without last season's Player of the Year Robert Pires.

Arsenal, now sponsored by O2, notched a top-flight record 14th consecutive win when they beat Birmingham 2-0 in the opener at Highbury with the second goal a sign of the electric one-touch football to come. Sol Campbell cleared from deep and the ball was quickly played through Vieira, Thierry Henry and Bergkamp to Sylvain Wiltord, who cut in from the left and curled into the far corner.

At West Ham, Joe Cole and Frédéric Kanouté put the home side 2-0 up. A fired-up Henry received a Vieira pass with his back to goal, flicked it around the defender, controlled with his thigh and fired a missile on the half-volley into the top corner. David Seaman saved a dubiously-given penalty from Kanouté before Wiltord passed into Nwankwo Kanu who held it up for the Frenchman to sidefoot into the corner and rescue a point on 88 minutes.

Against West Brom, it was Total Football as full-backs Ashley Cole and Lauren both scored in the first 20 minutes before Wiltord clipped over goalkeeper Russell Hoult. Cole's was an excellent outside-of-the-foot strike, helped by Hoult leaving an inviting proportion of the goal gaping. Cole then tried to leave a high hoof but the ball hit his toes and rolled to Scott Dobie, who nearly rejected the gift but his weak shot bobbled under Seaman's despairing dive. The left-back made amends by showing off his former winger prowess to beat two men and cross for Wiltord who again finished cleverly. It ended up 5-2 as Jérémie Aliadière scored his first and only league goal for the club.

The unbeaten run was again in doubt at Stamford Bridge when a Gianfranco Zola free-kick evaded everyone, including Seaman. Vieira was incorrectly given a second yellow card after Jesper Grønkjær kicked the bottom of his foot and his screams reverberated around the stadium. Yet again, the ten men raised their game and Kolo Touré, on for the injured Edu, capped off a hyperactive performance by heading in a rebound off Carlo Cudicini and celebrating wildly.

Arsenal beat Man City 2-1 with Wiltord finishing Bergkamp's perfect through-ball and an Henry Sidefoot Finish. In between, Nicolas Anelka, who was at his fourth club since leaving Highbury three years earlier, headed in a long cross. Charlton were dispatched 3-0 and Kanu poked in a 93rd-minute winner against Bolton to make it 2-1. It should have been a more routine win as chances were missed, including Henry hitting the post from the penalty spot, and Seaman again saw a high ball, this time a Gareth Farrelly cross, float over him. It proved at least one season too many for the goalkeeper formerly known as Safe Hands.

Even in the Champions League, Arsenal started dispatching teams relatively comfortably, winning their first three games against Borussia Dortmund (2-0), PSV Eindhoven (4-0) and Auxerre (1-0). The PSV game was a notable breakthrough as it was Arsenal's first away win in the competition in nine games. Non-Flying Dutchman Bergkamp made the 400km drive to play his first European away game since the 2000 UEFA Cup Final but, in a hostile stadium, Gilberto grabbed the headlines, scoring the fastest Champions League goal after only 20.7 seconds.

TYPICAL LINE-UP (4-4-2)

14 Henry / Wiltord / Jeffers
10 Bergkamp / Kanu

7 Pires / Ljungberg
4 Vieira / Edu
19 Gilberto / Parlour
8 Ljungberg / Wiltord / Parlour

3 Cole / van Bronckhorst
23 Campbell
5 Keown / Cygan
12 Lauren / Luzhny

1 Seaman / Taylor

Players in: Pascal Cygan, Gilberto Silva, *Rami Shaaban, Guillaume Warmuz*

Players out: Lee Dixon, Tony Adams, Alex Manninger, Richard Wright, Junichi Inamoto, Tomas Danilevičius, *Matthew Upson*

THE INVISIBLE WALL

As a defensive midfielder, Gilberto only scored 17 goals in six years, but he did score the winner on his debut in the 2002 Community Shield against Liverpool, struck Arsenal's (and the Champions League's) fastest-ever goal at 20.7 seconds against PSV Eindhoven in September 2002 and, on 19 August 2006, scored Arsenal's first competitive goal at the Emirates Stadium versus Aston Villa.

It was surprisingly easy at Elland Road as Wiltord, Kanu, Henry, Touré and others sliced through Leeds, winning 4-1 in a mesmerising display of one- and two-touch passing. Their manager Terry Venables was impressed: "Manchester United have been exceptional for ten years – but I've not seen anything as good as that." Arsenal were top of the league at the end of September, two points ahead of Liverpool and already six ahead of Man Utd in fourth.

In early October, Kanu got another two in a 3-1 win over Sunderland including a header to finish a classy move that involved a Vieira tackle and pass, a Freddie Ljungberg back-heel and Cole chip to the back post.

After 30 games, Arsenal finally lost a league game and it took something special. At Everton, where the run had begun ten months earlier, Ljungberg gave Arsenal an eighth-minute lead before Tomasz Radzinski smashed home from the edge of the box. On 90 minutes, 16-year-old Wayne Rooney famously introduced himself by picking up the ball 30 yards out, turning and curling into the top corner off the underside of the bar.

It was a goal that had a far greater effect than it should have done as Arsenal lost their next three matches 2-1 for their worst run in 19 years. In the Champions League, Auxerre silenced Highbury. 39-year-old Seaman – already under scrutiny after getting caught out by Ronaldinho's long-range free-kick in the 2002 World Cup and Macedonia scoring direct from a corner a couple of weeks earlier – was again beaten from distance, this time by Olivier Kapo. More happily, Pires made a welcome return seven months after his knee injury.

Old failings returned against Blackburn as Arsenal peppered the visitors' goal with 27 efforts, 14 of which were on target, only to be thwarted by the woodwork, goalline clearances and Brad Friedel making last-ditch saves despite a piece of knee cartilage popping out before kick-off. They lost a crazy game 2-1 as Edu scored at both ends and Dwight Yorke finished a counter-attack. A Tomáš Rosický penalty then gave Borussia Dortmund a win despite Henry curling a free-kick past Jens Lehmann. At least other results ensured qualification into the next stage of the Champions League.

Fortune turned at Fulham where Steve Marlet took a wild swing at a low corner but only managed to slice it into his own net. Wiltord finished a flowing move to give another 1-0 win against Newcastle.

On 16 November 2002, it was time for the North London derby, where Henry produced a moment so iconic they made a statue of it at the Emirates Stadium. He collected a clearance outside his own area, juggled and brought the ball down as he glided into the Spurs half, leaving players in his wake. The Frenchman kept going and going until he reached the area, turned inside Stephen Carr and Ledley King, and curled the ball left-footed into the bottom corner past Kasey Keller. Henry only needed 12 seconds to collect the ball at one end and finish at the other. Amazingly, he still had the energy to sprint all the way back to the Clock End and slide in front of the stunned and riled Spurs fans. Simon Davies was sent off soon after and Ljungberg and Wiltord finished the job for a 3-0 statement win.

At Southampton, it seemed to be business as usual as Vieira, Edu, Bergkamp and Wiltord knocked it around to tee up the Dutchman to sweep home a half-volley from the edge of the area. However, James Beattie thumped a low free-kick past Seaman from 25 yards, and Antti Niemi saved a one-on-one from Vieira and unbelievably blocked the Frenchman's two close-range follow-ups. A Cygan mistake let in Agustin Delgado and Campbell fouled him in the area trying to rescue the situation. Arsenal's defensive leader was sent off, as well as suspended for the upcoming Man Utd game, and Beattie dispatched the penalty. Arsenal then conceded a poor goal as neither Seaman nor a defender attacked a free-kick which was bundled home by Delgado from almost ground level at the back post. Pires got one back to make it 3-2 but it was another loss for the previously high-flying Champions.

Against Aston Villa, Pires opened the scoring by sidefooting a Bergkamp through-ball. Henry curled a free-kick into the top corner, as he had done in Rome four days previously, before showing his confidence with a Panenka penalty to give a 3-1 win. This set up the annual battle at Old Trafford at the start of December. Arsenal, with Keown returning after three months out, could not match the home team's intensity as utility man Phil Neville strangely got the better of Vieira in centre-midfield. Man Utd won 2-0 with goals from Juan Sebastián Verón and Paul Scholes, both of which came after Arsenal turned over possession deep in their own half.

Next it was already time for another North London derby, which proved trickier than the previous month's stroll. Christian Ziege scored a 30-yard free-kick and Cole twice made trademark goalline clearances. Luckily, Spurs goalkeeper Kasey Keller gave Arsenal a lifeline as he naively underestimated Henry's pace and came rushing off his line to bring the Frenchman down even though he was heading towards the corner-flag. Pires converted the penalty, scoring against Spurs for the fourth game in a row. In the second half, Seaman made a couple of good saves and Henry went on another 70-yard run, beating three players before teeing up Bergkamp, whose shot was blocked.

A 2-0 win over Middlesbrough, with a powerful diving header from Campbell and sidefoot finish from Pires, sent Arsenal to the top of the table, where they stayed after a hard-fought Boxing Day win at West Brom. Henry got a late winner out of the blue after Vieira blocked a clearance by Adam Chambers.

Three days later at Highbury, Liverpool took the lead on 70 minutes through a Danny Murphy penalty after Campbell had brought down Milan Baroš. Nine minutes later, Jeffers made the most of a John Arne Riise arm across him to win a penalty, which Henry buried, and

Gilberto missed a great chance late on to win the game. Arsenal capped off a successful Christmas and New Year period against Chelsea, helped by a Marcel Desailly own-goal. The game finished 3-2 with four goals in the last ten minutes. Giovanni van Bronckhorst drilled in an excellent angled shot and Cudicini fumbled Henry's effort, before Chelsea got two back, including old-boy Emmanuel Petit capitalising on a Seaman error.

At the start of 2003, Arsenal had a five-point advantage over Man Utd. Birmingham were on the end of a classic Wengerball display as Henry scored twice to reach 100 Arsenal goals, as Bergkamp had done the week before. Pires hit a sweetly-struck volley into the top corner and Lauren notched a header to make it 4-0. Ten-man West Ham were dealt with 3-1 as Henry scored a perfect hat-trick – right-foot penalty, back-post header and left-foot finish.

At Anfield, Arsenal let two crucial points slip when Emile Heskey was inexplicably left unmarked to head an equaliser in injury time. Earlier, Pires had buried a rebound after Jerzy Dudek had blocked from Henry, who had been played in by an excellent curled pass from Bergkamp. Riise drilled in for Liverpool before Bergkamp gave Arsenal the lead with a shot that deflected off Stéphane Henchoz.

Arsenal had other chances to kill the game and Henry ran Liverpool ragged, at one point picking the ball up in his own half and flying down the left wing past Henchoz and Jamie Carragher.

At home to Fulham, it was Arsenal that scored in injury time as Pires, who had earlier notched an unlikely far-post header, tapped in for a 2-1 win. Henry opened the scoring at Newcastle after being slipped in by Wiltord. However, early in the second half, Laurent Robert skipped through Arsenal's midfield and curled into the bottom corner. He was sent off five minutes later after blocking Bergkamp's attempts to take a quick free-kick. Newcastle manager Bobby Robson complained that Bergkamp had got him sent off but many teams were resorting to similar stalling tactics to interrupt Arsenal's flow, get men behind the ball and confidently deal with any set-pieces sent into the box, so it was refreshing to see the practice punished for once.

Arsenal turned on the style against Man City, racing to a 4-0 lead in 20 minutes. Bergkamp stroked home a Lauren through-ball, then Richard Dunne presented the ball to Henry and regretted it immediately as the Frenchman skinned him to set up Pires. Henry brought down a long ball and volleyed home left-footed. Campbell headed home a corner. Dunne was replaced at half-time to spare any further embarrassment. In the second half, Vieira played a one-two with Bergkamp and sidefooted calmly before Anelka made it 5-1.

RECORD-BREAKING RUNNERS-UP

Over 2001/02 and 2002/03, Arsenal set top-flight records for consecutive wins (14), games unbeaten (30), away games unbeaten (23) and games scored in (55). In 2002/03, they were top scorers in the league with 85, their best-ever in the Premier League, and netted 119 goals in all competitions.

Arsenal beat Charlton 2-0 to go eight points clear of Man Utd and Newcastle, although they had played a game more. The sun was out and it was traditionally Stage One Wenger teams' favourite time of the year. With nine games to go, Arsenal were favourites to regain their title but media hype of a Treble proved premature – seven weeks later, the eight-point lead had become a five-point deficit.

In the Champions League second group stage, Henry scored a brilliant hat-trick, Arsenal's first-ever in the competition, in the Stadio Olympico to earn a 3-1 comeback win over Roma.

The first was a cool Henry Sidefoot Finish, the second a left-foot half-volley to bury a loose ball and the third a curling free-kick into the top corner. Cygan had earlier appeared out of nowhere to block a thumping Francesco Totti volley on the line.

The promising start was not maintained as Arsenal drew their next four games, three at home, against Valencia, Ajax (twice) and Roma either 0-0 or 1-1. In the latter, Roma had Totti sent off after only 22 minutes. The failure to break down well-organised defences proved costly. It meant Arsenal needed a point in the last game at Spanish Champions Valencia, but it was déjà vu as John Carew headed the winner. An Henry Sidefoot Finish from outside the area had earlier cancelled out Carew's first strike. A brilliant team domestically with world-class players had failed to make their mark in Europe again.

Without Seaman, Campbell and Cole at Blackburn, it became a defensive crisis as Keown pulled a hamstring and Gilberto filled in at centre-back. Blackburn won 2-0 with strikes from Damien Duff and Tugay. Highbury was tense against Everton as Rooney scored again to cancel out Cygan's header past Richard Wright. However, a goal-kick was headed on twice to bounce around the Everton area where Vieira drilled it into the roof of the net for the winner.

Arsenal began April at struggling Aston Villa and failed to get the win they needed. Ljungberg tapped in a rebound from a Gilberto shot but a panicked Touré, trying to clear a corner from his own six-yard box, inexplicably lashed it into the roof of his net.

So in mid-April it was time for another massive late-season title showdown between the country's top two teams, this time at Highbury. Man Utd were three points ahead but had played a game more. On 24 minutes, Ruud van Nistelrooy beat Campbell on the left, sprinted in on goal and lifted the ball over Taylor's dive. Despite losing Vieira with a season-ending injury, Arsenal turned it around in the second half with two fortunate goals in ten minutes. The first came when Cole burst into the box and took a swing with his right foot. His shot was going wide until it deflected off Henry's calf and spun through Barthez's legs. Then Gilberto played a ball to an offside Henry, who calmly applied a Sidefoot Finish in front of a jubilant North Bank.

However, the celebrations lasted only 66 seconds as Ryan Giggs was left unmarked at the back post to head the equaliser – a recurring, and costly, theme in Arsenal's season. Campbell was sent off for 'elbowing' Ole Gunnar Solskjær, although it looked more like he put his arm out to shield the ball, and got a four-game suspension including the FA Cup Final. Although the game ended up a 2-2 draw, Alex Ferguson came onto the Highbury pitch and fist-pumped in front of the away fans, sensing his team had the momentum in the title race. He was soon proved right.

Arsenal beat Middlesbrough 2-0 with a nice finish from Wiltord and another top-corner free-kick from Henry. It was the same scoreline at Saturday lunchtime at Bolton with two goals just after half-time, Henry the provider for Wiltord and Pires. But then it all went wrong as, already without Vieira, Campbell and Edu, there were injuries to Ljungberg, Cygan and Lauren. "They were put out by bad tackles," Wenger complained – Jay-Jay Okocha's stamp on Ljungberg's ankle was particularly nasty. On 76 minutes, Bolton hit the post from a half-cleared corner and Youri Djorkaeff was left free to lift the rebound over Seaman. Seven minutes later, Keown could only glance a free-kick into his own goal to make it 2-2 and one of the most painful days ever under Wenger. At the end, Florent Laville was sent off by Andy D'Urso for a bad challenge on Cole. In the six minutes of injury time, Okocha did a rainbow flick over Parlour's head to wind down the clock and rub it in even further. Man Utd beat Spurs 2-0 the following day and took control of the title race.

Afterwards Wenger said, "I don't like the way Allardyce prepared that game with the referee. He put him under unbelievable pressure." The Bolton manager and mate of Ferguson had said that referees "showed a huge bias towards top teams" and that Arsenal "regularly intimidated referees." It was a landmark game for the "Arsenal don't like it up them" narrative as other British Football Managers subsequently followed the blueprint of a physical style, bad challenges, tactical fouls, wound-up home crowd, weak referee, and the targeting of Arsenal's vulnerability from set-pieces and crosses.

Relegation-threatened Leeds were the next visitors at Highbury. Harry Kewell brought down a long ball and smashed a half-volley past Seaman. Henry headed in a rebound from a Parlour shot but an Ian Harte free-kick after half-time put Leeds ahead again. Henry and Pires combined to set up Bergkamp but as Arsenal – who hit the woodwork four times in the match – pushed for the winner they needed, Viduka cut inside and buried an 88th-minute winner to make it 3-2. Leeds stayed up and, as in 1999, inflicted the final blow to Arsenal's title hopes.

There were still two league games left and Arsenal began their record 49 Undefeated run with a 6-1 thrashing of FA Cup Final opponents Southampton as both sides fielded rotated teams. Pires and 20-year-old Jermain Pennant scored hat-tricks, the highlight being Pires' instinctive curling lob over goalkeeper Paul Jones from 30 yards. At relegated Sunderland, it was Ljungberg's turn for a hat-trick as Arsenal won 4-0. Henry scored the first and teed up the Swede for the other three despite being only one goal behind van Nistelrooy in the Golden Boot race.

In the FA Cup, after two comfortable wins against Oxford (2-0) and Farnborough (5-1), Arsenal returned to Old Trafford. On a surprisingly sunny February day, it only took 47 seconds for Scholes to clatter Vieira from behind and another two minutes for him to do it again. After four minutes, van Nistelrooy took a high swinging kick at Keown but luckily did not make much contact. Predictably, neither were red-carded, both caused melees and Vieira was booked for dissent.

Giggs, presented with a completely open goal from the edge of the area after Keown slipped, unbelievably shovelled the ball over the bar with his right foot. Arsenal were the stronger team despite Henry and Bergkamp being rested and replaced by Wiltord and Jeffers. Edu's free-kick was deflected in off David Beckham and then the Brazilian slipped in Wiltord, who cut inside and sidefooted past Barthez to make it 2-0. Despite somehow finishing the match with 11 men, Ferguson without a hint of irony said, "Arsenal's players bullied the referee and got away with it." A furious Ferguson lost it in the dressing room and kicked a boot that hit Beckham

just above the eye, giving him a cut that needed two stitches.

The quarter-final was a pulsating game against Chelsea at Highbury. John Terry opened the scoring with a diving header before Cudicini saved an Henry penalty. Jeffers showed his fox-in-the-box credentials, tapping in after Celestine Babayaro took an air swing at what should have been a comfortable clearance. Soon after, Henry found yet another way to score. He broke a ragged offside trap, brought down Vieira's high ball with his back to goal, did a 180-degree pirouette that fooled Cudicini and rolled it into the empty net. With six minutes left, Frank Lampard made it 2-2 from a goalmouth scramble.

In the replay, Terry scored an own-goal off Vieira's cross, then the Frenchman broke through the midfield to play in Wiltord, who finished one-on-one. Cygan was sent off after 65 minutes and Terry headed a goal back before Lauren continued the tradition of Arsenal full-backs silencing Stamford Bridge. He picked up the ball just inside the Chelsea half, casually took it down the line to seemingly keep possession and kill time, then cut inside and drilled it inside the near post left-footed, prompting wild celebrations from his teammates. It was a counter-attacking masterclass and brilliant 3-1 win.

Arsenal made hard work of the semi-final against First Division Sheffield Utd. Referee Graham Poll first let a Campbell foul go unpunished then collided with Michael Tonge, leaving Vieira free to pick up the ball in the centre-circle. Arsenal, legitimately, played on and a while later Ljungberg fired the winner into the roof of the net. Furious United manager Neil Warnock was as measured as usual: "The manner in which we have lost this match is an absolute disgrace." Towards the end, Seaman made a famous save in his 1,000th senior game, clawing back a three-yard header from Paul Peschisolido that looked a certain goal.

So Arsenal went to Cardiff for the FA Cup Final for the third year running, this time to play Southampton. With the roof closed due to rain, it was the first 'indoor final'. Vieira, Edu and Cygan were injured and Campbell suspended leaving Keown and Oleh Luzhny as centre-backs.

After 38 minutes, a good move saw Ljungberg's shot blocked and the ball fall to Pires who finished from six yards. Arsenal had other efforts saved or blocked and, while not fully turning on the Wengerball style, deserved to win. On 94 minutes, Cole cleared a Beattie header off the line and back-to-back cups were secured. Seaman and Vieira jointly lifted the trophy, a happy finale to Safe Hands' Arsenal career.

Henry was voted both the PFA Players' Player of the Year and FWA Footballer of the Year. Arsenal fans sang, with some justification, "We've got the best player in the world." As Vieira had done for centre-midfielders a few years earlier, Henry redefined the role of a striker. As well as scoring 32 goals overall, he set a Premier League record of 20 assists, all from open play – a remarkable achievement for a striker and one that even specialist playmakers have failed to beat (Man City's Kevin De Bruyne equalled the record in 2019/20).

He could play on the last man, receive the ball in tight spaces, or come back into midfield or onto the left wing to burn defenders with his electric pace and play in the likes of Wiltord, Pires and Ljungberg, as well as scoring plenty of Henry Sidefoot Finishes, netbusters and now curling free-kicks. After him, top-level strikers could no longer be either a penalty box finisher or target man. They had to be quick, strong and technical, and occupy two or three defenders on their own as teams moved to playing one upfront.

The "shift of power" Wenger referenced after winning the previous season's title at Old Trafford had not happened. In footballing terms, the Arsenal 2002/03 side was a contender for the best team in history not to win the league. It was all too easy at times as they played brilliant attacking football and the media, other players and managers, and Wenger went heavy on the praise, especially between August and October. However, they dropped 14 points from winning positions in away matches. Early in the season, this was often due to complacency. In the run-in, it was due to pressure and lack of quality squad depth to cover injuries and the fixture pile-up brought about by going deep in three competitions.

Man Utd capitalised with a strong finish to the season. Wenger failed to bolster and freshen up a very good squad, in goal and central defence in particular. Improving his squad from a position of strength to keep everyone hungry and maintain competition for places was a hallmark of Ferguson. Wenger, on the other hand, stayed loyal to the players that had brought success and this trait was a key factor in Arsenal failing to win back-to-back titles during his reign as well as getting caught in a *Groundhog Day* loop during Stage Two and Three. Vieira later said, "His loyalty to his players is both his biggest strength and his biggest weakness."

2003/04
THE INVINCIBLES

Premier League	Winners
FA Cup	Semi-final
Champions League	Quarter-final
League Cup	Semi-final
Community Shield	Runners-up

PREMIER LEAGUE	PL	W	D	L	GF	GA	GD	PTS
1 ARSENAL	38	26	12	0	73	26	47	90
2 CHELSEA	38	24	7	7	67	30	37	79
3 MAN UTD	38	23	6	9	64	35	29	75
4 LIVERPOOL	38	16	12	10	55	37	18	60
5 NEWCASTLE	38	13	17	8	52	40	12	56
6 ASTON VILLA	38	15	11	12	48	44	4	56

Highlights: Winning the league at White Hart Lane; 4-2 comeback win against Liverpool; the Battle of Old Trafford; 5-1 in the San Siro; Thierry Henry's four goals versus Leeds; sealing the Invincibles season in a party atmosphere against Leicester

Lowlights: Getting knocked out of the Champions League by Chelsea and FA Cup by Man Utd in the space of four days

Player of the year: Peak Henry was one of the best players in the world

Top scorers: Henry 39 (30 in PL), Robert Pires 19 (14), Freddie Ljungberg 10 (3)

Goal of the season: Henry's crucial solo effort versus Liverpool, Highbury, Premier League

"We are unbeatable" sang the Highbury crowd on 15 May 2004 as Patrick Vieira lifted the Premier League trophy, but it was the Invincibles tag that eventually stuck for one of the greatest teams and seasons English football has seen. Won 26, drew 12, lost 0. Arsenal became only the second side to go an English top-flight season unbeaten after Preston North End in 1888-89, and that team only had to play 22 games not 38. A year after Arsène Wenger was ridiculed for saying that Arsenal could go the season undefeated, he was proved right.

The Invincibles' success was based on:

- A recognisable first 11, which surprisingly only started two Premier League games, containing up to six world-class players (Sol Campbell, Ashley Cole, Vieira, Robert Pires, Dennis Bergkamp and Thierry Henry) supplemented by strong squad back-ups.

- Tactical flexibility – they played a very loose 4-4-2 formation.

- Interchange of positions to confuse opponents and create space – Pires and Ljungberg would drift inside allowing the full-backs to be attacking weapons, especially Cole on the left; Bergkamp would drop deep to play precision passes to the likes of Henry, Pires and Ljungberg; and Henry would start from in-between the right-back and centre-back, often drifting left to leave space in the centre.

- Athletic defence shielded by two ball-winning centre-midfielders and two hard-working wide players.

- Rapid counter-attacks – as soon as they won the ball, three or four players (such as Henry, Pires, Freddie Ljungberg and Vieira) would surge forward in support.

- Pace all over the pitch.

- One- and two-touch pass and move.

- Peak Henry as the spearhead – a dribbler, supplier and lethal finisher all in one.

- A willingness to deliver early low crosses or shoot from outside the box.

In summer 2003, Russian billionaire Roman Abramovich bought Chelsea, already a team on the rise under managers Ruud Gullit and Gianluca Vialli, for £140m, paid off their debt and immediately funded a £111m spending spree. A few months later, Chelsea made a £40-50m bid for Henry, which was immediately rejected. Arsenal vice-chairman David Dein quipped that Abramovich had "parked his Russian tanks on our lawn and is firing £50 notes at us." Arsenal and Man Utd could no longer only worry about finishing above each other and know they would win the league.

In contrast, Arsenal were constrained by spending on their new stadium, but these were the days where Wenger unearthed cut-priced gems and turned them into stars – teenagers Cesc Fàbregas and Gaël Clichy were picked up for a combined £250,000. He hit upon a new defensive pairing in pre-season, finding a settled position for Kolo Touré alongside lynchpin Campbell. In typical Wenger style, he created a defence containing three converted midfielders, but they all proved masterstrokes as Lauren, Cole and Touré added positional sense to their ball-playing ability, athleticism and attacking instincts.

He also finally bought a quality goalkeeper in Jens Lehmann to replace David Seaman. A leader, strong character and organiser that demanded the highest standards around him, Lehmann played every minute of every game in the three main competitions.

In the Community Shield against Man Utd, Arsenal were back in their traditional yellow and blue away colours, unveiling a classy retro 1979 FA Cup Final kit. The game finished 1-1 as a 30-yard Henry free-kick cancelled out Mikaël Silvestre's header. Despite it being a sweltering day and far-from-full crowd, there was still aggro. Francis Jeffers signed off his Arsenal career with a red card after kicking Phil Neville. Eric Djemba-Djemba followed through studs up on Campbell's waist, and the centre-back reacted by back-

TYPICAL LINE-UP
(4-4-2)

14 Henry / Reyes Aliadière

10 Bergkamp / Wiltord Kanu

7 Pires / Reyes

19 Gilberto / Edu

4 Vieira / Parlour

8 Ljungberg / Parlour

3 Cole / Clichy

28 Touré / Cygan

23 Campbell / Keown

12 Lauren / Touré

1 Lehmann

Players in: Philippe Senderos, Jens Lehmann, Johan Djourou, Gaël Clichy, Cesc Fàbregas, *José Antonio Reyes*

Players out: David Seaman, Giovanni van Bronckhorst, Oleh Luzhny, Guillaume Warmuz

heeling him. Man Utd won 4-3 on penalties as Tim Howard saved from Giovanni van Bronckhorst and Pires.

Arsenal began the league season with a perfect August, beating Everton 2-1 through an Henry penalty and Pires tap-in, and despite Campbell being sent off for a contentious professional foul on Thomas Gravesen after 25 minutes. The Wengerball was in full flow in a 4-0 win at Middlesbrough. Ljungberg set up Henry and Sylvian Wiltord for tap-ins, Pires chipped for Gilberto Silva to drill in a volley, and Wiltord opened his body and guided in an Henry cross with a sidefoot volley. Aston Villa were beaten 2-0 at Highbury with second-half goals from Campbell and Henry.

At Man City, Lauren embarrassingly shinned a long ball past Lehmann before Wiltord equalised after typical interplay on the left between Pires and Cole. Then Ljungberg finished into an empty net after Seaman came out unconvincingly to challenge Pires and reaffirmed that time had caught up with the former Arsenal number one.

Against Portsmouth at Highbury, Teddy Sheringham headed the opener before Pires flicked the ball too far, hung out a leg and went down to con a penalty. Henry had to re-take the spot-kick due to encroachment but converted both times to make it a 1-1 draw that some

Invincibles critics like to put an asterisk alongside.

A few days later, the Champions League campaign got off to a bad start as Inter Milan silenced Highbury with three first-half goals. Henry had a penalty saved by Francesco Toldo and at the end of game Marco Materazzi and Javier Zanetti argued over who would get the Frenchman's shirt. It was the worst preparation for the following Sunday's trip to Old Trafford, the annual barometer for Arsenal's title chances.

Martin Keown replaced Campbell, whose father had passed away that week, and Wenger showed his intentions by picking the more industrious Ray Parlour and Ljungberg over Pires and Wiltord in midfield. The tactics worked as Arsenal held strong and limited Man Utd's chances to a Ryan Giggs free-kick that evaded everyone to hit the post and a Ruud van Nistelrooy header. Arsenal did not have a shot on target.

After 77 minutes, Vieira was booked for a foul on Quinton Fortune. Three minutes later, under a high ball, van Nistelrooy jumped all over Vieira. The Arsenal captain fell for the wind-up and kicked out. Although Vieira was well off target, van Nistelrooy jumped back theatrically and referee Steve Bennett gave both players yellow cards, meaning Vieira was sent off.

Arsenal players were incensed with the Dutchman. Just as it looked like the ten men had held out, their anger reached boiling point. In injury time,

Gary Neville crossed from the right and Diego Forlán threw himself to the ground under pressure from Keown. Bennett pointed to the spot. After lengthy protests from Arsenal players, van Nistelrooy, who had surprisingly missed his two previous penalties including Lehmann saving his effort in the Community Shield shootout, lined up to take the kick and add to Arsenal's sense of injustice. Lehmann did his best to distract his opponent, sidestepping along the goalline and waving his arms. Unbelievably, the Dutchman smashed his shot against the crossbar and seconds later the final whistle went.

Arsenal players' fury with the Dutchman's gamesmanship on both this and previous occasions, as well as the regularity with which they were on the wrong end of penalty and red card decisions in games between the two teams, came to a head. Keown led the way and comically jumped all over the Dutchman, while others including Parlour and Lauren pushed him around. Other clashes involved Lauren and Giggs as well as Cole and Cristiano Ronaldo.

Arsenal came off fired up with team spirit emboldened and having sent a message they would not be pushed around. They would deal with the repercussions later. It proved a pivotal moment in the season – a draw was a huge result as a late loss would have been tough to take so soon after the previous season's collapse.

The Battle of Old Trafford was one of the most infamous games in Premier League history. Yes, it was unsavoury, petulant and unsporting, but some of the reaction was hysterical – after all, no one came away with even a scratch. Arsenal received a fine of £175,000, the biggest ever dished out by the FA. Lauren (four games), Keown (three), Vieira (one) and Parlour (one) were banned and fined, while Cole, Giggs and Ronaldo were also fined.

Wenger, as always, defended his players: "I think van Nistelrooy does not help. Frankly, his attitude is always looking for provocation and diving. He looks a nice boy but I think on the pitch it's not always fair behaviour."

Importantly, Arsenal capitalised on the Old Trafford momentum by winning three tricky, and tight, games. On an entertaining Friday night at Highbury, Newcastle equalised twice as Henry benefited from a Titus Bramble slice and Gilberto headed in a free-kick. Ljungberg hit the woodwork for the third time this season, showing a range of chips and curlers, while Vieira and Cole went off injured. After 80 minutes, Jermaine Jenas inexplicably jumped for a corner with his arm up and conceded a penalty, which Henry 'Panenked' past Shay Given to make it 3-2.

Harry Kewell volleyed Liverpool into an early lead, but a Pires free-kick bounced off Sami Hyypiä into his own net. On 68 minutes, Pires again showed the Anfield crowd his class, cutting in from the left and curling a brilliant winner inside the far post. A confident Chelsea came to Highbury with new players and an unbeaten start to the season. A deflected Edu free-kick after five minutes was cancelled out by an impressive Hernán Crespo curler. With 15 minutes left, Carlo Cudicini missed Pires' low cross and it hit Henry's shin to give Arsenal a 2-1 win.

In the Champions League, Arsenal did not enjoy their long away trips, drawing 0-0 with Lokomotiv Moscow (not falling for an attempted honeytrap involving "Russian top models" who planned to tire them out the night before the game, according to Pascal Cygan) and losing 2-1 to Dynamo Kyiv, the second goal seeing Lehmann lose the ball outside his area.

Back in the Premier League, Paolo Di Canio scored a Panenka penalty of his own for Charlton. When Henry lined up a free-kick from 20 yards, the home side built a big wall and positioned the other players around the goalline; a route to goal looked impossible but Henry curled a brilliant strike into the top corner. A point was enough for Arsenal to be top at the end of October.

At Leeds, Arsenal repeated their 4-1 thrashing of the previous season. After eight minutes, Cole played a ball over the top for Henry to sprint away from the defence and score. Two more rapid counter-attacks ended with Pires and Henry finishes to make it 3-0 after half an hour.

However, Arsenal were struggling in Europe and needed to end the club-record run of six home games without a win. After missing numerous chances against Dynamo Kyiv, it looked like they were out of the competition when Henry flicked on and Cole came out of nowhere to bury a diving header in the 89th minute.

Spurs took a rare lead at Highbury after five minutes as the ball ricocheted into Darren Anderton's path. Spurs held on for over an hour until Kasey Keller saved a one-on-one from Henry and Pires buried the rebound for his customary North London derby goal. Ten minutes later, Ljungberg's shot from outside the box took a deflection to loop over Keller and earn a 2-1 win.

At Birmingham, injuries and the Old Trafford suspensions kicking in meant an unusual centre-midfield partnership of Edu and Pires. It did not matter as Arsenal's transition play was at its breath-taking best as Henry first set up Ljungberg after four minutes, then Bergkamp and Pires late on to seal a 3-0 win. The second goal started with Arsenal defending a corner; seconds later, the Dutchman dinked over Maik Taylor.

Two frustrating draws followed against Fulham (0-0) and Leicester (1-1), the latter when Cole was red-carded for a foul on Ben Thatcher, and Arsenal conceded a 90th-minute equaliser.

In Italy, only victory over Inter Milan would keep Arsenal in the Champions League. A precise Henry Sidefoot Finish opened the scoring before Christian Vieri equalised with a deflected shot. Four minutes into the second half, Henry twisted and turned on the left, and squared to Ljungberg to finish. In a crazy last ten minutes, an Henry-inspired Arsenal ran rampant against legendary defenders Fabio Cannavaro, Ivan Cordoba, Materazzi and Zanetti.

The highlight came when Campbell hoofed clear a corner, Parlour headed on and Henry picked the ball up in his own half. Zanetti did well to stay with the Frenchman and hold him up. But Henry went again, beat him on the outside and fired into the far corner left-footed. Edu added another and celebrated by banging on the Perspex doors in front of the away fans while two straight-faced *Carabinieri* stood by. Jérémie Aliadière joined in the fun, shouldering Jérémie Bréchet off the ball and setting up Pires.

On a famous night, the away fans chanted, "5-1 in the San Siro." It was the first time an Italian team had conceded five goals at home in the Champions

League, and Arsenal had finally showed the rest of Europe some classic Wengerball. Arsenal got the job done at Highbury against Lokomotiv Moscow with goals from Pires and Ljungberg, and after taking only one point from the first three games, they ended up winning the group.

Arsenal went top of the Premier League after beating Blackburn 1-0 as Touré, covering for Lauren at right-back, rampaged down the wing and teed up Bergkamp. On a rainy Saturday before Christmas, Arsenal travelled to Bolton with the memory of the previous season's lost title fresh in their minds. Lehmann and Arsenal looked to have survived the barrage of crosses and poached a win when Pires bobbled in a second-half rebound. However, on 83 minutes, the home team scored a typical Sam Allardyce goal – long free-kick, strong aerial challenge, first to the second ball and half-volley from the edge of the area by Henrik Pedersen. This year, Arsenal were satisfied with a 1-1 draw.

Seeing Vieira back in full flight on Boxing Day after two months of injury problems was a welcome sight for Arsenal fans. Not for Jody Craddock though. First, Vieira pressured him into an own-goal from a corner. Then Vieira robbed him and set up Henry. A Vieira tackle also set up the third, as Edu passed to Henry, who dropped his shoulder and drilled left-footed into the bottom-right corner, again proving he could finish with both feet. A 1-0 win at Southampton through a Pires finish from Henry's ball inside the right-back meant Arsenal reached the New Year unbeaten in the league. But they were only in second place, one point behind Man Utd, who had won six in a row, and three ahead of Chelsea.

Arsenal began their FA Cup defence with a difficult draw at Leeds. It started badly as Lehmann took a heavy touch and Mark Viduka blocked his clearance into the net. Arsenal recovered with a brilliant display of quickfire pass and move. Henry met Ljungberg's cross with a thumping sidefoot volley, then the Frenchman set up Edu and Pires. Another team move ended with Pires hanging up a ball for Touré to volley

home and yet another 4-1 win over Leeds.

At Everton, Kanu scored his first league goal of the season, but Tomasz Radzinski made it 1-1. Middlesbrough were easily dispatched 4-1 at Highbury. Danny Mills naively spent the game trying to wind up Henry, including sledging the Frenchman when he was preparing to take a penalty. Henry dispatched the kick and celebrated in Mills' face. Mills later tried to shepherd the ball out near the corner-flag, but Henry dragged the ball back, flicked it through Mills' legs and left him standing there to take in the schadenfreude of the 38,000 fans.

At Aston Villa, Henry checked with the referee before passing a free-kick into the empty part of the net while Thomas Sørensen was organising his wall. Manager David O'Leary complained, offering a very different opinion on the matter to when his Leeds player Ian Harte did the same to David Seaman in 2001. Henry then converted a penalty after a classic Kanu Dummy made a fool of three defenders and he was obstructed. The win took Arsenal top of the table, where they stayed for the rest of the season.

In the League Cup, Wenger continued his policy of blooding young players and giving game time to squad players. Fàbregas (becoming the

club's youngest player at 16 years and 177 days) and Clichy made their debuts on an entertaining night as First Division side Rotherham came to Highbury. After 120 minutes and a 1-1 draw, it took 22 penalties to separate the teams. Arsenal won the shootout 9-8, with Wiltord missing the first but scoring Arsenal's last. Subsequent wins came over Wolves (5-1 with Fàbregas becoming the club's youngest-ever scorer) and West Brom (2-0).

With the semi-final two-legged, Arsenal had to play Middlesbrough four times in less than four weeks. However, there would be no League Cup and full set of domestic trophies for Wenger as Arsenal lost 1-0 to a Juninho goal at home and 2-1 away as Keown was sent off and José Antonio Reyes scored an own-goal. It was the 20-year-old Spaniard's second game after signing from Sevilla in January to boost Arsenal's attacking firepower even further. They did beat the same team 4-1 in the FA Cup, notable for youth prospect David Bentley scoring a Bergkamp-esque chip.

Five wins out of five in February extended Arsenal's lead in the table. First came Man City on a wet Tuesday night. After seven minutes, Henry skidded a ball across the six-yard box which came off Michael Tarnat for an own-goal. Late on, Henry picked up the ball on the left and from 25 yards hit a tracer bullet into the top-right corner, another classic strike to add to the Frenchman's portfolio. Nicolas Anelka made it 2-1 on 89 minutes, which sparked the standard football procedure when a team scores a late goal and senses an improbable comeback – the scorer races into the net to retrieve the ball in the naive belief it will speed up the restart, while the winning team annoyingly hold on to the ball. This time the protagonists were Anelka and Cole. Surprisingly, and to the delight of the home crowd, Anelka was given a red card and Cole a yellow.

Arsenal went to Wolves and got an early lead through a Bergkamp special, the Dutchman cutting across a volley to send it into the bottom-right corner. Wolves equalised from a corner, but Pires slipped in Henry and Touré completed a 3-1 win. Henry then scored both goals against Southampton.

The tricky games came thick and fast as Arsenal faced Chelsea twice. In the FA Cup fifth round, Adrian Mutu gave the away side the lead from 20 yards before Reyes sent Highbury wild and Arsenal knocked Chelsea out of the FA Cup for the fourth year in a row. The Spaniard arrowed a sweet rising drive from outside the area into the top corner past Carlo Cudicini. Five minutes later, he sidefooted Vieira's ball past substitute Neil Sullivan. In the league at Stamford Bridge, Eidur Gudjohnsen gave Chelsea the lead after 27 seconds. Fifteen minutes later, Bergkamp's pass with the outside of his right foot

INVINCIBLE

WWWWDDWWWDWWWDDWD
WWDWWWWWWWWDWDW
DDDWW

carved Chelsea's defence open and was perfectly weighted for Vieira to burst on to and finish one-on-one. Sullivan then made a mess of a corner, leaving Edu to score the winner.

In the Champions League knockout, Arsenal beat Celta Vigo 3-2 in Spain. Edu, who was in excellent form and justifying his increased game time as strong cover for Vieira and Gilberto, scored twice, the second a 20-yard curler with his weaker right foot. Arsenal conceded twice from set-pieces, but Henry and Pires played a couple of rapid-fire one-twos, and the latter poked home. The home leg was a comfortable 2-0 win with Henry scoring twice, the first after a typical Bergkamp pirouette-and-flick assist.

At Highbury, it only took 100 seconds for Henry, Ljungberg and Pires to carve Charlton open. Minutes later, Henry made it two. Arsenal had 21 shots but a Claus Jensen free-kick invoked memories of last season's collapse and prompted a nervous last 30 minutes, especially when Jonatan Johansson hit the post in injury time with an overhead kick from outside the area.

Arsenal held on and at the end of March were nine points clear.

In the FA Cup quarter-final against Portsmouth, Arsenal gave another classic exhibition of rapid interplay, with Reyes slotting in well. Arsenal won 5-1 and when Henry, Vieira and Ljungberg were taken off after 70 minutes, the Fratton Park crowd gave them a standing ovation.

At Aston Villa, Henry curled another long-range free-kick and Pires notched another rebound, again showing the benefits of following up shots and being alert in the area. Against Bolton at home, Pires scored another of his specialities, a sidefoot curler from the inside-left position 20 yards out, as Arsenal won 2-1. It was their ninth league win a row, a run that coincided with them getting their first-choice line-up back on the pitch for the first time since before the Battle of Old Trafford. Man Utd, surprisingly, won just three in nine.

At the end of March, Arsenal faced Chelsea in the Champions League quarter-final with Treble talk in the air. Early in the second half, Lehmann came out of his area to deal with a long ball, but Gudjohnsen blocked his clearance and finished into the empty net. Five minutes later, Pires soared to head home a Cole cross. Marcel Desailly got booked twice late on and was sent off. With an away goal and home advantage to come, Arsenal were favourites to progress.

Then Man Utd came to Highbury hoping to de-rail Arsenal's title charge. In the tunnel, Vieira joked to Roy Keane, "Smile, man." The Man Utd captain replied, "I'd be smiling if I was 12 points clear as well." Henry scored another brilliant strike, this time with power and swerve to wrong-foot Roy Carroll from 30 yards. However, with five minutes left, Louis Saha was left unmarked to tap in a low cross. A 1-1 draw suited leaders Arsenal, but they missed the opportunity to get one over their rivals.

A week later, the two teams met again in the FA Cup semi-final at Villa Park. Wenger started with Aliadière instead of Henry, while van Nistelrooy was injured. After two minutes, Wes Brown headed off the line from Bergkamp. Edu chipped Carroll but it hit the bar and the goalkeeper saved Touré's follow-up. On the half-hour, Giggs squared for Paul Scholes, who buried it. A Vieira header from a free-kick brushed the post, but Arsenal were not at their free-flowing best. Henry, Reyes and Kanu came on in the second half and, within 15 minutes, Reyes got his first taste of how Man Utd would target him. Scholes crashed into him well after the ball had gone, scissoring and twisting his leg but luckily not causing serious injury. It was Arsenal's first FA Cup loss in 19 ties since the 2001 final.

Three days later, it was Chelsea in the Champions League. Just before

half-time, Highbury erupted as Reyes finished right-footed. Early in the second half, Claude Makélélé powered a long-range volley that Lehmann could not hold and Lampard levelled the tie. On 87 minutes, Highbury was stunned as left-back Wayne Bridge played a one-two with Gudjohnsen and calmly sidefooted past Lehmann.

It was a huge blow to Arsenal, not just to get knocked out by their Premier League rivals, but Wenger's iconic team, with world-class players at the height of their powers, would never have a better chance to win the Champions League. Monaco and Porto awaited in the semi-final and final. An improving Chelsea played well and maybe Arsenal were slightly complacent over the two games, perhaps understandably so given they had not lost to Chelsea for 17 games, but the matches between the two were getting tighter and Arsenal could not continue to rely on a goalkeeping error or unlikely moment of brilliance to get the win. Arsenal were also undone by a punishing schedule of seven tough games in 22 days, something teams in other leagues did not have to face as authorities rescheduled their domestic games around big Champions League fixtures.

With Arsenal going out of two competitions in four days, the "choker" accusations resurfaced. Three days later on Good Friday, Liverpool came to Highbury with Arsenal four points ahead of Chelsea but having played a game less. Would all the great football and accolades come to nothing like the previous season? A nervous Highbury crowd feared so after five minutes when Hyypiä headed in from a corner and again at half-time as Michael Owen gave Liverpool a 2-1 lead.

However, Arsenal were determined not to lose the title for the second year running. Four minutes into the second half, Ljungberg glanced an Henry pass into Pires' path and the French midfielder finished left-footed. A minute later, Henry seized the moment and raised the roof at a relieved Highbury. He picked the ball up ten yards inside the Liverpool half and rounded Dietmar Hamann, who failed in his efforts to stop him both legally and illegally. Henry then gave Jamie Carragher such twisted blood that he took out his teammate Igor Bišćan, and the Frenchman sidefooted past Jerzy Dudek. Henry later completed his hat-trick to make it 4-2 as Dudek saved his one-on-one effort, but the ball rebounded back off Henry into the net.

There would be no choke this year. Arsenal secured a point at Newcastle two days later with a 0-0 draw before they, and Henry, put on a Friday-night masterclass as they smashed Leeds 5-0. They beat the offside trap again and again, timing their run and pass to perfection. The first was Bergkamp to Pires, who curled home. Gilberto played in Henry twice. The Frenchman then scored a Panenka penalty. The best was saved for last when Henry raced on to a Pires layoff near halfway at such speed that he took out five defenders. Gary Kelly tripped Henry but the Frenchman was good enough to finish as he was falling. Four more goals for Henry, who loved playing against goalkeeper Paul Robinson. Arsenal scored 13 goals in three games against Leeds in 2003/04.

On Sunday, 25 April 2004, Chelsea lost in the early kick-off at Newcastle, meaning Arsenal only needed a draw at Spurs to win the title at White Hart Lane for the second time in their history. Arsenal did not waste any time. After three minutes, they cleared a Spurs corner. Henry raced away with the ball, passed inside the right-back for Bergkamp, who crossed low for Vieira to slide in and score a classic counter-attacking goal. Half an hour later, a brilliant spell of keep-ball ended with Bergkamp playing in Vieira on the left, who cut back for Pires to score.

On the hour, Jamie Redknapp drilled an excellent low drive. Four minutes into injury team, awaiting a corner, Robbie Keane wound up Lehmann and the German gave the referee the opportunity to give a dubious penalty. Keane converted, and he and the Spurs fans wildly celebrated the 2-2 draw; embarrassing given they had just witnessed their rivals win the title at their own ground. The ending was a brief disappointment for Arsenal players and fans, who wanted the win to reinforce their North London superiority, but the elation at winning the league soon took over. Despite being told not to celebrate on the pitch and inflame the crowd, the party started in front of the away section.

With the league secured, Wenger stressed the opportunity to create history and complete the season unbeaten. The players found it hard to keep up the intensity but secured draws against Birmingham and Portsmouth, the latter with a low Reyes volley and late Lehmann one-on-one save from Yakubu. At Fulham, the Spaniard tackled goalkeeper Edwin van der Sar to give a 1-0 win.

That just left Leicester at a sunny Highbury. Former Arsenal striker Paul Dickov did not read the script and gave the away side a 1-0 lead at half-time. Arsenal went up a gear to ensure history was made and the party could start in full. Henry scored a penalty and Bergkamp sliced open the defence to play in Vieira who rounded the goalkeeper. Wenger left it excruciatingly late to bring on Keown for his tenth game and a Premiership medal in his last season at the club. It was well deserved for the centre-back who always played with intensity and a burning desire to win – his smothering marking was a nightmare for opposing forwards. Clichy became the youngest player to win a Premier League medal, aged 18 years and 10 months.

The Invincibles season was Wenger's crowning achievement. Six players were selected in the PFA Team of the Year (Lauren, Campbell, Cole, Vieira, Pires and Henry). Henry won PFA Players' Player of the Year, FWA Footballer of the Year, Premier League Player of the Season, the Golden Boot and the European Golden Shoe, while Wenger was named LMA Manager of the Year and Premier League Manager of the Season.

Breaking Up The Band

Arsène Wenger spent years putting together one of British football's best-ever teams, winning two league titles and two FA Cups in three seasons, and peaking with the Invincibles season in 2003/04. However, instead of building from a position of strength, a squad where the quality ran deep was dismantled prematurely. It was not a conscious decision on Wenger's behalf. Some players' careers were winding down (Martin Keown, Ray Parlour, Nwankwo Kanu) but others left too early (Patrick Vieira, Edu and most notably Ashley Cole) as Arsenal entered Stage Two Wenger and its stadium-related financial constraints. Wenger was left to rebuild a new team but could not get enough quality around the likes of Cesc Fàbregas to challenge old foe Man Utd and newly petrodollar-fuelled Chelsea.

2004/05
END OF A GOLDEN ERA

Premier League	Second	
FA Cup	Winners	
Champions League	Round of 16	
League Cup	Quarter-final	
Community Shield	Winners	

PREMIER LEAGUE		PL	W	D	L	GF	GA	GD	PTS
1	CHELSEA	38	29	8	1	72	15	57	95
2	ARSENAL	38	25	8	5	87	36	51	83
3	MAN UTD	38	22	11	5	58	26	32	77
4	EVERTON	38	18	7	13	45	46	-1	61
5	LIVERPOOL	38	17	7	14	52	41	11	58
6	BOLTON	38	16	10	12	49	44	5	58

Highlights: Stealing the FA Cup on penalties after being dominated by Man Utd; stretching the unbeaten record to 49 games; winning crazy games 5-4 against Spurs and 5-3 against Middlesbrough; thrashing Everton 7-0 led by a Dennis Bergkamp masterclass

Lowlights: 2-0 loss at Old Trafford that triggered the Battle of the Buffet; losing 4-2 at home to Man Utd; dismissed by Bayern Munich in the Champions League first leg

Player of the year: Thierry Henry kept showcasing dazzling footwork and skill at a pace not seen before

Top scorers: Henry 30 (25 in PL), Robert Pires 17 (14), Freddie Ljungberg 14 (10), José Antonio Reyes 12 (9), Robin van Persie 10 (5)

Goal of the season: Reyes' right-foot drive against Middlesbrough finished a move that involved a Bergkamp nutmeg and classic pass, Highbury, Premier League

Arsène Wenger began his quest to defend the title for the first time by backing the Invincibles first-choice line-up – managing to hold on to Patrick Vieira despite the usual speculation of a move to Real Madrid – supplemented by young players Cesc Fàbregas, José Antonio Reyes, Robin van Persie, Philippe Senderos and Gaël Clichy. They were needed as senior squad players Nwankwo Kanu, Sylvain Wiltord, Ray Parlour and Martin Keown left for no fee.

In contrast, Chelsea owner Roman Abramovich went on another spending spree, bringing in Porto's Champions League-winning manager José Mourinho and a whole new spine in Petr Čech, Ricardo Carvalho, Tiago Mendes, Didier Drogba and Arjen Robben for £100m.

A 3-1 win in the Community Shield over Man Utd was a good omen for Arsenal, although both sides had players missing. Reyes dropped his shoulder twice to fool the defence and goalkeeper but missed the open goal with his right foot. He later made amends by setting up Gilberto Silva as well as scoring himself.

The title defence could hardly have started better as Arsenal won eight of their first nine games, stretching the unbeaten run to a record 49 games. They won 4-1 at Everton on the opening day with goals from Dennis Bergkamp, Reyes, Freddie Ljungberg and Robert Pires. Fàbregas, sporting a 1980s mullet, became Arsenal's youngest-ever Premier League player at 17 years and 103 days, and it was clear he was ready.

On a sunny Sunday, the club was presented with a golden Premier League replica trophy to honour the Invincibles' achievement. Middlesbrough were the visitors and equalling Nottingham Forest's 42-game unbeaten record was expected to be a formality. A long Reyes diagonal ball played in Thierry Henry, who lobbed Mark Schwarzer to open the scoring. Arsenal hit the woodwork twice before missed tackles let in Joseph-Désiré Job to smash the equaliser. Just after half-time, Pascal Cygan made a mess of a long ball and Jimmy Floyd Hasselbaink thumped it home. Jens Lehmann and Highbury were stunned again three minutes later when Franck Queudrue saw the goalkeeper out of position and shot from 25 yards into the gap.

Arsenal were not in the mood to let their record go, however, and Bergkamp drove forward and drilled into the bottom corner from just outside the area. Nine minutes later, Pires tapped in Henry's cross-shot. Arsenal won the ball back straight from the kick-off and played it to Reyes in the left corner of the box. The Spaniard cut inside and hammered a right-foot shot into the top corner to send Highbury wild. Late on, Pires cut back for Henry to seal a memorable 5-3 comeback win. Arsenal were electric in attack with numerous goalscoring threats. However, the defending was a worry.

Second-half goals from Henry, Gilberto and Reyes ensured a 3-0 win against Blackburn. Norwich had not lost at Carrow Road for eight months, but Arsenal dealt with them easily after Graham Poll only gave Lauren a yellow for a professional foul on Darren Huckerby and were 3-0 up at half-time. Henry turned on the afterburners on the left and squared for Reyes to tap in. The Frenchman headed home a Ljungberg cross. Pires swept in after Ljungberg robbed Adam Drury in the area. The game finished 4-1 as Bergkamp scored a late volley.

Against Fulham, referee Mark Halsey grabbed the headlines when he gave the home side a penalty after Andy Cole stretched for a ball as Ashley Cole came in from the side. Halsey realised he might have messed up when he saw the players' bewildered reactions. After Arsenal complaints and consulting with his assistant, he cancelled the penalty and restarted with a drop-ball. Reyes came on in the second half and instigated a move that saw Ljungberg fire across Edwin van der Sar. The Swede then forced an own-goal from Zat Knight before Bergkamp played in Reyes to finish one-on-one for a 3-0 win.

Bolton were the first team to take points off the Champions as an 85th-minute route-one goal from Henrik Pedersen gave them a 2-2 draw. At Man City, an instinctive flick by Cole with the

TYPICAL LINE-UP (4-4-2)

14 Henry / Reyes
10 Bergkamp / van Persie
7 Pires / Reyes
19 Gilberto / Edu
4 Vieira / Fàbregas / Flamini
8 Ljungberg / Pires / Fàbregas
3 Cole / Clichy
28 Touré / Cygan
23 Campbell / Senderos
12 Lauren
1 Lehmann / Almunia

Players in: Robin van Persie, Manuel Almunia, Mathieu Flamini, *Emmanuel Eboué*

Players out: Martin Keown, Ray Parlour, Nwankwo Kanu, Francis Jeffers, Sylvain Wiltord, Rami Shaaban

outside of his foot gave Arsenal a tough 1-0 win in the rain.

Arsenal cut Charlton apart in a 4-0 win. Ljungberg opened the scoring before Henry scored a memorable goal. On the six-yard box with his back to goal and defender Jon Fortune all over him, the Frenchman back-heeled it through Fortune's legs and into the net. Henry and Reyes both then scored fierce strikes.

Lee Hendrie opened the scoring for Aston Villa with a bobbling shot that Lehmann should have saved. Pires converted a penalty – in line with Henry's custom of not taking it when he was the person fouled – before Reyes set up an Henry Sidefoot Finish. An excellent team move ended with Pires sidefooting home. Arsenal had made a flying start, scoring 29 goals in nine games.

On 24 October 2004, 13 months after the Battle of Old Trafford, Arsenal returned to the scene of the crime, unbeaten in 49 league games. They were top of the table, two points ahead of Chelsea and 11 ahead of Man Utd in sixth. Wenger started with the in-form Reyes on the left ahead of Pires. Phil Neville replaced the ill Roy Keane in centre-midfield alongside Paul Scholes, while Wayne Rooney, signed for a teenage record £25.6m in the summer, played just behind Ruud van Nistelrooy upfront.

Man Utd's tactics were clear: aggression, rough up the 'weak young foreigner' Reyes using rotational fouling and stop Arsenal's free-flowing football at all costs. It was a template that proved successful on this occasion and in numerous subsequent games for the likes of Bolton and Stoke. However, it could not have worked without a terrible refereeing performance by Mike Riley:

1. Edu played in Ljungberg on a run from deep. The Swede got there before last-man Rio Ferdinand and would have had a one-on-one but Ferdinand barged him over. Red card? No, play on.

2. Reyes nutmegged Gary Neville and sprinted away. Neville turned and raked his studs down Reyes' calf. Yellow or red card? No. Riley had a chat with Neville, who patted him on the backside.

3. van Nistelrooy stamped on Cole's knee directly in front of the assistant. Red card? No, play on.

By half-time, Man Utd should have been playing with eight or nine men. 35 minutes in, Riley did get his cards out and, rightly, booked Cole for a foul on Rooney. Both Nevilles finally got booked for late fouls on Reyes. In terms of the football, Arsenal started well with Henry and Bergkamp having chances, and Kolo Touré and Sol Campbell blocking from Rooney and Ryan Giggs.

4. After 73 minutes, it was still goalless when Rooney pushed the ball past Campbell in the Arsenal area. Campbell initially put his leg out to

make a tackle, but quickly withdrew it. Rooney threw himself over. Yellow card for diving? No, penalty to Man Utd, the eighth consecutive game at Old Trafford that Riley had given a penalty to the home side. This time, van Nistelrooy beat Lehmann from the spot and celebrated, *Platoon*-style, on his knees.

5. Cole fouled Cristiano Ronaldo in the box. Penalty? No, play on.

Rooney finished a late counter-attack as Arsenal pushed for an equaliser to make it 2-0, giving Arsenal their first loss since May 2003. Wenger confronted van Nistelrooy in the tunnel, and it all kicked off between the two managers and sets of players. Amazingly, a slice of pizza landed on 63-year-old Alex Ferguson's face. Both clubs went into *omertà* mode, but viewers noticed that the previously-suited manager did his TV interviews in a tracksuit. Fàbregas confirmed rumours he was the culprit in 2017.

A furious Wenger said, "[Riley] decided the game, like we know he can do at Old Trafford." He added, "We know how Ruud van Nistelrooy behaves. He can only cheat people – we know him very well." The latter statement cost him a £15,000 FA fine. The Dutchman was banned for three games for his challenge on Cole.

The Battle of the Buffet was a huge psychological blow as Arsenal lost their way, winning only one of their next five league games. By the end of November, they were five points behind Chelsea.

INKED

In 2005, Ljungberg suffered a persistent hip injury that led to fears he may have contracted cancer. It transpired that he was suffering from blood poisoning caused by a rare allergic reaction to the ink when he got a tattoo. Ljungberg had surgery on the hip to remove the inflamed gland and missed four weeks of the season.

In the Champions League, Arsenal opened with a 1-0 win over PSV Eindhoven as Henry breezed into the box on the left and his pull-back came off Brazilian defender Alex. In Norway against Rosenborg, Ljungberg buried a loose ball after six minutes, but in the second half Roar Strand sidefooted into the roof of the net to frustrate Arsenal.

At Panathinaikos, Reyes flicked a clever ball through to Ljungberg, who dinked over the goalkeeper. Lehmann then came out of his box and headed clear, but Ezequiel González lobbed it back over him. Henry converted Cole's low cross but a late header from a corner made it 2-2. The reverse fixture at Highbury was also a disappointing draw as Henry's penalty was cancelled out by Cygan inadvertently diverting a long shot past Lehmann with his head.

At PSV, Arsenal conceded another set-piece header. Henry played into Ljungberg, who back-heeled for the Frenchman to finish hard and low.

In the second half, both Lauren and Vieira received second yellow cards, but the nine men hung on for the last 15 minutes to earn a 1-1 draw. Throughout the game, Mark van Bommel showcased his Scholes-like immunity from picking up cards as foul after foul of his went unpunished.

That left Arsenal needing to beat Rosenborg to qualify. Reyes settled any nerves after three minutes. Then Henry lobbed the onrushing goalkeeper and Fàbregas coolly cut inside and volleyed left-footed. The away side got one back, again from a set-piece, while Pires scored a penalty. Late on, van Persie dinked over the goalkeeper to give Arsenal a 5-1 win and top place in the group.

Arsenal drew three of the next four league games against Southampton (2-2), Crystal Palace (1-1) and West Brom (1-1). In the first of these, Henry hit the post with a penalty before finishing from Bergkamp's curled pass. But poor defending from set-pieces, noticeably without Campbell, allowed Rory Delap to score headers in the 80th and 85th minutes. van Persie rescued a point with the last kick of the game. His first

Premier League goal was a whipped left-footed strike from the right into the far corner, finishing that explained why Wenger planned to convert van Persie from left-winger to centre-forward as he had done so successfully with Henry.

Arsenal then went to White Hart Lane where Wenger had seen off another manager, Martin Jol replacing Jacques Santini. In a roller-coaster game with two open defences, Arsenal's attackers enjoyed themselves against their favourite goalkeeper Paul Robinson. Spurs took the lead from a set-piece but Henry equalised just before half-time after bringing down Lauren's long pass.

In the second half, Ljungberg drove into the box and was fouled by Noé Pamarot. Lauren confidently stroked the penalty to the goalkeeper's left. Five minutes later, Vieira won the ball in midfield, strode through Spurs' defence and sidefooted in. Within a minute, Arsenal's defence parted and Jermain Defoe fired into the top corner. Ljungberg made it 4-2 after Fàbregas' reverse pass fooled the defence. Ledley King headed a free-kick, but brilliant stop-start footwork from Pires left Pamarot flat-footed and he passed inside the post. Frédéric Kanouté made it 5-4 on 87 minutes, but Arsenal got the win.

At Anfield, Rafa Benítez's Liverpool won 2-1 with a 92nd-minute 25-yard swerving volley from Neil Mellor. Despite Vieira earlier equalising with a left-foot dink to finish off quickfire interplay between him, Henry and Pires, it was a lacklustre performance from the Champions.

Wenger tried to shake up his players, calling them into his office one by one, telling them their performances were not good enough. He also dropped Lehmann for Manuel Almunia against Birmingham. Worryingly, the nervy Spaniard had only three days earlier let a David Bellion shot through him in the League Cup at Man Utd. While Lehmann had made mistakes – often with his high-risk forays out of his area – Almunia added uncertainty to an already shaky defence. However, Arsenal won 3-0 to set up a big game against leaders Chelsea at Highbury.

Mathieu Flamini and Fàbregas partnered each other in midfield for the first time as Vieira was suspended and Gilberto and Edu injured. After two minutes, Reyes headed to Henry, who controlled and hit an instinctive volley left-footed past Petr Čech. John Terry equalised with a free header from a corner. Henry then scored a quick free-kick while Čech was lining up his wall. Chelsea were furious, but everyone had seen Henry do it the previous season with the referee's approval so they should have been prepared. After the break, Arsenal again lost the lead to a set-piece as William Gallas beat Cole to a long free-kick and headed across goal, where Eidur Gudjohnsen bundled in. Fàbregas sliced the defence open to play in Pires, who drew Čech and cut back for Henry. With two men on the line to beat, Henry leant back and unusually sent the ball high and wide with his left foot. The 2-2 draw suited leaders Chelsea.

Arsenal took maximum points from the Christmas fixtures as they found unlikely inspiration to make up for the lack of fluid football and Almunia kept three clean sheets. At Portsmouth, Campbell drove forward and lashed a 25-yarder. At Newcastle, Vieira hit a half-volley from a similar distance that swerved and dipped past Shay Given with the aid of a deflection.

On New Year's Day, Charlton's Talal El Karkouri hammered a free-kick into the top corner to cancel out Ljungberg's strike, but in the second half some flowing football returned. van Persie played to Fàbregas, who back-heeled into Ljungberg's path and the Swede fired across goalkeeper Dean Kiely. van Persie again showed his lethal left foot by burying a volley to make it 3-1.

Against Man City, Vieira lost the ball and Shaun Wright-Phillips hit a swerving 25-yarder. Ljungberg met an Henry overhead kick with a diving header, but a 1-1 draw was not enough for Arsenal. Bolton then unleashed an aerial bombardment to test Almunia and Arsenal's weak defence, and it paid off as Stelios Giannakopoulos scored a diving header. It was Arsenal's first-ever defeat at the Reebok Stadium and ended any realistic title hopes as they were ten points behind Chelsea.

49 UNDEFEATED

Won 36, drew 13, lost 0. Arsenal's record-breaking unbeaten league run eventually stretched to 49 games over three seasons, beating the previous best of 42 set by Nottingham Forest 26 years earlier. Their manager Brian Clough was impressed: "Arsenal caress a football the way I dreamed of caressing Marilyn Monroe." It started with a 6-1 hammering of Southampton in May 2003 and ended with 3-1 win over Aston Villa in October 2004 – 112 goals over 77 weeks. Thirty-three players featured with Henry leading the way at 48 starts and 39 goals.

After a 1-0 win over Newcastle, Man Utd visited Highbury at the start of February. Although they were no longer the top two teams in the country fighting for the title, the animosity was just as great. So great that, this time, the players clashed in Highbury's narrow tunnel before the game had even started. Vieira confronted Gary Neville and warned him against kicking his teammates like he had done to Reyes at Old Trafford. Roy Keane got involved and launched into a tirade at Vieira telling him, "I'll see you out there." Referee Graham Poll restored order but the players were fired up and atmosphere frenzied.

After three minutes, Cole dived as Keane pulled out of a tackle in the area, and Poll rightly waved away any penalty appeals. Vieira headed the opener from a corner after eight minutes. Ten minutes later, Giggs' shot was deflected in. Mikaël Silvestre brought down Pires in the area and Poll again declined to give a penalty, this time incorrectly. Henry slipped in Bergkamp to fire through Roy Carroll's legs and give Arsenal a 2-1 lead at half-time. Ronaldo equalised from wide left and 'shushed' the home fans who had been giving him stick. Five minutes later, Almunia came charging out of his area to the left-back position; Giggs easily beat him to the ball and squared for Ronaldo to tap into the empty net. Silvestre headbutted Ljungberg and was sent off. As Arsenal pushed for a late equaliser, they suffered the ignominy of defender John O'Shea chipping Almunia, the Irishman more stunned with his exquisite skill than anyone in the stadium. A 4-2 defeat and conceding three second-half goals to their hated rivals was a blow to Arsenal's pride.

Added to Arsenal's woes was the *News of the World* catching Cole and his agent at a London hotel meeting with Chelsea representatives including Mourinho. The story and the FA investigation into the illegal approach were the beginning of the end for relations between the full-back and the club/fans.

Arsenal then beat Aston Villa 3-1 with the Almunia experiment put on hold and Lehmann restored to the side. They outplayed the home side with the third goal seeing Henry beat two players on the right, hit a crossfield pass to Bergkamp, who caressed it first-time into Cole's path. The under-fire left-back hit a brilliant swerving volley from 20 yards. On Valentine's Day against Crystal Palace, Arsenal became the first English team to field a completely non-British squad. The heavily-criticised Wenger said, "I don't look at the passport of people, I look at their quality and their attitude." He had a point and the flowing football in a 5-1 win vindicated him; however, the lack of players coming through the Arsenal academy was a concern. Henry scored a curling strike after receiving a short corner and Vieira's dummy on goalkeeper Gábor Király would have made Kanu proud.

Reyes scored his first goal since October with a low 20-yard drive. The Battle of the Buffet kicking proved a watershed for Reyes. In his first year at the club, the Spaniard slotted in well, joining in Arsenal's quick interplay, slipping away from defenders with bursts of pace and skill, and finishing with his left foot. He scored six goals in ten league games before the Old Trafford game, but afterwards only netted three in 20.

It was an eventful few months for the 21-year-old. In October, Spain coach José Aragonés was filmed trying to motivate "the gypsy" using racist language in reference to Henry. Then in February, amid reports he was homesick, he fell for a prank by a Spanish radio station. Thinking he was talking to Real Madrid director of football Emilio Butragueño about a transfer, Reyes said, "I wish I was playing for Real Madrid" and "If I'm not [playing for Real], I'm going to have to carry on playing with some bad people."

At Southampton, David Prutton was given a second yellow card for a nasty tackle on Pires and went ballistic. In shades of Paolo Di Canio, he pushed referee Alan Wiley – who stayed on his feet – as he tried to get at the linesman who had pointed out his indiscretion, earning a ten-game ban. Ljungberg soon after opened the scoring and Arsenal were all set. However, after the break, already-booked van Persie stupidly lunged in on Graeme Le Saux to make it ten aside and Peter Crouch beat Lehmann to a corner to earn a draw. Wenger was furious with the Dutchman, saying he warned him at half-time that "when the home team has had a player sent off, the referee's under pressure. If anyone had to behave, it was him."

In the Champions League knockout, Arsenal went to Bayern Munich and were up against it after only four minutes. Touré got under a goalkeeper hoof and his header set up Claudio Pizarro to volley past Lehmann. The Peruvian then beat Touré to head in a cross. A Hasan Salihamidžić volley made it 3-0. On 88 minutes, Touré buried a loose ball to give Arsenal a lifeline.

In the return fixture, after 66 minutes, Cole launched a long ball to Henry, who brought it down and drilled past Oliver Khan left-footed. Lehmann kept Arsenal in it, but they did not seriously look like they would get the extra goal needed to go through. It was another disappointing exit from Europe.

Arsenal were down to third place at the start of March but went on a strong run, winning their next four games. Henry notched hat-tricks against Portsmouth (3-0) and Norwich (4-1). A 0-0 draw at Chelsea was followed by Reyes striking the winner in the North London derby.

van Persie and Edu goals gave a 2-0 win at West Brom before Arsenal dispatched Champions League finalists Liverpool 3-1. Pires curled a free-kick over the wall, before Reyes drove into the box and finished left-footed. Late on, Fàbregas poked home a classic Bergkamp cushioned pass.

The Iceman again pulled the strings as Arsenal smashed Everton 7-0, laying on goals for van Persie, Pires and Vieira, whose dinked finished was the best of the lot. Edu was given the penalty honours in his last game at Highbury before Bergkamp scored himself as the fans chanted, "One more year."

Arsenal secured second place with a creditable 83 points. Chelsea were a ruthless machine and broke the Arsenal-Man Utd duopoly, breaking records for goals conceded (15) and clean sheets (25). Arsenal were easily top scorers with 87 goals, as Henry won his third Golden Boot and second European Golden Shoe (this time jointly with Diego Forlán). However, they were poor defensively, hurt by injuries to Campbell (who only played 16 league games), Gilberto and Edu, and mistakes by both Lehmann and Almunia.

Arsenal began the FA Cup against Stoke, who were leading at half-time before good finishes from Reyes and van Persie sent Arsenal through. They then beat Wolves 2-0 with a Vieira penalty, after Henry was brought down, and a Ljungberg finish.

Sheffield Utd were the third Championship visitors in a row and a much-changed Arsenal team struggled. After 35 minutes, numerous players engaged in some push and shove, with Bergkamp singled out for a red card. Arsenal looked to have survived the opposition's set-piece threat when Pires tapped in a rebound off goalkeeper Paddy Kenny.

However, in the 89th minute, Senderos handled and Andy Gray scored the penalty. In the replay, injuries and suspensions saw a frontline of 17-year-old Arturo Lupoli and Ljungberg. Kenny made numerous saves and the game ended goalless after 120 minutes. Almunia was the hero in the shootout, saving two out of four penalties, as Lauren, Vieira, Ljungberg and Cole held their nerve.

Three days after the Champions League exit, Bolton were confident of ending Arsenal's season. However, three minutes in, Pires played in Ljungberg on a typical late run and the Swede lifted the ball over the advancing Jussi Jääskeläinen. Five minutes later, El Hadji Diouf slapped Lehmann and was sent off. At the end, Pires again teed up Ljungberg, who unbelievably skied the ball over an empty net from four yards for the miss of the season.

Arsenal were into their seventh FA Cup semi-final in eight years. On a sunny Cardiff day, Mark Hughes' Blackburn team attempted to kick Arsenal, and Vieira in particular, off the pitch. Just before half-time, Touré showed good skill on the left and hit a low ball across the six-yard box, which Pires buried. In between being fouled, Arsenal controlled the game, at one point knocking it around for 40 passes to chants of "olé." van Persie came on after 82 minutes and within eight minutes scored two classy goals. For the first, he turned one centre-back, beat the other and sidefooted into the bottom corner. For the second, he curled first time into the far corner, receiving an Andy Todd

forearm to his face as he turned away to celebrate.

The season finale was another clash between Arsenal and Man Utd, both looking for a trophy after Chelsea ended their nine-year title dominance. Arsenal had already lost three times to Man Utd this season and, for almost the first time in his reign, Wenger set up his team cautiously. He played a 4-5-1 formation with 36-year-old Bergkamp upfront on his own in the absence of the injured Henry, while Senderos kept his place ahead of fit-again Campbell.

Ronaldo immediately beat Lauren on the left wing and gave him a torrid time throughout. After 27 minutes, Lehmann saved a Rooney shot with his foot and Ferdinand put the rebound in but was rightly given offside. Two minutes later, Lehmann again saved from Rooney after van Nistelrooy beat Cole on the right. Man Utd dominated Arsenal, who – only a year after being crowned the Invincibles and beating all-comers with flowing football – struggled to get out of their own half.

In the second half, Lauren clattered Ronaldo and gave him a shove on the floor, then brought him down again and finally got booked. Rooney's mis-hit cross rattled the post, while Vieira blocked a Keane shot in front of the line. From the corner, a van Nistelrooy header from four yards looked sure to be the winner, but Ljungberg stretched on the line to head up onto the bar. In extra time, a van Persie free-kick finally forced Carroll to make a save. Lehmann saved from Scholes, and an unmarked van Nistelrooy headed over from seven yards. Right at the end, Reyes took out Ronaldo to earn his second yellow card and become only the second player to be sent off in an FA Cup Final.

Man Utd had eight efforts on target to Arsenal's one, with the corner count 12 to 1. Unbelievably, Lehmann and Arsenal held out and the FA Cup Final was settled on penalties for the first time.

van Nistelrooy and Lauren confidently dispatched their spot-kicks. Lehmann dived to his right to save from Scholes. Ljungberg put his almost down the middle, while van Persie swept high past Carroll's dive. Cole, at an FA hearing a few days earlier over the Chelsea tapping up, also sidefooted strongly. Keane scored to make it 4-4 and the two captains, who had been at each other a few months earlier in the Highbury tunnel, crossed paths briefly. Vieira stroked it high and to the left, Carroll guessed the right way, but the Arsenal leader's penalty was perfect.

It was the Great Cup Final Robbery Part II – the most one-sided FA Cup Final since Arsenal outplayed Liverpool in 2001, but this time Arsenal left with the trophy. Having been on the wrong end of that as well as other smash and grabs in the past, Arsenal players and fans did not care; in fact, getting one over their bitter rivals in such circumstances made it even sweeter. Vieira lifted the cup, Arsenal's third in four years, as *Song 2* by Blur rang out, and Ferguson and Man Utd players watched on in disbelief.

After a brilliant Invincibles start to the season, the Battle-of-the-Buffet loss derailed Arsenal much more than it should have done and the season tapered off into an end-of-an-era feel. Chelsea's oil money broke the Arsenal-Man Utd dominance, while key players were older (Pires, Ljungberg, Bergkamp), more injury-prone (Campbell, Ljungberg, Gilberto, Edu) or less motivated or distracted (Cole, Vieira, Edu).

Stage One Wenger saw Arsenal's best-ever teams and the best football Arsenal (and English football) fans had ever seen. Three Premier League titles, four FA Cups, two Doubles and one Invincibles season in eight years. On 21 May 2005, it ended fittingly with a trophy against fierce rivals Man Utd, sealed by Wenger's first signing Vieira with his last kick for the club. There was even a red card for old times' sake.

Off The Pitch

When Arsène Wenger joined Arsenal in 1996, they had a simple corporate structure where the manager worked closely with vice-chairmen David Dein, who was the de facto director of football responsible for negotiating transfers and wages. Once nicknamed the Bank of England club, they had a multi-owner model, where the shareholdings had been in a few English establishment families (the Bracewell-Smith and Hill-Wood families) for years and were passed on to the next generation.

Twenty-two years later, they had left the iconic Highbury Stadium and were playing in a relatively soulless – but cash cow – 60,000 seater named after the UAE's state-owned airline. They were 100% owned by an American billionaire who had little knowledge, interest or passion for football or the club. One that did not go to Arsenal's first European final in 13 years in 2019.

When Dein left early in Stage Two Wenger, the manager described it as a "sad day for Arsenal" and went on to assume responsibility for running almost all aspects of the club, becoming heavily involved in transfer and wage negotiations. It was too much for one man and a set-up with clear key-man risk and lack of succession planning.

In Stage Three, Arsenal's stagnation inspired CEO Ivan Gazidis' "catalyst for change" statement of intent. To avoid a repeat of the situation where all the power lay in one person, Arsenal over-compensated and went on a hiring spree at both the executive and coaching levels. Almost all of these hires left the club within a couple of years and in 2020 Arsenal reverted to something similar to the original manager-director model, with two former Wenger players in Mikel Arteta and Edu at the helm.

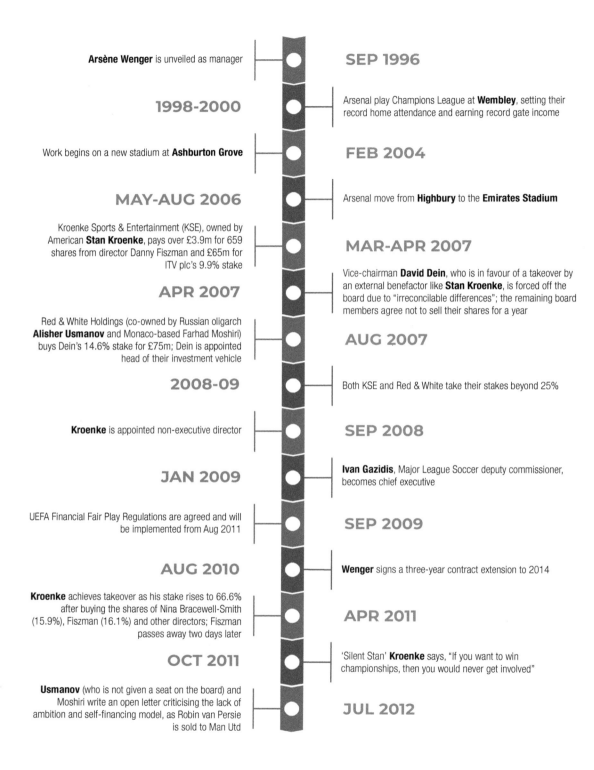

Arsène Wenger is unveiled as manager

SEP 1996

1998-2000

Arsenal play Champions League at **Wembley**, setting their record home attendance and earning record gate income

Work begins on a new stadium at **Ashburton Grove**

FEB 2004

MAY-AUG 2006

Arsenal move from **Highbury** to the **Emirates Stadium**

Kroenke Sports & Entertainment (KSE), owned by American **Stan Kroenke**, pays over £3.9m for 659 shares from director Danny Fiszman and £65m for ITV plc's 9.9% stake

MAR-APR 2007

APR 2007

Vice-chairman **David Dein**, who is in favour of a takeover by an external benefactor like **Stan Kroenke**, is forced off the board due to "irreconcilable differences"; the remaining board members agree not to sell their shares for a year

Red & White Holdings (co-owned by Russian oligarch **Alisher Usmanov** and Monaco-based Farhad Moshiri) buys Dein's 14.6% stake for £75m; Dein is appointed head of their investment vehicle

AUG 2007

2008-09

Both KSE and Red & White take their stakes beyond 25%

Kroenke is appointed non-executive director

SEP 2008

JAN 2009

Ivan Gazidis, Major League Soccer deputy commissioner, becomes chief executive

UEFA Financial Fair Play Regulations are agreed and will be implemented from Aug 2011

SEP 2009

AUG 2010

Wenger signs a three-year contract extension to 2014

Kroenke achieves takeover as his stake rises to 66.6% after buying the shares of Nina Bracewell-Smith (15.9%), Fiszman (16.1%) and other directors; Fiszman passes away two days later

APR 2011

OCT 2011

'Silent Stan' **Kroenke** says, "If you want to win championships, then you would never get involved"

Usmanov (who is not given a seat on the board) and Moshiri write an open letter criticising the lack of ambition and self-financing model, as Robin van Persie is sold to Man Utd

JUL 2012

Gazidis says, "In the next two years, we will have the financial resources to sit and compete among the leading clubs in the world, which is an extraordinary achievement"

OCT 2012

DEC 2012

Arsenal buy **StatDNA**, a US-based "sports data performance analysis" company, for £2.165m

Sir Chips Keswick is appointed club chairman following the 31-year reign of Peter Hill-Wood, ending the Hill-Wood family association with Arsenal since 1922

JUN 2013

MAY 2014

Wenger signs a three-year contract after winning the FA Cup, the club's first trophy for nine years

Arsenal's 2013/14 accounts reveal they paid £3m to KSE for "strategic and advisory services"

SEP 2014

SEP 2015

Arsenal's 2014/15 accounts reveal they again paid £3m to KSE for "strategic and advisory services"

Usmanov buys out Moshiri, who buys 49.9% of Everton

FEB 2016

APR 2017

Gazidis says the poor season will be "a catalyst for change"; Arsenal go on to fill numerous new roles at the executive and coaching levels such as head of recruitment, head of high performance and chief contract negotiator

Usmanov offers **Kroenke** £1bn for his 67% stake, valuing the club at £1.5bn, but Kroenke is not interested in selling

APR 2017

MAY 2017

Wenger signs a two-year contract after winning the FA Cup

Raúl Sanllehí, former Barcelona director of football, joins as head of football relations

FEB 2018

MAY 2018

Wenger leaves and Arsenal pay £17m to him and his staff; **Unai Emery** is appointed head coach

Kroenke buys Usmanov's 30% stake for £550m, valuing the club at £1.8bn, and becomes 100% owner

AUG 2018

SEP 2018

Gazidis announces he will join AC Milan, after earning over £20m in under ten years at Arsenal; **Sanllehí** is named head of football and **Vinai Venkatesham** managing director

Emery is sacked at a cost of £4m and replaced by **Mikel Arteta**

NOV-DEC 2019

AUG 2020

Sanllehí leaves and **Venkatesham** is named CEO

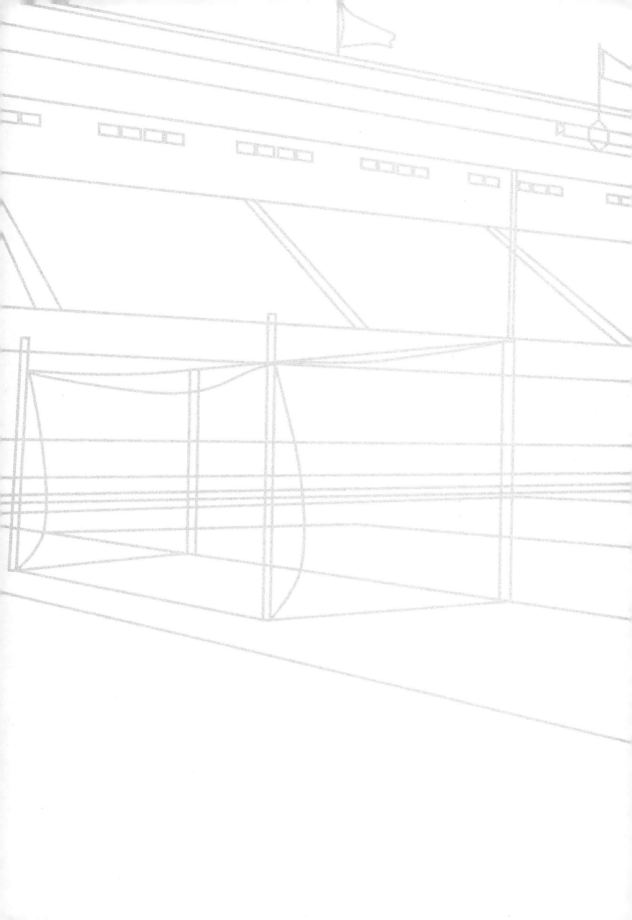

2005/06
PARIS, JE TE DÉTESTE; GOODBYE HIGHBURY

Premier League	Fourth
FA Cup	Fourth round
Champions League	Final
League Cup	Semi-final
Community Shield	Runners-up

PREMIER LEAGUE		PL	W	D	L	GF	GA	GD	PTS
1	CHELSEA	38	29	4	5	72	22	50	91
2	MAN UTD	38	25	8	5	72	34	38	83
3	LIVERPOOL	38	25	7	6	57	25	32	82
4	ARSENAL	38	20	7	11	68	31	37	67
5	TOTTENHAM	38	18	11	9	53	38	15	65
6	BLACKBURN ROVERS	38	19	6	13	51	42	9	63

Highlights: 1-0 in the Bernabéu; beating Juventus at a rocking Highbury; Jens Lehmann's penalty save at Villarreal put Arsenal into their first Champions League Final; Highbury farewell party featuring a Thierry Henry hat-trick

Lowlights: Losing the Champions League Final after being 14 minutes from glory; numerous bad away days meaning a league challenge was gone by Christmas; going out of both cups to Wigan and Bolton in five days

Player of the year: New captain Henry led from the front, scoring crucial goals time and again

Top scorers: Henry 33 (27 in PL), Robin van Persie 12 (5), Robert Pires 11 (7)

Goal of the season: Henry's brilliant solo effort versus Real Madrid, Bernabéu, Champions League

The Stage Two Wenger era began with the £13.75m sale of Arsenal's captain and best-ever midfielder Patrick Vieira to Juventus. It was a surprise when Arsène Wenger finally let the 29-year-old go as almost every previous summer featured an ultimately futile saga over whether the Frenchman would move to Real Madrid, Juventus or even Man Utd. Wenger felt Arsenal got a good price and had Cesc Fàbregas to step in.

How Arsenal missed Vieira dominating the midfield week after week. It is no surprise that his arrival and departure bookended the Stage One Wenger glory years, and the club's metamorphosis from "boring boring Arsenal" to "it's just like watching Brazil" would not have been possible without him.

He was always available to receive the ball in tight spaces and had the technique and strength to hold off and beat opponents. He made tackle after tackle, regularly sliding to extend a telescopic leg, and immediately initiated an attack by striding forward with the ball or releasing the attackers with the inside or outside of his right foot. He won countless headers to clear corners. His party piece of flicking a bouncing ball over his opposing midfielder's head and racing away – which Arsenal fans knew was coming but opponents seemed powerless to stop however much they craned their heads – got the crowd going and prompted the 'Vieira song' over and over.

Unlike rivals Chelsea and Man Utd, Arsenal's budget was tight as they financed the new stadium. However, Wenger had consistently shown he could unearth talent to replace top players. Most people had faith in his ability to build another successful team and continue to win silverware.

In the Community Shield, Arsenal lost 2-1 to Chelsea as Didier Drogba began his domination of Arsenal's defence and 'vaccination' of Philippe Senderos in particular. For Arsenal's last year at the Home of Football, they wore classy redcurrant shirts in a nod to the kit worn in their first season at Highbury in 1913. In the first game, Newcastle's Jermaine Jenas only lasted 32 minutes before being sent off for a scissor-tackle on Gilberto Silva. Arsenal made their one-man advantage tell late on with a Thierry Henry penalty and Robin van Persie close-range finish to an excellent counter-attack.

In Wenger's 500th game as manager, Drogba again got ahead of Senderos and a long ball hit his shin to fortuitously wrongfoot Jens Lehmann. A tight game ended 1-0 to the Champions, the manager's first loss to Chelsea in the Premier League. Arsenal beat Fulham 4-1 with two classic Henry one-on-one finishes and two surprising Pascal Cygan goals from set-pieces, prompting the Highbury crowd to sing,

"He's bald, he's shit, he plays when no one's fit. Cygan."

Arsenal, without Sol Campbell and Henry, started strongly at Middlesbrough but failed to take advantage and gave away two soft goals, losing 2-1. Campbell returned and scored two powerful headers to beat Everton 2-0. Against ten-man Birmingham, Arsenal needed a deflected van Persie shot to finally get past Maik Taylor. At West Brom, Arsenal took the lead with another centre-back, this time Senderos, getting on the end of a set-piece. However, when the ball fell to Nwankwo Kanu in the Arsenal box, the Nigerian unusually did not waste time with any dummies and thumped it into the roof of the net. In the second half, Darren Carter laced a volley into the top corner from 25 yards to give West Brom a 2-1 win.

Down in the unfamiliar territory of eighth place, some themes were developing: (1) injuries – six key players were missing and Freddie Ljungberg went off with a torn hamstring; (2) away-day blues – it was already Arsenal's third away loss of the season; and (3) no Henry, no 'va va voom' – the passing was still good, but his cutting-edge could not be replaced.

Henry was back against Man City, winning a penalty when he beat David James to the ball. Robert Pires buried the spot-kick into the top-left corner. Dennis Bergkamp won another penalty and Pires stepped up again. This time, he stopped his run and barely flicked

TYPICAL LINE-UP (4-4-2; 4-5-1 IN CL)

	14 Henry (Adebayor)		9 Reyes (Bergkamp, van Persie)	
7 Pires (Reyes, Ljungberg, Hleb)		19 Gilberto (Flamini)	15 Fàbregas (Diaby)	8 Ljungberg (Hleb, Fàbregas, Pires)
16 Flamini (Cole, Cygan, Clichy)		28 Touré	23 Campbell (Senderos)	12 Lauren (Eboué)
		1 Lehmann (Almunia)		

Players in: Nicklas Bendtner, Vito Mannone, Armand Traoré, Alexander Hleb, Alex Song, *Abou Diaby*, *Emmanuel Adebayor*, *Theo Walcott*

Players out: Jermaine Pennant, Stuart Taylor, Patrick Vieira, *David Bentley*, *Quincy Owusu-Abeyie*

the top of the ball. As Henry ran past the ball, Pires stood there unable to resist touching it again. The referee gave a free-kick as a bemused crowd looked on. It turned out the two Frenchmen were trying to recreate Johan Cruyff and Jesper Olsen's penalty for Ajax in 1982 and Pires meant to pass to the onrushing Henry. Arsenal won 1-0 and most people could see the funny side of it; for others, including Man City's Danny Mills, it made them angry and reinforced their 'arrogant Arsenal' narrative.

At White Hart Lane, Ledley King scored a bullet header early on, but on 77 minutes Paul Robinson flapped at a free-kick and Pires coolly volleyed the ball back for his eighth North London derby goal. It secured a point that proved crucial at the end of the season.

injury. Wenger's plans to ease him back late in the game changed after 15 minutes when José Antonio Reyes was injured. Six minutes later, Henry brought down a long ball from Kolo Touré, spun 180 degrees and hit a brilliant curling half-volley with the outside of his foot to equal Ian Wright's Arsenal goals record. In the second half, Pires curled an excellent through-ball to Henry, who controlled and fired home to make it 186 goals in 303 games, claiming the record outright.

Arsenal won the home game 3-0 with another Henry special, curling first-time from 25 yards. van Persie scored twice, including a left-foot netbuster from the edge of the area. An 88th-minute Pires penalty over ten-man Thun made it five wins from five and top place in the group.

Arsenal drew a comfortable group in the Champions League, although they needed an injury-time Bergkamp winner against FC Thun. The Dutchman won a hopeful long ball and sidefooted home. With the injuries mounting, Ljungberg played upfront at Ajax and showed his finishing credentials after only 80 seconds, dinking over the goalkeeper. Pires buried a penalty in the second half to secure another 2-1 win.

At Slavia Prague, Henry was on the bench after six weeks out with a groin

Arsenal rediscovered their goalscoring touch in November as they beat Sunderland 3-1 and in-form Wigan 3-2. Both games saw Henry net a brace and van Persie one. Against Blackburn, Fàbregas curled into the bottom corner from outside the area, then Pires threaded a perfect pass to tee up an Henry Sidefoot Finish. van Persie marauded down the right, cut inside two defenders and curled an unstoppable shot off the inside of the far post. Despite not being a consistent starter, the Dutchman was regularly showing his close control, sharpness around the box and lethal left foot that generated impressive sidefoot power.

At the start of December, Arsenal had moved up to second place, but Chelsea were 11 points ahead. Arsenal went to Bolton and again got bullied. Abdoulaye Faye headed the opener and Kevin Davies robbed Gilberto to set up Stelios Giannakopoulos. Henry hit the post with a left-foot volley and Lehmann made plenty of saves amid the aerial bombardment, but it finished 2-0. Ljungberg admitted, "You need to be ready for the fight at Bolton but some of our players did not stand up for it." It was a better performance at Newcastle, but Shay Given kept Arsenal out early on and the home side's physical approach paid dividends as Gilberto got his second yellow after 56 minutes and Alan Shearer was not punished for a two-footed lunge on Campbell. With eight minutes left, Nobby Solano fired the winner.

Against leaders Chelsea, Henry hit the post before Arjen Robben broke away and finished. Chelsea efficiently soaked up pressure and Joe Cole robbed Lauren in the left-back position, cut inside and curled into the bottom corner. Arsenal could match Chelsea in terms of football, but the leaders were now streets ahead in getting results as proven by their three victories over Arsenal in 2005/06. It was Arsenal's third league loss in a row, a first for Wenger.

On Boxing Day at Charlton, Reyes scored Arsenal's first league goal for a month as he followed up Henry's blocked effort to give a much-needed 1-0 win. Two days later, the flowing football returned in a 4-0 win against Portsmouth as Reyes, Bergkamp and Henry (two) scored in the first half. A 0-0 draw on New Year's Eve at Aston Villa left Arsenal sixth, behind Spurs and Wigan – times had changed.

The first meeting with Man Utd in the Stage Two Wenger era was an entertaining, but relatively trouble-free, affair. Arsenal should have had a penalty when Gary Neville took out Fàbregas from behind, but the two former heavyweight champions slugged out a 0-0 draw.

Against Middlesbrough and Steve McClaren's naive high line, Henry met a Ljungberg cross with a thumping sidefoot volley, then buried two one-on-ones. Pires scored a curler, Senderos and Gilberto powered headers, and silky but shot-shy Alexander Hleb scored his first goal for the club. It ended a 7-0 hammering as Reyes equalled Bergkamp's Premier League record of four assists in one game. However, in a microcosm of the season, the home silk was not followed by away steel as Arsenal lost 1-0 to Everton, with Fàbregas sent off at the end after clashing with Mikel Arteta.

In the League Cup, Wenger as usual gave chances to young prospects like Alex Song, Johan Djourou, Emmanuel Eboué, Arturo Lupoli and Quincy Owusu-Abeyie. Two 3-0 wins over Sunderland and Reading were followed by an entertaining night at Doncaster Rovers, where Gilberto made it 2-2 with almost the last kick of extra time. Almunia saved two penalties to send Arsenal into the semi-final for the second year running.

In the first leg at Wigan, Arsenal put in a tame display, losing 1-0 to a Paul Scharner header. At home, Wenger brought back the big guns. Stéphane Henchoz handled from Henry, and unlike in the 2001 FA Cup Final, a penalty was given. Mike Pollitt saved from Reyes, as well as attempts from Henry and others. In the second half, Arsenal finally broke through as Kerrea Gilbert burst down the right for what should have been his 15 minutes of Arsenal fame and crossed for Henry to head home. In extra time, van Persie curled a brilliant free-kick into the top corner. However, with one minute left, Senderos and Campbell failed to deal with a hoof forward and Jason Roberts sent Wigan through on away goals. Lauren injured his knee and, although it did not seem bad at the time, did not play for the club again. Arsenal had lost another quality player and crucially another character that teammates would want to go into battle with.

Four days later, Arsenal had to go back to Bolton in the FA Cup with ten players out injured, at the African Nations Cup or suspended. van Persie, playing upfront in a 4-5-1 formation, headed against the crossbar but, like the previous season, Stelios ghosted in to score a diving header. February had not begun and Arsenal were already out of both cups as well as the league, with only the Champions League and trying to get back into it by finishing fourth to play for.

On a Wednesday night against West Ham, Arsenal started strongly but Highbury was silenced as Campbell was beaten twice to let in Nigel Reo-Coker and Bobby Zamora. Henry got one back. Campbell failed to appear after half-time and the injury-hit defence saw midfielders Sebastian Larsson and Mathieu Flamini at left- and right-back. Arsenal pressured but Matthew Etherington made it 3-1, before Pires scored a late goal. Campbell had asked to be substituted and left the stadium immediately. He spent time at a friend's place in Brussels and returned to training five days later. In the days of little mental health awareness, there was not much sympathy from fans or the media for his personal issues or for 'walking out' on his team.

In the January transfer window, Wenger boosted the squad by signing

Abou Diaby, Emmanuel Adebayor and 16-year-old Theo Walcott. Adebayor made his debut at Birmingham and headed a rebound after 21 minutes. Fàbregas played in Henry, who fired his 200th Arsenal goal left-footed into the roof of the net to seal a rare away win. Bolton took an early lead through a Kevin Nolan lob and, after numerous saves by Jussi Jääskeläinen, Gilberto volleyed a deserved 93rd-minute equaliser.

At Anfield, Lehmann saved a Steven Gerrard penalty and late on a volley from Dietmar Hamann, but Luis García was first to react to give Liverpool a 1-0 win. It was the first outing for a back four of Eboué, Touré, Senderos and Flamini.

In poor form, especially away from home, and missing key players, expectations were low when Arsenal went to Real Madrid in the Champions League. Wenger went for a 4-5-1 formation, with Henry upfront supported from midfield by Reyes and Ljungberg, and the same makeshift defence used against Liverpool. Madrid were full of Galácticos – Roberto Carlos, Zinedine Zidane, David Beckham, Robinho and the Brazilian Ronaldo – and had won ten of their previous 11 games.

Surprisingly, Arsenal flew out of the blocks. Iker Casillas saved from Reyes

and Henry headed wide. Lehmann saved one-on-one from Beckham. Just after half-time, Henry picked up the ball in the centre-circle and turned to face a sea of white shirts. Undeterred, he drove forward, shrugged off Ronaldo, left Alvaro Mejia standing, skipped past Guti and his attempt to bring him down, raced into the area and, under pressure from Sergio Ramos, fired left foot into the bottom corner. An amazing goal that stunned the 80,000 Madrid fans. Arsenal created further chances and Lehmann made crucial saves. Arsenal were the first English team to win in the Bernabéu with a famous 1-0 victory that gave a much-needed boost to their disappointing season.

The following weekend, however, they were undone by the non-Galácticos of Blackburn, losing another away game in north England, this time 1-0. Given their league position, there were real worries Arsenal would have to win the Champions League to be in the competition the following season. At the start of March, the sun was out and Arsenal were away from home, but happily in London. They carved Fulham open, Henry scoring twice, and Adebayor and Fàbregas once each.

Madrid came to Highbury and the crowd was fired up, but wary of a comeback. Lehmann saved a Ronaldo header, Henry again tormented the Madrid defence and Reyes hit the crossbar. Raúl hit the post with a first-time effort from outside the area, the ball came back to him, and amazingly Lehmann scrambled to palm his follow-up onto the same post. At the end, with Casillas up for a corner, Pires broke away but his effort from inside his own half did not have the legs to reach the empty goal before Carlos got back. The whistle went soon after to end a thrilling goalless draw and Highbury was euphoric.

Third-placed Liverpool came to Highbury with Arsenal desperate to join them in the top four. Fàbregas sliced open their defence with a brilliant pass to Henry in his favourite inside-left position, taking out right-back Steve Finnan and centre-back Jamie Carragher. The Frenchman did the rest, curling inside the far post. Deep into the second half, Gerrard struck a long-range drive, Lehmann parried

and Garcia was again first to react. Xabi Alonso got his second caution and was sent off. Three minutes later, Gerrard played a back-pass and, in a repeat of England-France in Euro 2004, was stunned to see it was a perfect through-ball to Henry, who rounded Pepe Reina and made it 2-1. The Arsenal crowd chanted, "There's only one Steven Gerrard," and Arsenal moved two points behind Spurs in fourth.

Fulham and Aston Villa were dealt with comfortably 3-0 and 5-0. The latter was David Rocastle Day, one of the 'Highbury – The Final Salute' themed matchdays held throughout the season. Earlier in the season, these had been a useful distraction from the lack of league challenge. Now, there was some brilliant Wengerball and the chance to catch up Spurs to keep the fans enthused. Adebayor scored a header and Henry lobbed Thomas Sørensen. It got better as Adebayor cushioned a long ball for Henry, who curled into the top corner from outside the box. van Persie returned from injury and showed his quick feet – after rounding Sørensen, he was tight to the byline; everyone expected a cutback, but van Persie beat the goalkeeper again with a dragback and drilled the ball past two defenders from an angle. Diaby finished a counter-attack to score his first Arsenal goal.

Back in the Champions League, Arsenal had another daunting task against Juventus and Vieira. The former captain got a taste of his own medicine from an unlikely source when Pires surprised him, and everyone else, with a slide tackle on the halfway line. Pires quickly played it to Henry, who moved it to Fàbregas, whose shot into the bottom corner left Gianluigi Buffon flat-footed. Another quick move saw Fàbregas played in again, Buffon came out, and the Spaniard squared for Henry to finish into the empty net. The Italian leaders lost the plot in the last five minutes as Mauro Camoranesi and Jonathan Zebina were sent off for bad fouls. Arsenal had again raised their game against world-class players. On another memorable night, Highbury was rocking with the song "We're on our way, we're on our way, we're going to Paris" sung with increased belief.

In the second leg in Turin, Arsenal got the job done with a goalless draw to go through to the first Champions League semi-final in the club's history. The patched-up defence had formed some chemistry and kept Arsenal's eighth clean sheet in a row, a Champions League record.

The following weekend, Henry was rested on the bench as Man Utd won 2-0 with second-half goals from Wayne Rooney and Park Ji-sung. Touré got away with pushing a Rooney shot onto the post with a desperate diving 'save' after tripping over a prostrate Lehmann and performing a commando roll to quickly recover. At Portsmouth, Henry did a one-two with Adebayor and curled into the bottom corner. However, Lomana LuaLua equalised with a header from a free-kick and it ended

1-1. Campbell was welcomed back with an elbow that gave him a broken nose.

15 April 2006 was Dennis Bergkamp Day at Highbury, with West Brom the visitors. Hleb played a one-two with Henry and, unusually, put his foot through the ball to open the scoring. Arsenal were in control until Nigel Quashie drilled low into the bottom corner. The scene was set when Bergkamp was brought on. The Iceman did not let the crowd down, cutting back for Pires to score. With a minute left, he produced a Bergkamp Curler, a fitting final goal for the club.

Mid-April saw a historic week for Arsenal, with their first Champions League semi-final sandwiching a big North London derby. After beating more illustrious opponents in the previous rounds, Arsenal were the favourites against Villarreal. The Yellow Submarines were well organised and had the sublime Argentine playmaker Juan Riquelme pulling the strings, but were missing their first-choice centre-backs and goalkeeper. At Highbury, Wenger kept his Champions League 4-5-1 formation with Ljungberg, Pires and Hleb joining Henry when Arsenal broke.

Arsenal started well and threatened from set-pieces, Touré firing just wide. Pires played in Henry, who passed into the net, but was incorrectly

THE NOT-SO-FAMOUS BACK FOUR

Eboué, Touré, Senderos, Flamini. With three of the Invincibles back four – Lauren, Campbell and Cole – as well as replacements Clichy and Cygan out for long spells, Wenger cobbled together a young defence that helped keep a record ten consecutive clean sheets in the Champions League. Backed by Lehmann at his best and drilled in coaching sessions by Martin Keown, they kept out world-class players Zlatan Ibrahimović, David Trezeguet, Nedvěd, Brazilian Ronaldo, Zidane, Raúl and Diego Forlán. 24-year-old Touré was the oldest player and grew into the leadership role alongside Senderos. Right-footed centre-midfielder Flamini became a tenacious left-back, Arsenal's eighth of the season, while Eboué provided drive and pace on the right wing.

palms. Gilberto fouled José Mari but no penalty was given. In the second half, Arsenal pressured, with an Henry effort headed off the line, but had to settle for a 1-0 lead going into the second leg.

The following Saturday lunchtime, the sun was out as Spurs came to Highbury for the final time, four points ahead but having played a game more. With the Villarreal trip three days later, Wenger rotated heavily, bringing in van Persie, Adebayor, Reyes, Diaby and Djourou for Henry, Fàbregas, Ljungberg, Hleb, Eboué and Bergkamp. Michael Carrick slalomed through the defence, rounded Lehmann, but could only fire into the side-netting from an angle. After an hour, Wenger sent Henry and Fàbregas on, but soon after, Gilberto and Eboué collided, Eboué staying down. Spurs played on, as they had every right to do, and Edgar Davids squared for Robbie Keane to tap in. Wenger was furious and went head-to-head on the touchline with burly Spurs boss Martin Jol. With only six minutes left, Adebayor made a good run down the left, played in Henry, who took one touch to control and a second to flick with the outside of his right foot past Paul Robinson – a new finishing technique for Henry, who delivered when needed yet again. Highbury was relieved, but the 1-1 draw meant Spurs were favourites for fourth place.

Villarreal's El Madrigal held only 23,000 fans, but they made a lot of noise. The record-breaking defence changed as Campbell came back for the injured Senderos, and Flamini had

ruled offside. After 40 minutes, Henry retrieved a corner on the left and played a brilliant reverse pass to Hleb, who squared for Touré to slide in and cause Highbury to erupt. Free-kick specialist Riquelme stung Lehmann's

to be replaced after nine minutes by Gaël Clichy, himself returning from an injury sustained in November. Guillermo Franco and Diego Forlán were dangerous, but poor finishing and resolute defending put Arsenal on course for the tenth consecutive clean sheet that would ensure progress. At the other end, they did not look like getting an away goal. With two minutes left, Villarreal put the ball in the box. Clichy jumped, José Mari got his body in front of him and collapsed. It was not a foul, but, not for the last time in his career, Clichy had given the referee a chance to give the home side a crucial late penalty. A nervous-looking Riquelme, after kissing the ball for good luck, sidefooted to his right and Lehmann made a famous save to send Arsenal into their first Champions League Final.

Arsenal, however, had to forget about that as they faced three games in the first six days of May, and they needed to win them all to stand a chance of reeling in Spurs, who were seven points ahead but had played two more games. They dismissed relegated Sunderland with three goals in the first half. Notably, Ashley Cole came on for his first action since January.

With the game petering out, journeyman Dan Smith came on and tried to impress the home fans by 'putting himself about.' Fàbregas

managed to avoid his first lunge. Referee Dermot Gallagher's failure to punish the challenge proved costly as Diaby was not so lucky. Smith launched his studs at Diaby's ankle, which he fractured and dislocated, putting the 20-year-old out of the Champions League Final and, more seriously, causing him injuries that affected him for the rest of his career. Unbelievably, Gallagher only gave Smith a yellow card. Wenger, who had been warning for a long time that the 'get stuck into Arsenal' tactics would result in serious injury, was upset: "If you do that to a guy in the street, you go to jail."

At Man City, Henry played in Ljungberg, who finished left-footed, amazingly his first league goal of the season. David Sommeil equalised from a corner, but substitute Reyes scored two good finishes in six minutes.

That set up Arsenal's 2,010th and last game at Highbury on 7 May 2006 against Wigan. Spurs, who had been in fourth place since 3 December, were two points ahead and only needed to equal Arsenal's result to qualify for the Champions League for the first time since 1961. As Gooners headed to the iconic stadium for the final time, there were reports that the Spurs team had been up all night at their five-star Canary Wharf hotel with a bout of food poisoning, and they were trying to get their game at West Ham delayed or even postponed. However, both games went ahead simultaneously with a sunny Highbury looking good in blocks of red and white as the club had left special T-shirts on each seat for fans to wear.

- 1-0 (eight minutes): Pires scored from a corner and news quickly spread that West Ham had taken the lead against Spurs.

- 1-1 (ten minutes): The party atmosphere was interrupted by a Scharner header.

- 1-2 (32 minutes): David Thompson saw Lehmann anticipating a cross and curled a long-range free-kick into the gap to silence Highbury.

- 2-2 (34 minutes): Pires set up an Henry Sidefoot Finish.

- 2-2 (half-time): Spurs equalised and both games were level.

- 2-2 (55 minutes): Arsenal fans began conspiracy theories when one of their most hated opponents, Teddy Sheringham, missed a penalty for West Ham against his old club.

- 3-2 (56 minutes): Henry capitalised on a poor back-pass from Thompson and rounded Pollitt to put Arsenal ahead.

- 4-2 (76 minutes): Ljungberg was brought down, Henry buried the spot-kick and kissed the Highbury turf in front of the North Bank.

- 4-2 (79 minutes): As Bergkamp came on for his final appearance, Yossi Benayoun made it 2-1 to West Ham and Highbury was jubilant.

It was not a trophy or a title chase like Arsenal had become accustomed to, but the final game at Highbury had drama, an Henry hat-trick and a lasagne-fuelled Spurs choke that saw Arsenal overtake them to seal Champions League football for another year. Spurs also suffered the ignominy of having the shortest Premier League season in history at 40 games, having been knocked out of both cups at the first attempt and not being in Europe. A ceremony and fireworks gave players, past and present, and fans a chance to say goodbye to the legendary art deco stadium after 93 years.

The final year at Highbury was easily Arsenal's worst league season since Wenger had arrived, losing 11 games, nine away, and scoring only 68 goals, 19 fewer than the previous year. Away from home, they were often bullied, not helped by an almost constant injury crisis in defence. However, the second half of the season saw a brilliant Champions League run and surge to fourth place, with a new form of Wengerball helped by the arrivals of Hleb, Adebayor and Diaby, progress of Fàbregas, van Persie, Senderos and Eboué, and spearheaded by FWA and Premier League Player of the Year Henry. The captain also won a record fourth Golden Boot.

On 17 May 2006, ten days after the Highbury farewell, came the biggest game in Arsenal's history – their first Champions League Final, against Barcelona. More than 50,000 fans made the trip to Paris, some paying over £1,000 for a ticket to the Stade de France. Arsenal lined up 4-5-1 in their yellow away kit. Wenger selected Pires over Reyes, with Cole and Campbell back in defence. Frank Rijkaard's Spanish Champions were favourites and full of flair. They played 4-3-3 with Samuel Eto'o, Ronaldinho and Ludovic Giuly upfront, and Deco, Edmilson and Mark van Bommel in midfield keeping Xabi and Iniesta on the bench, alongside 18-year-old Lionel Messi, who was carrying a thigh injury.

Henry made a lively start, getting on the end of a low Eboué cross but Víctor Valdés blocked his effort. He then fired a shot from the edge of the area, which Valdés parried. After 17 minutes, Ronaldinho slipped in Eto'o, who had beaten the offside trap. Lehmann came racing out, but Eto'o toed it past him. The German goalkeeper tripped Eto'o just outside the area and Giuly passed into the empty net. However, the referee had already blown his whistle for a foul, so was left with no choice but to make Lehmann the first player to be sent off in a Champions League Final. Arsenal had to play over 70 minutes with ten men against one of the best passing teams around. The game plan was thrown out the window and Wenger sacrificed Pires, in his last

appearance in an Arsenal shirt, to bring on Almunia.

On 37 minutes, Eboué pushed the ball past Carlos Puyol on the right and took a dive. The referee bought it, Henry took the free-kick, and Campbell soared to head into the corner and give Arsenal an unlikely lead. Eto'o turned Campbell, but Almunia pushed his shot onto the post. At half-time, a famous victory was on the cards.

Unsurprisingly, Barcelona dominated the second half with 69% possession, but Arsenal were resolute, while hoping for counter-attacks. They got what they were looking for when Hleb played in Henry. It was a huge chance to make it 2-0. The Frenchman was just inside the box, right of centre, a situation where he usually thrived. However, he sidefooted a tired attempt that Valdés saved.

After 76 minutes, Iniesta played a pass on the left, which substitute Henrik Larsson flicked into Eto'o's path. Eboué had let him go and the Cameroonian, who was marginally offside, passed the ball inside the near post from close range. It was the first European goal Arsenal had conceded for 995 minutes and a huge blow to the tired ten men. Four minutes later, Larsson played a clever ball to substitute right-back Juliano Belletti, whose shot across the goal went through Almunia's legs and into the net off the inside off his shin. The lively Swede had changed the game with two assists, and Arsenal's legs were shot. Arsenal lost 2-1, their third consecutive European final loss (a trend that was extended by the 2018/19 Europa Cup Final).

Arsenal were only a painful 14 minutes from the biggest trophy in their history. It was an agonising defeat full of 'what-ifs'. That they lost to an excellent team with a bench full of talent was little consolation. Arsenal were only left with memories, including three famous Highbury nights, and wondering whether they would ever win the Champions League.

For Henry, it was another brilliant season as he drove a young Arsenal team to the final. Arsenal fans sang, "We've got the best player in the world." For a time, they were right. Every year between 2003 and 2006, he was voted in the top four in both the Ballon d'Or and FIFA World Player of the Year. He should have won at least once, in particular when losing to Juventus'

Pavel Nedvěd in 2003 and Italy's World Cup-winning captain Fabio Cannavaro in 2006.

Some critics accused him of being a 'big-game bottler'. This was harsh as he consistently stepped up with goals and moments of brilliance in crucial games against Man Utd, Chelsea, Liverpool and Spurs, as well as proving the difference against the likes of Brazil, Real Madrid, Juventus and Inter Milan. A goal in a major final for Arsenal or France was the one thing missing from his CV. It seemed an anomaly, especially as he was named man of the match in more than one of those games, and one that would have ended were it not for Henchoz's handball in the 2001 FA Cup Final, when Henry did everything right in rounding the goalkeeper and slotting goalwards. However, his chance in the Champions League Final was a massive opportunity to take his reputation to the next level and put to bed any criticism.

2006/07
HELLO EMIRATES; PROJECT YOUTH

Premier League		Fourth
FA Cup		Fifth round
Champions League		Round of 16
League Cup		Final

PREMIER LEAGUE		PL	W	D	L	GF	GA	GD	PTS
1	MAN UTD	38	28	5	5	83	27	56	89
2	CHELSEA	38	24	11	3	64	24	40	83
3	LIVERPOOL	38	20	8	10	57	27	30	68
4	ARSENAL	38	19	11	8	63	35	28	68
5	TOTTENHAM	38	17	9	12	57	54	3	60
6	EVERTON	38	15	13	10	52	36	16	58

Highlights: A young back-up team knocked out Spurs and others on the way to the League Cup Final; league double over Champions Man Utd; nine goals and two cup wins in a week at Anfield

Lowlights: Limp Champions League exit to PSV; losing a tight League Cup Final to Chelsea; beaten by Sheffield Utd despite centre-back Phil Jagielka playing in goal for 30 minutes; playing for fourth, not the title, from early in the season

Player of the year: Assist-master Cesc Fàbregas was the pivot and the leader of Project Youth aged 19

Top scorers: Robin van Persie 13 (11 in PL), Thierry Henry 12 (10), Emmanuel Adebayor 12 (8), Gilberto Silva 11 (10), Julio Baptista 11 (3)

Goal of the season: van Persie's flying volley versus Charlton, the Valley, Premier League

Seven years after deciding to leave Highbury, Arsenal finally moved to their new stadium at Ashburton Grove. The 60,000-seat arena was named the Emirates Stadium in a deal estimated at £100m, giving the airline stadium-naming rights for 15 years and shirt sponsorship for seven years. Arsenal fans were excited by the bigger crowds and better facilities, happy they had only moved less than 1km up the road, but sad at losing historic Highbury and entering a new corporate reality.

Arsène Wenger's tenth year began with the continued departure of Invincibles:

- Dennis Bergkamp retired aged 37.

- Robert Pires moved to Villarreal, a victim of Wenger's rigid policy of only offering one-year contracts to players over 30. At 32, the classy midfielder still had something to offer a young Arsenal team.

- 31-year-old Sol Campbell was released as he sought a "fresh challenge." A month later, he signed for Portsmouth. Wenger said, "It is a big surprise to me because he cancelled his contract to go abroad. Have you sold Portsmouth to a foreign country?" With two league titles and three FA Cups, the centre-back had vindicated his controversial move from Spurs.

- 29-year-old Lauren, who had been out for a year with a knee injury, was sold to Portsmouth in the winter transfer window.

- José Antonio Reyes was exchanged for Real Madrid's Júlio Baptista in a season-long loan deal. After a promising early impact and plenty of moments of quality, Reyes left an unfulfilled talent, although a Premier League and FA Cup winner. The 22-year-old Spaniard never settled to English life both on and off the pitch. Sadly, Reyes died in a car crash in 2019 aged 35.

- Most acrimoniously, Ashley Cole went to rivals Chelsea in exchange for William Gallas and £5m. A bitter Cole did himself no favours with his autobiography *My Defence* in which the 25-year-old said he almost swerved his car off the road when his agent told him Arsenal would only offer him £55,000/week not the £60,000 he was after (an amount that was double the UK's average *annual* income at the time and not a long way below the manager's salary). "I was trembling with anger," he wrote, adding that the Arsenal board had "fed him to the sharks" over the Chelsea tapping-up affair, for which he was eventually fined £75,000 by the Premier League. Neither Arsenal nor Cole handled the situation well. While players and agents negotiate with other clubs while under contract all the time, Cole had been caught red-handed with José Mourinho, of all people. At the time, many thought Arsenal had done a good swap in getting a French international plus cash. But they lost a world-class left-back that had been at Arsenal since he was nine, had years left at the top and should have formed the backbone of the post-Invincibles team.

Apart from Gallas and Baptista, the only major signing was Tomáš Rosický, who replaced Pires as number seven. Two excellent strikes in the 2006 World Cup for the Czech Republic boded well. Thierry Henry ended speculation of a move to Barcelona by signing a new contract. Cash-strapped Arsenal were reliant on a young squad replicating their 2006 Champions League form over a long season.

The Premier League opener on 19 August 2006 was the first competitive game at the Emirates. Back in red and white, Arsenal passed it around on the new surface, which was bigger than Highbury and in similar pristine condition. However, early in the second half, Aston Villa's Olof Mellberg gatecrashed the party and beat Jens Lehmann to head the first top-flight goal at the stadium. With six minutes left, substitute Theo Walcott, on for his Premier League debut despite having been selected in England's 2006 World Cup squad, crossed from the left and the ball fell to Gilberto, who volleyed into the roof of the net.

TYPICAL LINE-UP
(4-4-2/4-5-1)

14 Henry / van Persie / Aliadière

25 Adebayor / Baptista

7 Rosický / Ljungberg / Diaby

19 Gilberto / Flamini

4 Fàbregas / Diaby

13 Hleb / Ljungberg / Walcott

22 Clichy / Gallas / Hoyte

5 Touré / Senderos

10 Gallas / Djourou

27 Eboué / Hoyte

1 Lehmann / Almunia

Players in: Tomáš Rosický, Júlio Baptista (loan), William Gallas, Denílson

Players out: Dennis Bergkamp, Robert Pires, Ashley Cole, Sol Campbell, Pascal Cygan, José Antonio Reyes (loan), Sebastian Larsson, *Lauren*

A familiar failure to finish chances meant Arsenal lost to Man City for the first time in the Premier League. Henry had ten shots, Robin van Persie hit the post and Kolo Touré had a header cleared off the line. Justin Hoyte, playing left-back, clumsily fouled Trevor Sinclair and Joey Barton converted the penalty off the crossbar. It was a similar story at the Emirates against Middlesbrough. Arsenal dominated but James Morrison did a one-two with Yakubu and clipped past Jens Lehmann. The away side defended well and frustrated Arsenal. After an hour, George Boateng got his second yellow card and Emmanuel Eboué quickly won a penalty. Henry scored, but despite a triple substitution of Baptista, Rosický and Emmanuel Adebayor, it finished 1-1.

No wins, two goals and two points in three games was not the start of title contenders nor good preparation for a trip to Man Utd, who had won all three of their games. With Henry and van Persie injured, Wenger played a 4-1-4-1 formation with Gilberto protecting the defence and Adebayor upfront. After ten minutes, goalkeeper Tomasz Kuszczak tripped Adebayor and a rare away penalty at Old Trafford was given. However, Gilberto's standing foot slipped and Kuszczak saved. Then the goalkeeper pushed a header onto the post and Paul Scholes cleared on the line. Cristiano Ronaldo hit a close-range volley which Lehmann saved with his face.

Arsenal were breaking well with Cesc Fàbregas, now wearing Patrick Vieira's number-four shirt, pulling the strings. With six minutes left, the Spaniard robbed Ronaldo, drove forward and slipped in Adebayor, who stretched a long leg to toe it past Kuszczak. Ole Gunnar Solskjær fired a low drive that took a slight deflection and was stunned when Lehmann dived to tip it round the post. A big 1-0 win kickstarted Arsenal's season and offered hope that they would still be competitive in the Stage Two Wenger era.

In late-September sun, Arsenal got their first league win at the new stadium. It took an hour but a Gallas volley, Phil Jagielka own-goal and Henry header ensured a 3-0 defeat of Sheffield Utd. At Charlton, van Persie cancelled out Darren Bent's opener. Then the Dutchman scored what Wenger described as "the goal of a lifetime." Eboué hit a deep cross from the right. van Persie, running in at full speed, met the ball mid-air just outside the area to smash a swerving, dipping volley into the roof of the net. A memorable way to seal a feisty game 2-1.

Arsenal clicked into form, beating Watford 3-0 and Reading 4-0 to make it five wins in a row. Against Everton, van Persie curled a free-kick to give a 1-1 draw and leave them fifth.

Arsenal and West Ham played out a lively game in early November as both teams missed chances. With two minutes left and a goalless draw likely, Marlon Harewood finished a low cross. West Ham manager Alan Pardew's vigorous celebrations wound up Wenger, who handed him off dismissively, before the two squared up and had to be separated by the fourth official. Wenger occasionally surprised with an entertaining willingness to get physical on the touchline that belied his skinny frame and cerebral nature.

The following Sunday, the Emirates saw its first big game, against Liverpool. Alexander Hleb slipped in Fàbregas on the right, and the Spaniard squared for Flamini to bundle home. In the second half, a quick counter involved Fàbregas, Henry and van Persie, who flicked it into the path of Touré, the centre-back surprising everyone with his burst forward and assured finish. Gallas headed in a corner to seal a confidence-boosting 3-0 win.

Arsenal started strongly against Newcastle but the away team led at half-time after Kieron Dyer curled past Lehmann. Arsenal had developed a unique ability, which they maintained throughout the Stage Two Wenger era, to dominate possession, fail to convert it into goals and concede the opening goal out of nowhere. Henry came on for the injured van Persie and curled a brilliant free-kick in off the crossbar. Arsenal were unbeaten at the Emirates after ten games, but five of those were drawn.

At Bolton, Arsenal again played some good football. However, they gave Abdoulaye Faye a free run and jump to head a corner from only three yards. Nicolas Anelka cut inside from the left and unleashed a swerving drive past Lehmann. Just before half-time, stand-in captain Gilberto powered a header of his own. Freddie Ljungberg, Adebayor and Fàbregas hit the woodwork in the second half, but Ivan Campo played in Anelka to make it 3-1 and the fifth consecutive year without an Arsenal league win at Reebok Stadium.

According to Wenger, Arsenal's season had reached "the moment of truth." Despite van Persie crashing in another free-kick, they lost 2-1 to Fulham, with Philippe Senderos sent off for two yellow cards. The truth was Arsenal were not good enough to challenge for the title. At the end of November, they were sixth and already 16 points behind leaders Man Utd.

In the Champions League, an under-strength Arsenal dealt with the inconvenience of an August qualifying round against Dynamo Zagreb, winning 5-1 on aggregate. In the group stage, they began with a 2-1 win at Hamburg, whose goalkeeper Sascha Kirschstein was sent off after 12 minutes for bringing down van Persie. Gilberto converted the penalty and Rosický cracked a 25-yarder into the top corner. Boubacar Sanogo's late goal was the first Lehmann had conceded in the competition for 853 minutes, a record that stretched over three seasons. When Justin Hoyte replaced an injured Touré early on, Arsenal had 11 different nationalities on the pitch, showing Wenger's eclectic global recruitment policy.

Arsenal beat Porto 2-0 at home with goals from Henry and Hleb. However, they only took one point from two games against CSKA Moscow, losing 1-0 away and drawing 0-0 at home despite having 24 shots, including the miss of the season by Rosický, who managed to pass it straight to the goalkeeper from three yards despite having 90% of the goal open. At the Emirates, Hamburg's Rafael van der Vaart struck a 25-yarder into the top corner after four minutes. Fàbregas played in van Persie, who passed it home. Late on, Eboué drilled a shot from an angle and Walcott crossed for Baptista to head in and make it 3-1. Arsenal and Porto drew the final game 0-0 to send both teams through, Arsenal as group winners.

Back in the league, Spurs came to the Emirates hopeful of a rare win given Arsenal's poor form and the absence of the injured Henry. After 20 minutes, Touré chipped over the defence where Adebayor had stayed onside and sidefooted past Paul Robinson. Pascal Chimbonda was wrongly adjudged

to have fouled Rosický, and Gilberto drove the spot-kick into the bottom-left corner. In the second half, Jermaine Jenas fouled van Persie and this time Gilberto sidefooted the penalty into the bottom-right corner. It was a satisfying 3-0 win in the first Emirates derby.

Injury-hit Arsenal went to Champions Chelsea with a defence of Eboué, Senderos, Johan Djourou and Gaël Clichy, average age 22. At the other end in Chelsea blue was their ex-teammate Cole. Some Arsenal fans had gone to the trouble of printing 'Bank of Russia' £20 notes bearing his face, and the vitriol from the away fans as they waved them at their former hero was palpable. In a pulsating game in the rain, Chelsea were on top. However, Arsenal took the lead with only 12 minutes left when Hleb cut back for Mathieu Flamini, who swept it in off Henrique Hilario's weak palms. Six minutes later, Michael Essien swerved a 30-yard piledriver inside the post. There was still time for both Essien and Frank Lampard to hit the woodwork. It ended in a credible 1-1 away draw.

A few days later at Wigan, Adebayor poked home a winner after 88 minutes. The Emirates was again stunned when Portsmouth took a 2-0 lead through a Noe Pamarot header and Matt Taylor dipping volley either side of half-time. Adebayor was sent on and had an instant impact, finishing Walcott's low cross. Then Gilberto buried a loose ball to make it 2-2.

Just before Christmas, there was more Emirates entertainment against Blackburn. After again going behind, a Gilberto header, Hleb twist and turn, and Adebayor penalty made it 3-1. The visitors got one back, but van Persie twice finished well and Fàbregas nutmegged Robbie Savage in the corner and set up Flamini to give a 6-2 win.

On Boxing Day at Watford, Gilberto headed in again. For the Invincibles, the Invisible Wall often went unnoticed, getting his job done without fuss. In 2006/07, he stepped up to lead a young team from the front in Henry's injury absences, taking penalties, driving forward, covering at centre-back and scoring crucial goals. Watford quickly equalised, but van Persie scored a trademark late winner, cutting inside from the right and curling left-footed into the far corner.

Arsenal were without nine players at relegation-threatened Sheffield Utd. It was wet, muddy and cold, and the home crowd were up for it. Christian Nadé turned Touré, Lehmann came racing out and Nadé sidefooted past him. After an hour, goalkeeper Paddy Kenny pulled a muscle taking a goal-kick and was replaced by centre-back Jagielka. Embarrassingly, Arsenal barely tested the stand-in goalkeeper and lost 1-0. Arsenal ended 2006 in fifth place, 17 points behind leaders Man Utd.

KEEPER

For a football obsessive and economics graduate, Wenger's failure to realise the importance of a quality goalkeeper was strange. They were good value, had potentially long careers at the top and could cost or save teams significant points over a season. Of the following 17 shot-stoppers he signed after inheriting David Seaman, only Lehmann was a success: Alex Manninger, Richard Wright, Guillaume Warmuz, Rami Shaaban, Lehmann, Almunia, Mart Poom, Vito Mannone, Wojciech Szczęsny, Łukasz Fabiański, Sean McDermott, Emi Martínez, Dejan Iliev, Matt Macey, Hugo Keto, David Ospina and Petr Čech.

In the New Year, Henry returned after over a month out. He converted a penalty against Charlton after Osei Sankofa was sent off for a foul on van Persie and Arsenal breezed to a 4-0 win. Hoyte finished a one-two with Henry, and van Persie powered in a second penalty as well as dinked a one-on-one over Scott Carson.

At Blackburn, Savage twice hacked at Gilberto from behind and got the reaction he wanted when the Brazilian kicked out and was red-carded. The remaining ten men had to play 77 minutes in the wind and rain against a physical team. Just before half-time, Touré headed in an Henry free-kick. In the second half, Henry picked up the ball deep in his own half, carried it down the left wing and drew three players. He played it inside to Fàbregas, who controlled and returned it into Henry's path. The Frenchman did not need to break stride and curled from the edge of the box into the far corner, a brilliant counter-attacking goal and a performance reminiscent of the Stage One Wenger ten-man wins.

Next up at the Emirates were leaders Man Utd. Lehmann kept it goalless at half-time with saves from Wayne Rooney and Henrik Larsson. Early in the second half, Patrice Evra crossed, the ball flicked off Touré's head and Rooney dived in at the back post to head in. With Henry and Adebayor already on the pitch, Wenger brought on more attacking players in van Persie and Baptista. On 83 minutes, Fàbregas and Rosický won the ball on the right. The Little Mozart swung in a low cross, Henry tried to flick on, and van Persie slid in at the back post to rifle high past Edwin van der Sar.

On 93 minutes, Eboué played a one-two with Rosický on the right, crossed and Henry scored a rare header. The Arsenal fans went truly wild for the first time in their new home to celebrate a memorable 2-1 comeback. The downside was that van Persie broke a metatarsal when scoring and

his season was over; yet again, injury disrupted the Dutchman's momentum. When he did play, he was a goal threat with a minutes-per-goal rate up there with the league's more-heralded big-name strikers.

At Middlesbrough, Senderos was sent off again, this time for a professional foul on Yakubu, who converted the penalty. The ten men picked up a point when Adebayor headed on and Henry controlled and drilled home left-footed.

Wigan's visit to the Emirates in mid-February followed a familiar pattern. Arsenal dominated possession but were vulnerable when they did have to defend. Denny Landzaat hit a 30-yard screamer to give Wigan the lead. Lehmann's fingertips deflected an Emile Heskey one-on-one effort onto the inside of the post and kept the deficit to one goal. With ten minutes left, Flamini crossed low and it went in off Fitz Hall. Henry mockingly offered the ball to goalkeeper Chris Kirkland, who had been wasting time all game. A few minutes later, Adebayor played in Baptista, who crossed from the right, and Rosický stooped to head in from close range.

Referee Phil Dowd suddenly decided to crack down on time-wasting and punished Lehmann at his first attempt – he and the jubilant home fans did not care though as Arsenal sealed another late comeback. An injury-hit Arsenal earnt a more comfortable 2-1 win against Reading, the away goal coming late on. Arsenal had lost only once in 13 league games and were up to third.

In the League Cup, a young team with a sprinkling of more senior squad players beat West Brom 2-0 with both goals from Jérémie Aliadière. At Everton, James McFadden was sent off early on, and Arsenal finally took advantage when Adebayor soared to head the winner from a corner.

The week before Christmas, the 'B team' travelled to Anfield but the game was called off due to heavy fog. Arsenal had also drawn Liverpool in the FA Cup, meaning an Anfield double-header in January. In the FA Cup, the fired-up Saturday evening crowd was silenced when Rosický and Hleb exchanged passes, Hleb squared and the Little Mozart swept high past Jerzy Dudek from the edge of the area. Just before half-time, Arsenal passed it around, Rosický drove forward from the left and this time shot into the bottom corner. Dirk Kuyt flicked Peter Crouch's header past Manuel Almunia to give Liverpool a lifeline.

With six minutes left, an isolated Henry picked up the ball in the centre-circle. His initial instinct was to kill time and push Liverpool back, so he passed the ball 40 yards towards the touchline. Jamie Carragher had a five-yard start but he seemed to have a parachute on his back as the electric Henry reeled

him in. They arrived together, but Henry was too strong and sprinted away with the ball, leaving Carragher in a heap on the floor. Henry cut inside and finished into the far bottom corner. It was another outrageous piece of skill and pace from the Frenchman, and a clinical counter-attacking 3-1 win for Arsenal. Henry consistently 'vaccinated' Carragher when they faced each other, something the Liverpool legend readily conceded: "When he hit top gear and ran past you, it was like trying to chase after someone on a motorbike."

Four days later, the two sides met in the League Cup. Although the line-ups were much changed, Liverpool had an experienced spine in Sami Hyypiä, Steven Gerrard, Robbie Fowler and Craig Bellamy.

- 1-0: Aliadière raced on to a Touré long ball and beat Dudek.

- 1-1: Fowler equalised.

- 2-1: Baptista curled a free-kick over the wall and past a flat-footed Dudek.

- 3-1: A corner bounced off Alex Song into the net.

- 4-1: Aliadière and Baptista combined for the burly Brazilian to give Arsenal an incredible half-time lead.

- 5-1: Hyypiä fouled Aliadière, but Dudek saved Baptista's penalty. Not a problem for the Beast as he then beat Dudek from 25 yards to secure his hat-trick.

- 5-2: Gerrard cracked a volley from the edge of the area.

- 5-3: A Hyypiä header raised Liverpool hopes of a comeback.

- 6-3: Aliadière raced on to a long ball, waltzed past Gabriel Paletta and squared for Baptista.

An incredible night finished 6-3, the first time Liverpool had conceded six at Anfield for 77 years, Aliadière channelling his inner Henry and Baptista scoring four as well as missing a penalty.

The League Cup semi-final was a North London derby. Wenger kept faith with his young team, while Spurs fielded a strong team. The home side went 2-0 up when Dimitar Berbatov headed in after a mix-up between Almunia and Touré, then a free-kick went through Baptista's legs for an own-goal. However, the Beast barged his way through the defence to sidefoot in and then sealed the comeback when he tapped in Hoyte's cross after Robinson inexplicably came racing out of his goal.

In the second leg, Arsenal dominated and eventually broke through when substitute Rosický deceived the defence with a reverse pass and Adebayor sidefooted in left-footed. However, with five minutes left, Mido headed an equaliser, Spurs' first attempt on target. It went to extra time and Arsenal had to win it again. Ricardo Rocha decided to head a low Fàbregas cross from six inches off the ground – it did not work. Aliadière swivelled on to the loose ball and smashed it

high into the net. Then Adebayor won a header, Rosický drove at the defence and his shot hit the post but went in off Chimbonda to make it 3-1 on the night and 5-3 on aggregate.

Back in the FA Cup, Arsenal faced Bolton for the third year running. A Touré diving header made it 1-1 and meant an unwanted replay at Reebok Stadium. Good interplay ended with Adebayor scoring from a deflected left-foot strike. Baptista won a penalty, which Gilberto blazed over the bar. Adebayor robbed Campo on halfway, rounded goalkeeper Jussi Jääskeläinen and hit the post with the goal gaping. Arsenal paid for their profligacy as Bolton pumped one last corner into the box and Abdoulaye Meite took it to extra time.

Aliadière injected pace and played in fellow substitute Ljungberg. The Swede, who was just back from another injury and had lost acceleration, scored with a trademark right-to-left run beyond the defence and low left-footed finish. Tal Ben Haim was sent off. Aliadière played in Adebayor and, with Jääskeläinen again pushing up to leave his goal unguarded, Anelka made a cynical foul. Unbelievably, or perhaps with Adebayor's earlier open-goal miss in mind, the referee did not deem it a goalscoring opportunity and only gave Anelka a yellow card. Baptista also skied his penalty over the bar. Arsenal broke again and this time Baptista and Adebayor against Jääskeläinen were sufficient to seal a crazy game 3-1.

The following Sunday, Arsenal went to the Millennium Stadium for the League Cup Final against Chelsea, a chance for Wenger to win the trophy for the first time. The manager kept faith in his young team, the average age of 21 being the youngest ever to play in a major English final. Adebayor and Hleb were on the bench. Lehmann, Gallas, Gilberto and Ljungberg were available but not included in the squad. The Champions played their strongest team.

Arsenal started strongly and took the lead when Walcott linked with Abou Diaby and curled his first Arsenal goal. It did not last long as Michael Ballack played in Didier Drogba, who was in an offside position, and Arsenal's regular nemesis sidefooted past Almunia. After 83 minutes, Arjen Robben crossed from the left and Drogba got in front of Senderos to head the winner.

In injury time, John Obi Mikel fouled Touré and Arsenal's captain for the day went crazy. Fàbregas and Lampard had a wrestling match and everyone got involved in a typical 'footballer's brawl' – lots of pushing and shouting by a few and holding people back by most of the others. However, Eboué did thump Wayne Bridge on the back and was subsequently banned. Touré and Mikel were sent off, as was Adebayor.

Arsenal's young players had run Chelsea close. Diaby in particular, back from serious injury, showed his talent, turning Lampard and gliding away on one occasion with ease. Fàbregas' class was already known and Denílson showed in the cup run the potential to follow in his footsteps. Wenger stuck to his principles but Mourinho walked away with the trophy. In the end, the cup final experience given to the young players was hardly worth it as few of them made it at Arsenal. Playing Senderos against regular tormenter Drogba was a risk that backfired. It also completed an unfortunate full set of final losses for Wenger – Champions League, UEFA Cup, FA Cup and League Cup.

The following Wednesday, Arsenal went to Blackburn for the FA Cup fifth-round replay, the home game having ended in a rare goalless draw. With four minutes left, Benni McCarthy easily cut inside replacement right-back Senderos and hammered into the far corner to knock Arsenal out of the second cup in four days.

Arsenal were favourites in the Champions League knockout against PSV Eindhoven. In the away leg, Heurelho Gomes saved from Rosický, Henry and Fàbregas. After an hour, Édison Méndez skidded a shot past Lehmann from 25 yards to give PSV a 1-0 win. At home, PSV frustrated Arsenal but the tension was lifted in the second half when Adebayor flicked on a corner and the ball bounced off Alex to level the tie. Wenger brought on an unfit Henry, but the Frenchman was soon holding his groin.

SLOW STARTERS

Arsenal regularly started Emirates games with low intensity during Stage Two and Stage Three Wenger, in sharp contrast to Stage One when they used to fly out of the blocks and often had games wrapped up within 20 minutes. It allowed away teams to settle in, sit back, and let Arsenal pass it around the defence and midfield. Arsenal would often go to sleep and watch the visitors score on the break or at a set-piece with their first chance. It put pressure on them to chase the game, which they became good at, stepping up the urgency late on. In 19 league games at the Emirates in 2006/07, they conceded first on ten occasions, coming back to win four times and draw five times.

Arsenal were left with only a top-four finish to play for and they needed the Champions League revenues it provided to repay the stadium debt. They battled to a 1-0 win at Aston Villa as Diaby deflected in a Baptista shot. But then came two losses in Merseyside. In injury time at Everton, as hail lashed down, a corner bounced to Andrew Johnson, who volleyed in. The sun was out at Anfield where Crouch scored a perfect hat-trick to give Liverpool a 4-1 win and third place.

In early April, Arsenal were all over relegation-threatened West Ham when Bobby Zamora stretched for a long ball and lobbed Lehmann. "We've only had one shot," sang the West Ham fans as Arsenal hit the woodwork twice and had 30 attempts on goal, but Robert Green saved one-on-ones, volleys and close-range headers. Arsenal were left scratching their heads as West Ham became the first team to win at the Emirates.

After 83 minutes, Alex rose to head past a stranded Lehmann and last year's finalists limped out to a team that Liverpool beat 4-0 on aggregate in the next round. Arsenal's season was almost over in early March, having been knocked out of three cups in ten days. To make it worse, scans revealed Henry would miss the rest of the season with groin and stomach injuries.

Those three losses and a goalless draw at Newcastle meant Arsenal's new reality was battling fifth-place Bolton. Anelka opened the scoring, following up a long set-piece. Rosický equalised from close-range and Fàbregas twisted and turned before scoring the winner. Arsenal backed it up with a 3-1 win against Man City, Fàbregas cracking in a 20-yard volley.

That left three London derbies and a final game at Portsmouth. At White Hart Lane, second-half set-piece goals from Touré and Adebayor put Arsenal 2-1 ahead, but Jenas drilled a low equaliser in the 94th minute. It was a frustrating end for Arsenal, who had hit the woodwork three times. More late goals, this time from Adebayor and Gilberto, meant Arsenal beat Fulham 3-1.

Chelsea needed a win at the Emirates to stay in the title race. Late in the first half, Khalid Boulahrouz fouled Baptista and was sent off, the Arsenal fans waving their red season-ticket cardholders at him as he trudged off. Essien headed an equaliser and, despite an exciting second half, the game ended 1-1, meaning Man Utd were Champions.

Arsenal finished the season fourth after a goalless draw at Portsmouth as David James saved Baptista's penalty. It was an eventful season for the Beast – ten goals, six of which came in two League Cup games, three missed penalties, promising moments and fluffed chances – but he did not live up to his nickname nor his status as a Brazilian from Real Madrid.

A disappointing season proved Arsenal had firmly entered a new reality of competing for a top-four finish. They played lots of excellent passing football and, in beating Man Utd twice, showed they could match anyone on their day. Wenger said, "We create more chances than anyone in the league but we don't score as many and that tells you we waste chances."

Injuries to the best finishers Henry and van Persie, who only started 16 and 17 league games respectively, were a blow. It was the only season in Henry's eight at the club that he failed to hit at least 22 goals. Hleb and Rosický were good replacements for Ljungberg and Pires in terms of passing and movement, but neither had their finishing ability or consistent desire to get into the box and apply the killer touch.

Wenger had also, deliberately or not, evolved from physical and pacey players and electric transition play to a possession-based game reliant on short triangles and clever movement. They crossed less and had fewer players that could carry the ball. They were also more lightweight and vulnerable to counter-attacks and set-pieces.

St Totteringham's Day

SEASON	DATE	GAME	
1996/97	5 Apr	33	
1997/98	28 Mar	29	Earliest since 1959
1998/99	6 Apr	32	
1999/00	16 Apr	32	
2000/01	17 Apr	33	
2001/02	18 Mar	30	Earliest at the time
2002/03	24 Mar	31	
2003/04	13 Mar	28	The Invincibles bring it on in the lowest number of games ever
2004/05	2 Apr	31	
2005/06	7 May	38	Last day of season – lasagne; Arsenal beat Wigan 4-2 in Highbury's last game and overtake Spurs, who lose at West Ham
2006/07	21 Apr	35	Achieved at White Hart Lane in 2-2 draw
2007/08	9 Mar	29	Earliest ever
2008/09	11 Apr	32	
2009/10	9 May	38	Last day of season – Arsenal beat Fulham 4-0 as Spurs lose at Burnley
2010/11	7 May	35	
2011/12	13 May	38	Last day of season – mind the gap; Arsenal win 3-2 at West Brom and finish one point ahead after being ten behind in February
2012/13	19 May	38	Last day of season – Arsenal seal a nervy 1-0 win at Newcastle to finish one point ahead
2013/14	28 Apr	36	
2014/15	4 May	34	
2015/16	15 May	38	Last day of season – it's happened again; Arsenal beat Aston Villa 4-0 to overtake Spurs who lose 5-1 to relegated and ten-men Newcastle
2016/17			Cancelled – Spurs beat Arsenal 2-0 on 30 April to end 21-year run
2017/18			Cancelled when Arsenal lose at Old Trafford on 29 April

2007/08
BROKEN LEG AND BROKEN DREAMS

Premier League	Third
FA Cup	Fifth round
Champions League	Quarter-final
League Cup	Semi-final

PREMIER LEAGUE		PL	W	D	L	GF	GA	GD	PTS
1	MAN UTD	38	27	6	5	80	22	58	87
2	CHELSEA	38	25	10	3	65	26	39	85
3	ARSENAL	38	24	11	3	74	31	43	83
4	LIVERPOOL	38	21	13	4	67	28	39	76
5	EVERTON	38	19	8	11	55	33	22	65
6	ASTON VILLA	38	16	12	10	71	51	20	60

Highlights: Sublime football in the first two-thirds of the season took Arsenal top of the table; beating AC Milan in the San Siro; Nicklas Bendtner's six-second North London derby winner; Theo Walcott's 75-yard run to set up Emmanuel Adebayor at Anfield provided the ultimate one-minute high

Lowlights: Eduardo's leg-break at Birmingham, William Gallas' reaction and Arsenal's subsequent title meltdown; going out of the Champions League to Liverpool despite being the better side in both games; a makeshift team was hammered 4-0 at Old Trafford in the FA Cup

Player of the year: Talisman Cesc Fàbregas added goals to his brilliant passing

Top scorers: Adebayor 30 (24 in PL), Fàbregas 13 (7), Eduardo 12 (4)

Goal of the season: Adebayor's turn and thunderous volley versus Spurs, White Hart Lane, Premier League

In June 2007, Arsenal's – and the Premier League's – best-ever player Thierry Henry moved to Barcelona after scoring 226 goals in eight years. The captain cut a frustrated figure the previous season due to injuries and the team's drop in status. His departure was a blow and many predicted Arsenal's young squad would struggle. Another legend, Freddie Ljungberg, went to the West Ham 'retirement home', having scored 72 goals in nine years. Brazilian-born Croatian Eduardo da Silva and Frenchmen Bacary Sagna and Lassana Diarra came in and a £10m profit helped pay some of the stadium debt. Meanwhile, Man Utd's net spend of £52m saw the arrivals of Owen Hargreaves, Carlos Tevez, Nani and Anderson.

Arsène Wenger named William Gallas as the new captain, which took everyone, including Gilberto Silva, by surprise. The respected Invincible and Brazil captain said, "He didn't say anything to me and I just found out about it that evening when I saw it on the Arsenal website. I wasn't upset about not being captain, but I was about the way I learnt about it."

Only 52 seconds into the new season, Jens Lehmann gifted Fulham's David Healy a goal by bumbling his attempted pass to Gaël Clichy. With five minutes to go, Kolo Touré burst forward and won a penalty. Robin van Persie sidefooted into the top-right corner. In injury time, Cesc Fàbregas lofted a pass to Alexander Hleb, who twisted and turned before scoring the winner. At Blackburn, in this season's classy but untraditional away kit of white shirts and redcurrant shorts, van Persie scored after a goalmouth scramble. However, Lehmann let a weak shot from David Dunn through his hands and it ended 1-1.

Against Man City, Manuel Almunia came in for the injured Lehmann and Gilberto, who had lost his centre-midfield place to Mathieu Flamini, filled in at centre-back. van Persie unusually missed a penalty, Kasper Schmeichel saving his low drive. However, Arsenal got another late winner as Fàbregas finished high into the net from an angle. Slick passing produced a 3-1 win over Portsmouth with goals from Emmanuel Adebayor, Fàbregas and Tomáš Rosický despite Philippe Senderos becoming the first Arsenal player to be sent off at the Emirates after bringing down Nwankwo Kanu. The Swiss defender's clumsy style and lack of pace meant it was his third red card in ten months.

In a pulsating derby at White Hart Lane, 18-year-old Gareth Bale curled a free-kick to give Spurs the lead after 15 minutes. Hleb set up Abou Diaby, who hit the bar. Dimitar Berbatov rounded Almunia 30 yards out and when he tried to do the same to Touré with the goal gaping, the Ivorian produced the tackle of the season. Sagna cut back for Adebayor, who also crashed against the bar. Midway through the second half, Arsenal finally equalised when Adebayor beat Paul Robinson to a free-kick and headed in. Clichy blocked on the line from Berbatov. With ten minutes left, Arsenal broke and Fàbregas fired a long-range effort past Robinson. Darren Bent was played through and his scuffed effort dribbled embarrassingly wide. At the end, Fàbregas fizzed the ball into Adebayor just outside the area, where the number 25 flicked the ball up, swivelled and cracked a swerving volley high into the net to make it 3-1 and send Arsenal top of the table.

Arsenal ran riot in a 5-0 win over Derby with Diaby and Fàbregas firing 20-yarders and Adebayor scoring a hat-trick. As well as pulling the strings in midfield, Fàbregas was now shooting confidently and had scored in six games in a row. An early van Persie header gave a 1-0 win at West Ham.

Arsenal were 2-0 up and coasting against Roy Keane's Sunderland after only 15 minutes. The first came when van Persie hammered a 25-yard free-kick off the underside of the bar. However, Sunderland stunned the home crowd by drawing level. Touré, whose preferred shooting range was 30-40 yards, also rattled the woodwork from distance, but the ball stayed out. With ten minutes left, Theo Walcott squared and van Persie scored the winner. Against Bolton, a Touré long-ranger did find the back of the net and Arsenal won 2-0.

TYPICAL LINE-UP
(4-4-2)

25 Adebayor — Bendtner

11 van Persie — Eduardo

7 Rosický — Diaby / Hleb

13 Hleb — Eboué / Walcott

4 Fàbregas — Gilberto

16 Flamini — Diarra / Hleb

22 Clichy

3 Sagna — Touré

5 Touré — Senderos

10 Gallas

24 Almunia — Lehmann

Players in: Łukasz Fabiański, Eduardo da Silva, Bacary Sagna, Lassana Diarra

Players out: Thierry Henry, Freddie Ljungberg, José Antonio Reyes, Jérémie Aliadière, Arturo Lupoli, *Lassana Diarra*

Arsenal's entertaining pass-and-move football had produced eight wins and one draw from their first nine games. Critics said they had had an easy fixture list – the next two games against Liverpool, who were also unbeaten, and Man Utd were chances to answer them.

van Persie, who had started the season well alongside Adebayor with seven goals in ten games, yet again saw his momentum stalled by injury. A damaged knee kept him out for three months, bar a couple of comeback attempts, and he barely put a run of games together in the rest of the season.

At Anfield, Wenger went 4-5-1 with Hleb behind Adebayor. Steven Gerrard drilled in a low free-kick after seven minutes. Emmanuel Eboué rattled the post and Fàbregas put the rebound wide with plenty of open goal to aim at. Then Hleb, with socks halfway down his calves in throwback style, showed his class. He received the ball on the left, allowed play to unfold, drew four players and flicked a perfect through-ball to Fàbregas, who stabbed past Pepe Reina. Fàbregas then curled onto the post and this time Nicklas Bendtner skied the rebound with the goal gaping. It was an excellent performance with impressive interplay between Fàbregas, Hleb and Rosický that should have brought more than one point.

At the start of November, Man Utd came to the Emirates level on points at the top of the table, although Arsenal had played a game less. Just before half-time, a low Cristiano Ronaldo cross went in off Gallas. Fàbregas equalised but with ten minutes left Patrice Evra squared for Ronaldo to score what looked like the winner. In injury time, Clichy crossed, Walcott played it back across and Gallas showed his finishing ability to guide in despite Edwin van der Sar pushing it out from behind the line. It was a club-record 25 games unbeaten in all competitions.

At Reading, a good move on the right ended with Flamini's first goal of the season. Adebayor sidefooted the second and Hleb typically took his time before shooting for the third. It ended 3-1. Arsenal could not break through against Wigan until Gallas burst forward and headed at the near post with seven minutes left. Soon after, a Rosický drive made it 2-0.

Arsenal went behind at Aston Villa but Flamini hammered a left-foot volley and Adebayor soared to make it 2-1. Wenger said, "We played the ball through needles and it was very difficult for Aston Villa."

In the Champions League qualifying round, Arsenal beat Sparta Prague 5-0 on aggregate with Rosický scoring against his first club and a mulleted

Eduardo opening his account with a nice volley on the stretch.

In the group stage, Arsenal had an impressive 3-0 win over Juande Ramos' Sevilla with goals from Fàbregas, van Persie and Eduardo. A strong van Persie finish into the roof of the net gave a 1-0 win at Steaua București. Then Slavia Prague were the unfortunate recipients of a brilliant display of Wengerball as Arsenal equalled the Champions League record win. Fàbregas and Walcott scored twice in a 7-0 rout, and it could have been more. A subdued goalless draw in Prague guaranteed qualification.

Arsenal's club-record unbeaten run ended at 28 in Seville, where they lost 3-1 despite Eduardo giving them the lead with a composed finish. A 2-1 win over Steaua meant they finished second in the group behind Sevilla.

Against Newcastle, Adebayor opened the scoring after four minutes with a variation of his brilliant Spurs volley, this time using his chest to control and striking from inside the area. In the second half, Arsenal failed to clear and Steven Taylor made it 1-1. Middlesbrough was Arsenal's third away game in eight days. After four minutes, Touré unnecessarily fouled Jérémie Aliadière as he was racing away from goal and Stewart Downing converted the penalty. Tuncay scored

from a corner in the second half while Rosický got one back late on. The 2-1 loss ended Arsenal's unbeaten run of 22 league matches and meant only one point from two games in which they badly missed three of their first-choice midfield – Fàbregas, Hleb and Flamini – as well as van Persie. However, they still led Man Utd by one point and Chelsea by three.

In mid-December, Chelsea, now managed by Avram Grant, came to the Emirates without Didier Drogba, but with Ashley Cole for the first time. Arsenal fans gave their former man, who they dubbed 'Cashley', an unwelcome reception and it set the tone for a niggly game. Just before half-time, Petr Čech got under a corner and Gallas headed into the empty net against his old club. Shaun Wright-Phillips screwed a close-range volley wide and Arsenal missed chances or had goals disallowed on the break. Fàbregas and Cole clashed at the end, and Arsenal beat Chelsea for the first time in 11 games to reclaim top spot.

Just before Christmas, Spurs came to the Emirates with yet another manager, Sevilla's Ramos replacing Martin Jol. Just after half-time, Fàbregas drove forward, exchanged passes with Rosický and back-heeled to Adebayor, who scored with an Henry Sidefoot Finish. Robbie Keane hit the bar but then set up Berbatov to equalise. Touré fouled Berbatov to give Spurs a penalty. Keane put it to his left and Almunia saved to huge cheers. With 15 minutes left and Fàbregas lining up to take a corner, Wenger sent Bendtner on for Eboué. A record six seconds later, the 19-year-old Dane soared to head a famous winner, his first Premier League goal.

A Boxing Day goalless draw against Portsmouth was the first time Arsenal failed to score in the league. At Everton, Wenger paired Eduardo and Bendtner upfront, ending the brief 4-5-1 experiment. The home side took the lead through Tim Cahill. Just after half-time, Eduardo twice showcased his finishing prowess to turn the game. For the first he got on to a speculative Clichy long ball, for the second his clever flick left Phil Jagielka on the floor. Bendtner, in his first Premier League start, got a second yellow card to give Everton hope, but Adebayor robbed Tim Howard and tapped in. Everton then went down to ten men when Mikel Arteta swung an arm at Fàbregas and a Rosický drive made it 4-1. Arsenal ended 2007 top of the table by two points.

In the League Cup, Arsenal's even younger team, which included Łukasz Fabiański, Alex Song, Armand Traoré, Kieran Gibbs, Denílson and Bendtner, again had fun, often against more experienced sides. They beat both Newcastle and Sheffield Utd 3-0 and Blackburn 3-2 with Eduardo scoring four typically cool finishes.

Like the previous season, the semi-final was a two-legged North London derby. After a 1-1 draw at the Emirates, Wenger added Sagna, Gallas, Gilberto and Hleb to the side, but Spurs' first team sensed the opportunity. Jermaine Jenas opened the scoring and Bendtner headed an own-goal. Spurs added two more before Adebayor came on and cracked a shot into the top corner. Then a running feud between Adebayor and Bendtner saw Adebayor land a 'footballer's headbutt' on the Dane, leaving him with a bloody nose. Bendtner was understandably furious and Gallas and Flamini had to keep the two apart. Spurs won 5-1, their first North London derby win in 22 attempts going back to November 1999.

More worrying were the cracks in the squad, as Adebayor-Bendtner was not the only personality clash. Lehmann, unimpressed at not regaining his place from Almunia when he returned from injury, said, "To be sitting on the bench behind somebody who only started to play when he was 30 is not funny." The outspoken German added, "I think – and this is aimed at my dear manager – one shouldn't humiliate players for too long." Five months later, Almunia responded: "To have someone here who hates me is just amazing. Every morning I wake up, I know it is going to be the same. But I don't care anymore. I come into training and work with Łukasz Fabiański and Vito Mannone. They are better than him anyway."

While it was not obvious on the pitch, centre-backs Gallas and Touré also did not communicate. The Ivorian refused to reveal why, saying: "If we start talking about that, then it will be a big story." At least the midfield four were good mates. Managing conflict was not Wenger's strong point and Arsenal had lost the senior players from the George Graham era or the likes of Patrick Vieira to maintain discipline and keep the squad united for the common cause.

Two minutes into the New Year's Day game versus West Ham, Eduardo chested a cross and volleyed home. Adebayor made it a comfortable 2-0 win. Against Birmingham, it looked to be a similar story when Adebayor's penalty opened the scoring. However, Arsenal switched off from a corner and a 1-1 draw meant they dropped two points.

They followed up with a trio of 3-0 wins in a week against Fulham, Newcastle in the FA Cup and Newcastle again in the league. Adebayor was on fire with five goals – three towering headers, a meandering run and right-foot finish, and a left-foot drive. Flamini hit a brilliant 25-yard drive into the top corner in the last game. It did not seem serious at the time, but Rosický suffered a tendon injury that triggered 18 months out of the game.

KNUCKLE DUSTER

17-year-old reserve left-back Armand Traoré revealed that he went to the North London derby at White Hart Lane to watch and was arrested with a knuckle duster in his pocket: "I was convinced someone might recognise me. I thought if a Spurs fan did, then I needed to be ready if something happened... As I walked into the stadium, the police found it on me and I ended up in custody for more than ten hours. I didn't see a ball kicked. Eventually they released me."

It was a breakout season for Adebayor. While Arsenal fans' song "Give him the ball and he will score" was not entirely accurate, his finishing was more composed, his aerial ability provided Arsenal with a rare threat from crosses and his rangy running was an outlet to release pressure.

In January, after only five months and 13 games, Diarra moved to Portsmouth due to concern about his lack of game time ahead of Euro 2008. For France, Diarra was a regular, while Flamini only got three caps. For Arsenal, the Fàbregas-Flamini partnership was a major success in 2007-08. With a small squad and still in all four competitions, letting a quality player go was a mistake.

At the start of February at Man City, Sagna pulled back for Adebayor to score. The big striker then headed back across goal to Eduardo, who chested, swivelled and volleyed in. Man City got one back but Arsenal broke and Adebayor made it 3-1. In the absence of van Persie, it was important that the Adebayor-Eduardo partnership thrived. Eduardo, who now had 12 goals and nine assists, impressed with a good touch, sharp movement and composed finishing.

Senderos powered in an early header against Blackburn and Adebayor made it 2-0 at the end, his 12th goal in nine games. A strong run of six wins and one draw had put Arsenal five points clear with 12 games to play, including trips to Old Trafford and Stamford Bridge.

The games came thick and fast. With nine players injured, another three carrying knocks and a game against Champions League holders AC Milan a few days later, Arsenal could have done without an FA Cup fifth-round tie at Old Trafford. They certainly played like it. Man Utd won 4-0 as Eboué was sent off for a high foot on Evra, and Nani, who had given right-back Justin Hoyte a tough time, showboated in the second half to rub it in.

Arsenal were the better team at the Emirates against Milan but did not create many clear-cut chances. Right at the end, Walcott did well on the right and his cross took out goalkeeper Zeljko Kalac, leaving Adebayor with an open goal from three yards, but he headed up against the bar. A 0-0 draw left work to do in the San Siro.

The following Saturday lunchtime on 23 February 2008, the season, and Stage Two Wenger era, had its defining moment. The game was three minutes old when Birmingham's Martin Taylor flew studs first into Eduardo's shin. The reaction of the players signalled the severity of the incident. The striker was given oxygen and treated on the pitch for eight minutes while being comforted by Sagna before being stretchered off. His teammates were visibly upset and many could not look at his broken leg and dislocated ankle. Sky refused to replay the incident. An Arsenal player had yet again suffered a career-threatening injury from a pumped-up inferior player testing the 'they don't like it up them' theory. Mike Dean sent Taylor off, but the traumatised Arsenal players were zombies for the rest of the half and James McFadden opened the scoring from a free-kick.

In the second half, Arsenal turned the game around. Adebayor beat goalkeeper Maik Taylor to a corner and Walcott flicked in for his first Premier League goal after 30 games. Five minutes later, he got another, robbing Liam Ridgewell on the right, cutting inside and striking left-footed into the bottom corner from the edge of the area. With ten minutes left, Adebayor was through on goal with Bendtner in support. Instead of giving his teammate a tap-in to secure the win, Adebayor shot and Taylor saved.

Four minutes into injury time, the ball was in Arsenal's left-back area but there was no danger. However, Clichy, who had not seen Stuart Parnaby, dawdled. Parnaby closed him down and Clichy made a panicked tackle, toeing the ball away. Parnaby threw himself over and Dein pointed to the spot. McFadden buried the penalty to make it 2-2, while a furious Gallas stayed on the halfway line and kicked advertising hoardings instead of looking to clear a potential rebound. It should not have been a penalty but Clichy – a very good full-back but susceptible to brain fades and moments of ball-watching – gave an opportunity for the player to go down, the crowd to scream and the referee to 'even it up' after already sending off a home player. Arsenal were agonisingly close to a comeback win and showing the mental resolve many accused them of lacking.

After the game, Gallas sat alone in the middle of the pitch until Wenger consoled him. According to Lehmann, "In the dressing room, Gallas came to blows with Gilberto, who accused him of seeking attention in a daft manner – the row dragged on for the remainder of the season."

An upset Wenger said, "This guy should never play football again. What is he doing on the football pitch? I've gone along with the idea for a long time that to stop Arsenal, you have to kick Arsenal. I knew that was coming for a long time now." He later retracted, "On reflection, I feel my comments about Martin Taylor were excessive. I said what I did immediately after the game in the heat of the moment." Birmingham manager Alex McLeish's defence of his player was predictable and one Arsenal would hear again two years later: "Martin is not that type of player."

Arsenal were still top with a lead of three points over Man Utd. However, Aston Villa went ahead at the Emirates when Senderos put a low Gabriel Agbonlahor cross into his own net. With seconds left, Clichy pumped in a cross, Adebayor headed back and Bendtner sidefooted an equaliser.

As they had done four years earlier, Arsenal faced the daunting task of getting a result in the San Siro, this time against an AC Milan team containing Alessandro Nesta, Paolo Maldini, Andrea Pirlo, Kaka and Filippo Inzaghi. With Hleb playing behind Adebayor and Fàbregas running the midfield, they put in a controlled away performance to rank alongside the club's best in Europe. After 84 minutes, Fàbregas, who had already hit the

THE ARSENAL SHIRT NUMBER MYSTERY

By 2007/08, Arsenal's shirt numbers started to go astray to the dismay of purists. Centre-back Gallas took Dennis Bergkamp's number ten, centre-midfielder Diaby wore Lee Dixon's old number two, while the actual right-back Sagna wore a traditional left-back's number three, previously worn by Ashley Cole and Nigel Winterburn. Future anomalies included left-back André Santos in a winger's number 11.

bar, hit a drive from 30 yards that swerved into the bottom-left corner. In injury time, Walcott used his pace on the right and squared for Adebayor, prompting the away fans to sing "2-0 in the San Siro." Arsenal were the first English team to beat Milan away.

The following Sunday, Arsenal went to the less-glamorous JJB Stadium, where the pitch was in a shocking condition due to its shared use with the Wigan Warriors rugby league team. In the first minute, Fàbregas played in Adebayor, but Chris Kirkland saved his one-on-one effort. Arsenal created few other chances until the end, when the

goalkeeper blocked from Fàbregas. A 0-0 draw meant two more points were dropped.

It was a familiar story when Middlesbrough came to the Emirates. Adebayor scored, but the goal was disallowed for offside even though the ball came to him off Middlesbrough's George Boateng. Arsenal went to sleep on a long ball and Aliadière sidefooted the opener. Eboué and Fàbregas both hit the woodwork. With five minutes left, Touré headed the equaliser from a corner. Mido was then sent off for a ridiculously-high kung-fu kick that caught Clichy.

Crucially, it was the fourth draw in a row against mid- or lower-table opposition that Arsenal expected to beat. Arsenal were now second, three points behind Man Utd, and two ahead of Chelsea, who were the next opposition at Stamford Bridge. It was a battle between Arsenal's short passing and Chelsea's more direct and physical play. Fifteen minutes into the second half, Sagna scored his first Arsenal goal with a glancing header at the near post. However, he then had to go off with an ankle injury, another significant loss as Sagna was an excellent replacement for Lauren, albeit a different type of player as he was more of a natural defender than converted midfielder. Arsenal failed to deal with a long ball and it fell to Drogba, who blasted past Almunia. With ten minutes to go, another long ball was flicked on by Anelka and Drogba scored the winner. It was only Arsenal's second league defeat of the season, but a campaign that promised so much had hit the wall.

It got worse at a wet Bolton, where Arsenal were losing 2-0 at half-time and down to ten men after Diaby had been sent off for a studs-up challenge. However, after an hour, Gallas ghosted in at the back post to bury a corner. Six minutes later, Gary Cahill fouled Hleb and van Persie equalised from the penalty spot. A minute into injury time, Hleb cut back for Fàbregas and his shot was deflected three times, finally going in off Jlloyd Samuel to make it 3-2 and send the away fans wild. After five weeks without a win and criticism of their mentality, a late ten-man comeback win at Arsenal's least favourite ground was a much-needed boost.

At the start of April, Arsenal were (mathematically at least) still in the two big competitions and faced Liverpool three times in six days. In the Champions League quarter-final at the Emirates, Adebayor opened the scoring with a header from a corner. Three minutes later, Gerrard waltzed past Touré on the Arsenal right and squared for Dirk Kuyt to make it 1-1. In the second half, Hleb dribbled past five players into the box. Kuyt pulled him back but the referee inexplicably gave a corner instead of a penalty. Then Adebayor skipped down the left and crossed for Bendtner, but

Reina palmed the ball away. Fàbregas stabbed the loose ball towards the unguarded net, only to see Bendtner save a goal on the line as he clumsily tried to jump out of the way. A good Arsenal performance somehow ended in a draw and advantage Liverpool.

In the league the following Saturday lunchtime, both teams rotated. Crouch scored a low volley from outside the area and Bendtner soared to head a Fàbregas free-kick so it again ended 1-1.

At Anfield, Wenger again moved Touré to right-back to replace the injured Sagna and played Senderos and Gallas in the middle of defence. Arsenal rediscovered their brilliant early-season Wengerball to calm the intimidating atmosphere. After 13 minutes, Hleb found Diaby in the inside-right position and the Frenchman drilled the opener low inside the near post. Twenty minutes later, as a corner was swung in, Senderos was not even looking at the ball and lost Sami Hyypiä, who buried a header into the top corner. Midway through the second half, Liverpool took the lead when Arsenal failed to deal with a long goal-kick, Fernando Torres turning and firing in. Adebayor sliced wide when put through by a brilliant pass from Hleb.

After 84 minutes, Gerrard took an air-swing at a volley on the edge of the Arsenal area. Substitute Walcott picked up the ball and sprinted forward. He beat Xabi Alonso and Fabio Aurelio, kept going, evaded the retreating Javier Mascherano, then went outside Hyypiä on the edge of the box. Walcott had run 75 yards in ten seconds and taken out the entire Liverpool team. He squared, where Arsenal had three players lined up, and Adebayor made it 3-3 on aggregate. It was an unbelievable assist that Henry would have been proud of. The celebrations were exuberant.

Arsenal just had to hold on for six minutes plus injury time to go through on away goals. However, some players had not switched on when Liverpool kicked off, allowing Ryan Babel to pick up the ball deep inside the Arsenal half. He got ahead of Touré and into the box. Gallas was there to deal with him, but Touré's pursuit was clumsy. He did not foul him in the area, but Babel threw himself over and inevitably a penalty was given. Gerrard dispatched it. Arsenal's high lasted only a minute and the comedown was brutal. Right at the end, Arsenal piled forward for a free-kick, Liverpool cleared and Babel made it 4-2, and 5-3 on aggregate.

Arsenal paid for Sagna's injury as the drop in quality from their first-choice defence to the back-ups was big. An edgy Senderos was no longer the solid presence that formed part of a Champions League record defence two years earlier and Touré was much more effective at centre-back than right-back. Over two pulsating matches, Arsenal played some excellent football and created plenty of chances. However, at crucial moments, poor decisions, lack of composure or bad refereeing decisions cost them. It was Stage Two Wenger in microcosm.

Arsenal then went to league leaders Man Utd and needed to win to have a chance of reeling them in. Just after half-time, van Persie whipped in a cross, Adebayor stooped to head and the ball went in off his hand. Six minutes later, Arsenal undid their good work. Michael Carrick bobbled a volley and Gallas handled the ball, a rare defensive mistake by the Frenchman in 2007/08. Ronaldo scored the penalty and Owen Hargreaves curled a free-kick to make it 2-1 to Man Utd.

Arsenal beat Reading 2-0 with goals from Adebayor and Gilberto. They then hammered Derby for the second time of the season. It ended 6-2 with substitute Adebayor scoring another hat-trick against the cellar-dwellers. Two 1-0 wins over Everton and Sunderland left Arsenal third at the end of the season, four points behind Champions Man Utd. They were unbeaten at home and only lost three games. Fàbregas was voted PFA Young Player of the Year and he, Sagna, Adebayor and Clichy were named in the PFA Team of the Year.

Wenger built a brilliant young team with most players aged 18-24. The departure of Henry, a dominant and demanding figure who let people know when they did not meet his standards on the pitch, freed up some of the junior teammates and allowed them to take more responsibility.

They played a sublime new form of Wengerball, featuring technical players, short sharp passing, perpetual motion, the belief to play out of tight situations and constant probing to break teams down. Adebayor gave them an aerial threat as full-backs Clichy and Sagna bombed up and down the flanks. At the heart of it were the midfield four of Fàbregas, Flamini, Rosický and Hleb. Fàbregas added goals to his 17 assists in the Premier League. Flamini provided the bite alongside him to be the perfect foil. Hleb was outstanding, a master of receiving and holding on to the ball in tight spaces, creating space for others and mazy dribbles. Rosický added thrust and energy.

In the first two-thirds of the season, Arsenal played the best football of the Stage Two and Three Wenger eras. However, they won nothing, leaving a host of 'what-if' questions. Winning the title with a young, cheaply-put-together team over big-spenders Man Utd and Chelsea would have been an achievement as great as the Invincibles season. Instead it was top of his lengthy near misses list alongside the 2006 Champions League. The headline reason they were left empty-handed was the team's, and Gallas', Birmingham meltdown. It became the symbol of Arsenal's collapse – the day they lost their striker, captain and the title – but it was not as simple as that and was instead due to a combination of factors:

- Arsenal's lack of winning mentality and footballing nous meant they made crucial mistakes at key moments or failed to see games through – for example, Clichy and Touré's penalty give-aways at Birmingham and Anfield respectively; Adebayor not giving Bendtner an open goal to make it 3-1 in the same game; the players not refocusing after scoring a late goal at Anfield; not being able to defend leads in tight games.

- The small squad and lack of quality after the first 14-15 players. Refreshing the squad in January like Wenger did by adding José Antonio Reyes in 2003/04 would have been a boost for the title run-in and the cups. Instead, Wenger weakened it by letting Diarra go.

- Long-term injuries to key players van Persie, Rosický and Eduardo, who only started 13-15 league games each. Both the Adebayor-van Persie and Adebayor-Eduardo partnerships were struck down as soon as they developed. The almost-iconic first-choice midfield four only started together twice in the league.

- Failure to grind out a win when not playing well – with only one win in eight from the Birmingham game, including four draws in a row against teams that sat back, Arsenal lacked a 'Ljungberg of 2002' to step up with a crucial goal.

- The at-times weak defence, especially when the first-choice four were broken up, conceded unnecessary goals from counter-attacks or long balls.

2008/09
SEMI-FINAL SEIZURE

Premier League	Fourth
FA Cup	Semi-final
Champions League	Semi-final
League Cup	Quarter-final

PREMIER LEAGUE		PL	W	D	L	GF	GA	GD	PTS
1	MAN UTD	38	28	6	4	68	24	44	90
2	LIVERPOOL	38	25	11	2	77	27	50	86
3	CHELSEA	38	25	8	5	68	24	44	83
4	ARSENAL	38	20	12	6	68	37	31	72
5	EVERTON	38	17	12	9	55	37	18	63
6	ASTON VILLA	38	17	11	10	54	48	6	62

Highlights: Andrey Arshavin's four brilliant strikes at Anfield; 7-6 penalty shootout win against Roma; beating Villarreal in the Champions League quarter-final; 2-1 victories against Man Utd and Chelsea; Eduardo's goalscoring comeback; Vela Chips

Lowlights: Outplayed by Man Utd in both Champions League semi-final legs; losing FA Cup semi-final (with in-form Arshavin on the bench) to Chelsea; conceding poor late goals to draw 4-4 against both Spurs and Liverpool; getting bullied at Stoke

Player of the year: Robin van Persie finally had an injury-free season and showed his class with 20 goals and 17 assists

Top scorers: van Persie 20 (11 in PL), Emmanuel Adebayor 16 (10), Nicklas Bendtner 15 (9)

Goal of the season: Arshavin's rocket, his second, versus Liverpool, Anfield, Premier League

When Arsenal's 2007/08 title hopes faded after leading for two-thirds of the season, many thought it was a year too early for a young team that could play opponents off the pitch with sublime passing football. Add two or three players to improve the squad depth and Arsenal would surely take the next step.

However, Arsène Wenger's Project Youth was torn apart when Mathieu Flamini turned down a new contract and went to AC Milan on a free transfer while Alexander Hleb could not resist the lure of Barcelona. Cesc Fàbregas was last man standing of the almost-iconic midfield four as Tomáš Rosický's hamstring-tendon injury surprisingly kept him out for the entire 2008/09 season. Invincibles Jens Lehmann and Gilberto Silva, who had become bit-part players, also left. With Eduardo recovering from a broken leg, Wenger had to start all over again.

New signing Samir Nasri had similar ball-playing ability to Hleb as well as two-footed shooting ability, but Arsenal would have loved to have both in the same midfield. A year later, after limited game time in a famous Treble-winning midfield of Xavi, Andrés Iniesta and Sergio Busquets, Hleb lamented, "Of course I regret leaving Arsenal. I was playing every week for one of the most exciting sides in Europe, a team which was always in the top four in the Premier League and were Champions League contenders. Also, I was being guided by one of the best coaches in the world in Arsène Wenger... No player

ever gets worse under Wenger. For me, leaving Arsenal was not a good move."

Wenger also pulled off a coup in persuading 17-year-old Aaron Ramsey to choose Arsenal over Man Utd. Alex Ferguson quickly got his own back when Wenger took centre-back Mikaël Silvestre off his hands, even paying a fee for a 31-year-old who had seen his best days.

The competitive landscape got tougher with the introduction of another oil-rich competitor when Man City were taken over by the Abu Dhabi United Group, transforming them into one of the world's richest clubs.

Arsenal opened the Premier League season with a lunchtime 1-0 win against West Brom. In a controversial Nike home kit without the traditional white sleeves, Nasri only took four minutes to get off the mark and finish a typical Arsenal one- and two-touch move on the left. The new yellow and navy away kit was better received, given its 1989 retro style. A lightweight midfield of Theo Walcott, Denílson, Emmanuel Eboué and Nasri started at Fulham. Brede Hangeland beat William Gallas and Denílson to stab in a corner and, apart from Emmanuel Adebayor heading against the post, Arsenal's possession ended with little threat. After the 1-0 loss, Wenger worryingly said, "I believe they wanted it a bit more than us in the first half and the corner [when they scored] shows that."

Fàbregas was back for the visit of Newcastle. Robin van Persie dispatched a penalty and then scored from an Eboué back-heel. Denílson finished off a team move to make it 3-0. At Blackburn, Walcott cut in from the left past two defenders and played in van Persie, who poked it home. Walcott, who had shown the confidence to switch from number 32 to Thierry Henry's number 14 shirt, was fresh off becoming the youngest English player to score a hat-trick in a 4-1 win in Croatia. Adebayor netted a hat-trick of his own to make it 4-1 with a header, penalty and one-on-one finish from Ramsey's through-ball. Jack Wilshere came on with six minutes left to become the club's youngest-ever league player, aged 16 years 256 days.

The following weekend at Bolton, the home side predictably took the lead from a corner when Kevin Davies scored. Eboué scored his first league goal as Arsenal's passing prised open the defence. A minute later, quick interplay ended with Denílson squaring from the left and Nicklas Bendtner slid in to make it 2-1. Late on, Walcott led a counter-attack and Adebayor set up Denílson to seal a 3-1 win. Arsenal's third win in a row at the Reebok Stadium put the Bolton bogey to rest.

Promoted Hull came to the Emirates in good form. A shot-shy Arsenal knocked the ball around but only led 1-0 after Walcott burst down the right and his

TYPICAL LINE-UP (4-4-2/4-2-3-1)

11 van Persie / Bendtner	25 Adebayor
8 Nasri / Arshavin	14 Walcott / Eboué
4 Fàbregas / Diaby	15 Denílson / Song
22 Clichy / Gibbs	5 Touré / Silvestre	10 Gallas / Djourou	3 Sagna / Eboué
1 Almunia / Fabiański			

Players in: Aaron Ramsey, Samir Nasri, Amaury Bischoff, Mikaël Silvestre, *Andrey Arshavin*

Players out: Jens Lehmann, Mathieu Flamini, Alexander Hleb, Gilberto Silva, Justin Hoyte, Philippe Senderos (loan)

low cross came off Paul McShane for an own-goal. Ten minutes later, Geovanni cut inside and hit an unstoppable swerving shot from 30 yards. Daniel Cousin then beat Gallas to a corner and headed in. Gallas rattled the crossbar with a header of his own, but Hull became only the second team to win at the Emirates.

Arsenal then struggled to break down Sunderland's defensive formation and paid the price near the end when Grant Leadbitter's shot from 20 yards flew in off the crossbar. A 93rd-minute Fàbregas header from a corner rescued a point, but Arsenal's title credentials were not looking strong.

Back at the Emirates, Leon Osman gave Everton a half-time lead. Nasri drilled the equaliser into the bottom corner from 20 yards and van Persie nodded in a rebound. Walcott sealed a 3-1 win late on after a one-two with Abou Diaby. Arsenal outplayed West Ham but needed Julien Faubert to deflect in an own-goal to get the breakthrough. In injury time, Adebayor made it 2-0 after collecting a raking pass from Bendtner and rounding Robert Green.

At the end of October, Spurs came to the Emirates bottom of the league and with yet another manager, Harry Redknapp replacing Juande Ramos. Ex-Arsenal player David Bentley hit a speculative volley from 40 yards, which

Manuel Almunia could only help into the net due to poor footwork and a weak wrist. Silvestre and Gallas headers from van Persie set-pieces made it 2-1 to Arsenal just after half-time. van Persie was again the provider with a brilliant curling through-ball to Nasri, who lifted it over goalkeeper Heurelho Gomes and Adebayor beat Alan Hutton to prod into the empty net. It was Adebayor's eighth North London derby goal, equalling Robert Pires and Alan Sunderland's club record. Minutes later, Almunia spilt a shot and Darren Bent was first to react to make it 3-2. However, the two-goal lead was restored straight away when Arsenal won the ball back and van Persie fired in with his right foot.

The home crowd were jubilant and sang "You'll never play here again" at the Spurs players and half-empty away section. With 89 minutes gone, Gaël Clichy slipped, Jermaine Jenas drove forward unchallenged and curled in from outside the area. It seemed inconsequential as there was only injury time left. Gomes took a goal-kick, there was a game of head-ball, and Luka Modrić turned and hit a volley that was deflected onto the post. Yet again, it was a Spurs player, not an Arsenal defender, following up, as Aaron Lennon slid home the rebound to make it an unbelievable 4-4 draw.

A Stage Two Wenger team had again shown a weak mentality, poor game management and unwillingness to carry out the boring aspects of the game. When Gomes' goal-kick landed in the 94th minute, most teams would have ten or 11 players behind the ball, tightly marking opposition players and scrapping to clear it to seal victory. In contrast, Arsenal had four players out of the game near or past the halfway line, leaving three Spurs players unmarked in midfield.

Arsenal then went to the Britannia Stadium, where newly-promoted Stoke were building a fortress by following the Bolton template with the added weapon of Rory Delap's 'extreme throw-ins'. A throw anywhere in the attacking half was as good as a free-kick as Delap's slingshot technique pinged the ball into the area where their numerous big men would cause havoc. Arsenal were now a lightweight team with few six-footers and a goalkeeper that did not command his area – only Bacary Sagna was a strong defensive header of the ball. It was no surprise 11 minutes in when Delap launched a missile 45 yards and Ricardo Fuller beat Kolo Touré to head in. In the second half, a throw reached the back post and Seyi Olofinjana chested in. van Persie came on and was sent off 12 minutes later when he barged goalkeeper Thomas Sørensen over. Clichy scored his first Arsenal goal at the end with a low 20-yard drive to make it 2-1.

Arsenal left battered and bruised as Sagna, Adebayor and Walcott all suffered injuries as a result of fouls. Wenger was fuming: "I read that my team were not brave. They are brave and, for me, you need to have more courage to play football when you know that someone is tackling you from behind without any intention to play the ball. The only intention is to hurt. The brave one is not the one who tackles from behind the player who tries to play football. That is the coward." The worst challenge was Ryan Shawcross' studs through the back of Adebayor that put the striker out for three weeks with an ankle injury – a yellow or red card in normal circumstances, even more so considering Adebayor and the ball were off the pitch at the time and Shawcross had no right to even attempt a challenge. The referee took no action – the sort of weak decision that ended up with much more severe repercussions 15 months later for Ramsey.

However, Sørensen's assessment was also fair: "Arsenal have shown in the past that they are a fantastic football side, but they are just lacking that bit of physicality. When Chelsea came here, they matched us in the challenges, but Arsenal weren't quite there. That's the difference. Arsenal lack that bit of spine that you need."

Arsenal then faced Man Utd at the Emirates. Nasri showed his technical ability with two 20-yard strikes, the first a left-footed half-volley that went in off Gary Neville, the second a right-footed effort after Fàbregas opened up the defence. Rafael da Silva volleyed one back, but Arsenal survived an anxious six minutes of injury time to record a confidence-boosting 2-1 win.

Arsenal were quickly brought back down to earth. Fifth-placed Aston Villa created plenty of chances at the Emirates with Almunia saving an Ashley Young penalty. Halfway through the second half, Young crossed and Clichy headed into his own net. Ten minutes later, Gabriel Agbonlahor beat Gallas – as well as Silvestre who barely broke into a jog – to a hoof and volleyed past Almunia.

Gallas then did an interview where he broke the football club code not to air dirty linen in public. "We are not brave enough in battle. I think we need to be soldiers. To be champions, you have to play big matches every weekend and fight." He revealed "a problem at half-time of the 4-4 draw with Tottenham" and that there was a disruptive influence in the team.

It was a partly self-serving act by Arsenal's captain ("I'm trying to defend myself a bit without giving names. Otherwise I'm taking it all [the blame]."), whose form and leadership were under scrutiny since his Birmingham meltdown. While some of his criticisms had merit – the players' weak mentality and "[Big contracts] make the difference, perhaps. You can rest on your laurels, that's for sure." – he could have delivered them in private.

Gallas was dropped for the visit to struggling Man City. Walcott was out for three months after having a shoulder operation while Fàbregas,

Touré and Adebayor were also missing. Gavin Hoyte made his only Premier League appearance at right-back against Robinho and a centre-back pairing of Johan Djourou and Silvestre were given a torrid time. A mix-up between Clichy and Silvestre led to Stephen Ireland opening the scoring. Robinho coolly scooped the ball over Almunia. Djourou clumsily fouled Daniel Sturridge and the striker converted the penalty to make it 3-0.

Wenger named 21-year-old Fàbregas as the new captain, with Gallas restored to the side as Arsenal tried to press reset on their season at Stamford Bridge. Ominously, Djourou diverted a low cross into his own net. In the second half, an Almunia free-kick initiated some head-tennis and the ball fell to Denílson, who played in van Persie. The Dutchman, who was in an offside position, smashed it past Petr Čech with his right foot. Three minutes later, Fàbregas played a long free-kick into the Chelsea area, Adebayor won the header, and van Persie spun and fired into the bottom corner to make it 2-1. Arsenal had beaten Chelsea at their own game – two long balls, winning headers to keep the ball alive and van Persie playing the Didier Drogba assassin role. The usual suspects of Chelsea, Liverpool, Man Utd and Arsenal made up the top four in the league, but Arsenal were seven points off the top.

In the League Cup, Łukasz Fabiański, Kieran Gibbs, Ramsey, Wilshere, Carlos Vela and Jay Simpson were this year's up-and-coming players. Arsenal's youngest-ever team, average age 18.5, hammered Sheffield Utd 6-0. Wilshere got his first goal with a drive from the edge of the area, but Vela was the star with a hat-trick of cool finishes. The second was memorable as he chested a pass from Gibbs, leaving defender Chris Morgan in his wake, and casually dinked the ball over a flapping Paddy Kenny.

Arsenal then beat Wigan 3-0 with Simpson scoring twice and Fabiański making a brilliant double save. Chris Kirkland made save after save until he too was left standing by the Vela Chip. The fun ended on a cold night in Burnley when Arsenal lost 2-0.

At the start of December, attention turned to Eboué, who received disgraceful treatment from the Emirates crowd. Adebayor gave Arsenal an early lead against Wigan that ultimately sealed a 1-0 win. Eboué, who was returning after five weeks in the treatment room, was a first-half replacement for the injured Nasri in the unfamiliar position of left-midfield. The Ivorian had a nightmare, constantly

ASK ARSHAVIN

The enigmatic Russian, who later named his son Arseny Arshavin after Arsène Wenger, broke the mould for a footballer and the Ask Arshavin section of his website was always entertaining with such gems as:

Hi, Andrey, in what order would you place the following animals: a tiger, a cow, a pig, a horse, a sheep?

AA: A pig – it will always get the last place! A tiger, a cow, a horse, a sheep. And I'll repeat that a pig is always the last one, because it is a pig.

Andrey, are you frightened of bears?

AA: On the contrary, I like bears.

Hi Andrey! Please tell me, in your opinion, what is the most important thing for a footballer these days?

AA: I think the most important thing is a head, not only for a footballer but for any person.

giving the ball away and even managing to tackle Touré at one point. Some Arsenal fans started to boo him.

With his confidence shot, he suffered the substitute's ignominy of being replaced himself. The mob mentality in the crowd took over and large sections cheered when they saw his number held up and booed him as he walked off the pitch wiping a tear from his eye.

It was a shocking lack of fan support for a player that was clearly struggling with his game. Eboué's Arsenal career got off to a promising start as right-back in the 2005/06 record-breaking Champions League team. He then became more of a utility player, mostly playing right-midfield, capable of great bursts down the right but often frustrating fans with his lack of calmness when in a good position and his penchant for trying to win free-kicks or penalties. Even Wenger said later in the season, "When Eboué gets in front of goal, he usually loses composure."

Arsenal could only draw at Middlesbrough after Adebayor headed the opener. Jérémie Aliadière again scored against his old club, celebrating vigorously. Arsenal took the lead against leaders Liverpool with a brilliant goal. Nasri pinged a 50-yard diagonal to van Persie, who chested it down and dragged it away from Jamie Carragher with his left foot, then hammered home with his right. However, a straightforward hoof caught out Gallas and Djourou, leaving Robbie Keane to fire a half-volley into the roof of the net. It got worse on half-time when Fàbregas went off with injured knee ligaments, which put the new captain out for over three months. Adebayor

was harshly given a second yellow card when shielding the ball, but the ten men held on well for a draw.

In the Champions League qualifying round, Arsenal faced FC Twente, managed by ex-England boss Steve McClaren. The Dutch fans sang *You'll Never Walk Alone* but it was no Anfield as Arsenal won 2-0 away, then 4-0 at home.

The group stages opened with a tough trip to Dynamo Kyiv, where a late Gallas tap-in earnt a 1-1 draw. More impressive was a 4-0 dismantling of Portuguese Champions Porto. Adebayor pulled back for van Persie to open the scoring, then the Togolese striker headed in a corner. van Persie dummied a defender and toe-poked past the goalkeeper, while Adebayor converted a penalty.

Arsenal calmed the intimidating Fenerbahçe crowd with two goals in the first 11 minutes, Adebayor and Walcott finishing Fàbregas through-balls. The home side got one back when a shot deflected off Silvestre, but Diaby soon made it 3-1 with a left-footed finish. The Frenchman was excellent in a roaming role behind Adebayor, one of those too-rare times where he was fully fit and showed his quick feet and ability to glide away from players that left everyone wondering what might have been. Song laced a volley and substitute

Ramsey hit a low drive to score his first Arsenal goal. An entertaining game with excellent attacking play and below-par defending finished 5-2. Surprisingly, the return fixture at the Emirates ended 0-0 with van Persie rattling the woodwork.

With only three minutes left against Dynamo Kyiv, substitute Bendtner chested down a long Fàbregas pass and drilled in with his pink left boot to ensure qualification for the knockout stage. A 2-0 loss in Porto, where Eboué received a warm reception from Arsenal's travelling fans just days after the home fans had booed him against Wigan, meant Arsenal finished second in the group.

Back in the league, there was plenty of Boxing Day entertainment at Aston Villa. Villa hit the woodwork three times before Denílson won a tackle on the edge of the box and fired in left-footed. Agbonlahor beat Almunia to a cross, but Sagna produced a brilliant overhead kick on the line to clear. Diaby then showed his class, nutmegging Curtis Davis with a flick on the right touchline, passing to Eboué, bursting forward to receive the return ball and sidefooting high into the net. "Two shots, we've only had two shots," sang the away fans. van Persie hit the post and Gallas gave away a penalty that Gareth Barry converted. Referee Lee Mason interrupted the game to force the arguing managers, Wenger and Martin O'Neill, to make up and shake hands like schoolkids. In injury time, the ball fell to Zat Knight, who drilled in to make it 2-2.

Arsenal struggled to break down Portsmouth and Bolton's deep defensive blocks at the Emirates, but eventually Gallas and Bendtner scored late winners to give 1-0 wins. At Hull, Adebayor's header was cancelled out by Cousin and the home fans turned up the noise. However, with less than ten minutes left, van Persie slipped in Nasri, who fired in left-footed. Soon after, Bendtner sealed the points after a one-two with van Persie, the Dutchman's third assist of the game.

Everton took the lead through a typical Tim Cahill header, but out of nowhere Arsenal scored an injury-time equaliser when Diaby hit a diagonal ball to van Persie, who chested down and buried a volley from a tight angle. Arsenal extended their unbeaten run to 13 games in February, but only managed four goalless draws against West Ham, Sunderland and Fulham at the Emirates and away at Spurs. Failing to score for four consecutive games was unheard of in previous Wenger years.

With a top-four finish and Champions League football in doubt, Arsenal signed Andrey Arshavin, who had impressed at Euro 2008 with Russia, for £15m. At White Hart Lane, Eboué was sent off after 37 minutes for kicking Luca Modrić, giving Spurs their best chance to beat Arsenal in the league for

KNOCK ON WOOD

As well as scoring 20 goals, van Persie rattled the woodwork 16 times in 2008/09. It was a regular theme for the Dutchman, who hit the frame of the goal a record 44 times in his Premier League career yet still boasted an elite minutes-per-goal rate.

did Julio Baptista. The ex-Arsenal man gave a reminder of his Premier League, not League Cup, finishing by missing his kick from eight yards.

The game went to penalties and Eduardo's effort was saved. Mirko Vučinić's attempt at a dummy went wrong and Almunia easily saved. van Persie, Walcott, Nasri and Denílson held their nerve, making it 4-4 and sudden death. Touré and Sagna scored comfortably, but so did Roma players. Diaby converted and Max Tonetto skied his effort over the bar, as well as the surrounding running track, into the Roma stands. Arsenal players celebrated their 7-6 penalty win with gusto, having come through a pressure situation in a hostile atmosphere.

In the FA Cup, two van Persie goals secured a 3-1 win over Plymouth. After a goalless draw at Cardiff, Eduardo made his first start in a year in the replay, scoring a header and then winning and scoring a penalty to the delight of him, his teammates and the fans. Bendtner scored a header from a corner and van Persie made it 4-0 with a right-foot finish.

ten years. However, the ten men held out, with Almunia blocking a one-on-one from Modrić at the end. Alongside Arshavin on the bench, Eduardo was a welcome sight, 350 days after his leg-break. Arsenal were only fifth at the end of February, five points behind Aston Villa.

In the Champions League round of 16, Arsenal faced Roma with Nasri playing behind van Persie, and Eboué and Bendtner unlikely wingers. Arshavin was cup-tied and unavailable. van Persie won and buried a penalty at the Emirates, and it finished 1-0 with the two wingers missing one-on-ones. Wenger kept the same formation in the Stadio Olimpico and, after ten minutes, poor defending allowed Juan to level the tie. Almunia kept Arsenal in it, as

Wenger rotated in the next round, making Eduardo captain and giving Vela another chance to get his pitching wedge out, the victim this time being Burnley goalkeeper Brian Jensen. The Championship side, looking to knock

Arsenal out of the second cup in the season, were outclassed as Eduardo added a brilliant improvised volley with the outside of his heel. Wenger was impressed: "It was as if Eduardo was playing football on the beach." Late on, Song backheeled to Eboué who fired in to make it 3-1.

Hull came to the Emirates in the quarter-final and took the lead when Nicky Barmby's volley was deflected in off Djourou. The away side hung on, wasting time when possible, but Arsenal equalised after 74 minutes when Bendtner caused problems in the box, the ball falling to Arshavin, who kept his cool and squared for van Persie to sidefoot in. The comeback was complete ten minutes later when Boaz Myhill failed to deal with a Nasri free-kick and Gallas, who was in an offside position, headed in from three yards.

Perma-tanned Hull manager Phil Brown did not take the loss well and criticised the injured Fàbregas for coming onto the pitch at the end to celebrate the win, even questioning his choice of clothing (a hooded leather jacket, jeans and trainers). He also accused the Spaniard of spitting at assistant Brian Horton, a claim that Fàbregas denied and was cleared of by the FA. Brown's case was not helped by his inconsistent and changing accounts of the incident in various interviews.

Arsenal went to West Brom in March, where Bendtner cut in from the right and curled a low left-foot shot to score the team's first Premier League goal for four weeks. However, three minutes later, Chris Brunt fired a free-kick through a weak wall. Arsenal got their first win in six games when Touré headed a free-kick and Bendtner took down a long ball from Touré and volleyed in.

The Emirates Premier League goal drought was broken after only 75 seconds against Blackburn as a low Walcott cross pinballed in off André Ooijer. In the second half, Arshavin scored his first Arsenal goal and it was special. Coming in off the left wing, a stepover bemused Danny Simpson. Left with a tight angle and seemingly few options, Arshavin curled a brilliant finish high into the net past Paul Robinson. Late on, substitute Eboué tapped in after Robinson saved from Arshavin and converted a penalty to continue his rehabilitation. The 4-0 win moved Arsenal up to fourth.

At Newcastle, Almunia gave away a penalty but made amends by saving Obafemi Martins' weak effort. In the second half, Bendtner headed the opener but Martins equalised immediately. Diaby played a one-two with van Persie, burst into the box and hammered it high into the net. Arsenal made it 3-1 with a low Nasri drive. An Adebayor double then gave a 2-0 home win over Man City. The winning run continued at Wigan as Arsenal came from behind to win 4-1 with goals from Walcott, Silvestre, Arshavin and Alex Song.

In the Champions League quarter-final, Arsenal returned to Villarreal and the home side took the lead after ten minutes through a Marcos Senna 30-yarder into the top corner. Arsenal improved after the break. Fàbregas floated a pass to Adebayor, who chested and scored a brilliant overhead kick. The good news was that Fàbregas was back, the bad that Gallas and Clichy suffered season-ending injuries.

In the second leg, the Arsenal fans welcomed Villarreal's Robert Pires to the Emirates. Ten minutes in, a Fàbregas flick played in Walcott, who calmly dinked over goalkeeper Diego Lopez. In the second half, van Persie set up Adebayor and the striker poked home to prompt a touchline jig from Wenger. Walcott won a penalty and Sebastián Ledesma was dismissed for complaining. van Persie sidefooted home to cap an emphatic 4-1 aggregate win and send Arsenal into their second-ever Champions League semi-final.

In mid-April, Arsenal had two chances of winning their first trophy for four years. For the FA Cup semi-final on a poor pitch at the new Wembley Stadium, injuries forced Wenger into an unfamiliar back five of Fabiański,

Eboué, Touré, Silvestre and Gibbs. Leaving Arshavin on the bench was entirely Wenger's decision however. With Arshavin cup-tied for the Champions League, and Arsenal having no chance of winning the league and eight points clear of fifth, it was unclear what Wenger was saving his in-form player for. The 5'6" Russian was settling in, having scored two and assisting five goals in his first seven starts from a wide position.

Fabiański showed nervous decision-making after only a few minutes, racing out of his area and allowing Drogba to head over him towards goal, but Gibbs got back to clear. After 18 minutes, Gibbs chipped to the back post and Walcott hit a controlled left-foot volley that deflected in off Ashley Cole. Before half-time, Florent Malouda cut inside Eboué and equalised into the bottom corner. Anelka hit the post. Arshavin was brought on after 75 minutes, though it was top scorer van Persie that was replaced. With 84 minutes gone, Frank Lampard pumped the ball forward. Silvestre's attempt at staying with Drogba was half-hearted and when Fabiański again came charging out, Drogba easily rounded him and got his usual goal. Arsenal hardly tested Petr Čech, who had conceded seven goals in the previous week in nervous performances against Bolton and Liverpool. As in the 2007 League Cup Final, Walcott had opened the scoring, but Chelsea proved the streetwise team and won 2-1.

The following Tuesday at Anfield came one of the most famous games in Premier League history as Liverpool needed to beat Arsenal to overtake Man Utd at the top of the table:

- 1-0 (39 minutes): Nasri played in Fàbregas on the right, who cut back for Arshavin to sidefoot left-footed into the roof of the net.

- 1-1 (49 minutes): Dirk Kuyt chipped to the penalty spot, where an unmarked Fernando Torres headed in.

- 1-2 (56 minutes): Arsenal were caught trying to play it out from the back, Kuyt chipped to the back post and Yossi Benayoun bundled it over the line.

- 2-2 (67 minutes): Arshavin robbed Álvaro Arbeloa and hammered a brilliant right-footed drive from outside the area with a bit of cut to take it away from Pepe Reina and inside the far post.

- 3-2 (70 minutes): A clearance went straight to Arshavin, who controlled and hit it right-footed under Reina. Arshavin wheeled away with three fingers held up and an incredulous look on his face, not realising it would get even more ridiculous.

- 3-3 (72 minutes): Torres toyed with Silvestre and fired into the bottom corner.

- 4-3 (90 minutes): Fabiański punched a corner and the ball fell to Walcott who, in a remarkable echo of the Champions League quarter-final a year earlier, raced 50 yards into the Liverpool half. Arshavin showed impressive pace and desire to keep up. Walcott squared for the Russian, who took a touch and fired left-footed high into the net. Four shots and four goals for Arshavin, who held four fingers up with an even more disbelieving expression.

- 4-4 (93 minutes): Xabi Alonso lofted the ball into the box, where Arsenal had only four defenders marking six attackers. The lack of cover would have been amazing if Arsenal had not shown such negligence in similar situations over and over again. The ball was headed back across and Benayoun fired into the net.

A crazy night finished Liverpool 4 Arshavin 4. Arshavin had shown his two-footed firepower and what the team missed in the FA Cup semi-final the previous Saturday, while Arsenal's unnecessary panic and poor defence had again led to an inability to close out a game.

Arsenal beat Middlesbrough 2-0 with Fàbregas scoring twice, the first ending a brilliant team move that sliced the defence apart. A 3-0 win at Portsmouth guaranteed a top-four finish and Champions League football for another year. Bendtner scored a header and a penalty, which was given after a challenge on Arshavin despite the Russian signalling it was not a foul.

That left the Champions League, where three of the remaining four teams were English. At Old Trafford, Almunia had the night of his life. Man Utd were all over Arsenal, but the goalkeeper made save after save from Wayne Rooney, Cristiano Ronaldo, Carlos Tevez and others. He was only beaten when John O'Shea thumped home a cross, a 1-0 deficit meaning Arsenal were still in the tie.

As the home leg kicked off, a boisterous Emirates crowd had high hopes of turning it around. After all, Arsenal had not conceded a goal at home in this year's competition. However, eight minutes later, the upbeat atmosphere was killed. Ronaldo pulled the ball back, Gibbs slipped and Park Ji-sung beat Almunia. Three minutes later, Ronaldo cracked a swerving, dipping free-kick from 35 yards that saw Almunia undo his excellent work of the first leg. Man Utd broke clinically in the second half and Ronaldo made it 3-0. Darren Fletcher brought down Fàbregas and was sent off, putting him out of the final. van Persie smashed the spot-kick into the top corner but Arsenal went out 4-1 on aggregate.

Man Utd left-back Patrice Evra gave a damning verdict: "It was 11 men against 11 children… Football today is not only about playing well, it's about winning trophies. Everybody talks about the way Arsenal play but, at the end of the day, it's about winning silverware." The Premier League Champions had given Arsenal a lesson in both games.

Arsenal then had another big Emirates loss against Chelsea, going down 4-1 in a lacklustre display. They did better at a sunny Old Trafford, a game that had an end-of-season feel and finished 0-0. The season ended on a high note with a 4-1 win over Stoke as van Persie closed out with a double.

The Dutchman finally played a full season and was able to show his class as a striker, vindicating Wenger's decision to convert him from winger. He finished with 20 goals and also had the most assists in the league alongside Lampard at ten. His left foot had always been lethal, but he had relied on it heavily, even describing his right as his "chocolate leg." In 2008/09, he regularly struck with his right foot, giving him the option to go either side of defenders, one of the few players in Stages Two and Three Wenger that made a noticeable improvement to an aspect of their game.

It was one of Arsenal's worst league campaigns so far under Wenger as an indifferent start to the season quickly ended any title hopes, but a 21-game unbeaten run beginning with a rare win at Stamford Bridge propelled them to a top-four finish. Arshavin's arrival at the start of February was key as the Russian provided extra creativity with his low centre of gravity and technical excellence.

Two semi-finals, Champions League qualification, some memorable football and brilliant goals would have qualified as an excellent season for most teams, but Stage Two Wenger sides always suffered from expectations raised during Stage One.

Although Wenger's transfer funds were limited, he failed to address clear weaknesses in the squad during the summer transfer window, in goal, central defence and midfield in particular. The 'anti-Darwinism' reasoning he gave a year later went some way to explaining why Arsenal lacked a winner's mentality and infuriated many fans: "I have been criticised for not hiring Xabi Alonso or Gareth Barry. But if I signed them, I would have killed Song, Diaby and Denílson."

The Curious Case of Theo Walcott

Three FA Cups. 108 goals in 397 games. Joint 15th in the club's all-time scorer list. 12 years of service. 270 Premier League appearances, the third highest under Arsène Wenger only behind Dennis Bergkamp (277) and Patrick Vieira (276).

You would expect someone with that history to be a club legend. But when Theo Walcott was sold to Everton for £20m in January 2018, it was the right move for both the player and club, and there was little sadness among Arsenal fans. It was easy to forget he was 28 as he seemed a perennial youngster that every year people hoped this would be the season he would fulfil his potential.

Unfortunately, Walcott hardly developed his game and became a posterchild for Arsenal's stagnation in Stages Two and Three Wenger. He almost always made the same run off the ball (away from his teammate, looking for a pass inside the left-back) and with the ball (outside the left-back). Teams soon learnt this and defended deep and narrow to nullify his express pace. Why did Walcott never fake that run to create space and come short for the ball or to keep defenders guessing? Why didn't he improve his left foot so he had the option of coming inside and shooting? He did this once, scoring what should have been the winner against Birmingham in the game where Eduardo's leg was broken. Unfortunately for Walcott, not for the last time, his potentially

game-changing moment was quickly overshadowed and forgotten as Arsenal blew their 2007/08 title chance.

He also suffered from the game's tactical trend to play one upfront – he might have done a good job using his pace to play off a target man – as he was not a conventional winger or technical or strong enough to lead the line on his own and play with his back to goal. His crossing did improve and he became an assured finisher one-on-one calmly dinking over the diving goalkeeper or from the inside-right position firing hard and low into the opposite corner. And he had plenty of memorable moments:

- Scoring the opener in the 2007 League Cup Final against Chelsea.

- A pitch-length dribble at Anfield to set up Emmanuel Adebayor in the 2008 Champions League quarter-final (immediately overshadowed as Arsenal conceded a penalty and were knocked out).

- Coming on and sparking a second-half comeback from 2-0 down against a brilliant Barcelona team in 2010.

- Scoring two goals as Arsenal came back from 2-0 down to win the North London derby 5-2 in 2012.

- Deceiving defenders by falling over before getting up and drilling home in a crazy 5-3 win at Stamford Bridge in 2011/12.

- 21 goals and 14 assists in 2012/13.
- Grinning and signalling the 2-0 score with his hands to the Spurs fans from a stretcher after tearing his anterior cruciate ligament in 2014.
- Scoring the opener in the 2015 FA Cup Final against Aston Villa.

Walcott seemed a nice guy and maybe did not have the drive to push himself: to get in front of a marker and on the end of a cross; to be more aggressive in tackling or pressing the opposition; to use his pace to help out the defence rather than jogging back and waiting for a counter-attack; or to be involved for the entire 90 minutes, week in week out, rather than be satisfied with one or two contributions per game.

Arsène Wenger's 'go-and-express-yourself' management style did not help. Maybe under a demanding micro-manager, Walcott would have developed his game and adopted more of a winning mentality. This characteristic was highlighted against Sunderland in 2016 when Walcott unbelievably jumped over the ball and out of a tackle with Younès Kaboul that could have presented him with an open goal late in a dull 0-0 game – something the likes of Dennis Bergkamp or Ian Wright would never dream of.

After the 2009 Champions League semi-final defeat by Man Utd, their left-back Patrice Evra said it was "men against children" – Walcott was a chief suspect as he often used to go missing in tough games and hardly touch the ball. However, it is harsh to single out Walcott for the 'no-learning, no-changing' trend during Stages Two and Three Wenger as there were many others this applied to, including Emmanuel Eboué, Denílson, Wojciech Szczęsny, Kieran Gibbs, Alex Oxlade-Chamberlain and Alex Iwobi.

There was a systematic issue in the management, coaching and culture during this time as many players started their Arsenal careers promisingly before stagnating or regressing. Numerous players confirmed this after they left including Cesc Fàbregas ("And then you lose a game, you're in the bus like this, destroyed, and then you hear some players laughing, thinking about where they will be going out later. This was going on for a few years."), Petr Čech ("It will sound strange but I think generally at Arsenal there is not enough pressure."), Szczęsny ("I couldn't say from a technical standpoint that I improved in any way from when I became first-choice at Arsenal until the day I left for Roma.") and André Santos ("They lost and were laughing on the bus already.")

2009/10
IT'S THE HOPE THAT KILLS

Premier League		Third
FA Cup		Fourth round
Champions League		Quarter-final
League Cup		Quarter-final

PREMIER LEAGUE		PL	W	D	L	GF	GA	GD	PTS
1	CHELSEA	38	27	5	6	103	32	71	86
2	MAN UTD	38	27	4	7	86	28	58	85
3	ARSENAL	38	23	6	9	83	41	42	75
4	TOTTENHAM	38	21	7	10	67	41	26	70
5	MAN CITY	38	18	13	7	73	45	28	67
6	ASTON VILLA	38	17	13	8	52	39	13	64

Highlights: Coming back from 2-0 down after being given the runaround by a brilliant Barcelona; the 11-second North London derby; beating Porto 5-0 in the Champions League; doing the double over Liverpool; thrashing Everton 6-1 on the opening day

Lowlights: Stoke's Ryan Shawcross breaking Aaron Ramsey's leg; losing all four games against title rivals Man Utd and Chelsea; dropping points every time Arsenal got back into title contention, most noticeably after topping the table in March; disappointing cup exits at Stoke and Man City

Player of the year: Captain Cesc Fàbregas led the way with 19 goals and 20 assists in only 36 appearances

Top scorers: Fàbregas 19 (15 in PL), Andrey Arshavin 12 (10), Nicklas Bendtner 12 (6), Robin van Persie 10 (9)

Goal of the season: Samir Nasri jinked past three defenders and fired in against Porto, the Emirates, Champions League

In July 2009, Arsenal maintained their status as a selling club when Man City continued their spending spree and paid a healthy £41m for Kolo Touré and Emmanuel Adebayor. Adebayor had not been as prolific, or as hard-running, following his breakout season in 2007/08 and signing a new contract. Arsenal replaced Touré with Belgian international Thomas Vermaelen, but made no other additions to a squad that came fourth, lacked a reliable goalkeeper and had weak back-ups in numerous positions. Frustratingly, Samir Nasri would miss the first two months of the season after fracturing his fibula when trying to tackle Abou Diaby in pre-season training.

The season opened at Everton, where Arsène Wenger followed the Barcelona trend and unveiled a 4-3-3 formation with Alex Song as defensive midfielder and Robin van Persie the pivot upfront. Denílson struck a 25-yarder into the top corner and Vermaelen marked an impressive debut by heading in a van Persie free-kick. Centre-back partner William Gallas followed suit to make it 3-1 at half-time. Cesc Fàbregas scored two in the second half and substitute Eduardo tapped in for an encouraging 6-1 win.

In the Champions League, Arsenal comfortably negotiated a tricky qualifying round against Celtic, dominating both legs to show the difference in quality at the top of the English and Scottish leagues. The two away goals had some fortune, however,

with a Fàbregas free-kick deflecting off Gallas' back and a Gary Caldwell own-goal. The 3-1 home win was marked by controversy when Eduardo nicked the ball past goalkeeper Artur Boruc and went down. Celtic were furious when a penalty was given, which Eduardo calmly scored.

After the game, Celtic, the Scottish Football Association and media's campaign about Eduardo's 'cheating' went into overdrive and UEFA gave him a two-game ban for "deceiving the referee." Arsenal appealed, with Wenger calling it a "witch-hunt" and rightly noting British football and the media's *omertà* when a local player did the same thing. The ban was overturned and UEFA's much-needed 'crackdown' on diving was short-lived.

In the league, Arsenal got off to another flyer against Portsmouth as Eduardo embarrassed right-back Marc Wilson with the playground trick of pushing the ball one side and running the other, then cut back for Diaby to sidefoot into the roof of the net. Minutes later, Diaby got his second as Emmanuel Eboué broke the offside trap and squared. Younès Kaboul pulled one back when he outjumped Manuel Almunia and headed in from one yard. However, a free-kick went in off Gallas' face and Aaron Ramsey coolly buried a one-on-one to make it 4-1.

Arsenal, in their new midnight blue away shirts, then faced their first big test of the season at Old Trafford. Without the injured Fàbregas, Wenger adjusted the line-up to 4-2-3-1 with Song and Denílson sitting in midfield. Darren Fletcher chopped down Andrey Arshavin in the area, but away penalties at Old Trafford in the Alex Ferguson era were rare. The game continued and Arshavin fired a brilliant drive from 25 yards into the top-left corner, celebrating with his trademark finger to the lips. Ben Foster made a crucial save with his foot from van Persie.

The Cristiano Ronaldo-less Man Utd posed little threat, but they did not need to as Arsenal self-destructed. With an hour gone, Wayne Rooney chased an over-hit through-ball on the left-side of the area. There was little danger until Almunia came flying out and gave Rooney an 'Eduardo-Celtic opportunity' he could not refuse – the Man Utd striker reached the ball first, toed it into touch and collapsed over Almunia's arm. This time, Mike Dean gave a penalty, which Rooney sidefooted in. Minutes later, van Persie curled a free-kick from wide onto the crossbar and, at the other end, Ryan Giggs sent in a free-kick that Diaby inexplicably headed into his own goal.

Five minutes into injury time, van Persie put the ball into the net, but it was ruled out for offside against Gallas. Dean sent a frustrated Wenger to the stands for having the temerity to kick a water bottle. With nowhere obvious to go, Wenger went onto a platform above

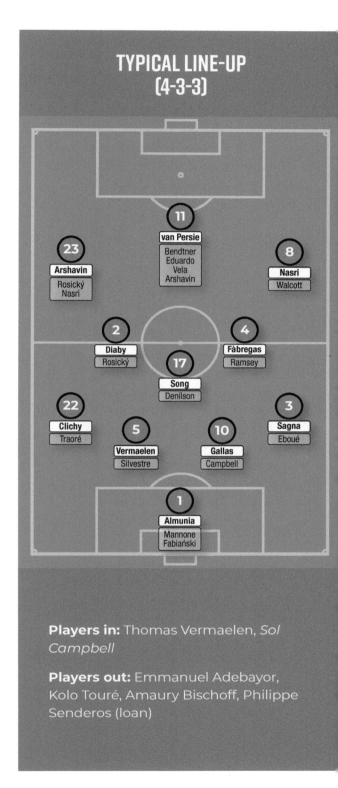

**TYPICAL LINE-UP
(4-3-3)**

11 van Persie
Bendtner
Eduardo
Vela
Arshavin

23 Arshavin
Rosický
Nasri

8 Nasri
Walcott

2 Diaby
Rosický

4 Fàbregas
Ramsey

17 Song
Denílson

22 Clichy
Traoré

5 Vermaelen
Silvestre

10 Gallas
Campbell

3 Sagna
Eboué

1 Almunia
Mannone
Fabiański

Players in: Thomas Vermaelen, *Sol Campbell*

Players out: Emmanuel Adebayor, Kolo Touré, Amaury Bischoff, Philippe Senderos (loan)

the substitute benches and stood alone surrounded by cheering home fans. He struck a famous arms outstretched pose to make a mockery of the situation, and his messiah-like stance became an iconic image of the Premier League era. Throughout the game, as he had done for a decade, Wenger had to endure thousands of Man Utd fans singing "Arsène Wenger is a paedophile" at him. Man Utd officials were slow to condemn the disgraceful abuse and ineffective in stopping their fans from repeating it.

Crucially, Arsenal had gifted two goals to their title rivals and lost 2-1. With Man Utd leading the foul count 21-15, but behind on yellow cards 3-6, Wenger outed their persistent fouling, led by Fletcher, to break up Arsenal's rhythm: "I have seen a player make 20 fouls without getting a yellow card. If you have seen the game, you don't need me to tell you who but their player gets away without a yellow card. It's quite amazing."

Two weeks later, Arsenal, and controversy, returned to Manchester. The Arsenal fans gave Adebayor stick throughout the game. The striker was fired up, at one point stamping on ex-strike partner van Persie's head, drawing blood with a glancing blow that subsequently earnt a three-game ban. Man City took the lead when Micah Richards' header went in via the post and Almunia's back. van Persie equalised after half-time with a low right-footed shot.

However, Arsenal again capitulated, conceding three goals in 12 minutes. The second was an Adebayor header and the striker sprinted the length of the pitch to slide in front of the away fans, causing a furious, and hypocritical, reaction from many of them. Adebayor also cleared a Diaby shot off the line, beat four players on one run and led the line superbly – he was an excellent striker when he was in the mood (and not offside; he holds the Premier League record for being caught offside 328 times). There was still time for substitute Tomáš Rosický, in his first Arsenal appearance for 20 months, to make it 4-2 and van Persie to curl against the post.

Arsenal got back to winning ways with a 4-0 cruise against Wigan, Vermaelen showing his goalscoring instincts with a header from a corner and a left-footed curler into the top corner from the edge of the area. Arsenal beat Fulham 1-0 as van Persie finished well from a Fàbregas lofted pass and Vito Mannone, replacing the ill Almunia, made impressive saves.

At the start of October, Wenger became the club's longest-serving manager with a game that highlighted the good and bad of his 13-year reign. Arsenal's defence was quickly exposed by the route-one football of Sam Allardyce's Blackburn as goalkeeper Paul Robinson launched a long free-kick and Steven Nzonzi beat Vermaelen to loop a header over Mannone. The centre-back made amends with a thumping drive from 25 yards. David Dunn gave Blackburn a 2-1 lead when his effort deflected off Gallas.

However, the Wengerball – orchestrated by Fàbregas, who equalled Dennis Bergkamp and José Antonio Reyes' Premier League record of four assists in one game – clicked into gear as the Spaniard played in van Persie and Arshavin for left-footed finishes. Fàbregas then struck an excellent volley with the outside of his left foot and kissed the badge to answer speculation of a move back to Barcelona. Substitutes Theo Walcott and Nicklas Bendtner added nice finishes to make it 6-2.

Another home win came against Birmingham as Song played in van Persie, a fruitful combination over the next three years, and Diaby buried a Rosický cross into the roof of the net. Mannone flapped at a cross and Lee Bowyer made it 2-1. van Persie cracked the crossbar from a free-kick inside the area and Arshavin settled nerves late on by cutting inside from the left and passing into the corner to make it 3-1.

At West Ham, van Persie volleyed into an open goal after Robert Green missed a cross and Gallas headed a corner as Arsenal cruised to a 2-0 half-time lead. However, after 74 minutes, Mannone palmed a free-kick back into trouble and Carlton Cole headed in. Six minutes later, Song unnecessarily fouled Cole and Alessandro Diamanti buried the penalty to make it 2-2 and two dropped points.

The following week, Spurs came to the Emirates level on points and striker Robbie Keane was bullish: "But now I think it's certainly even and if you look at the squads, I think that our bench is probably a little bit stronger than theirs at the moment." For 42 minutes, he had a point. Then Bacary Sagna whipped in a low cross and van Persie beat Ledley King to stud the ball past Heurelho Gomes. Amazingly, 11 seconds later, with the crowd still celebrating and TV coverage showing replays of van Persie's goal, Fàbregas had the ball in the net again. Spurs had kicked off and given the ball away. Fàbregas collected it in the centre circle, waltzed between Tom Huddlestone and Wilson Palacios, toed it past King's sliding challenge and sidefooted into the bottom corner from the edge of the area, a famous derby goal from the Arsenal captain.

Arsenal dominated the rest of the game and made it 3-0 in the second half when Sagna crossed, King and Gomes missed the ball to complete their nightmare performances, and van Persie tapped in. Keane was taken off to the Arsenal fans' delight after 65 minutes.

The goals kept coming at Wolves where Arsenal won 4-1 with two own-goals and Fàbregas and Arshavin strikes. They were up to second, two points behind Chelsea as the league broke for an international break – one that proved costly as van Persie injured ankle ligaments playing for the Netherlands in a friendly against Italy. Despite trying horse placenta treatment in Serbia, the Dutchman was out for five months, yet again seeing his season effectively ended when in fine form – he already had eight goals and eight assists in the first quarter of the campaign.

Five minutes into the Champions League group stage, Arsenal were already 2-0 down to Standard Liège. However, Bendtner fired in just before half-time and Vermaelen and Eduardo finished set-pieces from close range to complete a late 3-2 comeback win. At the Emirates, Arsenal could not get past Olympiacos goalkeeper Antonis Nikopolidis until van Persie finished an excellent move involving Fàbregas and Eduardo. Arshavin made it 2-0 with a clever flick.

Arsenal were looking good for an away win against AZ Alkmaar after slick passing from Arshavin and van Persie set up Fàbregas. With 93 minutes gone, the home side pumped a free-kick into the box, won the header and David Mendes da Silva smashed a volley to equalise. The home tie was a 4-1 breeze for Arsenal after Sergio Romero let in a Fàbregas dribbler. Nasri, Fàbregas and Diaby scored with good finishes, the latter coming after an Eduardo

back-heel on the halfway line played in Arshavin.

Arsenal beat Standard Liège 2-0 to ensure they won the group. Nasri scored the first and Denílson hit a swerving shot from 30 yards that goalkeeper Sinan Bolat waved in.

At Sunderland, Eduardo led the line in place of van Persie, but Arsenal failed to score for the first time in the season. Darren Bent netted in the second half to inflict a damaging 1-0 loss. The following week, Arsenal had a chance to prove their title credentials with the visit of Chelsea. Ashley Cole silenced the boos of the home fans with two crosses that set up goals, the first Didier Drogba guided in on the volley, while the second went in off Vermaelen's shin. Chelsea were too strong and Arsenal's possession counted for little. Late on, Drogba scored yet another goal past Almunia, this time a sidefooted free-kick. The 3-0 loss meant the gap had jumped to 11 points, although Arsenal had a game in hand.

With Arsenal's bogey month of November out of the way, their form returned. Wenger surprisingly moved Arshavin to centre-forward in the absence of van Persie and Bendtner. The diminutive Russian was much better running with the ball, looking to play in teammates or create shooting opportunities for himself than play with his back to goal, but he did a good job. Against Stoke, he won a penalty that Thomas Sørensen saved from Fàbregas. Arshavin then cut in from the left and drove low into the far corner. Ramsey made it 2-0 with another low shot.

At Anfield, Arsenal failed to deal with a free-kick and Dirk Kuyt scored the opener. At half-time, an angry Wenger shocked the players with a rare tongue-lashing, telling them they were "not fit to wear the shirt." It worked, as five minutes into the second half, Nasri's low cross went in off Glen Johnson for an own-goal. Eight minutes later, Fàbregas crossed and the ball came to Arshavin, who cut inside and cracked a shot from 16 yards in off the post. This time, Arshavin's Anfield arrow earnt three points, Arsenal's first win there in five years. At Burnley, Fàbregas weaved through the defence and opened the scoring. However, Vermaelen gave away a penalty and specialist Graham Alexander toe-poked it down the middle. It ended a 1-1 draw with Fàbregas taken off with a hamstring injury.

Against Hull, Denílson curled an excellent free-kick over the wall. Eduardo and Diaby completed a 3-0 win. Arsenal struggled to get the breakthrough against Aston Villa just after Christmas, prompting Wenger to bring on Fàbregas after 57 minutes. Arsenal's talisman did not disappoint in a 27-minute match-winning cameo, curling a free-kick over the wall and finishing a counter-attack. Worryingly,

LORD BENDTNER

At the start of the 2009/10 season, Bendtner changed shirt number from 26 to 52 saying at the time it was "a special number to me personally" and more recently "because of a professional fortune-teller my mum knows" contradicting reports it was a reference to his weekly salary (no room for the three zeroes). The Dane's self-confidence was off the charts as confirmed in a club test, according to Arsenal sport psychologist Jacques Crevoisier. Bendtner was a useful back-up striker if given the right service, especially from crosses, His nine years at the club brought a decent 47 goals in 83 starts and 88 substitute appearances, not helped by Wenger's strange phase of deploying the 6'4" target man out wide.

stretching for the second goal caused more hamstring problems and Fàbregas had to go off. Diaby sealed a 3-0 win by curling into the bottom corner.

Arsenal then cruised to a 4-1 win at bottom-of-the-table Portsmouth. Eduardo's free-kick was deflected into the corner, even though there was a defender on the line to cover that side. Nasri fired a low drive, Ramsey cut inside and hit an even better strike with his left foot, and Song netted a rare header. Five wins and a draw in December meant Arsenal ended the year back in title contention.

In the League Cup, Arsenal's policies of unveiling exciting youth players and cheap ticket prices were rewarded with a 56,000 crowd against Championship side West Brom. Wojciech Szczęsny made his debut as ex-Arsenal prospect Jerome Thomas gave Jack Wilshere a push in the face and was red-carded. Sánchez Watt and Carlos Vela scored to make it a 2-0 win.

In the next round, Arsenal won an entertaining game against Liverpool 2-1 with two excellent left-foot strikes from Fran Mérida and Bendtner. The run was ended in the quarter-final by the extra firepower of Man City, who scored three second-half goals, including two excellent strikes by Carlos Tevez and Shaun Wright-Phillips. The media made a big fuss of Wenger not shaking hands with opposing manager and regular bête noir Mark Hughes. Wenger was often a bad loser, but why should he hang around to shake the hand of someone that had been abusing and provoking him for the previous 90 minutes?

In the FA Cup, West Ham's Diamanti beat Mikaël Silvestre's attempt to play him offside and finished as the centre-back jogged back with no attempt to redeem the situation. However, Arsenal fought back with Ramsey firing left-footed into the corner and Eduardo sealing a 2-1 win with a looping header past a flapping Green.

A mid-winter visit to Stoke in the next round was not the draw Arsenal wanted. With ten injuries, a makeshift side featuring numerous reserve players, as well as Sol Campbell playing his first game for the club since the 2006 Champions League Final and only his second game of the season, the outcome was almost inevitable. It only took a minute for Stoke to convert a Rory Delap throw-in as Ricardo Fuller beat Łukasz Fabiański to head in. Denílson equalised with a deflected shot, but Stoke scored two goals in the last 20 minutes. A small squad, a fixture pile-up, injuries and Wenger going all-in on the two big, but hardest to win, competitions meant Arsenal risked extending their five trophy-less years.

35-year-old Campbell had been training with Arsenal after an aborted spell at League Two Notts County when Wenger re-signed him for the rest of the season, something of a turnaround for a manager that previously believed players were on the downtrend once they hit 30. With Gallas and Vermaelen both suffering injuries, Johan Djourou out for the season and Silvestre one of Wenger's worst-ever signings, Campbell played 13 games and again answered the doubters with his winner's mentality, strength and defensive nous.

Early in January, the Emirates was one of the few grounds to survive the 'Big Freeze of 2010'. Everton took the lead as Leon Osman was left unmarked to head in a corner. Denílson equalised with a deflected shot. In the second half, as the snow fell, Arsenal chased a winner. Unbelievably, after 81 minutes, they left no defender back and Steven Pienaar raced from the halfway line to dink over Almunia. Denílson then had the ball in the centre circle with no one around him and mysteriously collapsed on the floor as if shot by a sniper. He did not hold on to the ball to stop the game, Everton played on and Almunia made a crucial save from James Vaughan. In injury time, the ball fell to substitute Rosický, who hit a trademark outside-of-the-right-foot shot; another deflection took it over Tim Howard's dive and the game finished 2-2. It was a welcome point in the end as the conditions suited a physical Everton team and Arsenal were without Song and Fàbregas in midfield, yet a missed opportunity to close the gap at the top.

Arsenal then had a double-header against Bolton. At the Reebok Stadium, they sliced the home team apart in Owen Coyle's first game in charge and won 2-0 with goals from Fàbregas and Mérida. Three days later, the Emirates crowd expected a repeat but Bolton were 2-0 up within half an hour. Just before half-time, Rosický cracked in from 20 yards to fire up the crowd. In the second half, Gallas fouled Mark Davies but the referee waved play on. It was played to Fàbregas, who drove between Jussi Jääskeläinen's legs from a narrow angle. Vermaelen smashed a half-volley and Arshavin finished after a one-two with Eduardo, a goal that took Arsenal top of the table on goal difference. Then a frustrating 0-0 draw at Aston Villa saw both Fàbregas and Rosický hit the woodwork.

An impressive nine-game unbeaten run had put Arsenal back in touch with the leaders at the end of January, but Man Utd, Chelsea and Liverpool were their next three games. After 30 minutes, Man Utd's Nani waltzed past half-hearted challenges from Gaël Clichy, Nasri and Denílson, and chipped to the back post, where Almunia could only palm the ball into his own net. Minutes later, the Emirates crowd was stunned again when Man Utd cleared an Arsenal corner to Nani. Rooney's desire was far greater than some of Arsenal's covering players as he ran 70 yards to burst on to Nani's pass and finish low. In the second half, Man Utd again exposed Arsenal on the counter-attack, Park Ji-sung racing in unchallenged to score. It finished 3-1 as Vermaelen pulled one back with a volley.

At the same time as Park was bearing in on Arsenal's goal, Denílson was ambling back and being overtaken

NORTH LONDON IS RED

Arsenal and Arsène Wenger went more than a decade and a record 20 games without losing a league game to Spurs between November 1999 and April 2010. Such was the dominance that Thierry Henry never lost a North London derby in eight years at the club. Wenger saw off ten Spurs managers with only Harry Redknapp's side mounting some resistance (Arsenal won two, drew two, lost three). Then Wenger's Stage Three decline coincided with Spurs' rise under Mauricio Pochettino, against whom Wenger only came out on top once in eight derbies. Overall, Wenger had an impressive record against Spurs, winning 23 and losing nine with 20 draws.

At Stamford Bridge, it was a similar story as Chelsea and Drogba clinically dispatched Arsenal 2-0. The first came as Arsenal ball-watched from a corner and the second when Drogba cut inside and fired in left-footed. Arsenal had lost all four games to their title rivals and were nine points off the lead. Yet again though, they picked themselves up and went on another run. Against Liverpool, Diaby headed in a Rosický cross from close range after 72 minutes and Arsenal hung on for a 1-0 win. Arsenal missed plenty of chances against Sunderland before Bendtner opened the scoring. Fàbregas made it 2-0 at the end with a penalty.

At the end of February, Arsenal went to Stoke and for the third time in four years saw a young player taken to hospital with a serious leg injury inflicted by a bad foul. As usual, Stoke took the lead from a Delap throw-in, Ryan Shawcross flicking on and Danny Pugh heading in after seven minutes. An excellent Bendtner header made it 1-1.

With an hour gone, the ball ran away from Shawcross in the middle of the pitch. Ramsey was there first and played the ball. Shawcross flew in and connected with Ramsey's shin. Ramsey's leg was "left at a right-angle" – he had broken his tibia and fibula. The Arsenal players were distraught and, having seen it happen

by the referee, a shocking attitude that Wenger had allowed to develop in the Brazilian and others. Before the game, the manager had challenged his players to prove they were "mentally prepared" to go for the title – they were not and afterwards he was unusually critical. "We were completely not at our level. Why? I believe there are some mental reasons in there."

twice before to a teammate, angry. At least two players were sick on the pitch. Arsenal players and Stoke's Glen Whelan comforted the 19-year-old while medics gave him oxygen. Shawcross was red-carded and walked off upset having seen and heard the damage done. Like at Birmingham, TV producers did not show replays of the incident.

The game restarted after seven minutes. With 89 minutes gone, Pugh handled a pass in the area. Captain Fàbregas dispatched the penalty and slapped his leg three times, one each for Diaby, Eduardo and Ramsey. Soon after, Fàbregas squared for Vermaelen to score his eighth of the season and make it 3-1. It was Arsenal's first win at Stoke for 28 years.

Afterwards, an emotional Wenger said, "I didn't see many bad tackles in the game but this one was horrendous." Another comment proved sadly prescient: "This is the third player – Eduardo, Diaby and now Ramsey – we've lost to tackles that are unacceptable, and spare me the articles tomorrow about how nice Shawcross is because we had all that with Eduardo." Ramsey and Arsenal had to hear constant straw-man arguments from Stoke officials and players as well as ex-players turned pundits that Shawcross did not mean to hurt him and was "not that type of player." No one was saying Shawcross set out to break Ramsey's leg, but a player is responsible for their actions and Shawcross, who two years earlier

had injured Adebayor's ankle with a bad foul when the ball and player were not even on the pitch, decided against pulling out of a challenge that he was not going to make.

Like Martin Taylor in 2008, the FA gave Shawcross a standard three-game ban while Ramsey was out for the best part of a year. If the FA had taken retrospective action against Dan Smith (who was only booked for his foul on Diaby) commensurate with the recklessness of the challenge and damage caused, maybe Taylor would have reined himself in. If the FA had punished Taylor, or Shawcross after the Adebayor incident, appropriately, perhaps the Stoke player would have stayed on his feet when he lost the ball.

Wenger had been complaining for years about the bad fouls that his players had been subjected to and the lack of protection from referees, and while sometimes they were lightweight in physical games against the likes of Stoke and Bolton, sadly he was again vindicated. It was noticeable that all three leg breaks had in common:

- Occurred in front of a boisterous home crowd. Consistently weak 'homer' refereeing enabled players to make challenges they would not attempt or get away with if they were playing for the visiting side.

- An inferior lower-table team managed by a British Football Manager and trying to make up for technical deficiencies by following the "Arsenal don't like it up them" narrative.

- Perpetuated by a fired-up journeyman.

In the Champions League knockout at Porto, things got off to a bad start for an injury-hit side when Fabiański gifted the opener, pushing a low cross into the net. Campbell, like on his previous European appearance in the final three years earlier, headed in a set-piece. After half-time, the Arsenal back-line had another collective brain fade. Fabiański picked up the ball after Campbell touched it back to him, then compounded his error by giving the ball to the referee. While Arsenal defenders stood around looking at each other instead of preventing a quick free-kick, Porto did exactly that and Radamel Falcao scored an easy goal. How many more times could "naivety" be used to excuse Wenger Stage Two teams' poor game management or ability to self-destruct?

At the Emirates, Bendtner poked home to give Arsenal the start they were looking for, then sidefooted in Arshavin's low cross. There seemed no danger when Nasri had the ball on the right touchline under pressure. However, he jinked back, cut inside, slalomed past three defenders and drove into the far corner for a classic European goal. Arshavin played in Eboué on the counter-attack and the Ivorian kept calm to round the goalkeeper and score. Bendtner

dispatched a late penalty to seal his hat-trick and an impressive 5-0 win that sent Arsenal into the quarter-finals.

At the start of March, Nasri lifted an excellent pass over a packed Burnley defence and Fàbregas finished first-time. However, Arsenal's talisman again went off injured soon after. David Nugent was left unmarked to equalise and Bendtner's missed chances seemed like they would prove costly. However, Walcott cut inside from the right for a rare time and scored left-footed. Near the end, Arshavin made it 3-1. At Hull, the Russian burst between two defenders and volleyed in, but Jimmy Bullard dispatched a penalty. George Boateng was sent off near half-time for taking out Sagna, but it was still level after 93 minutes when Boaz Myhill could only parry Denílson's swerving long-range shot and Bendtner scored an important late winner.

Denílson opened the scoring against West Ham and Arsenal were in control until Vermaelen and Guillermo Franco chased a long ball. Both players went down, Vermaelen was sent off – surprisingly, Arsenal's only red card of the season – and a penalty given. Almunia made an excellent save from Diamanti and Fàbregas scored a late penalty to make it 2-0. Unbelievably, six wins in a row and slip-ups by rivals meant Arsenal were briefly top of the table.

Arsenal then returned to St Andrew's for the first time since Eduardo's leg was broken. A tight game opened up with ten minutes left when Nasri drilled a low shot past Joe Hart from 25 yards. However, two minutes into injury time, Birmingham played a free-kick into the area. Sagna's clearance rebounded off Kevin Phillips towards goal, where Almunia let it through his hands. It was déjà vu as Arsenal's title hopes were again dealt a late, partially self-inflicted, blow at Birmingham.

In the Champions League quarter-final, European Champions Barcelona came to the Emirates and put on a *tiki taka* masterclass. Arsenal were used to dominating the ball, but they could barely get it off the Barcelona carousel. Amazingly, it was 0-0 at half-time as Almunia made save after save. However, straight after the break, Zlatan Ibrahimović twice broke Arsenal's jagged offside trap. For the first, Almunia came rushing out and the Swede lobbed him. For the second, Ibrahimović smashed into the roof of the net. It looked like it could get embarrassing. However, after 66 minutes, Walcott came on and his pace had an immediate impact, getting in on the right to sidefoot under Víctor Valdés' dive. With five minutes to go, Carles Puyol brought down Fàbregas. The hobbling Spaniard drilled it down the middle, despite having a fractured fibula, to give Arsenal the unlikeliest of 2-2 draws. It was a famous

comeback that set the Emirates off. However, it came at a big cost as the risk to play the injured Fàbregas and Gallas backfired and their seasons were effectively over, along with Arshavin's.

Arsenal then dominated Wolves but missed chance after chance. Karl Henry was sent off with 20 minutes to go after sliding in on Rosický. In the 94th minute, Sagna hit one last cross and Bendtner headed another late winner to keep Arsenal within three points of the leaders.

In Camp Nou, Walcott started and quickly justified Barcelona's concerns about his pace. Diaby played him in, Walcott squared and Bendtner scored at the second attempt. However, order was restored within minutes when Lionel Messi hammered into the top corner. The Argentine 'vaccinated' Arsenal, like he had done to numerous others, with four sublime finishes. It ended 4-1 and could have been many more as Arsenal were outplayed by a brilliant team. "He is like a PlayStation. He is the best in the world by some distance," Wenger admired.

The following Wednesday, Arsenal went to White Hart Lane with their title chances on the line. After ten minutes, Almunia punched a corner he should have caught. Thirty yards out, left-back Danny Rose, who was making his Premier League debut, sent it back with a ferocious volley.

Almunia could have saved it, but it flew into the roof of the net. Just after half-time, Jermain Defoe's pass sliced open Arsenal's defence and Gareth Bale made it 2-0. Wenger sent on van Persie for his first action in five months and the Dutchman was an instant threat. However, the often-unreliable Gomes was a man possessed and made brilliant saves. Late on, Bendtner tapped in, but Spurs finally won a North London league derby.

Surprisingly, Spurs then gave Arsenal a title lifeline by beating Chelsea. An injury-hit Arsenal went to Wigan and took a 2-0 lead with goals either side of half-time from Walcott and Silvestre. However, Arsenal started coasting, thinking the game was won. Wenger brought on Mérida rather than van Persie. With 80 minutes gone, Arsenal's midfield went AWOL and Ben Watson got one back. Fabiański dropped a corner onto Titus Bramble's head and the embarrassing capitulation was complete when Charles N'Zogbia cracked in from the edge of the area to make it 3-2. Wenger was furious: "I believe that we were not focused and were not disciplined and we got caught. In football, you have to keep focused for 90 minutes." This was not a new issue – why had Wenger not instilled that discipline and focus, especially when there was a title to be won?

The season petered out with a tame goalless draw against Man City, where the Emirates gave Patrick Vieira a standing ovation when he replaced boo-boy Adebayor, and a 2-1 loss at Blackburn. This meant Arsenal still needed a point on the last day of the season to finish third above Spurs. They easily beat a weakened Fulham 4-0 with Arshavin robbing goalkeeper Mark Schwarzer and scoring into the empty net from an angle. van Persie gave a reminder of what Arsenal had missed and there was the trademark icing-on-the-cake Vela Chip.

Arsenal exceeded most people's expectations at the start of the year and, in some ways, Wenger did an impressive job mounting a title challenge with many unreliable or inconsistent players. Injuries again took their toll – van Persie was a huge loss and Arsenal badly missed his two-footed finishing and set-piece quality. It was a big drop in quality from Fàbregas to Denílson, van Persie to post-leg-break Eduardo, Vela or Bendtner, Gallas or Vermaelen to Silvestre, and Sagna to Eboué.

Wenger did not have the funds of his richer rivals, but good goalkeepers were not expensive in this era. Arsenal had assembled a trio of keepers that made blunders too frequently, caused uncertainty and cost points. Also, the weak mentality, slack work rate and soft defence were issues under Wenger's remit. Frustratingly, every time Arsenal put together an excellent run that got them back into the title race, they lost consecutive games, the weaknesses coming to the surface in the four losses to Chelsea and Man Utd.

2010/11
LEAGUE CUP CHOKE

Premier League	Fourth
FA Cup	Quarter-final
Champions League	Round of 16
League Cup	Final

PREMIER LEAGUE		PL	W	D	L	GF	GA	GD	PTS
1	MAN UTD	38	23	11	4	78	37	41	80
2	CHELSEA	38	21	8	9	69	33	36	71
3	MAN CITY	38	21	8	9	60	33	27	71
4	ARSENAL	38	19	11	8	72	43	29	68
5	TOTTENHAM	38	16	14	8	55	46	9	62
6	LIVERPOOL	38	17	7	14	59	44	15	58

Highlights: Famous 2-1 win over Barcelona got the Emirates rocking; 4-1 defeat of Spurs in the League Cup; beating Man Utd and Chelsea at home

Lowlights: Blowing the League Cup Final against relegated Birmingham; drawing with Newcastle after leading 4-0; knocked out of Champions League in Barcelona after Robin van Persie red card; FA Cup loss to a Man Utd team containing seven defenders; 2-0 up, 3-2 down to Spurs; Emmanuel Eboué giving Liverpool a 112th-minute penalty equaliser

Player of the year: 19-year-old Jack Wilshere made his England debut, became an Arsenal regular and was PFA Young Player of the Year

Top scorers: van Persie 22 (18 in PL), Samir Nasri 15 (10), Theo Walcott 13 (9), Marouane Chamakh 11 (7), Andrey Arshavin 10 (6)

Goal of the season: Carlos Vela finished a 24-pass spell of one- and two-touch Wengerball versus Bolton, the Emirates, Premier League

After five trophy-less years, questions were starting to be asked about Arsène Wenger, the club's most successful manager, and his entertaining but brittle nearly-men. A quiet transfer window did little to add the necessary quality, experience and steel. Arsenal made a couple of bids for Fulham's Mark Schwarzer, a solid and experienced Premier League goalkeeper, but their familiar indecisiveness and refusal to pay £1-2m more prevented them closing the deal and they again started the season with Manuel Almunia as number one.

At centre-back, Laurent Koscielny, who had only one year of top-flight experience, and Sébastien Squillaci replaced William Gallas, Philippe Senderos, Mikaël Silvestre and Sol Campbell. Upfront, Wenger finally signed out-of-contract Marouane Chamakh on a free transfer after refusing to pay Bordeaux's asking price in the two previous windows. Eduardo went to Shakhtar Donetsk having shown only glimpses of his 2007/08 goalscoring form after his leg-break.

Arsenal faced a tricky Monday lunchtime start at Anfield, but they were given a one-man advantage near half-time when Joe Cole was sent off for a two-footed foul on Koscielny. However, David N'Gog cracked a drive from an angle past Almunia. It looked like being the winner until injury time when Chamakh headed a cross against the post and Pepe Reina fumbled the rebound over the line. There was still time for Koscielny to get a second

yellow card, an eventful debut for the Frenchman, who had been stretchered off after the Cole challenge, and one that summed up his Arsenal career – excellent front-foot defending, sharp recovery pace, good on the ball but intermittent costly misjudgements.

Arsenal outclassed newly-promoted Blackpool 6-0 as Theo Walcott scored a hat-trick of assured finishes from the inside-right position and Chamakh opened his account. At Blackburn, the Englishman did it again, drilling the first from an angle. Blackburn equalised before Bacary Sagna went marauding down the right and squared for 2010 World Cup Winner Cesc Fàbregas, whose shot was blocked by Walcott. Andrey Arshavin sidefooted the rebound past the goalkeeper and three defenders on the line.

The international break again proved costly as Robin van Persie picked up ankle damage that cost him two months and Thomas Vermaelen an Achilles injury that put him out until the end of the season and meant a regular centre-back pairing of Johan Djourou and Koscielny. Against Bolton, Koscielny opened the scoring from a corner but later his weak header led to the equaliser. Chamakh headed in to make it 2-1 before Gary Cahill went through the back of him and was sent off. Owen Coyle, not Sam Allardyce, was the manager but Bolton still knew how to leave their mark – Paul Robinson had earlier planted his studs on Abou Diaby's shin, causing yet another injury to the unfortunate Frenchman. Alex

Song finished a counter-attack with a clever dink over Adam Bogdan and icing-on-the-cake specialist Carlos Vela finished a brilliant 24-pass spell of possession soundtracked by the crowd's "olés."

In the Champions League, Arsenal faced some long trips but not top teams. They hammered Braga 6-0 with Fàbregas running the show and scoring twice. Chamakh won another penalty and fired a goal after a Jack Wilshere back-heel. It was the perfect set-up for substitute Vela to score two crowd-pleasing goals, including a trademark Vela Chip.

At Partizan Belgrade, Wilshere set up Arshavin to open the scoring in a hostile atmosphere, but the home side equalised through a Cléo penalty. Chamakh was brought down and Marko Jovanović sent off. The usually-composed Arshavin put his laces through the penalty and Vladimir Stojkovic saved. However, the one-man advantage eventually told as Chamakh headed Tomáš Rosický's cross onto the bar and nodded in the rebound. Squillaci headed in a corner to make it 3-1 and there was still time for Kieran Gibbs to give away a third penalty; this time, new first-choice goalkeeper Łukasz Fabiański saved from Cléo.

Arsenal cruised to a 5-1 win over Shakhtar Donetsk helped by a

TYPICAL LINE-UP
(4-2-3-1)

10 van Persie — Chamakh / Bendtner

23 Arshavin — Nasri

8 Nasri — Walcott / Rosický / Bendtner

4 Fàbregas — Rosický / Ramsey

19 Wilshere — Diaby

17 Song — Denilson

22 Clichy — Gibbs

6 Koscielny — Vermaelen

20 Djourou — Squillaci

3 Sagna — Eboué

53 Szczęsny — Almunia / Fabiański

Players in: Marouane Chamakh, Laurent Koscielny, Sébastien Squillaci, *Ryo Miyaichi, Wellington Silva, Jens Lehmann*

Players out: William Gallas, Philippe Senderos, Mikaël Silvestre, Sol Campbell, Eduardo da Silva, Fran Mérida

goalkeeping fumble, a penalty gift courtesy of blatant linebacker grappling and a Wilshere dink after a slick one-two with Rosický. Eduardo came on for the visitors and scored a half-volley that was warmly received by the home crowd singing his name. In Donetsk, Walcott raced clear from halfway and coolly buried an Henry Sidefoot Finish. However, the home side came back and Eduardo scored the winner after Gaël Clichy had one of his brain fades. The home players and crowd went wild except the ex-Arsenal man, who did not celebrate.

At Braga, Fàbregas went off with a recurrence of his hamstring problems and Arsenal ended with ten men when Emmanuel Eboué was injured with all three substitutes used. The home side, nicknamed Os Arsenalistas in their Arsenal-esque kit, produced a shock 2-0 win as Matheus scored two excellent breakaway finishes.

Having opened with three wins, Arsenal's qualification was in doubt and they needed to beat Partizan Belgrade at home to qualify. van Persie dispatched a penalty but Cléo's deflected shot was not in the script. With 20 minutes to go, Walcott chested down and volleyed well, then Samir Nasri fired in left-footed for a 3-1 win that saw Arsenal qualify second in the group.

At Sunderland in the league, Fàbregas scored a freak goal from 40 yards when he stuck out a leg to block Anton Ferdinand's clearance and the ball flew over Simon Mignolet. Early in the second half, Song unnecessarily body-checked Steed Malbranque and was given his second yellow card. Nasri won a penalty but Rosický blazed it over the bar. With 95 minutes gone, Sunderland launched one last ball into the box. It just needed an Arsenal player to attack the hanging ball but no one challenged. After a scramble, Darren Bent rifled in to make it a frustrating 1-1 draw.

In late September, promoted West Brom came to the Emirates and took advantage of a complacent Fàbregas-less Arsenal. Late in the first half, Almunia came charging out to give away a penalty but redeemed himself by saving from Chris Brunt. It did not act as a wake-up call as weak defending, midfielders not tracking back and two more mistakes from Almunia saw West Brom take a deserved 3-0 lead. Nasri twisted and turned in the box to get one back and scored another on 90 minutes but it ended 3-2 to West Brom.

It was a familiar story at Stamford Bridge as Ashely Cole squared for Didier Drogba to flick in and make it 13 goals in 15 games against Arsenal. Arsenal played some good football, but Alex leathered a late free-kick high into the net to put Chelsea 2-0 up and open a seven-point gap between the two teams. With one point in three games,

Arsenal desperately needed a win against a Birmingham side featuring Alexander Hleb. However, the away side took the lead through a Nikola Žigić header. Chamakh continued his remarkable penalty-winning run with a *Platoon* fall from Scott Dann's foul. Early in the second half, Chamakh scored the winner. In injury time, Wilshere, who had set up both goals through bursts forward and one-twos, was sent off for a lunge on Žigić.

At Man City, Chamakh drew last-man Dedryck Boyata into a foul and red card after only four minutes. Arsenal beat the big spenders 3-0 with goals from Nasri, Song and Nicklas Bendtner and despite Fàbregas having a penalty saved by Joe Hart. A late Song header against West Ham broke the deadlock and kept Arsenal in second place at the end of October.

In the League Cup, Arsenal faced a trip to White Hart Lane. Given the North London rivalry and 5-1 loss two years earlier in the same competition, a game which Spurs embarrassingly released a DVD of, Wenger did not rotate as much as usual. An excellent move on the left ended with Wilshere firing across goal and Henri Lansbury made it 1-0. Arsenal should have been out of sight as Wilshere ran the midfield and Spurs could only stop him by fouling. However, a poor offside trap let in Robbie Keane and his sidefooted

effort went through Fabiański's hands. In the first six minutes of extra time, Nasri and Chamakh both won penalties that Nasri dispatched calmly. Arshavin fired in left-footed to make it 4-1 and the away fans sang, "Shall we make a DVD?"

The fun continued at Newcastle when Ryan Taylor headed off the line onto the back of his own goalkeeper Tim Krul's head and into the goal. Bendtner cut inside and hammered into the far corner while Walcott scored two one-on-ones to complete an impressive 4-0 win. A 2-0 win against Wigan put Arsenal into the semi-final and they were strong favourites to get the trophy monkey off their back.

It did not go to plan in the first leg as Championship strugglers Ipswich won 1-0. In the second leg, Arsenal finally broke Ipswich's resistance in the second half when Bendtner cut in from the left and curled into the far corner. Koscielny headed in a corner and Fàbregas confirmed Arsenal's Wembley place with a 3-1 aggregate win.

Back in the league in early November, Arsenal hit the bar twice against Newcastle but their goalkeeping issues were again exposed when Andy Carroll beat the onrushing Fabiański to a long free-kick. Late on, Koscielny brought down Nile Ranger and Mike Dean gave

him the second red of his short Arsenal career.

Fabiański showed his shot-saving ability at Wolves as Chamakh's goals in the first and last minute earnt a 2-0 win. Three more points came in a 2-1 win at Everton, where Sagna crashed a rare strike into the roof of the net.

Ex-Arsenal captain Gallas was now in Spurs white and Nasri refused to shake his hand before the North London derby at the Emirates. After 45 minutes, Arsenal's title pursuit was back on as they were 2-0 up with goals from Nasri and Chamakh. However, Gareth Bale took advantage of poor defending and Fàbregas inexplicably put his hand up in the wall to block a Rafael van der Vaart free-kick; the Dutchman dispatched the penalty. With four minutes left, Younès Kaboul glanced in a free-kick to make it 3-2, another embarrassing capitulation in Stage Two Wenger. It was Spurs' first win at Arsenal for 17 years (19 games in all competitions).

Arsenal bounced back in an entertaining game at Aston Villa, where they faced another old boy in Robert Pires. Arshavin drove in from the left and fired low into the far corner and Nasri volleyed in a corner to make it 2-0. Ciaran Clark got one back with a volley. Rosický played a through-ball worthy of his number-seven predecessor Pires and Chamakh poked home. Clark got another one but Wilshere drove forward and ended up diving to head home Chamakh's lob for a 4-2 win.

At the start of December, things were looking up. Arsenal were top of the league ahead of Man Utd, van Persie was back and Nasri was on fire. The quick-footed Frenchman scored two brilliant goals against Fulham. First, he jinked inside twice to leave defenders sprawling and finished left-footed. Second, he beat two defenders, rounded Mark Schwarzer and curled in from an angle. That set up a big test for Arsenal at Old Trafford, where the pre-match talk turned to the Arsenal players' attire. Nasri and Chamakh, among other foreign Premier League players, had become prominent snood wearers and the fleecy neck-warmers did not help Arsenal's soft image. Alex Ferguson said, "Real men don't wear things like that," while Rio Ferdinand tweeted "U won't see a Man Utd player wearing a SNOOD." The debate ended when the attire was banned in 2011 for safety reasons.

With Fabiański injured, 20-year-old Wojciech Szczęsny made his Premier League debut in a tight game. Predictably, Man Utd came out on top as Park Ji-sung guided a deflected shot with his head over the Polish goalkeeper. Wayne Rooney blazed a penalty high into the crowd and the game finished 1-0.

Chelsea, who were on an unusually poor run, were Arsenal's next opponents. A brilliant ten-minute spell either side of half-time fired up the Emirates Christmas crowd as Song, Fàbregas and Walcott put Arsenal 3-0 up. Chelsea got a goal back but Arsenal finally beat one of Man Utd and Chelsea after a run of ten defeats and one draw. Two nights later, Wigan took the lead through a penalty. Arsenal turned it around as Arshavin scored a brilliant acrobatic volley and Bendtner sidefooted in. Charles N'Zogbia was sent off for headbutting Wilshere but late on Arsenal's weakness at set-pieces was exposed and the 2-2 equaliser went in off Squillaci.

Arsenal began 2011 in third place behind the two Manchester clubs. They secured a comfortable 3-0 win at Birmingham and were frustrated by the woodwork and goalkeeper Joe Hart to only draw 0-0 against Man City. At the end, Sagna and Pablo Zabaleta locked horns and their 'footballer's headbutts' earnt them both red cards.

At West Ham, Walcott took advantage of left-back Wayne Bridge's nightmare debut to score one, assist another and win a penalty from the former Chelsea nemesis. van Persie was back in the goals with a double. The Dutchman then fired his first-ever hat-trick against Wigan, the second a typical left-foot volley from a raking Fàbregas pass. The only surprise was when the Dutchman, an excellent penalty taker, fired over the bar from 12 yards.

TASER

Arsenal and France teammates Nasri and Gallas had a long-running beef and Gallas later told a bizarre story where some of Nasri's associates asked him to go for a talk with Nasri. Gallas did not go, saying: "At the same time, I glanced inside and I saw someone crouched down with a bag. In the bag, there were tasers. I didn't know why. But luckily I was with people that day because I do not know what could have happened."

In the FA Cup, Arsenal struggled to put away Championship side Leeds and nearly paid the price. However, in a game of two penalties, Fàbregas' 90th-minute spot-kick sent the tie to an unwanted replay in a busy January. Arsenal's class told at Elland Road and they won 3-1, the third featuring Bendtner in his now regular role on the wing crossing for van Persie to head home.

The Dane opened the scoring against Huddersfield in the fourth round, but even the League One side managed to expose Arsenal's weaknesses. Right-back Jack Hunt was allowed to run 50 yards past three token challenges before Squillaci blocked him and was sent off. Alan Lee outjumped the defence from a corner, but substitute Fàbregas dispatched another late penalty for a 2-1 win.

At the start of February, Arsenal were second in the league, five points behind Man Utd, and in contention in all four competitions. The league challenge looked over when Everton's Louis Saha scored from a clearly offside position, the referee strangely allowing the goal to stand because Koscielny got a touch to Séamus Coleman's pass to Saha. With 20 minutes to go, Arshavin and Koscielny scored to relieve the Emirates tension and secure what felt like a significant comeback win.

It only took one minute at Newcastle for van Persie to slice open the defence and play in Walcott, who finished comfortably. Two minutes later, Djourou headed in a free-kick. Walcott drove a low cross from the right and van Persie buried right-footed. The Dutchman then bulleted in a header from a Sagna cross to make it 4-0 after 26 minutes. It was a brilliant start reminiscent of so many during the Stage One Wenger years where the game was over well before half-time. However, this was a Stage Two Wenger team and they had the ability to shoot themselves in the foot.

Just after half-time, Joey Barton went through Diaby. A player from a more cynical team would have rolled around the floor while his teammates rushed to the referee to pressure him into sending Barton off, as he should have been. Instead Diaby, who was well aware of the dangers of a nasty challenge, jumped up and grabbed Barton's neck and pushed him over (and then pushed Kevin Nolan when he got involved). The Newcastle wind-up merchant had got what he wanted and Diaby was sent off.

With 68 minutes gone, Koscielny made an unnecessary attempt to win the ball from Leon Best who had his back to goal and was going nowhere. Barton sidefooted the penalty past Szczęsny. Nolan put Szczęsny in a headlock but, unlike Diaby, no action was taken. Seven minutes later, Clichy was outjumped and Best buried the loose ball to make it 4-2. Newcastle launched another set-piece into the box and substitute Rosický, despite having already seen that referee Phil Dowd was not in a mood to blend into the background, put his hands on Mike Williamson's back and gave away another spot-kick. This time, Barton beat Szczęsny with a Panenka and the home fans that had not left at half-time were wild with the belief they were witnessing a once-in-a-lifetime event. On 87 minutes, Arsenal cleared another free-kick but Cheick Tioté smashed a left-footed volley into the bottom corner from 25 yards, his only ever goal for the club in 156 games. It finished 4-4.

It was one of the most embarrassing days since Wenger took over and a chance blown to move within two points of leaders Man Utd. Champions do not let four-goal leads slip. However, the writing had been on the wall for a while: 4-2 up versus Spurs with minutes to go, drew 4-4; 2-0 up with ten minutes to go at Wigan, lost 3-2; 2-0 up against Spurs, lost 3-2. The failings were familiar – poor game management; weakness at set-pieces due to a lack of height in the team (especially after Djourou went off injured and Diaby was sent off) and having few players bar Sagna that relished an aerial battle; basic individual errors under pressure; and players giving the referee a chance to make big decisions.

The following Saturday was a happier affair as van Persie continued his brilliant form to score a double against Wolves. It was back to the Champions League the following Wednesday and another showpiece tie against Barcelona, one of the best club sides in history, in front of a buzzing Emirates crowd. Barcelona were again strong but did not dominate possession as much as the previous year. However, after Lionel Messi missed a one-on-one, they took the lead when the Argentine played in David Villa, who was played onside by Clichy. Messi surprisingly missed another chance in the second half before Arsenal sprang into life. Clichy chipped a great pass

right-footed to van Persie on the left and the Dutchman surprised Victor Valdés by hammering a volley from the tightest of angles inside the near post. Five minutes later, Arsenal unleashed a devastating counter-attack from Wilshere to Fàbregas to Nasri. The Frenchman bided his time before cutting back to the onrushing Arshavin, who coolly sidefooted the winner. The crowd erupted as Arshavin ran away lifting his shirt to reveal a T-shirt of himself doing his trademark finger-to-the-lips celebration.

Only 11 days after one of Wenger's most embarrassing matches came one of his greatest victories and the most famous night at the Emirates. For 19-year-old Wilshere, it was a breakout performance against a legendary midfield of Xavi, Andrés Iniesta and Sergio Busquets where he showed his ability to play on the half-turn, keep possession in tight spaces and burst past opponents.

The opposition and Arsenal line-up were very different the following weekend as they went to Leyton Orient in the FA Cup. Rosický headed his first goal in 13 months but in the 89th minute Jonathan Téhoué beat two challenges and drilled the equaliser.

Arsenal beat Stoke 1-0 the following Wednesday but it was a costly night as Fàbregas and Walcott went off injured and were out of Sunday's League Cup Final. Arsenal were still big favourites against Birmingham, who were hovering just above the relegation

PENALTY

Arsenal won 16 penalties in all competitions in 2010/11, scoring 12. Chamakh was the king of winning them with a dramatic, but effective, knee-collapsing technique.

a microcosm of the Dutchman's Arsenal career so far.

Keith Fahey drilled against the post, while Nasri did his best to make things happen in Fàbregas' absence. Man-of-the-match Ben Foster made crucial saves as Arsenal had 20 attempts on goal to Birmingham's 11. Wenger took off Arshavin, relying on Bendtner and Chamakh to supply a winner. With 89 minutes gone, a Foster hoof was destined for Szczęsny to collect unchallenged until Koscielny went to clear, then pulled out. Szczęsny fumbled the ball into the path of substitute Obafemi Martins to score the easiest winner imaginable. It was agony for Koscielny, Szczęsny and Arsenal, dealt a psychological blow that killed their season and arguably took years to recover from, and provided untold schadenfreude for rival fans.

Arsenal beat Leyton Orient in the FA Cup replay 5-0 with a Bendtner hat-trick, but could only draw 0-0 against Sunderland in the league. The season was on the brink and Arsenal faced one of the most challenging tasks in football – a trip to Pep Guardiola's Barcelona. Fàbregas and van Persie were rushed back from injury. It started badly when Szczęsny dislocated a finger saving a free-kick and was replaced by Almunia. Barcelona dominated with 61% possession and were relentless in hounding Arsenal

zone. It may have only been the League Cup but they could not have asked for a better opportunity to end their six-year trophy drought, a spell that was not unusual for most clubs but a lifetime for a manager that had raised the bar with seven trophies in the nine Stage One Wenger years.

Within minutes, Szczęsny brought down Lee Bowyer in the area but was fortunate to see Bowyer had been given offside – incorrectly as Clichy had again been out of sync with his defensive colleagues. Half an hour in, Arsenal were again outdone at a corner as Birmingham won the first ball and 6'7" Žigić beat Szczęsny and his defenders to head the opener. Just before half-time, Wilshere rattled the crossbar from outside the area. Arshavin collected the ball on the right, beat two players and crossed for van Persie to hook in on the volley with his right foot. Crucially, he was injured in the process and struggled until being replaced in the second half,

and winning the ball back. Their only failing was a lack of clinical finishing and it took until just before half-time for them to take the lead through Messi after Fàbregas tried a back-heel just outside his own area. Early in the second half, Sergio Busquets headed a corner into his own net and Arsenal were somehow leading 3-2 on aggregate.

Minutes later, van Persie received a through-ball, was given offside and struck a shot into the side-netting. Referee Massimo Busacca gave the Dutchman a second yellow card for time-wasting, an unbelievable decision as van Persie argued he did not hear the whistle in the 95,000-crowd Camp Nou and, even if he did, he shot within one second like players did every week without punishment. Arsenal held out for 15 minutes but Xavi finished a brilliant move and Messi buried a penalty to make it 3-1, and 4-3 on aggregate. Right at the end, Wilshere played in Bendtner for a great chance to seal the ultimate smash and grab. However, the ungainly Dane took a poor touch that allowed Javier Mascherano to make a tackle. Arsenal had still not had an effort on goal versus the home side's 19. For the second year running, they went out of the Champions League at Camp Nou; as well as regretting Bendtner's miss and van Persie's sending off, they paid the price for coming second in a group they should have won.

Four days later, Arsenal went to Old Trafford in the FA Cup and embarrassingly lost 2-0 to a team containing seven defenders. Man Utd, who were chasing a potential treble, rotated heavily with a high-energy but low-quality midfield of full-backs John O'Shea and the da Silva twins alongside reserve Darron Gibson. Fabio and Rooney scored the goals and Paul Scholes came on for a typically feisty cameo and as usual managed to avoid a red card. Wenger said, "I liked the pitch, I liked the referee, I did not like Paul Scholes' tackles." Arsenal were out of their third cup in two weeks.

The league title was still possible however. Arsenal went 2-0 down at West Brom, the second when Squillaci failed to clear a long ball and Almunia came charging out of his area to leave his goal unguarded for Peter Odemwingie to roll in. Arsenal secured a late comeback with a quality Arshavin left-footed volley and van Persie scoring from a tackle in the six-yard box. They then dropped two points for the third game in a row with a goalless draw with Blackburn.

41-year-old Jens Lehmann, who had been re-signed on a short-term deal to cover for the goalkeeping injury crisis, became Arsenal's second-oldest player ever when Almunia was hurt during the warm-up at Blackpool. The Invincible must have been shocked at playing behind a defence of Eboué, Squillaci, Koscielny and Clichy after being used to a back-line of warriors Lauren, Sol Campbell, Kolo Touré and Ashley Cole. Arsenal won 3-1 in the sun with goals from Diaby, Eboué and van Persie.

Arsenal were frustrated by Liverpool at the Emirates but in a game that saw a long delay due to a head injury to Jamie Carragher, they finally made the breakthrough when van Persie slotted a penalty in the 98th minute. Unbelievably, there was still time for Arsenal to hit the self-destruct button. They cleared a free-kick and, as the ball bounced to safety and everyone waited for the final whistle, Eboué clambered all over Lucas Leiva to give Liverpool a penalty that Dirk Kuyt scored with the last kick of the game in the 112th minute.

Despite a run of one win and four draws, Arsenal still had a chance at the title but they needed all three points at White Hart Lane. It started perfectly when Fàbregas played in Walcott for an Henry Sidefoot Finish. Two minutes later, Rafael van der Vaart was free to make it 1-1. Nasri drilled a low shot from outside the area to put Arsenal 2-1 ahead after only 12 minutes. It was a pulsating game and van Persie gave Arsenal a two-goal cushion on 40 minutes but it did not last until half-time as Tom Huddlestone struck the cleanest of strikes from 25 yards. Spurs' comeback was complete in the second half when Szczęsny came charging out to foul Aaron Lennon and give away

an unnecessary penalty, which van der Vaart dispatched. The Pole made an excellent save late on to keep the score at 3-3.

At Bolton, the home side scored their usual goal from a corner while Szczęsny saved a weak Kevin Davies penalty. van Persie equalised after a one-two with Fàbregas. With 90 minutes gone, Tamir Cohen beat Djourou to head the winner from another corner and Arsenal's title hopes were over.

With the pressure off, Arsenal beat eventual Champions Man Utd at the Emirates when van Persie cut back to Aaron Ramsey to sidefoot into the bottom corner. It was a big moment for the Welshman, who had had short loan spells at Nottingham Forest and Cardiff to rebuild his fitness. He then started at Stoke, 14 months after having his leg snapped there, but the home side inevitably scored from a set-piece and won 3-1. The season finished with a 2-1 home loss to Aston Villa and 2-2 draw with Fulham, where van Persie scored for a Premier League record ninth consecutive away game, to leave Arsenal in fourth place.

Arsenal showed that on their day they could match the top teams, but it ended up a season to forget as a talented but fragile team capitulated from February onwards with the League Cup Final upset and only two leagues victories in the last 11 games. Frustratingly, the weaknesses were plain to see – after the Stoke loss, Wenger himself said, "We have conceded, I think, 21 from set-pieces and only 17 in open play. That is something we have to correct. It is the easiest thing to correct in the game but you still must understand the flight of the ball and want to be first to the ball." However, Wenger did not address it on the training ground or by buying taller, more aggressive players.

There was also his strange habit of playing players out of position. Arshavin, who in-between the moments of quality did himself no favours with a lethargic attitude, was frustrated at playing on the wing instead of his preferred central playmaker role. Even more infuriating was the regular sight of Bendtner – a one-paced 6'4" striker with no dribbling skills but good heading ability – playing out wide.

The wait to sign Chamakh was strange from a manager that previously stockpiled technique, pace and power, and the Moroccan offered little more than Bendtner apart from an uncanny penalty-winning ability and less controversy; however, why not play either of the target men centrally and give them the crosses they thrived on?

The mitigating circumstances were yet again injuries as the Vermaelen-Fàbregas-van Persie spine as well as Gibbs, Diaby, Walcott, Bendtner and the three goalkeepers were regulars in the treatment room. van Persie, who was now fittingly wearing Bergkamp's number-ten shirt, scored 18 goals in 19 league starts and was two goals away from the Premier League Golden Boot despite only playing half the season.

Favourite Combos

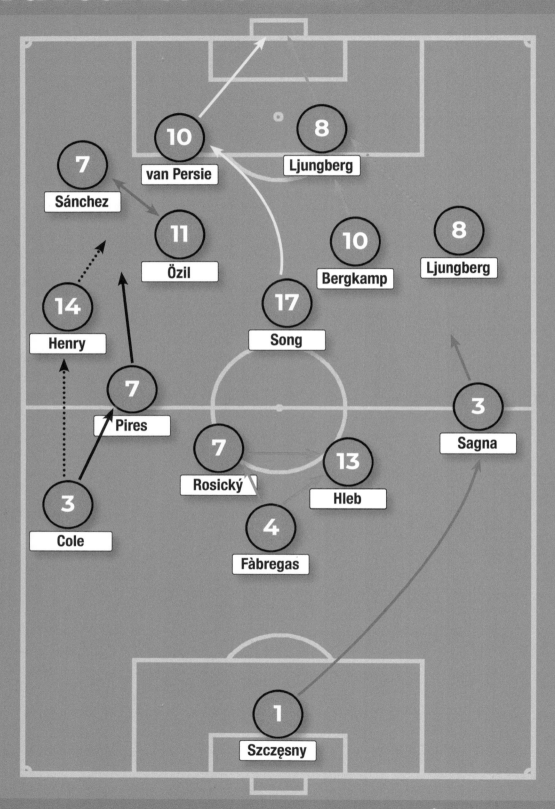

Movement of ball   Movement of player

2011/12
8-2

Premier League	Third	
FA Cup	Fifth round	
Champions League	Round of 16	
League Cup	Quarter-final	

PREMIER LEAGUE		PL	W	D	L	GF	GA	GD	PTS
1	MAN CITY	38	28	5	5	93	29	64	89
2	MAN UTD	38	28	5	5	89	33	56	89
3	ARSENAL	38	21	7	10	74	49	25	70
4	TOTTENHAM	38	20	9	9	66	41	25	69
5	NEWCASTLE	38	19	8	11	56	51	5	65
6	CHELSEA	38	18	10	10	65	46	19	64

Highlights: Beating Chelsea 5-3 in a crazy game at Stamford Bridge; 2-0 down, 5-2 up against Spurs; Thierry Henry's six-week return and goal against Leeds; last-day-of-season 3-2 win at West Brom to finish fourth above Spurs after being ten points behind them; beating champions Man City 1-0

Lowlights: Not being ready for the start of the season led to three losses in five games including an 8-2 humiliation at Old Trafford, which was followed by a desperate late transfer window trolley dash; hammered 4-0 in Milan

Player of the year: PFA and FWA Player of the Year Robin van Persie stayed fit and showed he was a world-class striker with 37 goals

Top scorers: van Persie 37 (30 in PL); Theo Walcott 11 (8)

Goal of the season: van Persie's flying volley from Alex Song's lofted pass versus Everton, the Emirates, Premier League

In July 2011, Arsène Wenger was defiant: "For example, you talk about Fàbregas leaving, Nasri leaving. If you give that message out, you cannot pretend you are a big club, because a big club first of all holds on to its big players and gives a message out to all the other big clubs that they just cannot come in and take away from you."

Wenger's hubris as well as his and the board's indecisiveness meant Arsenal began their 125th year ill-prepared as Cesc Fàbregas and Samir Nasri were left out of the side at Newcastle. The only new signings were Ivory Coast winger Gervinho and 17-year-old attacking midfielder Alex Oxlade-Chamberlain. A 0-0 draw saw Arsenal players – and the referee – again take Joey Barton's bait. Alex Song received a three-game ban for stamping on Barton, while Gervinho and Barton grappled after the Newcastle man accused Gervinho of diving to win a penalty (he was clipped). With no sense of irony, Barton threw himself to the ground and got Gervinho sent off on his debut – why had no one warned the new man about the five-star wind-up merchant?

In the first home game against Liverpool, Wenger selected Nasri, who could have gone through the motions but played well in his last game for the club. In the second half, Emmanuel Frimpong was sent off on his first start for flying into challenges twice while substitute Ignasi Miquel, on for the injured Laurent Koscielny, hit a clearance against Aaron Ramsey that looped into the Arsenal net. Luis Suárez made it 2-0 at the end.

Having let the transfer sagas drag on all summer, 24-year-old Fàbregas inevitably returned to Barcelona and Nasri joined the last Invincible Gaël Clichy in signing for Man City. Fàbregas was a serial winner with Spain in the World Cup and European Championships but had won nothing at club level since the 2005 FA Cup. It was no surprise he wanted to join a brilliant Barcelona team as Arsenal paid the price for surrounding him by too few players that matched his quality and elite mentality – something that the Spaniard confirmed in 2020: "Sometimes, I used to go home after we lost and I used to cry. I used to suffer, I used to spend sleepless nights suffering. And then you lose a game, you're in the bus like this, destroyed, and then you hear some players laughing, thinking about where they will be going out later. This was going on for a few years." While Arsenal had got the better of some deals with Barcelona, this was the second time in four years – Thierry Henry being the first – that the Spanish team had signed a world-class player from Arsenal for below the market rate.

Poor preparation, suspensions and injuries (including an ankle stress fracture that caused Jack Wilshere to miss the entire season and various injuries meant Abou Diaby effectively suffered the same fate). Surely things could not get any worse. Arsenal went to Old Trafford and the fans were laughing pre-match as Man City thrashed Spurs 5-1 on Nasri's debut. However, there was concern when they saw Arsenal's inexperienced and weak line-up. Koscielny was accompanied in defence by Johan Djourou and full-backs Carl Jenkinson and Armand Traoré, while Francis Coquelin made his debut in centre-midfield. However, Man Utd had their own injury problems and the average age of their line-up was slightly younger.

The tone was set when Danny Welbeck brushed aside a meek Djourou to head a bouncing ball past Szczęsny. Walcott won a penalty, but David de Gea saved new captain van Persie's unusually tame effort. 19-year-old right-back Jenkinson had a torrid time on his second start and was left isolated by his teammates. Ashley Young was allowed to keep cutting in onto his right foot and was made to look a Ballon D'Or contender with two curling strikes. In between Wayne Rooney stroking in two free-kicks, Walcott put one through de Gea's legs to make it 3-1 at half-time and give Arsenal some hope. But Arsenal were all over the place and a far-from-vintage Man Utd team with a centre-midfield pairing of Anderson and Tom Cleverley had a field day. It was 6-2 when Jenkinson got his second yellow and made it three games, three red cards for Arsenal. Walcott went to right-back and gave away a penalty for Rooney to seal his hat-trick. Coquelin, who had done OK, was taken off for poor Oxlade-Chamberlain to make his debut.

TYPICAL LINE-UP
(4-2-3-1)

10 van Persie — Chamakh / Walcott

27 Gervinho — Arshavin / Benayoun

14 Walcott — Gervinho / Ox-Chamberlain

16 Ramsey — Rosický

8 Arteta

17 Song

28 Gibbs — Santos

6 Koscielny — Vermaelen

4 Mertesacker — Djourou

3 Sagna — Djourou

13 Szczęsny

Players in: Carl Jenkinson, Jon Toral, Héctor Bellerín, Gervinho, Alex Oxlade-Chamberlain, Joel Campbell, Park Chu-young, André Santos, Per Mertesacker, Mikel Arteta, Yossi Benayoun (loan), *Thomas Eisfeld*, *Thierry Henry* (loan)

Players out: Gaël Clichy, Cesc Fàbregas, Emmanuel Eboué, Samir Nasri, Armand Traoré, Denílson (loan), Carlos Vela (loan), Nicklas Bendtner (loan), *Andrey Arshavin* (loan)

It ended up 8-2, a complete humiliation. Even Wenger's former bitter rival Alex Ferguson later admitted he felt sorry for him. Arsenal had not conceded eight goals in a league game since 1896. Experienced players like Arshavin, Rosický and Walcott gave their younger teammates little help or guidance. Traoré was sold two days later to QPR. Szczęsny escaped criticism as he was offered little protection but he conceded three goals from outside the area.

Had Wenger jumped the shark? Not being ready for the start of the season was neglection of duty. The 6-1 mauling at Old Trafford in 2001 was embarrassing, the League Cup Final loss to Birmingham was devasting, but getting smashed 8-2 by the team that Arsenal used to trade blows with in title-deciding blockbusters was Wenger's lowest day at the club and a result that few managers would survive.

It forced Arsenal into a frenzied trolley dash in the last two days of the transfer window that brought in Brazilian left-back André Santos, German centre-back Per Mertesacker, Spanish midfielder Mikel Arteta, Israeli midfielder Yossi Benayoun and South Korean striker Park Chu-young.

Mertesacker and Arteta made their debuts as a much-changed team beat Swansea 1-0. Arsenal had the promoted

side's goalkeeper Michel Vorm to thank as he threw the ball against the heels of his own defender; Arshavin accepted the gift and converted into the empty net from an angle.

At Blackburn, Arsenal dominated the first half and led 2-1 as Gervinho and Arteta opened their accounts well. However, Arsenal's set-piece and organisational frailties remained despite the change of personnel as Blackburn stunned them with three goals, including own-goals from Song and Koscielny. In a frenetic finish, substitute Chamakh bulleted a header to make it 4-3, but he and Mertesacker both missed the target with late headers. Arsenal finally found some form in a 3-0 win over Bolton, van Persie scoring twice as David Wheater was sent off for the away side.

At the start of October, Arsenal went to White Hart Lane for a frantic derby. Emmanuel Adebayor, now in white, teed up Rafael van der Vaart, who chested down and volleyed home. Song drove down the left and squared for Ramsey to equalise. Midway through the second half, Kyle Walker drilled a low shot from 25 yards that was almost in the middle of the goal, but Szczęsny failed to get behind it and Spurs won 2-1. Arsenal had lost four of their first seven league games, relegation form that left them in 16th position. In addition, their best defender – Bacary Sagna – had broken his leg after landing awkwardly and was out for four months.

Arsenal finally found some form after the international break, beating Sunderland 2-1 as van Persie scored after 30 seconds and then got the winner with a curling free-kick. The Dutchman again made the difference against Stoke, despite carrying a knock, as he came on with the score 1-1 and netted twice from Gervinho cutbacks. Arsenal then went to a sunny Stamford Bridge for a Premier League classic:

- 0-0 (11 minutes): Walcott teed up Gervinho with a great cross but the Ivorian scuffed it wide.

- 0-1 (14 minutes): Frank Lampard headed the opener.

- 1-1 (36 minutes): Ramsey sliced open Chelsea's defence with a brilliant disguised pass to Gervinho, who gave van Persie an open goal to score.

- 1-2 (45 minutes): John Terry beat Arsenal defenders to volley in a corner.

- 2-2 (49 minutes): Song played in Santos on the left and he passed the ball through Petr Čech's legs. Chelsea had earlier successfully targeted the left-back, who in taking the number 11 shirt had foreshadowed his preference for attacking over defending.

- 2-2 (50 minutes): Szczęsny charged out of his area and took out Ashley Cole, fortunately only receiving a yellow card.

- 3-2 (55 minutes): Walcott cut in from the right and fell over, causing four defenders to freeze. The Englishman, however, got up and fired in at the near post.

- 3-3 (80 minutes): Mata's deflected shot from 25 yards levelled the match again.

- 4-3 (85 minutes): Last man Terry inexplicably slipped and was left face down in the turf, much to non-Chelsea fans' delight, as van Persie pounced to waltz round Čech and unleash his dirt-off-the-shoulder celebration.

- 5-3 (92 minutes): Arsenal kept piling forward and van Persie thumped a left-foot shot through Čech to complete a memorable hat-trick and spark wild celebrations. A 'basketball' game had showed the best and worst of Arsenal – their firepower led by van Persie as well as Walcott having one of his most productive games, but defenders and midfielders going AWOL.

Arsenal then cruised to a 3-0 win over West Brom with goals from van Persie, the returning Vermaelen and Arteta. At Norwich, Mertesacker was slow to deal with a hoof and Steve Morison opened the scoring. However, Arsenal's talisman again bailed them out. First, Gervinho tried to flick in Walcott's low cross and missed completely; luckily, van Persie was waiting to show him how it was done. Then, the Dutchman classily dinked right-footed when one-on-one to make it 2-1, his tenth goal in five league games and Arsenal's fifth consecutive win. A 1-1 draw against Fulham, where Vermaelen scored at both ends, meant Arsenal moved up the table to fifth.

The Champions League qualifier was no walkover this year with fourth-placed Serie A finishers Udinese. Walcott finished a Ramsey cross to give a 1-0 win at home. In Italy, an Antonio Di Natale header levelled the tie, but Gervinho beat his man on the left and pulled back for van Persie to score. Szczęsny made a crucial penalty save from Di Natale and Walcott sealed a 3-1 win to put Arsenal into the group stages, where they got another tricky draw.

First was a visit to German Champions Borussia Dortmund. Arsenal looked set for an impressive win in front of an intimidating 75,000 fans when Walcott played in van Persie, who finished right-footed. However, after 88 minutes, Ivan Perišić met a clearance with a brilliant swerving volley into the top corner and it ended up a credible 1-1 draw.

The lively Oxlade-Chamberlain finished well with his left foot against Olympiacos and Santos made it 2-0. The Greek side headed one back and then the bar saved Arsenal from dropping more points. In Marseille, substitute Ramsey drilled an important winner in injury time. After a 0-0

draw at home against the French team, Arsenal hosted Dortmund. Song left three defenders for dead and crossed for van Persie to head in. The Dutchman got his second from a corner and, after a late Dortmund goal, the game finished 2-1. It meant Arsenal would finish top of a difficult group.

Arsenal lost a dead rubber in Olympiacos 3-1, where substitute goalkeeper Vito Mannone, retreating back into his area after heading clear, forgot a goalkeeper is allowed to use their hands. His panicked attempt to volley the ball was uncoordinated and comical, and the ball dribbled past him into the net.

In the League Cup, Oxlade-Chamberlain showed his long-range shooting ability in a 3-1 win over Shrewsbury. In the next round, Arshavin teed up Park to curl a Pires-esque winner from the inside-left position, a finish worthy of his number-nine shirt but a 'false flag' for those thinking Wenger had unearthed another gem – the Korean was barely seen again, playing a total of seven minutes in the Premier League. Man City knocked Arsenal out in the quarter-final with Sergio Agüero scoring in a 1-0 win.

December started at Wigan, where Arteta set up an easy 4-0 win with a swerving 25-yarder. Vermaelen headed in a corner with Gervinho and van Persie sealing the win. Against Everton, Song lofted a ball over the defence to the inside-left position, where van Persie struck a typically clean flying volley into the opposite corner. With Song taking on more of a roaming midfield role following the arrival of Arteta, the Song-van Persie combination was becoming a fruitful one. After a run of eight wins and one draw, Arsenal lost 1-0 at leaders Man City. At Aston Villa, Benayoun headed a late Christmas winner from a corner. A 1-1 draw against Wolves was followed by a New Year's Eve game against QPR, where van Persie swept in Arshavin's pass to earn a 1-0 win.

Arsenal's strong run after their dreadful start saw them begin 2012 in fourth place, nine points off the top. They lost 2-1 at Fulham, however, when the home side scored two late goals from crosses after Djourou was sent off for receiving two yellow cards.

The club received a boost when Henry, who was now playing for New York Red Bulls, re-joined the club on a two-month loan during the Major League Soccer off-season. Henry provided cover for Gervinho and Chamakh, who were playing in the African Nations Cup. Chamakh was hardly featuring anyway – he had started well at Arsenal, scoring 11 in 22 games, but then lost confidence and was no competition for van Persie when the Dutchman returned from injury, scoring only four in the next 46 games. The Moroccan was slow for a striker and had weak shooting ability;

ALMOST SIGNED

Claude Makélélé, Zlatan Ibrahimović, Gigi Buffon, Didier Drogba, Cristiano Ronaldo, Pep Guardiola, Yaya Touré, Lionel Messi, Gerard Piqué, Carlos Tevez, Vincent Kompany, Javier Mascherano, Gareth Bale, Xabi Alonso, Gareth Barry, Mark Schwarzer, Gary Cahill, Raphaël Varane, Eden Hazard, Juan Mata, Paul Pogba, Yann M'Vila, Luis Suárez, Gonzalo Higuaín, Demba Ba, David Villa, Virgil van Dijk, N'Golo Kanté, Jamie Vardy, Riyad Mahrez, Jadon Sancho, Kylian Mbappé, Thomas Lemar.

however, he thrived on crosses, which were rare in Wenger Stage Two teams.

In the FA Cup, Arsenal were 2-0 down to Aston Villa but scored three in seven stirring minutes, including two van Persie penalties. Against Leeds in the fourth round, Henry replaced Chamakh after 68 minutes. Ten minutes later, Song found the Arsenal legend in his favourite inside-left position. Henry was a bit bigger around the waist, had a beard and was wearing the number 12 shirt, but the Henry Sidefoot Finish was the same. The winner sent the Emirates crowd delirious and Henry celebrated wildly along the touchline.

Back in the league, Arsenal played out another end-to-end game at Swansea. van Persie and Walcott goals made it 2-2 but Danny Graham was left free to score a one-on-one winner. Against Man Utd, the visitors took the lead with an Antonio Valencia header. Arsenal played well in the second half, finally equalising with an excellent counter-attack initiated by a Koscielny tackle in his own box and ended three passes later by a low van Persie drive. Wenger brought Arshavin on for Oxlade-Chamberlain; with the youngster an attacking threat and having just provided an assist, van Persie and many in the Emirates crowd registered their disapproval for almost the first time in his tenure. Instead of pushing on for a win, Arsenal's habit of switching off defensively allowed Valencia an easy path into the box and Welbeck scored the winner.

Three consecutive losses and a goalless draw at Bolton left Arsenal in seventh place and struggling to qualify for the Champions League. A 7-1 hammering of ten-man Blackburn lifted the mood in the sub-zero Emirates as van Persie got a hat-trick against his favourite opponents and Oxlade-Chamberlain scored two. Arsenal were unusually clinical, scoring with seven of their eight shots on target against perennial whipping boy Paul Robinson.

At Sunderland, Mertesacker went down on a cow-field pitch clutching his ankle. James McClean did not hang around to check on the German's ankle ligaments, running in on goal to fire the opener. The German, who been almost ever-present until then, missed the rest of the season. Ramsey hit a low equaliser that went in off both posts. After 91 minutes, Henry cushioned in an excellent Arshavin cross to score another crucial winner before returning to the US.

In the Champions League, Arsenal went to Serie A leaders Milan optimistic of repeating past San Siro glories. However, after 15 minutes, Kevin-Prince Boateng hammered in a volley and what followed was one-way traffic. Robinho scored two and Zlatan Ibrahimović dispatched a penalty to make it 4-0, the club's heaviest European defeat, and effectively put Arsenal out of the competition for another year. A few days later, confirmation that the trophy drought would be extended for a seventh year came at Sunderland where a lacklustre Arsenal lost 2-0 in the FA Cup.

That prompted Wenger's infamous statement that "The first trophy is to finish in the top four. And that's still possible. I believe finishing fourth is vital for us, so let's focus on that." It was an infuriating resetting of expectations and a small-club mentality. On the latter note, it was the North London derby and Spurs fans were enjoying their ten-point lead over Arsenal with "Mind the Gap" London Underground T-shirts, memes and jokes.

A must-win game for Arsenal's Champions League qualification hopes started terribly after only four minutes when Arsenal's defence gave Louis Saha the freedom of the Emirates and his shot looped slowly in off Vermaelen. Half an hour later, Gareth Bale beat Szczęsny to a one-on-one and threw himself over. Mike Dean gave a penalty which Adebayor netted to the fury of the home fans to make it 2-0. Arsenal's season had collapsed yet again and their local rivals were putting the final nail in the coffin.

Sagna had had enough. After van Persie hit the post, Arteta chipped into the box and the French right-back attacked the ball to bullet a header past Brad Friedel. Minutes later, van Persie collected a ball on the edge of the box, twisted onto his left foot and curled a brilliant shot into the corner to make it 2-2 and raise the roof on the Emirates.

Six minutes into the second half, Rosický burst forward and played it to Sagna, who hit a low cross that the Little Mozart flicked in for his first goal in 50 league games. As Spurs pressed for an equaliser, Arsenal countered and Walcott dinked in. Three minutes later, Song played in Walcott and he got his second to make it 5-2, two excellent finishes for a player lucky to be on the pitch after a terrible first half. It was an incredible comeback with five goals in 27 minutes as Arsenal ran rampant and Spurs capitulated. The last 20 minutes were played in a party atmosphere in the winter sun and Scott Parker was sent off after receiving a second yellow card for a foul on Vermaelen. However, with ten games left, the gap was still seven points.

At Anfield, it was Suárez that made the most of Szczęsny's tendency to rush out and commit himself. This time, the goalkeeper made amends with a brilliant double save from Dirk Kuyt's penalty and follow-up. Then own-goal specialist Koscielny gave Liverpool the lead – the usually-impressive defender often took up a poor position at the front post, leaving too big a channel between him and the goalline and leading to him slicing in crosses. Arsenal's goal was bombarded but saved by Szczęsny and the woodwork. Out of nowhere, Sagna curled in a long cross and van Persie headed in. They completed the ultimate smash-and-grab win in the 92nd minute with a familiar combination – Song lofted a ball to the inside-left position, where van Persie had peeled off to volley another excellent strike.

Then came the return leg against Milan where a Koscielny header after seven minutes got the crowd going. Oxlade-Chamberlain, playing in centre-midfield due to injuries, drove Arsenal forward. Rosický sidefooted in at the near post and van Persie crashed in a penalty to make it 3-0 at half-time and put Arsenal on the brink of a remarkable comeback. In the second half, Christian Abbiati saved a deflected

CANNON FODDER

Paul Robinson was Arsenal's favourite goalkeeper to play against throughout the Wenger era as they put 69 goals past him in 24 games for Leeds, Spurs and Blackburn. The 7-1 mauling of Blackburn in 2011/12 was the 13th time that Robinson conceded more than three goals in a match against Arsenal. Henry in particular tormented the goalkeeper, beating him 11 times. In those 24 games, Robinson only kept two clean sheets and won three times.

Gervinho shot with his legs then crucially stopped van Persie's dinked rebound effort just as everyone was about to celebrate. Milan regained composure and Arsenal were out.

At the end of February, Arshavin was loaned back to Zenit Saint Petersburg for the rest of the season. His Arsenal career had become a waste of an exceptional talent – he provided plenty of moments of quality, but there could have been many more if he had shown more application and featured more often as a number ten rather than winger or wide midfielder.

Back in the league, Newcastle's Hatem Ben Arfa gave them the lead,

but van Persie equalised within a minute. The Arsenal players and fans were frustrated by their own missed chances and the away side's cynical attempts to kill the game, goalkeeper Tim Krul in particular wasting time at every opportunity. With 95 minutes gone, Newcastle tried to keep the ball in Arsenal's corner instead of going for a winner. However, their negative tactics cost them as Arsenal broke upfield, Walcott crossed and Vermaelen, who had sprinted 80 yards to join the attack, buried the loose ball to send the Emirates wild yet again. van Persie channelled Henry versus Chris Kirkland from five years earlier and mocked Krul, who suddenly showed remarkable urgency to get on with the game. Arsenal's fourth consecutive comeback win was a Premier League record.

The centre-back got another winner in a 1-0 victory at Everton. Arsenal strolled to a 3-0 win against Aston Villa, their seventh in a row, capped off by Arteta firing a Ronaldo-esque free-kick into the top corner from 30 yards. However, the run came to an end at relegation-threatened QPR, who won 2-1 as Samba Diakité took advantage of a Vermaelen slip.

At the start of April, Arsenal outplayed title challengers Man City, hitting the woodwork three times. With the game heading for a draw, Arteta won the ball in the midfield and hit a low swerving winner from 25 yards. The Spaniard was one of the few Arsenal players, along with van Persie and Oxlade-Chamberlain, with the inclination and technique to shoot from distance, something Wenger discouraged as he believed the results were inefficient.

At Wolves, Sébastien Bassong brought down Walcott after eight minutes and was red-carded. van Persie dinked the penalty down the middle and minutes later set up Walcott to kill the game. The lively Benayoun, who justifiably got increased game time in the last third of the season, made it 3-0 in the second half. Arsenal conceded two soft early goals to Wigan who won 2-1 despite Vermaelen heading his sixth of the season. A goalless draw at home to Chelsea and 1-1 draw at Stoke left Arsenal in third place, one point above Spurs and two above Newcastle.

Against Norwich, Benayoun curled into the top corner after two minutes. Wesley Hoolahan equalised soon after with a shot that Szczęsny should have saved. Norwich silenced the home crowd in the second half, taking the lead when Grant Holt's strike looped off Gibbs. As usual, van Persie bailed them out. He volleyed from another lofted Song pass and then drilled a loose ball in with his right foot. However, his teammates threw away his good work within minutes when they lost the ball in midfield and a pass over the top took out Arsenal's zigzag offside trap, allowing Steve Morison to make it 3-3.

At the end, van Persie was about to score his hat-trick and the winner into an empty net when Kyle Naughton pushed him. Inexplicably, referee Anthony Taylor waved play on. Sagna sustained another leg-break, which ruled him out of the 2012 Euros, cruel fate for a player willing to put his body on the line week after week.

That left another tense last day of the season when Arsenal went to West Brom having to match the results of Spurs and Newcastle. Four minutes in, goalkeeper Marton Fulop got confused where the penalty area was, allowing Benayoun to nick the ball from him and score an easy opener. However, Arsenal's porous midfield and defence always gave teams a chance and West Brom were 2-1 up after 15 minutes. Santos drilled a shot through Fulop's weak wrists to equalise.

In the second half, the goalkeeper's nightmare was complete when he got a punch wrong and it dropped to Koscielny to poke in. Arsenal could not rely on Spurs failing this time as they were beating Fulham. With 91 minutes gone, substitute Gibbs made a crucial £25m last-ditch tackle on Billy Jones and Arsenal won 3-2, stuttering to a third-place finish and Champions League qualification. With Chelsea gaining a place in the competition as holders, Spurs were pushed into the Europa League. Nasri and Clichy were vindicated as Man City won the league in the final minutes of the season.

The exciting run-in, comebacks, late goals and third place salvaged some pride and gave fans plenty to cheer after the shocking start to the season, but it should not have overshadowed the management failure that put Arsenal in that position and led to the Old Trafford humiliation. It also showed Arsenal's tendency to do well when the pressure was off – the near reversal against Milan a case in point.

Captain van Persie carried the team time and again, winning the PFA and FWA Player of the Year as well as the Premier League Golden Boot with 30 goals, equalling Henry's Invincibles total. He scored 37 overall with the next highest scorer Walcott on 11, such was Arsenal's dependence on the Dutchman.

In Song, Arsenal had finally found a strong holding player in the middle but this season he started marauding like a box-to-box midfielder. Whether it was Song's own initiative or at Wenger's urging – and despite his excellent link-up play and 14 assists – it was to Arsenal's detriment. They conceded 49 league goals, 20 more than champions Man City, and suffered a huge ten Premier League defeats as teams exploited the big gaps between individual defenders and between the defence and midfield, while the lack of midfield press negated Arsenal's attempts to play a high line. Playing behind them was not easy but Szczęsny had a low 64% save rate.

A team that could not shut up shop or win 1-0 would always struggle long term. Wenger's approach was later confirmed by Sébastien Squillaci: "The style of play was a bit like Spain's. It was very open, and often we found ourselves defending in the middle one-on-one with the opposition attackers. It was never easy. It was very attacking. But that was the club's philosophy. I talked about it with coach Wenger. He told me, 'I know it's difficult, but I want us to play like this, I want the attacking players to have more freedom and less defensive work'."

2012/13
TOP-FOUR TROPHY
DÉJÀ VU

Premier League	Fourth
FA Cup	Fifth round
Champions League	Round of 16
League Cup	Quarter-final

PREMIER LEAGUE		PL	W	D	L	GF	GA	GD	PTS
1	MAN UTD	38	28	5	5	86	43	43	89
2	MAN CITY	38	23	9	6	66	34	32	78
3	CHELSEA	38	22	9	7	75	39	36	75
4	ARSENAL	38	21	10	7	72	37	35	73
5	TOTTENHAM	38	21	9	8	66	46	20	72
6	EVERTON	38	16	15	7	55	40	15	63

Highlights: Thrashing Spurs 5-2 for the second season running; unbeaten ten-game run-in culminating in a last-day-of-season 1-0 win at Newcastle to finish fourth above Spurs after being seven points behind them; beating Reading 7-5 after being 4-0 down on a crazy League Cup night; 7-3 win over Newcastle

Lowlights: Limping out of both cups to lower-league teams; 3-1 home loss to Bayern Munich; losing 2-1 at White Hart Lane; no wins, two draws and four losses against the top three

Player of the year: Santi Cazorla – the classy two-footed playmaker scored 12 and assisted 14

Top scorers: Theo Walcott 21 (14 in PL); Olivier Giroud 17 (11); Lukas Podolski 16 (11); Cazorla 12 (12)

Goal of the season: Podolski's van Persie-esque dipping volley versus Montpellier, the Emirates, Champions League

On 4 July 2012, Robin van Persie wrote a letter to Arsenal fans on his website: "As announced earlier this year I had a meeting with the Boss and Mr Gazidis after the season. This was a meeting about the club's future strategy and their policy. Financial terms or a contract have not been discussed, since that is not my priority at all. I personally have had a great season but my goal has been to win trophies with the team and to bring the club back to its glory days. Out of my huge respect for Mr Wenger, the players and the fans I don't want to go into any details, but unfortunately in this meeting it has again become clear to me that we in many aspects disagree on the way Arsenal FC should move forward. I've thought long and hard about it, but I have decided not to extend my contract."

With only one year left on his contract, he was inevitably sold a month later. That the destination was Man Utd, and not overseas, was a surprise and provided an outlet for fans' anger, not helped by their former striker saying, "I always listen to the little boy inside of me in these situations – when you have to make the harder decisions in life. What does he want? That boy was screaming for Man United." However, it only deflected from the fact that Arsenal had again failed to convince their captain and world-class player that they were serious about making the necessary changes to compete at the top level. The Dutchman was understandably fed up of scoring a great goal only to see his defence and midfield throw it away. He left as the club's eighth-highest goalscorer with 132 goals and, like Cesc Fàbregas, just a solitary FA Cup medal in eight years.

However, Arsenal did finally sign established – although only attacking – players in German international Lukas Podolski, Ligue 1 Champion and top scorer Olivier Giroud, and Spanish playmaker Santi Cazorla. After losing Alex Song to Barcelona, Arsène Wenger reinvented Mikel Arteta as a holding midfielder.

Nicklas Bendtner managed to get a season-long loan at Juventus, whose director general Giuseppe Marotta welcomed him with, "Clearly he isn't the top player we wanted, but we needed reinforcements." Bendtner, who suffered injuries and was arrested for drink-driving and banned by Denmark for six months, was joined by former Gunner Nicolas Anelka in January – the pair took home Series A medals despite a combined 11 league appearances and zero goals. Not surprisingly, the Italian Champions did not take up the option to make the Bendtner deal permanent.

Former centre-back Steve Bould became assistant manager replacing Pat Rice, who retired after 48 years at the club as player, youth-team coach, caretaker manager and assistant manager. Bould's relationship with Wenger, on the sidelines at least, was not a chatty one.

The van Persie-less era began with two frustrating goalless draws. Arsenal had 23 shots against Sunderland, the best chance falling to Giroud, who worryingly put a one-on-one wide with his weaker right foot. At a sunny Stoke, Arsenal sported their new purple and black hooped away kit. Giroud could have played Aaron Ramsey in late on, but went for a long-range effort from out wide which landed on the roof of the net.

Arsenal finally got off the mark against Brendan Rodgers' Liverpool when Cazorla, who had made an impressive start to his Arsenal career, played in Podolski. The German, who had relieved Park Chu-young of the number-nine shirt despite mostly playing wide left, finished well. The two new signings combined again and this time Cazorla fired in low from the left. It was an impressive 2-0 win at Anfield with man-of-the-match Abou Diaby showing his immense talent – close control to receive the ball in tight spaces, skill and pace to glide away from opponents, and good forward passing.

Arsenal hammered Southampton 6-1 as Podolski curled a van Persie-esque free-kick into the top corner and the newly-promoted side scored two own-goals. The away goal was a gift for Danny Fox as Wojciech Szczęsny dropped an easy cross unchallenged.

TYPICAL LINE-UP
(4-2-3-1)

12 Giroud — Podolski, Walcott

9 Podolski — Cazorla

14 Walcott — Gervinho, Ox-Chamberlain

19 Cazorla — Rosický

10 Wilshere — Ramsey

8 Arteta — Diaby

28 Gibbs — Santos, Monreal

6 Koscielny — Vermaelen

4 Mertesacker

3 Sagna — Jenkinson

1 Szczęsny — Mannone, Fabiański

Players in: Lukas Podolski, Olivier Giroud, Santi Cazorla, *Nacho Monreal*

Players out: Robin van Persie, Alex Song, Carlos Vela, Manuel Almunia, Henri Lansbury, Denílson (loan), Nicklas Bendtner (loan), *Marouane Chamakh* (loan), *Johan Djourou* (loan), *André Santos* (loan)

Arsenal then faced two tricky tests. At Champions Man City, Ramsey played a perfect pass inside Gaël Clichy for Gervinho to run on to one-on-one. However, after scoring three goals in two games in a brief spell leading the line, the Ivorian was back to his infuriating worst and his touch was so heavy Joe Hart collected easily. It did not get better as Gervinho skied shots high and wide or dribbled them. Gervinho had rare dribbling ability, but no consistent end-product due to poor decision-making and inability to strike a ball cleanly. Just before half-time, Vito Mannone came out for a corner but got under the ball and Joleon Lescott headed the opener. With ten minutes left, a corner fell to Laurent Koscielny and he fired a deserved equaliser into the roof of the net. The game finished 1-1 as Mannone made an excellent late save from Vincent Kompany and Sergio Agüero surprisingly rolled the rebound wide.

Arsenal started brightly against Champions League winners Chelsea, but gave away a poor goal as Fernando Torres, whose marker Koscielny had his back to the incoming free-kick, volleyed in. Gervinho fired in the equaliser. After half-time, new captain Thomas Vermaelen slid in to give away another unnecessary free-kick and Juan Mata's cross went straight past Arsenal's defenders and Mannone to give the league leaders a 2-1 win.

In the Champions League, Podolski and Gervinho goals earnt a 2-1 comeback win in Montpellier. Arsenal again faced Olympiacos, winning 3-1 with second-half goals from Podolski and Ramsey.

At the Emirates against Schalke, Wenger's decision to play Gervinho as a 'false nine' did not work, while Jefferson Farfán had the freedom of the right wing as André Santos effectively operated as a 'false three'. In the second half, Schalke won two consecutive headers and it fell to an unmarked Klaas-Jan Huntelaar to drill past Mannone. Ten minutes later, Schalke transitioned the ball to Farfán and he crossed low for Ibrahim Afellay to seal a 2-0 win. There were boos at the end, although it was Arsenal's first home loss to an overseas team in 46 matches since Inter Milan at Highbury in 2003.

In the return fixture in Germany, Arsenal took a 2-0 lead through Theo Walcott and Giroud, but Huntelaar and Farfán made it 2-2 to keep the Germans top of the group. Arsenal beat Montpellier 2-0 at home with Podolski playing a one-two with Giroud and meeting the looping return pass with a brilliant dipping volley. It meant they had reached the knockout stage for a 13th consecutive season. However, they missed the chance to top the group, and get a potentially easier draw in the knockout round, when they lost their final group game to Olympiacos for the third time in four years. The Greek side outplayed a weakened Arsenal team, winning 2-1 as Schalke's draw against Montpellier meant an Arsenal win would have seen them top the table.

Arsenal started October with a visit to West Ham. After 20 minutes, Mohamed Diamé nutmegged Ramsey on the left and curled an excellent strike into the far top corner. Just before half-time, Podolski fizzed a ball across the area and Giroud stretched at the near post to volley his first Premier League goal. Deep into the second half, substitute Walcott started and ended a counter-attack. Five minutes later, Cazorla scored a brilliant dipping drive from 25 yards with his left foot to seal a 3-1 win.

However, a toothless Arsenal then lost 1-0 at Norwich as Mannone spilt a shot from distance and Grant Holt beat a static defence to the rebound. To no avail, Wenger threw on Alex Oxlade-Chamberlain (who only lasted nine minutes before having to go off injured), Arshavin and Serge Gnabry (at 17 years and 98 days the second-youngest player to play in the Premier League for Arsenal after Jack Wilshere).

At the club's fractious AGM, where owner Stan Kroenke and chief executive Ivan Gazidis were heckled by some shareholders, Wenger repeated his top-four trophy comment: "For me,

there are five 'trophies' – the first is to win the Premier League, the second is to win the Champions League, the third is to qualify for the Champions League, the fourth is to win the FA Cup and the fifth is to win the League Cup. I say that because if you want to attract the best players, they do not ask 'did you win the League Cup?', they ask you 'do you play in the Champions League?'." Wenger's overall point was valid as Arsenal needed the Champions League revenue and all teams had now downgraded the cups by fielding second-string players, but calling fourth place a trophy encouraged a loser's mentality, gave his players and the club a pass for their failure to compete for actual trophies, and led to over-the-top celebrations at the end of certain seasons.

Arsenal welcomed back Bacary Sagna and Jack Wilshere for the visit of QPR. It was the Englishman's, now wearing the number-ten shirt, first game for 17 months. A cold Emirates burst to life after 80 minutes when Stéphane Mbia was sent off for kicking Vermaelen and an offside Arteta poked home after a scramble to give a 1-0 relief win.

Arsenal then went to Man Utd six points behind the second-placed team. However, the gulf was bigger than that and it only took three minutes to be laid bare – an innocuous cross came in from the right, but Arsenal's new captain Vermaelen miskicked his clearance under little pressure; former captain van Persie did not miskick, striking a volley into the bottom corner with his right foot. The Dutchman did the 'hands up, I'm not celebrating' celebration, but it was the sort of moment that reminded him why he left. Wayne Rooney scuffed a penalty wide. As the players left the pitch at half-time, Santos further riled Arsenal fans by swapping shirts with van Persie. In the second half, Wilshere got his second yellow card for leaving his studs on Patrice Evra, and soon after Evra beat the Arsenal defence to head the second. Cazorla curled an excellent consolation in injury time, only Arsenal's second effort on target in the entire game, and Man Utd won 2-1.

Arsenal took a 2-0 lead against Fulham at the Emirates as Giroud powered a header from a corner and Podolski finished from an Arteta cutback. However, Dimitar Berbatov headed a corner in and then teed up Alexander Kačaniklić to head the equaliser. The classy Bulgarian then made it 3-2 by stroking a penalty into the corner. Giroud levelled it up almost immediately with another good header. In the 94th minute, Arsenal won a penalty when an Arshavin cross hit John Arne Riise's hand, but Mark Schwarzer saved Arteta's low effort and it ended 3-3.

The North London derby began badly when Per Mertesacker inexplicably stepped out of the defensive line and left a hole for Jermain Defoe to exploit. Szczęsny saved his effort but Emmanuel Adebayor tapped in the rebound. However, the game turned

when Adebayor slid in with his studs up on Cazorla and, much to the delight of the home fans who had been booing him for the 18 minutes he was on the pitch, was red-carded. Walcott hit a hanging cross and Mertesacker for once soared to head his first Arsenal goal into the top corner. Podolski's deflected shot bobbled in and Giroud finished Cazorla's low cross to make it 3-1 at half-time. Cazorla slid in to bury Podolski's cross before Gareth Bale made it 4-2 with a right-footed drive. Walcott put the seal on the Emirates party by unbelievably giving Arsenal their second 5-2 win over Spurs in nine months.

However, Arsenal's push up the table was halted by two flat draws against Aston Villa and Everton. Arsenal were desperate for a win against visitors Swansea but in the 88th minute Michu sliced open the defence with a one-two and sidefooted past Szczęsny. As Arsenal pushed for an equaliser, Carl Jenkinson was robbed on the halfway line and Michu, having the season of his life, confidently made it 2-0. The home fans booed as Arsenal were down to tenth, their worst start to a season under Wenger.

In the League Cup, Arsenal dealt with League One strugglers Coventry 6-1 as Giroud got his first goal and also had a penalty saved, Arshavin provided a reminder of his class with his only goal of the season and Walcott scored twice.

The next round saw a trip to relegation-threatened Reading and one of the craziest nights in the cup's history. In a completely-changed line-up from the league games, Wenger gave rare starts to forgotten men Arshavin and Chamakh as well as 'contract-rebel' Walcott.

- 0-4 (37 minutes): Arsenal's back-up players did little to press their first-team claims, the defence being particularly shambolic, as Reading cruised to a 4-0 lead, with the goals including a typical Koscielny own-goal from in front of the near post and Emi Martínez seeing a 'save' spin behind him into his own net.

- 1-4 (45 minutes): Arshavin played Walcott through the middle and he coolly dinked to pull one back.

- 2-4 (64 minutes): Substitute Giroud stooped to net a brilliant header from a corner.

- 3-4 (89 minutes): Surprisingly, given the defending on show and Arsenal's improvised 4-2-4 formation, there were no goals at either end for 25 minutes. Then Koscielny buried another header from a corner.

- 4-4 (95 minutes): Arsenal launched the ball into the box one last time, it fell to Walcott, who poked it goalwards, where it was blocked from just behind the line. Jenkinson dispatched the follow-up to erase any doubt. It finished 4-4 after normal

TREATMENT ROOM

Stage One Wenger players were known for their next-level athleticism and stamina; Stage Two and Three players were known as brittle. Nothing could be done about the three leg-breaks from shocking fouls, but the number of muscle injuries and time they took players out for were an outlier in English football. It raised major questions about Arsenal's training methods and back-room staff. The club's injury updates became a running joke as players who had "minor" injuries and would be "out for a couple of weeks" were not seen for months. The club did not address this issue until well into Stage Three.

time and the buzzing Giroud and Francis Coquelin threw their shirts into the away section. They then sheepishly had to ask for them back after being informed that there was extra time to come.

- 5-4 (103 minutes): Chamakh took a rare shot from outside the area and it was a good one, hard and low.

- 5-5 (115 minutes): Pavel Pogrebnyak was left unmarked to head in from close range.

- 6-5 (121 minutes): Arshavin drove down the left and drilled a shot that was stopped on the line. Walcott buried the rebound to seal his hat-trick.

- 7-5 (124 minutes): Arsenal hoofed clear, Chris Gunter missed his header completely and, to seal the win and cap off the madness, Chamakh lobbed Adam Federici from 30 yards. It was brilliant entertainment and the most goals ever scored in a League Cup match.

The quarter-final against Bradford City, now playing in the bottom tier of English football, was a less riveting, and more painful, evening. With no league game the following weekend, Wenger played a strong team, but Garry Thompson gave the home side the lead from a set-piece after 16 minutes. Gervinho sealed YouTube fame by failing to put in a low Kieran Gibbs cross from three yards with an open goal beckoning – an embarrassing miss that prompted the chant "Premier League, you're having a laugh" from the Bradford supporters. With two minutes left, Vermaelen headed a Cazorla cross to take it to extra time. With no further goals, it went to penalties, and the League Two side showed more nerve to win 3–2 as only Wilshere and Oxlade-Chamberlain scored, while Cazorla, Chamakh and Vermaelen missed. It was the first time that Arsenal had been knocked out of the competition by a lower-league club.

In early December, there was a nervous atmosphere at the Emirates as Arsenal faced West Brom having won only four of their last 13 matches in all competitions. Their fortunes turned when Cazorla cut inside Steven Reid and went down to win a penalty that even Wenger struggled to justify afterwards. Arteta stroked the ball down the middle and scored another spot-kick in the second half after Oxlade-Chamberlain was actually fouled. The Spaniard was doing his best in his new deeper role with good passing and intelligent positional play to make interceptions.

Arsenal went back to the Madejski Stadium with post-Bradford pride to restore and the attacks again dominated as a Cazorla hat-trick meant this time they beat Reading 5-2. Just before Christmas, an Arteta penalty gave a 1-0 win at Wigan.

Walcott, who had become vocal about wanting to play central striker rather than winger, had not been starting games as he and Arsenal struggled to agree a new contract, with his existing one expiring at the end of the season. He and his agents were holding out from a position of power, knowing that the club's management would be castigated if they let another established player leave, and this time for free. But he was no van Persie or Fàbregas and the panic among some fans, which saw a ridiculous #SignDaTing campaign trend online, showed how Arsenal's star had fallen.

Arsenal and Newcastle put on some post-Christmas entertainment on a cold night in North London. Walcott, who started in the striker position he wanted to play, finished a counter-attack with an Henry Sidefoot Finish. Demba Ba levelled just before half-time with a free-kick that was deflected off a ducking Wilshere. It was 1-1 at half-time and there was no sign of the mayhem to come.

Just after the break, Oxlade-Chamberlain fired in from the edge of the area; however, Sylvain Marveaux was left all alone to tap in and make it 2-2. Wilshere drove down the left and chipped to the back post and it eventually fell to Podolski to nod in. Within five minutes, Newcastle equalised for the third time when Gibbs switched off and left Ba to volley in. Gibbs did better going forwards and cut back for Walcott to bury his second into the roof of the net. Giroud came on and Walcott returned to the right wing, where he crossed for the Frenchman to seal the game with a diving header. Two minutes later, Giroud drove a rare right-footed strike and Arsenal led 6-3.

In injury time, Walcott took a short free-kick in the left corner and, instead of running down the clock, drove into the box past four half-hearted challenges, repeated his Chelsea trick of falling and getting up while everyone else froze,

and dinked over Tim Krul to make it 7-3. A great night for Walcott with a hat-trick and two assists prompting the home fans to chant "Sign him up."

Arsenal ended 2012 in fifth place and in another 'top-four trophy' battle with Spurs and the likes of Everton. The transfer window was a tacit admission of the poor recruitment of previous years as Santos and Chamakh were loaned out, and Spanish left-back Nacho Monreal was brought in to provide competition for Gibbs. Walcott finally signed a bumper new contract as Arsenal blinked and almost doubled his salary to make him one of the top earners. There were high hopes for the British Core, which also included Wilshere, Ramsey, Oxlade-Chamberlain, Gibbs and Jenkinson, who had all signed long-term contracts; however, they did not turn out to be a Man Utd Class of 92 success story.

After a New Year's Day 1-1 draw at Southampton, Arsenal went to Swansea in the FA Cup. Michu again scored the opener, before Arsenal went 2-1 up with late goals from Podolski and Gibbs, who replicated Podolski's Montpellier one-two with Giroud and volley, just from closer range. However, Danny Graham sent it to a replay in the 87th minute as Arsenal failed to clear a corner. Arsenal won an entertaining replay 1-0 with a late Wilshere finish.

HOLE IN THE MIDDLE

Between 2008 and 2016, Wenger did not sign a recognised central-midfielder except Mathieu Flamini in 2013, who was out of contract and training at his old club to maintain fitness. He instead converted attacking ball-players like Arteta and Cazorla, who were excellent at recycling the ball, but not equipped at tackling, pressuring opponents and winning headers, nor had the physical presence that almost all teams now had in the middle of the pitch – a trend Wenger himself started with the signings of strong and tall ball-playing midfielders like Patrick Vieira, Emmanuel Petit and Gilberto Silva. Arsenal's defenders were regularly criticised, but the lack of serious midfield cover often left them vulnerable.

Optimism over keeping the unbeaten run going faded after nine minutes against a strong Man City team when Koscielny was sent off for a linebacker challenge on Edin Džeko. Szczęsny deflected Džeko's penalty with his feet onto the post and grabbed the ball on the line, but Milner soon smashed the opener and then crossed for Džeko to make it 2-0. It ended up ten aside when Kompany was sent off after Wilshere drove through the midfield and, in what became a sadly common sight for the Englishman, overran the ball and attracted a hefty challenge that he did little to evade.

On a snowy day at Chelsea, Walcott played in Giroud, who drilled it just wide. The French striker had been finding his feet, and the net, but he was not a 'one-chance, one-goal' striker. Soon after, Ramires fouled Coquelin in midfield and, with no free-kick given, Mata capitalised on Sagna being out of position to open the scoring. Szczęsny then fouled Ramires and Frank Lampard converted the penalty to make it 2-0 with only 16 minutes gone. After half-time, Walcott finished a one-on-one, but Chelsea held on.

Arsenal finally got their first win in 2013 when they took West Ham apart with four goals in eight free-flowing second-half minutes. It finished 5-1 with Podolski scoring a left-foot hammer from 25 yards and Giroud getting a double.

Back in the FA Cup, Arsenal faced Championship side Brighton and a pumped-up home crowd. Giroud scored two good goals but the home side took advantage of Arsenal's ramshackle back five to equalise twice. After 85 minutes, Walcott's volley was deflected in to send Arsenal through with a 3-2 win.

Liverpool came to the Emirates and were 2-0 up after 60 minutes when Jordan Henderson scored after some penalty-box pinball. Henderson was the only Liverpool player in the area while Arsenal had six – either making half-hearted or clumsy challenges or simply standing and watching. However, Giroud made it five goals in three games by heading a Wilshere free-kick and two minutes later the Frenchman cushioned a pass to Walcott, who leathered the equaliser with the outside of his right foot. It was a pulsating 2-2 draw, but Arsenal were down in sixth.

Arsenal got a much-needed 1-0 win over Stoke with a deflected Podolski free-kick. It was the same score at Sunderland after Cazorla drilled the opener left-footed. Jenkinson was sent off, but Arsenal held on for the last 30 minutes as Ramsey did an admirable job at right-back and Szczęsny made two excellent close-range saves.

In the FA Cup fifth round, Championship side Blackburn blunted Arsenal's rotated side with a low block. Arsenal fans had seen this story before in Stage Two Wenger as their horseshoe-shaped passing patterns failed to penetrate a well-organised and crowded defence. They failed to mix it up with crosses or shots from outside the area, apart from a Tomáš Rosický drive that rattled the crossbar, threatened little from 16 corners and lacked clinical finishing from their 26 efforts on goal. After 72 minutes, Blackburn broke, Szczęsny palmed the shot into the dangerzone and Colin Kazim-Richards scuffed the rebound in off the post. It was the first

time in his 17 years that Wenger had lost in the FA Cup to lower-league opposition and an embarrassing double cup exit after the Bradford ignominy.

Three days later, Bayern Munich visited the Emirates in the Champions League. Walcott, not Giroud, was chosen to lead the line. After only seven minutes, Toni Kroos volleyed a cross from the edge of the area into the ground and past Szczęsny in a flash. After 21 minutes, Arsenal's zonal markers were statues as Daniel van Buyten headed a corner at the near post and Szczęsny could only palm it to Thomas Müller to make it 2-0. Early in the second half, Manuel Neuer got caught in no-man's land at a corner and it bounced for Podolski to nod in against his old club. Mario Mandžukić made it 3-1. Bayern's power, pace, skill and ruthlessness were reminiscent of Stage One Wenger teams; they were far too good for a Stage Two Wenger team.

Cazorla showed his two-footed prowess with both goals in a 2-1 win over Aston Villa, setting up a North London derby with Champions League football on the line. Giroud had the first chance, but his lack of pace and confidence in his right foot allowed Jan Vertonghen to get back and block. Gareth Bale easily broke Arsenal's offside trap and made no mistake. There was an action replay two minutes later as Arsenal again tried to play a high line. There was no communication between the defenders and Vermaelen seemed oblivious to the Spurs runner, this time Aaron Lennon, who made it 2-0. Early in the second half, Mertesacker glanced in a free-kick, but it finished 2-1. Arsenal were five and seven points behind fourth- and third-placed Chelsea and Spurs.

With the season at a new low, Wenger took action by dropping slip-sliding captain Vermaelen for a Mertesacker-Koscielny partnership and replacing Szczęsny with Łukasz Fabiański. In Munich, Giroud opened the scoring after three minutes to raise hopes of an unlikely turnaround. Bayern had most of the chances as both teams feared conceding the next goal. On 86 minutes, Koscielny headed in a corner to make it 3-3 on aggregate, but with Bayern ahead on away goals. Neuer held on to the ball, Arsenal players piled in to retrieve it and there was an entertaining bundle in the back of the net. The German side held on, and went on to win the trophy, as Arsenal became the first team to beat Bayern at the Allianz Arena all season. They had restored some pride, but it again suggested that they were a team that performed when the pressure was off.

With the high line gone, Arsenal's new-look back five kept a clean sheet at Swansea when Monreal and Gervinho goals gave a 2-0 win. Arsenal again disposed of Reading, a 4-1 win making it 16 goals against them in three games this season. At a sunny West Brom, Rosický scored a close-range diving header, then got his second when he followed up his own saved volley. Arsenal had an anxious last 20 minutes when Mertesacker was sent off for a last-man foul and James Morrison converted the penalty. However, they held on for a 2-1 win.

Against Norwich, Michael Turner scored with a free header as Arsenal's zonal marking again failed. With only five minutes left, Arsenal were heading to defeat when they got a penalty for a foul from a corner and Arteta scored. Three minutes later, Oxlade-Chamberlain burst into the box and squared for Giroud to slide in. Podolski scored from the edge of the box to seal an excellent late comeback and Arsenal's fourth win in a row took them briefly up to third.

Everton came to the Emirates with Champions League ambitions of their own. However, an entertaining and fractious game ended 0-0 as Giroud spurned the best chances. Arsenal kept their momentum going at ten-man Fulham as Steve Sidwell was sent off after only 12 minutes for going studs up on Arteta. From a free-kick, Koscielny won the first header and his centre-back partner Mertesacker had an easy finish to make it 1-0 win. Giroud got a red card of his own, and three-match ban, right at the end.

Man Utd visited having already clinched the title and Arsenal players gave them a chastening guard of honour onto the pitch. van Persie had been vindicated by playing a leading role, winning the Golden Boot for the second consecutive year and ousting British media favourite Rooney to a supporting role. Alex Ferguson retired, and by winning his 13th title with a far-from-elite squad, showed his unparalleled winning mentality one last time. After only two minutes, Rosický slipped in Walcott and he opened the scoring. Just before half-time, Sagna gave the ball to van Persie and compounded his error by sliding in on the Dutchman to give away a penalty. Sagna made a surprising number of mistakes in 2012/13 – in seven years at the club, it was the only season that he did not put in at least seven-out-of-ten performances week in week out. van Persie buried the penalty and it finished 1-1.

With three games left, Arsenal had edged into fourth. After only 20 seconds against bottom-of-the-table QPR, Arteta played in Walcott and he scored the club's fastest-ever Premier League goal to earn a 1-0 win. It ended up the Englishman's best season as he finished top scorer with 21 confident finishes and 16 assists in 43 games.

Wigan came to a wet Emirates days after winning the FA Cup and were playing for Premier League survival. A Podolski header was cancelled out by a Shaun Maloney free-kick that Szczęsny was slow to cover. In the second half, Arsenal cruised to a 4-1 win with goals from Walcott, Podolski and Ramsey sending Wigan down. Cazorla equalled the Premier League record – shared by six others including Dennis

Bergkamp, José Antonio Reyes and Fàbregas – of four assists in one game.

That left another tense last-day-of-season battle for Champions League football. This time, Arsenal went to Newcastle and, one point ahead of Spurs, knew a win would be enough. For the second season running, Koscielny got the crucial goal as he hooked in a loose ball from a free-kick and Arsenal pipped Spurs to fourth place. A nervy 1-0 win sparked vigorous celebrations from the manager and players as the fans sang, "Are you watching, Tottenham?" It sealed an excellent run-in of eight wins and two draws where Arsenal reined in their usual attacking football and became more resolute, led by the Mertesacker-Koscielny partnership, only conceding five goals in ten games.

Wenger Stage Two ended after following a now-familiar pattern: best player and captain left; season started badly; the Wengerball picked up; long-term injuries to talented players (Rosický and Diaby only played 31 games in total); ability to shoot themselves in the foot with basic individual errors; knocked out of cups and then Champions League in knockout round; thrived on a fourth-place chase to reel in Spurs and pip them on the line; feel-good factor returned and sparked optimism for the following season.

With their world-class striker leaving, Arsenal were again playing catch up just to stand still as new players were scouted and incorporated into the team. Giroud was not a van Persie replacement, but would have been an excellent back-up and foil to the Dutchman. It was just one of the what-if questions left unanswered – what if Arsenal had kept van Persie and signed Giroud, what if they organised and focused defensively for 90 minutes throughout the season, and what if they signed a reliable central midfielder and goalkeeper?

The Captain's Curse

The evolution of club captains over Arsène Wenger's 22-year reign was symbolic of the three Wenger stages as well as his disregard for the role. From warriors Tony Adams and Patrick Vieira in Stage One, to best players-in-the-playground Thierry Henry, Cesc Fàbregas and Robin van Persie in Stage Two, to injured or ageing Thomas Vermaelen, Mikel Arteta and Per Mertesacker in Stage Three.

Invincibles leader Vieira was the natural heir to club legend Adams, who captained title-winning teams in three different decades. While different characters, both left everything on the pitch and were men that teammates would follow into battle.

In Stage Two, Wenger usually gave the captaincy to the best player, sometimes partly to placate them from leaving. However, they soon did. After Henry, Wenger took a gamble in giving the armband to William Gallas, hoping his experience with France and as a serial trophy winner at Chelsea would rub off on his Project Youth youngsters. However, Gallas' Birmingham meltdown was widely derided and his on-pitch team-talk before the Chelsea game a month later came across as attention-seeking. The move backfired as a divisive figure failed to harmonise a squad that had numerous personality clashes.

Stage Three introduced the concept of the non-playing captain – a not unpredictable scenario given Vermaelen, Arteta and Mertesacker's injury problems. Between 22 November 2014 and 14 October 2017, Arsenal went an incredible 110 consecutive Premier League games without the club captain in their starting line-up. A common criticism of Arsenal during the Stage Two and Three Wenger years was that they lacked leaders – it did not help when the captain was in the stands, as he was 87% of the time in Wenger's last five years.

The honour of following in the footsteps of club legends such as Frank McLintock was regularly diminished as the armband was tossed, admittedly often when playing rotated teams in FA Cup and League Cup matches, to the most senior player or whoever had played the most games for the club. This resulted in unlikely characters such as Theo Walcott, Manuel Almunia and Andrey Arshavin leading the team into battle.

The situation reached a nadir in January 2016 when – with Arsenal chasing the title – Walcott was allowed to lead the team out against Chelsea to mark his tenth anniversary at the club – sentimentality is not the hallmark of champions and Arsenal lost 1-0 as regular captain Mertesacker was sent off after 18 minutes. They also forgot to name a captain for the second half against Man City in April 2017 after Koscielny went off injured at half-time. Wenger's successor Unai Emery took the situation to a new low with his five-captains model.

Club captain	Credentials/style	Big moment(s)	Trophies	Why end?	Years
Tony Adams 1988-2002	Warrior; inspirational; vocal; organiser; chatty with referee	Volleying home in front of the North Bank as Arsenal clinched the 1998 Premier League versus Everton – one of four titles in three different decades		Retired on a high with another Double	14
Patrick Vieira 2002-05	Warrior; led by example; first to back a teammate up	Scoring the goal against Leicester that sealed the Invincibles season and the FA Cup-winning penalty versus Man Utd with his last kick for the club		Sold to Juventus	3
Thierry Henry 2005-07	Best player; demanding; sometimes moody with teammates that did not meet his high standards	Driving a young Arsenal team to the 2006 Champions League Final		Went to Barcelona for a new challenge	2
William Gallas 2007-Nov 2008	Experience of winning the league at Chelsea	Led a young team well initially until his on-pitch meltdown at Birmingham as Arsenal's title bid unravelled		Publicly criticised teammates' mentality	1.5
Cesc Fàbregas Nov 2008-11	Best player; never hid; feisty; hated losing	The 21-year-old talisman of Project Youth played on with a broken leg against Barcelona		Wanted to return to Barcelona	2.5
Robin van Persie 2011-12	Best player; led by example; drove a weak team forward with his performances	Bailing out the team numerous times with quality finishes, often just before or after Arsenal had conceded a sloppy goal; winning the Golden Boot and Player of the Year to drive Arsenal to third		Wanted to move to Man Utd	1
Thomas Vermaelen 2012-14	Strong defensive and goalscoring start to his Arsenal career but then injured or sidelined	Lifting the 2014 FA Cup despite being an unused sub in the final – only started 13 of 56 games in 2013-14 due to injury and the Mertesacker-Koscielny partnership		Sold to Barcelona	2
Mikel Arteta 2014-16	Respected but past his best and mostly injured	Lifted the 2015 FA Cup despite not being in the match-day squad – started 13 of 110 games in two seasons		Retired	2
Per Mertesacker 2016-18	World Cup winner but past his best and mostly injured	Lifted the 2017 FA Cup – the Mertesacker Final – after not playing all season – started 11 of 114 games in two seasons		Retired	2

2013/14
FA CUP

Premier League	Fourth	
FA Cup	Winners	
Champions League	Round of 16	
League Cup	Fourth round	

PREMIER LEAGUE		PL	W	D	L	GF	GA	GD	PTS
1	MAN CITY	38	27	5	6	102	37	65	86
2	LIVERPOOL	38	26	6	6	101	50	51	84
3	CHELSEA	38	25	7	6	71	27	44	82
4	ARSENAL	38	24	7	7	68	41	27	79
5	EVERTON	38	21	9	8	61	39	22	72
6	TOTTENHAM	38	21	6	11	55	51	4	69

Highlights: Extra-time FA Cup Final win over Hull despite being 2-0 down after eight minutes; statement signing of Mesut Özil lifted the mood; overrunning Napoli in a barnstorming opening 20 minutes; "1-0 to the Arsenal" at Borussia Dortmund; three clean sheets and three wins against Spurs; assured 2-0 win over Liverpool

Lowlights: Thrashed 5-1 and 6-0 at rivals Liverpool and Chelsea; losing to Man City 6-3 and Everton 3-0; lacklustre loss at Stoke with title still on the line; going out of Champions League to Bayern Munich in round of 16 again

Player of the year: Aaron Ramsey capped off a 16-goal breakthrough season with the Cup Final winner

Top scorers: Olivier Giroud 22 (16 in PL), Ramsey 16 (10), Lukas Podolski 12 (8)

Goal of the season: Jack Wilshere finished a famous Wengerball move versus Norwich, the Emirates, Premier League

With the sun out for the first game of the season, a fixture Arsenal had not lost for 13 years, the home fans would normally have been excited for the year ahead. However, there was widespread frustration at the lack of signings, and it did not take much for the atmosphere to turn sour as a 3-1 loss to Aston Villa provoked boos and chants demanding the club spend money.

The 2013 summer was another one dominated by transfer speculation. However, this year it was about who would be signed, not who would leave. The year before, chief executive Ivan Gazidis had signalled a new era as sponsorship and kit deals tied to the stadium move or simply poor value expired and were upgraded and the club put their faith in the UEFA Financial Fair Play Regulations: "In the next two years, we will have the financial resources to sit and compete among the leading clubs in the world, which is an extraordinary achievement." He doubled down at the end of the 2012/13 season: "The fact is this year we are beginning to see something we have been planning for some time, which is the escalation in our financial firepower." He also put the onus on reluctant-spender Arsène Wenger: "He has new tools available to him financially and I think he'll make good use of them."

Argentine forward Gonzalo Higuaín looked set to sign from Real Madrid, but Napoli took advantage of Arsenal dithering over the price and the possibility of capturing Luis Suárez.

Arsenal got wind of a buyout clause in the Uruguayan's contract and offered Liverpool £40m + £1. Liverpool rejected it and made Arsenal a laughing stock by publicising the offer, with owner John Henry tweeting, "What do you think they're smoking over there at Emirates?"

Against Villa, the season started well as after six minutes Alex Oxlade-Chamberlain surged down the left and crossed low for Olivier Giroud to sweep home. However, 15 minutes later, Gabby Agbonlahor burst through a hole in Arsenal's centre and Wojciech Szczęsny rushed out and fouled him. The ball fell to Andreas Weimann, whose effort hit the side-netting. Despite playing the advantage, referee Anthony Taylor then awarded a penalty. Szczęsny saved Christian Benteke's soft spot-kick but the rebound bounced up nicely for the striker to head in.

In the second half, Laurent Koscielny made a good sliding tackle on Agbonlahor, but Taylor gave another penalty, as well as a yellow card to the defender. Benteke only needed one attempt this time and Villa were ahead 2-1. Taylor was not done as he gave Koscielny a second yellow for a routine foul. Despite playing 25 minutes with ten men, Arsenal had 64% possession, but Villa were efficient on the counter-attack and made it 3-1. The crowd's angry boos were aimed at the referee, the board and, increasingly, the manager.

The knives were out as Arsenal faced a difficult Champions League qualifier in Fenerbahçe and the prospect of going out before the group stage. Koscielny's season already seemed cursed as he got a kick in the face and was taken to hospital pouring with blood. Arsenal, unusually wearing red shirts and blue shorts, sprang into life in the second half led by Aaron Ramsey, who slipped in Theo Walcott to cross low for Kieran Gibbs and then fired the second from 20 yards. A Giroud penalty sealed an impressive 3-0 win. The second leg saw a 2-0 win with a Ramsey double, the second of which was an instinctive sidefoot volley.

Arsenal unveiled a smart new yellow-and-blue away kit at Fulham. Giroud opened the scoring before Lukas Podolski rattled a rebound from the edge of the area past goalkeeper David Stockdale and three defenders. The German drilled another in the second half to give Arsenal a 3-1 win. As Wenger once said, "If there's one you want to see in front of the goal in a shooting position, it's him." Unfortunately, Podolski then picked up a hamstring injury that sidelined him for three and a half months.

Then a much-hyped Spurs team came to the Emirates with £110m of new signings, funded by the sale of Gareth Bale to Real Madrid. Arsenal had only added French under-20 international Yaya Sanogo for a nominal fee and out-of-contract Mathieu Flamini, who was training with the squad to keep fit. However, Spurs had bought quantity

**TYPICAL LINE-UP
(4-2-3-1)**

Players in: Mesut Özil, Yaya Sanogo, Mathieu Flamini, *Kim Källström* (loan)

Players out: Andrey Arshavin, Gervinho, Marouane Chamakh, Denílson, Sébastien Squillaci, André Santos, Vito Mannone

not quality. After 23 minutes, Walcott crossed low from the right. In his early Arsenal career, Giroud often missed near-post chances when they came from the right, but was prolific from the left as either way he would use his left foot. This time, however, he produced an exquisite flick with the outside of his favourite foot and the ball spun past Hugo Lloris at the near post for Giroud's fourth goal in five games. Flamini came on for his first Arsenal game in five years and quickly got stuck in. Arsenal held on, finishing with four full-backs on the pitch, for an excellent 1-0 win.

On 2 September, the last day of the transfer window, Arsenal smashed their transfer record and signed assist-master Mesut Özil from Real Madrid for £42.4m, as the Spanish club looked to fund their Bale purchase. It was a statement signing, the second-highest fee in British history and an acknowledged world-class player from one of the top clubs in Europe. Stage Three Wenger had begun.

In mid-September, Arsenal fans got their first chance to see Özil in action against Sunderland, and their spirits were lifted after only ten minutes as he brought down a Gibbs pass with a classy touch and squared for Giroud to open the scoring for the fourth league game in a row. Just after half-time, Craig Gardner equalised from the penalty spot after Koscielny had dived in on Adam Johnson. Then man-of-the-match Ramsey cracked another volley from the edge of the area and finished excellent interplay between himself, Özil and Giroud to make it 3-1.

Arsenal beat Stoke at their own game by scoring three goals from Özil set-pieces. Ramsey netted a rebound off goalkeeper Asmir Begović, while Per Mertesacker and Bacary Sagna scored looping headers. At Swansea, 18-year-old Serge Gnabry became Arsenal's second-youngest Premier League scorer after Cesc Fàbregas with a confident finish that should have been the first of many for the club. Ramsey buried a classic end-to-end move that started with Szczęsny, featured a Ramsey flick, a strong Jack Wilshere tackle and a Giroud back-heel. It was the Welshman's eighth goal in eight games and, although Swansea got one back late on, a 2-1 win put Arsenal top of the table. Arsenal's run of away wins ended at eight, equalling the 2001/02 title-winning team's league record, when they drew 1-1 with West Brom. Wilshere, often a reluctant shooter, smashed a 25-yarder.

The English midfielder found the net again in the next game versus Norwich, and it was Stage Three Wengerball at its finest. It started in the Arsenal half and featured a blur of passes and one-twos between Santi Cazorla, Wilshere and Giroud, the second of which saw Giroud and Wilshere trade instinctive flicks. Wilshere ran on to the final ball to finish right-footed to score the

BBC Goal of the Season. Goal-hungry Ramsey left defenders sprawling by dropping his shoulder twice and finishing. An Özil double, including a rare header, sealed a 4-1 win.

At Crystal Palace, Gnabry won a penalty that Mikel Arteta converted. The Spaniard was then sent off for a professional foul on Marouane Chamakh just inside his own half. It was a dubious decision as Chamakh's heavy touch pushed the ball towards the corner, not goal, and he ran across Arteta, causing them both to go down. However, Arteta should have remembered his former teammate's red card- and penalty-inducing ability. Szczęsny made two excellent close-range saves and, late on, Ramsey crossed for Giroud to seal a hard-fought 2-0 win.

After going out of the League Cup 2-0 to Chelsea, Arsenal faced a tough November beginning with a first-versus-second battle with Brendan Rodgers' Liverpool. Cazorla opened the scoring after heading a bouncing cross onto the post and volleying the rebound into the net with typically-assured technique. Özil found Ramsey 25 yards out and the Welshman added another to his one-man goal-of-the-season competition with a brilliant swerving half-volley over Simon Mignolet's dive. Arsenal were five points clear at the top of the table and the first day of the season was a distant memory.

In the Champions League, Arsenal were drawn in the 'group of death' with Borussia Dortmund, Napoli and Marseille. In Marseille, Walcott volleyed a loose ball into the roof of the net and Ramsey again drove in from the edge of the area. Marseille got a late penalty but it was an important 2-1 win for Arsenal.

An unbeaten Napoli looked a tougher test but Arsenal raced out of the blocks and produced a brilliant half of flowing football. After eight minutes, Ramsey pulled the ball back to the edge of the area at pace, where Özil nonchalantly sidefooted it first-time high into the net for his first Arsenal goal. Seven minutes later, Özil drove into the box on the right and cut back for Giroud to make it 2-0. It was an impressive tenth consecutive win.

Then Jürgen Klopp's 'heavy metal' Dortmund side came to the Emirates. Ramsey lost the ball on the edge of his area and Henrikh Mkhitaryan hit it past a flat-footed Szczęsny. Rosický cracked a left-foot volley from 25 yards that looked sure to go in until Mats Hummels appeared on the line to block. Just before half-time, defender Neven Subotic and goalkeeper Roman Weidenfeller made a mess of a Sagna cross, leaving Giroud to smash into an empty net. In the second half, Arsenal pressed for the winner and Cazorla clipped the crossbar with a curling effort. However, with ten minutes to go, Dortmund applied the sucker-punch as Robert Lewandowski was left alone to volley the 2-1 winner. The Polish hitman was lucky to be on the pitch after earlier only getting a yellow card for an elbow to Koscielny's mouth.

In the return fixture, Arsenal silenced the Yellow Wall with an uncharacteristic smash and grab of their own. They withstood Dortmund's attacks, kept possession and scored with their first effort on goal in the 62nd minute, a Ramsey header. Arsenal became the first English team to win at the Westfalenstadion and Wenger said, "We were light metal."

It only took 30 seconds for Wilshere to open the scoring against Marseille, as he curled into the far corner from the inside-right position. Steve Mandanda saved a weak penalty from Özil before Wilshere completed his first double for a 2-0 win that meant Arsenal went to Napoli needing to avoid a three-goal defeat to qualify. It was going to plan in Italy until Higuaín scored after 73 minutes and Arteta received his second yellow card soon after. Fortunately, Rafa Benítez's side seemed to settle for that, relying on the Marseille-Dortmund game remaining 1-1. In the 92nd minute, Napoli made it 2-0, but Dortmund got a late goal of their own to leave three teams on 12 points and Arsenal to qualify in second place on goal difference. A draw or win would have meant more straightforward knockout

opponents; instead they again faced holders Bayern Munich.

In mid-November, Arsenal had a great chance to overcome their Old Trafford inferiority complex as David Moyes' Man Utd were struggling in eighth. The Arsenal squad had been hit by a virus, with Mertesacker and Rosický unable to play, but it did not excuse a lacklustre performance that saw 60% sterile possession, only two shots on target and Robin van Persie head the winner.

Arsenal got back on track against Mauricio Pochettino's third-placed Southampton when Giroud embarrassed goalkeeper Artur Boruc by easily thwarting his cumbersome double attempt at a Cruyff Turn and scoring into the empty net. The Frenchman made it 2-0 with a penalty. At Cardiff, Özil again supplied the bullets for Ramsey twice and Flamini once to crack impressive finishes. The 3-0 win kept Arsenal four points ahead at the top of the table with a tough December to come. With that in mind, Wenger made changes for the visit of Hull, including giving Nicklas Bendtner his first start in the league for two and a half years. It only took two minutes for the Dane to head the opener and set up a 2-0 win, Arsenal's 11th in 13 since the opening day.

Four days later saw an entertaining game between Arsenal and Roberto

Martínez's Everton. Özil gave Arsenal the lead after 80 minutes, but within four minutes substitute Gerard Deulofeu smashed a shot past Szczęsny's late dive. With the last kick of the game, Giroud rattled the crossbar with a swerving volley from 25 yards – Arsenal were inches from a seven-point lead.

Next up was an early kick-off at Man City, who were averaging four goals a game at home. They soon matched that. Agüero volleyed the opener from a corner as Koscielny went to sleep. Walcott, who was back from injury for his first start since September, bobbled an equaliser. After Álvaro Negredo and Fernandinho made it 3-1, Walcott scored an impressive curler from the inside-right to raise hopes of an unlikely comeback. It remained a basketball game as Man City pounced on Arsenal errors and Yaya Touré, David Silva and Samir Nasri outnumbered and outplayed them in midfield. It ended up 6-3 as Arsenal, who were not helped by the referee and linesmen, could have scored more – Giroud in particular had one of his bad days; however, so could Man City as only seven of their 22 efforts were on target.

Chelsea parked the bus at a wet Emirates. Wenger unusually made no substitutions and Giroud had a great chance at the end but sliced wide and struck a familiar pose – prostrate with head down in the turf. José Mourinho got the draw he wanted as the players left the pitch to chants of "Boring boring Chelsea."

On Boxing Day, Szczęsny spilt a shot and gifted West Ham's Carlton Cole the opener. Arsenal produced a strong second-half comeback though as Walcott scored rare left-foot and headed finishes. Podolski returned and thumped a typical left-footer, but crucially Ramsey suffered a thigh strain. Giroud, who had not scored for seven games, headed the winner in a scrappy match at Newcastle before two late goals from Bendtner and Walcott earnt a 2-0 win over Cardiff. Arsenal were top again and had earnt the most points in the Premier League in 2013 – could they do the same in a season?

In the FA Cup, Arsenal were drawn against their North London rivals.

Spurs' latest manager Tim Sherwood picked a 4-4-2 formation and they were overrun in midfield. Gnabry showed pace, dribbling ability and a composed final ball, most crucially when he teed up Cazorla, who hit a sweet strike with his left foot to open the scoring. In the second half, Rosický robbed last-man Danny Rose on the halfway line and the 33-year-old had the legs to race towards goal and skill to dink over Lloris. The celebrations on and off the pitch were huge, and the home fans reminded Spurs' manager of his boyhood allegiance with chants of "Tim Sherwood's a Gooner."

Walcott, playing as striker, was given the freedom of the Emirates by Spurs' back-line and his speed was a constant threat. Sadly, with ten minutes left, he stepped on the ball when making a tackle and ruptured his anterior cruciate ligament. Despite the serious injury, as he was carried past the Spurs fans on a stretcher, Walcott sat up with a cheeky grin and mockingly signalled the 2-0 scoreline with his hands. It was a memorable North London derby moment that endeared him to Arsenal fans almost as much as any of his goals.

However, it was a blow as Giroud was left to carry the striker burden and Arsenal had lost the one player that could run in behind. With midfielders Ramsey, Wilshere, Oxlade-Chamberlain and Abou Diaby also injured to various degrees, the January transfer window offered the chance to strengthen for a title push. However, there was no activity until the final day of the month

when Arsenal signed 31-year-old Kim Källström. Unbelievably, the Swedish midfielder's medical revealed damaged vertebrae, incurred while training on a Dubai beach, but Arsenal had left it so late, they went through with the deal anyway.

Arsenal got the job done in the next two league games, winning 2-1 at Aston Villa and 2-0 against Fulham, a Cazorla double in the latter showcasing the Spaniard's two-footed prowess. They then dispatched League One side Coventry in the FA Cup 4-0 with a Podolski brace.

At Southampton, José Fonte headed the home side into the lead, but Arsenal turned it around with a Giroud flick and Cazorla bobbler. However, minutes later, Adam Lallana equalised. With ten minutes left, Flamini was sent off for a two-footed foul and Arsenal were grateful for a 2-2 draw. Against Crystal Palace, Oxlade-Chamberlain made his first start since injuring knee ligaments on the opening day of the season and netted a double to give a 2-0 win.

After a run of six wins and two draws, Arsenal were top of the table. Mertesacker said, "February could be the season-defining month with a lot of crucial games coming up." He was right. Arsenal went to Anfield in the early kick-off with a chance to make a statement. From the kick-off, Mertesacker unnecessarily fouled Suárez and an unmarked Martin Škrtel kneed in the free-kick. Nine minutes later, the centre-back headed in a corner, again under little pressure. Jordan Henderson robbed Özil on halfway and a quick transition ended with Daniel Sturridge making it 3-0. The game was over at 1.05pm.

Liverpool were rampant while Arsenal capitulated. No one on the pitch or the sidelines addressed the suicidal high line, midfielders piling forward or the lack of fight. Liverpool picked them off at will, surprisingly only scoring two more through Raheem Sterling. It ended in a humiliating 5-1 loss as Arteta converted a penalty, and yet again Arsenal's mental fragility was questioned. The Gunners were knocked off the top and Liverpool went on a title charge, winning 11 consecutive matches. Four days later, a traumatised Arsenal played out a goalless draw with a cautious Man Utd team.

Arsenal had to play Liverpool again, this time in the FA Cup at the Emirates. They had not fully learnt the lessons from Anfield as Liverpool again opened with a high tempo and twice played in Sturridge behind a flat defence. Luckily, both chances were on his weaker right foot. A free-kick fell to Oxlade-Chamberlain and he buried it. In the second half, the Ox cut back for Podolski to finish with his right foot. Gerrard got one back with a penalty, but Arsenal held out thanks to saves from cup goalkeeper Łukasz Fabiański

and referee Howard Webb not giving another penalty despite Oxlade-Chamberlain clattering Suárez.

Against Champions League holders Bayern Munich, now managed by Pep Guardiola, Wenger surprisingly gave Sanogo only his second start ahead of Giroud, who had made the tabloids with some late-night hotel shenanigans before the Crystal Palace match, and Podolski. Arsenal started strongly as Özil checked inside Jérôme Boateng and drew a penalty in the eighth minute. As he did against Marseille, Arsenal's record signing used a stuttering run-up and stroked a weak effort that was easily saved, this time by German teammate Manuel Neuer. Eight minutes before half-time, Toni Kroos chipped over Arsenal's defence, Arjen Robben beat the onrushing Szczęsny to the ball and the goalkeeper took him out to earn a red card. Although David Alaba hit the outside of the post with the spot-kick, they proved two key moments. Not surprisingly, Bayern then dominated with Kroos running the show and Arsenal's ten men only having 12% possession in the second half. Kroos curled into the top corner from 20 yards and at the end Thomas Müller made it 2-0 with a header.

Arsenal got their title bid back on track with a 4-1 win over Sunderland at the end of February, the highlight of which

THE MAN WITH THE BROKEN BACK

The FA Cup semi-final penalty shootout win was Arsenal's seventh successful shootout in eight since the 2000 UEFA Cup Final against Galatasaray. This was not necessarily due to meticulous preparation. Källström revealed how he came to be one of the takers after the draw against Wigan: "I hear Wenger shouting in French: "Kim, do you take penalties?" "Yeah, I'd be glad to take one." "Good. You're second." The Swede only featured four times after Wenger signed him despite the medical revealing three vertebral fractures. "Although my contribution was small in the 120-year history of the club, it was a highlight for me. The greatest 15 minutes of my life..." Like Fàbregas and van Persie before him, Källström left with a single FA Cup winner's medal.

was Rosický finishing a brilliant team move with a one-two with Giroud and dinked finish – Wilshere's goal against Norwich was no fluke. Arsenal then went to Stoke in second place, one point behind Chelsea. However, they put in a lacklustre performance and lost 1-0 to a poor team, although one that was always fired up for a home game against a Wenger team. The manager said Arsenal were "too selfish" as they only registered two shots on target and lost to a second-half Jonathan Walters penalty.

Arsenal again looked to the FA Cup for relief, although they faced another tricky tie against an Everton side in good form. Cazorla played in Özil for his first goal in three months, but Romelu Lukaku tapped in the equaliser from a counter-attack. In the second half, Oxlade-Chamberlain won a penalty off Gareth Barry, which Arteta dispatched to the left. Mark Clattenburg made him retake it as Giroud had encroached and Arteta calmly passed it to the right. Substitute Giroud scored two in three minutes – the second of which was an end-to-end move involving Cazorla, Rosický and Özil – to make it 4-1 and Arsenal fans expectantly sang, "She wore a yellow ribbon."

For the second year running, Arsenal went to Bayern looking for an unlikely turnaround. This year, however, it was never on as the Bundesliga leaders controlled the tie. In the second half, Bastien Schweinsteiger opened the scoring, but two minutes later Podolski got away with a push on Philip Lahm and hit a rocket into the roof of the net from a tight angle. At the end, Robben – who Wenger called "a great player but also a good diver" – won a penalty off Koscielny. However, Fabiański pushed Thomas Müller's effort onto the post and as the ball rolled invitingly on the line, the goalkeeper brilliantly palmed it away from a sliding Müller. It finished 3-1 on aggregate and Arsenal went out in the last 16 for the fourth year running.

A few days later, Arsenal went to Spurs and took only 72 seconds to silence White Hart Lane. The ball bounced back to Rosický on the right corner of the penalty area and he leathered a trademark *trivela* into the far top corner. The Little Mozart was showing a liking for North London derby moments like his number-seven predecessor Robert Pires. Mertesacker and Koscielny, who blocked a Nacer Chadli shot off the line after Szczęsny had missed a cross, led a resolute defensive effort and Arsenal held on to win 1-0, their first victory at White Hart Lane for over six years. With Chelsea losing to Aston Villa, the gap was back to four points and Arsenal had a game in hand.

That set up a huge top-of-the-table clash at Stamford Bridge – Wenger's 1,000th game in charge – on the back of an increasingly nasty war of words between two managers that did not like each other, culminating in Mourinho labelling Wenger a "specialist in failure." The sun was out for the 12.45pm kick-off and immediately Giroud's effort was saved by Petr Čech. After four minutes, Oxlade-Chamberlain lost the ball in midfield, Chelsea broke and Samuel Eto'o curled left-footed past Szczęsny. Three minutes later, Cazorla was tackled on halfway and André Schürrle shot past Szczęsny's non-dive.

It was a wild start, but it had only just begun. Chelsea broke again, Eden Hazard shot and Oxlade-Chamberlain got fingertips to it with a panicked diving save, even though the ball was actually going just wide. Referee Andre Marriner sent off a bewildered Gibbs, despite the Ox telling Marriner he was the one that should go. Hazard stroked in the penalty to make it 3-0 after 17 minutes. It was embarrassing for both Marriner and Arsenal as yet another away fixture was effectively over before lunchtime. Chelsea scored three more as they capitalised on individual mistakes and a ragged Arsenal. Wenger's milestone ended in humiliation – his joint-highest margin of defeat and Chelsea's biggest win over Arsenal – and any serious title pretensions were blown away.

In Arsenal's game in hand, substitute Podolski looked to have led a comeback win against relegation-threatened Swansea with a goal and assist for Giroud in the space of three minutes. However, in the 90th minute, Leon Brittan drove into the box, Mertesacker toed it on to Szczęsny and it rebounded off Flamini to trickle into an empty net for a farcical own-goal. It could have got worse in the 94th minute as referee Lee Probert blew the final whistle with Jonathan de Guzman through on goal. It finished 2-2 to the fury of the Swansea players. Another draw followed against Man City as Flamini cancelled out David Silva's opener.

April began with another early kick-off away from home. The outcome was familiar as Arsenal were outplayed at Everton, losing 3-0. It meant they had won no league games against the top five and they now had to focus on preventing Everton from overtaking them in fourth rather than the title.

There was still the FA Cup to play and Arsenal were favourites in the semi-final against Championship side and holders Wigan. Wembley was red and white with more than 50,000 Arsenal fans in the 82,000 crowd. Arsenal dominated possession but it was mostly slow passing as the occasion seemed to get to them again. After 63 minutes, Mertesacker dived in on Callum McManaman and Jordi Gómez converted the penalty.

Wenger brought on Giroud to replace Podolski, not Sanogo, sparking dissent among Arsenal fans. Sanogo was raw and enthusiastic, but not of the technical quality required. Arsenal pressed for an equaliser as journalists honed their Wenger obituaries. Scott Carson pushed a Gibbs header onto the post and from the resultant corner, the ball fell to Oxlade-Chamberlain,

who scuffed a volley back in. It came to Mertesacker, who redeemed himself by stooping to head the bouncing ball in. In extra time, Oxlade-Chamberlain crashed a shot against the crossbar, but it went to penalties. Fabiański saved the first two from Gary Caldwell and Jack Collison, while Arteta, Källström, Giroud and Cazorla scored comfortably and the relief was palpable.

Arsenal beat West Ham 3-1 with two typical Podolski strikes. The other goal was not typical Arsenal as Thomas Vermaelen played a long ball into the box that Giroud took down with a Bergkamp-esque touch and drilled in right-footed. They then dispatched FA Cup Final opponents Hull 3-0 in blustery conditions as Podolski scored another double and Ramsey showed what Arsenal had missed over the previous months. A third consecutive win, this time 3-0 against Newcastle, meant Champions League football was secured and Arsenal could relax in the last two games ahead of the cup final.

Giroud got his 22nd goal of the season as Arsenal beat West Brom 1-0, meaning they were unbeaten at home in the league since the opening day. Against relegated Norwich, Wilshere returned from a foot injury for the final 30 minutes, while Diaby came on for his first game in 14 months. Arsenal won 2-0 as Ramsey hammered another brilliant volley and Carl Jenkinson celebrated his first goal like a true boyhood Arsenal fan.

Arsenal finished fourth, seven points behind Champions Man City. Having topped the table for 128 days of the season, they had regrets, although not as many as Liverpool who were five points clear at the top with three matches to go.

That left the FA Cup Final on 17 May 2014. Arsenal were back at Wembley, having never left London during the entire competition, and 'only' had to beat Hull, a team they had already dispatched 2-0 and 3-0 in the league. However, any complacency was quickly wiped away:

- 0-1 (4 minutes): Hull floated a corner to the edge of the area, Tom Huddlestone volleyed and James Chester diverted it in.

- 0-2 (8 minutes): Arsenal cleared a free-kick, Hull crossed it back in, Alex Bruce headed against the post and Curtis Davies buried the rebound. It was Birmingham 2011 all over again. A shell-shocked Arsenal were heading for their fourth consecutive loss in a final.

- 0-2 (13 minutes): Bruce headed a looping header goalwards and Gibbs crucially headed off the line. Hull's centre-backs were having a field day against Arsenal's ball-watching zonal markers.

- 1-2 (17 minutes): Cazorla curled a brilliant 30-yard free-kick that Allan McGregor could only tip onto the underside of the bar and in.

- 1-2 (43 minutes): Matty Fryatt was through on goal after outmuscling Koscielny, but referee Probert awarded a free-kick to Arsenal.

- 1-2 (58 minutes): Giroud chased a high ball in the box and Huddlestone pulled him back by the neck. No penalty given.

- 1-2 (61 minutes): Wenger went two upfront, bringing on Sanogo for Podolski. Arsenal were on top but without the injured Walcott and Oxlade-Chamberlain's pace, Hull's five-man defence crowded out Giroud and faced little wide threat. The extra presence in the box and Sanogo's unpredictability and mobility caused plenty of mayhem.

- 1-2 (64 minutes): Sanogo flicked on a corner and it hit Jake Livermore's outstretched arm. No penalty given.

- 1-2 (68 minutes): Cazorla cut inside Davies on the right side of the area, and the defender took out the Spaniard. No penalty given.

- 2-2 (71 minutes): Sagna headed a corner towards goal and Koscielny hooked in to again show his poacher's instinct and eye for an important goal.

- 2-2 (79 minutes): Sanogo poked it across goal and the best chance of the game fell to Gibbs, who hit a wild effort over the bar from seven yards.

- 2-2 (80 minutes): Ramsey squared for Cazorla, who was lining up to shoot until David Meyler nudged him over. No penalty given.

- 2-2 (94 minutes): Giroud soared to head a Ramsey cross against the bar as it remained one-way traffic in extra time.

- 2-2 (105 minutes): Rosický and Wilshere came on for Özil and Cazorla and added zip against a tired defence.

- 3-2 (109 minutes): The ball bounced off Sanogo, Giroud back-heeled, Ramsey burst into the box and finished with an instinctive low-backlift half-volley into the bottom corner.

- 3-2 (116 minutes): Mertesacker comically fell over, gifting the ball to Sone Aluko. The striker rounded Fabiański, who had charged out of his area in a throwback to the 2007 League Cup Final, and shot from wide left. Fortunately, Aluko was no Didier Drogba and the ball rolled agonisingly wide of the empty net and the retreating Gibbs.

- 3-2 (121 minutes): Wilshere played in Rosický whose shot was blocked on the line.

At the final whistle, there was a huge outpouring of both relief and joy from the fans, players and Wenger. Substitute and club captain Vermaelen lifted the cup, Wenger threw his red Arsenal tie into the crowd, and the players soaked him with champagne and gave him the bumps. It was his fifth FA Cup win and Arsenal's record-equalling 11th.

After years of criticising Arsenal for not winning a trophy, cynics now argued that it was only the FA Cup, it was only Hull, they were lucky and they had four home draws. 250,000 fans at the Islington parade disagreed. Arsenal won a trophy, beating three top-five teams on the way. They also overcame a 2-0 deficit and a referee that failed to award multiple penalties. Two weeks later, Wenger signed a three-year contract – it would have been a lot harder to have done so on the back of a loss to Wigan or Hull and another trophy failure.

It was a successful season as, although Arsenal again finished fourth and again were knocked out of the Champions League in the first knockout round, they got the trophy monkey off their back and registered their highest points total and best title challenge since 2007/08. Along the way, they played sublime football and scored numerous classic goals. They led the league for much of the campaign, but not during the business end of the season as the Anfield thrashing in February derailed them, with only two wins in the following eight games. Injuries, the reliance on Giroud upfront and poor results against the top teams prevented them from reaching the next level.

Ramsey was the standout player with his drive, energy and desire to make third-man runs off Giroud. He scored 16 goals including volleys and long-range strikes. The previously-maligned player won over the fans and was badly missed during his more-than-three-month injury absence, only playing 23 of the 38 league games.

Giroud's 22 goals and ten assists were a good – but not elite – return, often coming in streaks followed by dry spells. He was an excellent target man and pivot, but his lack of pace limited Arsenal's vertical threat. Almost everything went into Giroud's feet with his back to goal. With the likes of Özil, Ramsey, Cazorla, Wilshere and Rosický buzzing around, zipping short passes to each other, it led to some brilliant football. Against more organised teams, it resulted in sterile possession in front of the defence. Giroud was unfairly asked to carry a heavy burden as Arsenal went into the season with Sanogo and Bendtner as back-up strikers, and Wenger did not rate Podolski at centre-forward.

Arsenal were exposed against the top-five Premier League teams, particularly away from home where they conceded 20 goals in four games. The failure to adjust tactics was frustrating as Wenger's 'go-out-and-play' message led to a familiar pattern where the opponent would press in midfield, force a turnover and quickly overload a ragged defence. Why not adopt a more pragmatic approach, in particular at the start of games, by restraining the full-backs and midfield and limiting the tight interplay to the last third of the pitch?

Defensively, Arsenal were generally better. Szczęsny and Gibbs were more consistent, with the Polish goalkeeper joint winner of the Premier League Golden Glove for most clean sheets with Čech. Key was the Koscielny-Mertesacker centre-back partnership, which relegated captain Vermaelen to the bench and played to each other's strengths – Koscielny's sharp front-foot defending and Mertesacker's positional sense and reading of the game; impressively, the BFG conceded just 12 fouls in the league all season.

Özil finished the season with seven goals and 14 assists, creating a chance every 28 minutes. After an excellent start where he galvanised the players and fans with his silky touches and passing as well as intelligent movement to find space and create it for others, he faded in the second half of the season. He had a good, but not £42.4m, season as Arsenal learnt that he was not the man for the big occasion or someone that would carry a team on his shoulders – a symbolic signing to kick off Stage Three Wenger in every way.

2014/15
FA CUP REPEAT

Premier League	Third
FA Cup	Winners
Champions League	Round of 16
League Cup	Third round
Community Shield	Winners

PREMIER LEAGUE	PL	W	D	L	GF	GA	GD	PTS
1 CHELSEA	38	26	9	3	73	32	41	87
2 MAN CITY	38	24	7	7	83	38	45	79
3 ARSENAL	38	22	9	7	71	36	35	75
4 MAN UTD	38	20	10	8	62	37	25	70
5 TOTTENHAM	38	19	7	12	58	53	5	64
6 LIVERPOOL	38	18	8	12	52	48	4	62

Highlights: Hammering Aston Villa 4-0 to secure back-to-back FA Cups; long-awaited tactical and disciplined away win at Man City; FA Cup quarter-final win at Old Trafford; 4-1 cruise against Liverpool

Lowlights: 3-1 home defeat to Monaco; two wins in first eight games meaning the title was gone by November; blowing a 3-0 lead against Anderlecht; gifting a poor Man Utd a 2-1 win; limp away losses at Stoke and Southampton

Player of the year: Alexis Sánchez added quality, drive and energy to Arsenal's attack, with 25 goals and 12 assists

Top scorers: Sánchez 25 (16 in PL), Olivier Giroud 19 (14), Aaron Ramsey 10 (6)

Goal of the season: Ramsey drilled a searing left-footed volley from 30 yards versus Galatasaray, Türk Telekom Stadium, Champions League

New captain Mikel Arteta lifted more silverware at Wembley when Arsenal beat Champions Man City 3-0 in the Community Shield with good finishes from Santi Cazorla, Aaron Ramsey and Olivier Giroud. Along with the marquee signing of Alexis Sánchez from Barcelona for £34m, there was optimism that the 2014 FA Cup win would be a springboard for more success.

A busy transfer window saw Thomas Vermaelen sold to Barcelona and out-of-contract Bacary Sagna and Łukasz Fabiański sign for Man City and Swansea respectively. Sagna was replaced by his rival French right-back Mathieu Debuchy – seeing a quality defender leave for free and paying £12m for a replacement who was only two years younger was not great business. After seven years of committed service, for most of which he was the best right-back in the league, the 31-year-old Sagna was finally rewarded with a trophy in his final game and deserved a last payday. In the latter part of his Arsenal career, Fabiański lost the nerves exhibited in his early performances and rarely let the team down – he went on to be a consistent and assured goalkeeper for Swansea, West Ham and Poland. In came 19-year-old centre-back Calum Chambers and Colombian international goalkeeper David Ospina.

Now playing in Puma's too-tight shirts after they replaced Nike as kit manufacturer, Arsenal opened up against Crystal Palace without World Cup winners Mesut Özil, Per Mertesacker and Lukas Podolski. The away side were manager-less as Tony Pulis had left two days earlier. It looked like another bad first day of the season when Brede Hangeland headed the opener. Laurent Koscielny equalised with a header of his own and on 89 minutes Jason Puncheon got his second yellow card. It gave Arsenal the momentum and Ramsey tapped in a rebound for their first opening weekend win since 2009.

Arsenal still seemed to be on their summer holidays when they went 2-0 down at Everton. Giroud came on at half-time and made an impact. After 83 minutes Ramsey finished Cazorla's low cross and on 90 Giroud headed to make it 2-2. Unfortunately, there was still time for the striker to break his tibia when he innocuously blocked a clearance by Sylvain Distin, putting him out for three months.

Arsenal faced a precarious Champions League qualifier against Beşiktaş. The away leg finished goalless as Demba Ba embarrassed Wojciech Szczęsny and hit the bar from the kick-off and Ramsey was sent off late on for two bookings. At the Emirates, Arsenal were lucky not to concede two penalties and Sánchez sidefooted a crucial first goal. Debuchy, sporting a Travis Bickle mohawk, was unlucky to receive a second yellow card and Arsenal saw out a nervy last 15 minutes to take their usual place in the group stages.

At promoted Leicester, Sánchez scored again but a Leonardo Ulloa header quickly made it 1-1. Despite 68% possession, Arsenal did not create many clear chances, not helped by Yaya Sanogo's lack of finesse upfront. Two days later, Arsenal signed Danny Welbeck from Man Utd on the last day of the transfer window.

Welbeck made his debut against Man City and soon had a chance to make his mark when one-on-one with Joe Hart, but his pitching-wedged effort rebounded off the post. Jesús Navas crossed low and Sergio Agüero lost Mathieu Flamini to open the scoring. In the second half, Jack Wilshere easily beat Gaël Clichy on the right and coolly dinked past Hart right-footed. Ten minutes later, Wilshere headed back into the box and Sánchez showed perfect technique to volley sidefooted high past Hart. In a frenetic finish, Debuchy was taken off on a stretcher with an ankle injury that put him out for three months, Martín Demichelis headed in a corner, both Arsenal posts were struck and Samir Nasri had a goal disallowed for offside. A pulsating game finished 2-2.

At Aston Villa, Arsenal clicked in a three-minute blitz before half-time: Welbeck's through-ball set up Özil and he passed it home; Özil crossed low for Welbeck to net his first Arsenal goal; and Aly Cissokho deflected in Kieran

TYPICAL LINE-UP
(4-2-3-1)

12
Giroud
Welbeck
Sànchez
Walcott

17
Sànchez
Cazorla
Özil

16
Ramsey
Sànchez
Ox-Chamberlain
Walcott

11
Özil
Ramsey
Rosický

19
Cazorla
Wilshere

34
Coquelin
Flamini
Arteta

18
Monreal
Gibbs

6
Koscielny
Monreal

4
Mertesacker
Gabriel

39
Bellerín
Chambers
Debuchy

13
Ospina
Szczęsny

Players in: Alexis Sánchez, Mathieu Debuchy, David Ospina, Calum Chambers, Danny Welbeck, *Krystian Bielik*, *Gabriel Paulista*

Players out: Thomas Vermaelen, Bacary Sagna, Łukasz Fabiański, Nicklas Bendtner, Chu-young, Thomas Eisfeld, Johan Djourou, *Lukas Podolski* (loan), *Yaya Sanogo* (loan)

Gibbs' shot to make it 3-0. Arsenal then went out of the League Cup to Southampton, losing 2-1 as Sánchez curled a brilliant free-kick into the top corner, but Nathaniel Clyne hammered an even better long-range effort.

Arsenal dominated the North London derby at the Emirates despite having to replace both Arteta and Ramsey in the first half due to calf and hamstring injuries, a regular issue for the latter. However, Spurs took the lead in the second half when Christian Eriksen robbed substitute Flamini and Nacer Chadli slotted home. Alex Oxlade-Chamberlain sidefooted a deserved equaliser helped by a classic Welbeck 'assist', the Englishman throwing off defenders with his clumsy air-shot. Despite the shot count being 16-6, it ended 1-1 and Wilshere also suffered an ankle injury.

At the start of October, Arsenal went to leaders Chelsea looking to answer questions about their away form in big games and kickstart a title chase. The home side featured Cesc Fàbregas – the ex-captain wanted to return to Arsenal but Arsène Wenger did not take up the club's first option to re-sign him from Barcelona. After 20 minutes, in a challenge that had nothing to do with the ball, Gary Cahill clattered Sánchez in front of the two benches. To Wenger's fury, Martin Atkinson only produced a yellow card. The two managers exchanged words and Wenger pushed José Mourinho. With Wenger safely back in his own technical area, Mourinho beckoned

him to come back. Wenger accepted the invitation, leaned over Mourinho and threateningly stuck his head in his face before the two were separated again.

It fired up the Arsenal away fans, who sang, "There's only one Arsène Wenger," but not the players. Eden Hazard dribbled through the middle, was brought down by Koscielny and stroked in the penalty. In the second half, Fàbregas played a long ball to Diego Costa, who lobbed Szczęsny to make it 2-0. Arsenal had played some good football, but defensively Chelsea were too savvy and did not allow one shot on target. In addition, Özil picked up a knee injury that ruled him out for three months. Afterwards, Wenger was unrepentant: "Was it a push? A little one. You can see when I really try to push."

Arsenal then had a more inviting run of fixtures to start picking up points. Sánchez opened the scoring against Hull with a stepover and drilled shot from the inside-right. However, Mohamed Diamé ran through the Arsenal defence, aided by pulling back Flamini, and levelled, then Abel Hernández beat Mertesacker to head Hull into the lead. In injury time, Sánchez dribbled into the box and set up Welbeck to poke in and make it 2-2. Arsenal had won only two of the first eight games and were seventh, 11 points behind the leaders.

At Borussia Dortmund in the Champions League, the home side dominated as 19-year-old Héctor Bellerín had a tough full debut. Ciro Immobile beat ineffective challenges from Gibbs and Koscielny before future Arsenal captain Pierre-Emerick Aubameyang made it 2-0.

Arsenal beat Galatasaray 4-1 as Welbeck sidefooted from Sánchez's reverse pass, impressively outmuscled Felipe Melo and finished, and dinked to complete his first senior hat-trick. With Arsenal coasting and the away fans bringing the noise and flares, Szczęsny could not resist taking out Burak Yılmaz, leaving Arsenal to play the last 30 minutes with ten men.

Arsenal were facing defeat in Anderlecht, but on 89 minutes Gibbs sidefoot-volleyed a cross from Debuchy and two minutes later Podolski fired in from close range to make it 2-1. The reverse fixture at the Emirates seemed more straightforward as Arsenal took a 3-0 lead in the rain. Arteta scored with a Panenka penalty, Sánchez's free-kick came back off the wall and he thumped it back on the volley with disdain, and Oxlade-Chamberlain surged past his man and sidefooted in.

Anderlecht got two back with 20 minutes left. With Nacho Monreal a makeshift centre-back and Flamini already on for an injured Arteta, Wenger had mostly attacking options left on the bench; however, bringing on Rosický and Podolski was not a way to tighten things up. After 90 minutes, Aleksandar Mitrović dived in front of Mertesacker to make it 3-3. Anderlecht manager Besnik Hasi hit the nail on the head: "Maybe Arsenal thought that they were on top and they could get more goals and they could have fun in front of the public."

Dortmund came to the Emirates top of the group but surprisingly third from bottom in the Bundesliga. With Giroud and Welbeck injured, Wenger chose Sanogo to lead the line. After 73 seconds, and before late-arriving fans had a chance to groan at his selection, Sanogo juggled the ball, back-heeled to Cazorla, accepted the return pass with a heavy touch and stretched to pass it between Roman Weidenfeller's legs. It was his first goal in 19 appearances, but the ungainly striker only featured once more in an Arsenal shirt. In the second half, Sánchez cut inside and curled into the far corner to make it 2-0 and seal Arsenal's place in the knockout stages for the 15th year running. However, the captain's curse struck again as Arteta's season ended with an ankle injury.

In Istanbul, Arsenal again beat Galatasaray 4-1 as Podolski and Ramsey netted doubles. The highlight was Ramsey returning a cleared corner with a stunning left-foot volley from 30 yards that was still rising when it flew into the top corner. The win meant Arsenal finished second behind Dortmund and could have been drawn against usual foes Barcelona or Bayern Munich; instead they got Monaco.

Arsenal beat Sunderland 2-0 courtesy of Sánchez's tireless pressing. First, he robbed Wes Brown and dinked over Vito Mannone. Then, he pressured the former Arsenal goalkeeper into a mistake and scored. The Chilean again led the way against Burnley, scoring two in a 3-0 win, while Chambers poked in his first for the club.

The rain lashed down at Swansea and Chambers was lucky not concede a penalty after pushing Wilfried Bony. In the second half, Arsenal launched a swift counter-attack and Welbeck squared for Sánchez to score his sixth in four league games. However, Gylfi Sigurdsson curled a brilliant free-kick past Szczęsny to equalise. Two minutes later, Jefferson Montero went past Chambers like he was not there, as he had done all game, and crossed for substitute Bafétimbi Gomis to rise above Monreal and head the winner with his first touch.

The rapid Ecuadorian winger 'vaccinated' Chambers, exposing the defender's lack of pace as well as his tendency to turn his back on the ball. One back-heel nutmeg left Chambers on the floor. Much was made of centre-back Chambers' versatility, but he was not a top-level right-back unless he had no designated winger to face and

he lacked the mobility to play holding midfielder. However, like Carl Jenkinson at Old Trafford in the 8-2 game in 2011, a young player was hung out to dry – Oxlade-Chamberlain in front of him provided little support, captain and right-sided centre-back Mertesacker did not intervene, and Wenger did not change the formation or put Chambers out of his misery until the 90th minute (despite having speedster Bellerín on the bench).

Next up was Arsenal-Man Utd, where sixth versus seventh was a far cry from the Battle Royale games of Stage One Wenger. It was a perfect chance for Arsenal to improve a record of one win in 14 games against Man Utd – Louis van Gaal had a defensive injury crisis and fielded inexperienced centre-backs Tyler Blackett and Paddy McNair alongside Chris Smalling in a makeshift back five; they had not won away all season; and they were the poorest Man Utd team in memory.

Arsenal dominated. Welbeck played in Wilshere, who hit a soft effort from eight yards that David de Gea saved. Welbeck missed a header and had a one-on-one blocked. Wilshere yet again suffered a serious injury as a result of a driving run and showing the ball to a defender; McNair did the damage with his studs crunching Wilshere's ankle and putting him out for five months. In a rare Man Utd attack, Szczęsny collided with Gibbs when punching a cross, Antonio Valencia fired it back in and a prostrate Gibbs dangled out a leg to divert a ball that was going wide into the net. Man Utd were 1-0 up without having a shot on target.

After 85 minutes, Man Utd did have their first effort on target when a counter-attack left Wayne Rooney to dink over substitute goalkeeper Emi Martínez and make it 2-0. Wenger seemed flummoxed, like it had never happened before: "I don't know why we had nobody at the back at all – you could see straight away that giving a two against one in your own half means you will be punished against these players." Five minutes into injury time, a returning Giroud hit a brilliant, but forgotten, half-volley from the edge of the area into the top corner to make it 2-1. It left Arsenal in eighth with 17 points from 12 games – their lowest total for 32 years.

Arsenal, and a struggling Mertesacker, welcomed back Koscielny after an Achilles problem and won 1-0 at West Brom with a soaring Welbeck header, his first goal in six games. Prominent in the away section was a banner stating, "Arsène, Thanks for the memories, But it's time to say goodbye." Against Southampton, Arsenal finally beat Fraser Forster as Sánchez scored a late winner to give another 1-0 win and move them up to sixth in early December.

Arsenal then went to Stoke looking to address a record of one win in eight games. Although Mark Hughes had replaced Tony Pulis, Arsenal knew what to expect – a physical day, direct early balls to target man Peter Crouch

SUBSTITUTION BY NUMBERS

Wenger's substitutions in Stage Three were so predictable that, however bad the team or certain players were playing or how the tactical battles across the pitch were panning out, regular watchers knew he would not proactively change things until his preferred 70th-minute mark. He had an unflinching belief in his players' ability to come good or turn it around as the opposition tired, which often worked when Arsenal were chasing a late winner. He rarely went radical with an early change, noticed something in the opposition's set-up to exploit or counter, and did not put a player out of their misery when they were being 'vaccinated', most notably Calum Chambers at Swansea in 2014. The average times of Wenger's Premier League changes in Stage Three were a predictable 68, 76 and 81 minutes (excluding changes forced by injury).

and lots of crosses. With Chambers partnering Mertesacker at centre-back, Arsenal needed their 6'6" World Cup winner to stand firm and win the first couple of headers to lay down a marker. Instead, Crouch was able to bring the first high ball down and was unchallenged for the second. Steven N'Zonzi crossed, Chambers missed it and it fell to Crouch to score after 19 seconds. Half an hour later, Jonathan Walters crossed past Gibbs' half-hearted attempt to block and Mertesacker watched as Bojan ran behind him to make it 2-0. Walters made it 3-0 at half-time as he smashed in after Stoke won the first header from a corner.

Unusually, Wenger made half-time changes, moving Flamini to right-back, Oxlade-Chamberlain to centre-midfield and bringing on Welbeck. A Cazorla penalty and excellent Ramsey volley in the space of three minutes lifted hopes of a comeback, but Chambers was given a second yellow card and it ended 3-2. Sadly, Wenger was subjected to boos and abuse from some Arsenal fans at the train station after the game.

Any tension among the Emirates fans was lifted against Newcastle as Giroud scored a towering header and near-post flick. Cazorla chipped a classy finish and Panenka penalty as a 4-1 win sparked chants of "There's only one Arsène Wenger."

In the pre-Christmas game at Anfield, Debuchy headed an equaliser with the last touch of the first half, only a minute after Philippe Coutinho's opener. Arsenal took an unlikely lead in the second half as quickfire passing between Giroud and Cazorla ended with the Frenchman firing between Brad Jones' legs. Arsenal had been unusually clinical, scoring with their first two efforts on target. Liverpool went down to ten men late on when Fabio Borini was sent off for leaving studs on Cazorla's chest and ripping his shirt, but an unchallenged Martin Škrtel powered a header from a corner to make it 2-2 in the 97th minute. Arsenal had conceded another late Anfield equaliser; that Mertesacker had inexplicably ducked under the cross, although he probably could not have reached it, made it all the more galling.

On Boxing Day, Sánchez had a weak penalty saved by QPR's Robert Green but headed the opener from a Gibbs cross. Arsenal had to play most of the second half with ten men after Giroud was sent off for a 'footballer's headbutt' on Nedum Onuoha. Sánchez teed up Rosický, making his first league start of the season, to sidefoot in from the edge of the area. QPR got one back but it finished 2-1. Two days later, Francis Coquelin made his first start of the season at West Ham after being recalled from a loan at Championship side Charlton Athletic. A Cazorla penalty and Welbeck tap-in gave Arsenal another 2-1 win. It left Arsenal fifth at the end of 2014, well behind frontrunners Chelsea and Man City.

On New Year's Day, Arsenal were outplayed and outrun at Southampton, who were helped by two Szczęsny errors. First, the Pole came out of his goal, unnecessarily giving Sadio Mané an empty net to expertly curl into from near the byline. Then a floored Szczęsny kicked a loose ball straight to Dušan Tadić, who poked in to make it 2-0. The home side also hit the woodwork twice and had another cleared off the line. The goalkeeper was fined for smoking in the showers after the game – the beginning of the end of his Arsenal career as Ospina replaced him as number one.

The FA Cup third round saw a repeat of the previous year's final against Hull, but it was more comfortable for Arsenal as Mertesacker and Sánchez goals ensured a 2-0 win. Theo Walcott made his first start for exactly a year since he injured his knee.

As usual, the home fixture against Stoke was a completely different affair to the away one and Arsenal won 3-0 with a Sánchez brace. Özil returned from injury as a substitute, but the unlucky Debuchy suffered a dislocated shoulder as Marko Arnautović nudged him while he was mid-air and the ball was heading out of play – a dangerous 'free hit' that referees and the FA consistently allowed. With train delays announced to the away fans, the Arsenal fans gleefully sang, "Three-nil and you can't go home."

In the January transfer window, Arsenal recruited a much-needed centre-back in Brazilian Gabriel Paulista while Podolski was loaned to Inter Milan. Like Andrey Arshavin before him, the German was a highly-talented player that Wenger had not got the best out of. His 31 goals came every 150 minutes on average, an exceptional rate for a wide player who rarely played 90 minutes. However, the popular German offered little away from the final third, a trait highlighted by Sánchez's high-energy desire to win the ball back and help out his left-back.

In mid-January, Arsenal went to Man City, who were unbeaten in their last 12 games. Wenger selected Ospina in goal and Coquelin as holding midfielder. Something was different – Arsenal defended in numbers, full-backs Bellerín and Monreal held their position when the other one attacked, and the midfield worked hard to protect the back four. After 22 minutes, Monreal played a one-two with Giroud and won a penalty off Kompany that Cazorla sidefooted past Hart. In the second half, Giroud nodded in a Cazorla free-kick to seal a landmark 2-0 win despite only having 35% possession. It was one of the few times that Wenger adopted a pragmatic game plan to suit the situation and the opposition.

The tenacious Coquelin made a significant impact, with 11 clearances and six interceptions. Cazorla beat him

IF ONLY

Poor Abou Diaby's fledgling career was brutally interrupted by Sunderland's Dan Smith, whose foul caused damage that required three ankle surgeries. The supremely-talented Frenchman subsequently suffered constant muscular injuries as well as rupturing his anterior cruciate ligament, tearing his medial ligament, and requiring further surgeries to his ankle and foot. He suffered 42 injuries to 12 different body parts in nine and a half years at the club. After playing a decent number of games in 2007/08, 2008/09 and 2009/10, and featuring in the 2010 World Cup, Diaby only made 22 appearances in his last four seasons as he kept undergoing lengthy rehabilitation in the gym, only to suffer a relapse or other issue. He was out for a total of 222 weeks, more than four years. The Frenchman retired aged 32 after two seasons and six games at Marseille, having been able to show only glimpses of his skill during his career.

Coquelin-Cazorla centre-midfield partnership and a turning point in the season.

It only took 89 seconds for Walcott to fire the opener in the FA Cup at Brighton. Rosický then played a brilliant reverse pass and Özil made it 2-0. The Championship side got one back before the Little Mozart jinked past a couple of challenges, made a no-look pass to Giroud, who dinked it to the edge of the area, where Rosický hammered a brilliant volley. The number seven was not a great goalscorer, but he was a scorer of great goals. Brighton got another but Arsenal saw out a 3-2 win.

Arsenal made it three wins and three clean sheets in a row in the league as they hammered Aston Villa 5-0. The goals were high quality including a classy Özil flick that set Giroud free to dink over Brad Guzan and Bellerín sidefooting his first-ever from 25 yards.

In the North London derby, Wenger faced his 11th Spurs manager in Mauricio Pochettino. Arsenal started well when Welbeck burst down the right and crossed. Giroud scuffed his effort, but it fell to Özil who guided it in. In the second half, Eric Dier flicked on a corner, Ospina saved, but Harry Kane swept it in. With a draw looking likely after 86 minutes, Koscielny lost Kane and the Spurs striker powered in a header to make it 2-1 and push Arsenal down to sixth in the league.

Three nights later, Arsenal beat bottom-of-the-table Leicester 2-1 as

to man of the match as the Spaniard put on a masterclass of ball retention and dribbling out of tight spaces. It was the beginning of the successful

Koscielny sidefooted in a corner and Walcott followed up a rare Özil drive with his laces that was too powerful for Mark Schwarzer to hold – the German should have shot more as he had the technique. Back in the FA Cup, Arsenal faced another Championship team in Middlesbrough. Two Giroud near-post finishes in three minutes ensured a 2-0 win.

An all-yellow – bar blue sleeves – Arsenal took a two-goal lead at Crystal Palace in the first half. Glenn Murray got one back after 94 minutes and still had time to hit the post, but a 2-1 win moved Arsenal up to third.

Having drawn unfancied Monaco, the famous Champions League music was greeted with gusto at the Emirates. Arsenal started well but Wenger's former club grew increasingly confident. After 38 minutes, Geoffrey Kondogbia hit a drive from 25 yards that deflected off Mertesacker and past a wrong-footed Ospina. Early in the second half, an Arsenal attack broke down, Mertesacker abandoned his defensive post to try and win the ball in midfield, leaving Anthony Martial acres of space to run into. The winger fed Dimitar Berbatov, who drove in to make it 2-0.

Giroud had a nightmare, failing to hit the target with six efforts, the last of which he skied over from eight yards

and prompted Wenger to replace him with Walcott. The Englishman had an effort blocked by goalkeeper Danijel Subašić and Welbeck, with the goal at his mercy, managed to hit the rebound against his prostrate teammate and over the bar. On 90 minutes, a corner fell to Oxlade-Chamberlain outside the area and he expertly curled the ball high into the net. A 2-1 deficit could have been turned around in Monaco. However, three minutes later, the Ox lost the ball and a pumped-up Arsenal had again pushed forward and exposed Mertesacker to a pacey counter-attack. Yannick Carrasco shot low through Ospina's weak wrist and a talented and well-drilled Monaco won 3-1. Wenger said, "We missed chances and were suicidal defensively."

Giroud's fortunes improved when he volleyed in a corner right-footed against Everton. A late Rosický drive was deflected in to seal a 2-0 win. Giroud poached another at QPR and Sánchez got his first in seven matches. Charlie Austin scored late to make it 2-1 but Arsenal secured their seventh win in eight games.

Into early March, Arsenal faced a testing Monday night FA Cup quarter-final at Old Trafford, where they had not won for over eight years. Arsenal pinged the ball about, Oxlade-Chamberlain danced past three challenges on the edge of the box and fed Monreal in the space created. The left-back calmly sidefooted past de Gea. Minutes later, an unmarked Rooney headed in to make it 1-1. On the hour mark, Antonio Valencia scuffed a back-pass, Welbeck toed it past de Gea, netted and had no hesitation in celebrating against his former club, to the delight of the 9,000 travelling Arsenal fans.

de Gea made two brilliant saves while Ángel Di María was given a yellow card for diving and a second one immediately after for grabbing referee Michael Oliver's shirt – decisions not seen at Old Trafford in the Alex Ferguson era. It was another impressive away win and Wenger was vindicated in starting Welbeck as striker.

The one- and two-touch Wengerball was dialled up to 11 for the visit of West Ham. First, Özil, Ramsey and Giroud exchanged rapid passes before Giroud laced the ball into the top-left corner. Second, Giroud dummied a throw-in, played a one-two with Ramsey and the Welshman sidefooted in. Third, Giroud played a one-two with Cazorla, who squared for substitute Flamini to tap in with his first touch. A 3-0 win put pressure on second-placed Man City.

In good form, Arsenal went to Monaco optimistic of an unlikely turnaround. The French side sat back, leaving Arsenal with 70% possession. After 35 minutes, Subašić blocked Giroud's effort and the Frenchman smashed the loose ball into the net. After 79 minutes, Ramsey drilled a second and Arsenal needed one more to qualify.

Sánchez came close with a header, but it finished 3-3 on aggregate and nearly-men Arsenal went out on away goals, having come close to a famous second-leg turnaround for the third time in four years.

Giroud scored twice from set-pieces in the space of four minutes against his favourite opponents Newcastle. Arsenal again saw off a comeback attempt and won 2-1. At the start of April, Arsenal entertained a Luis Suárez-less Liverpool, who were not the title-chasing side of the year before. Late in the first half, Bellerín was ushered inside by Alberto Moreno and curled left-footed into the far corner. Özil curled a free-kick into the same corner and Sánchez made it three in eight minutes with a thunderbolt from the edge of the area. Giroud sealed a 4-1 win at the end with another excellent strike – the striker had been on fire since his Monaco nightmare and had scored ten in ten games. Arsenal were now second behind runaway leaders Chelsea. A 1-0 win, Arsenal's eighth in a row, at Burnley kept them there.

Arsenal returned to a sunny Wembley for the FA Cup semi-final against Championship side Reading. Özil curled a pass to Sánchez, who kept his cool and opened the scoring. Arsenal were on top, but Gibbs lost Garath McCleary at the back post and Szczęsny could only help his volley over the line.

Late on, Ramsey had only a defender on the line to beat from an angle but fired against the post. For the second year running, Arsenal's semi-final went to extra time. Sánchez cut inside on the left and his shot dribbled through Adam Federici's legs, a tough ending for the goalkeeper that had kept his team in it with several crucial saves. There was no need for penalties this year as it finished 2-1 and Arsenal had another final to look forward to.

Arsenal's winning run came to an end as an organised Chelsea extended their Arsenal shut-out to eight hours. Arsenal had only one shot on target in the two Chelsea games in 2014/15. At the final whistle, the home fans again greeted the goalless draw with chants of "Boring boring Chelsea." However, John Terry celebrated as Chelsea, and Fàbregas with 18 assists, closed in on the title.

Arsenal cruised to a 3-1 win at Hull with two goals from Sánchez and one from Ramsey. Wilshere came on for his first appearance since November. Swansea's Fabiański made several saves in his Emirates return and late on Gomis outjumped Monreal to give the away side a 1-0 win. 36% of the goals Arsenal conceded in 2014/15 came from headers.

It was third versus fourth as Arsenal returned to Old Trafford. Man Utd took the lead in an end-of-season affair through Ander Herrera in a first half where Arsenal had zero shots. Giroud looked sure to have the first when a retreating Phil Jones lost his balance and went down in instalments. Not to be deterred, the defender crawled across the turf, launched himself full length and headed the ball off Giroud's toes. It won no points for style, but plenty for foolhardiness, improvisation and effectiveness as it bounced off a bemused Giroud and out for a goal-kick. Jones' unique style again saw him go viral. After 82 minutes, substitute Walcott's cross deflected in off Blackett and earnt a fortunate 1-1 draw, Arsenal's first point at Old Trafford in six years.

A 0-0 draw against Sunderland meant Arsenal needed a point on the final day against West Brom to finish third. Walcott, making his first start for two months, only took five minutes to unleash a brilliant angled drive into the roof of the net. Nine minutes later, he poked in a second. Wilshere, also making a rare start, smashed a volley from 20 yards into the top corner. The goal won the midfielder BBC Goal of the Season for the second year running as Arsenal fans mobilised their prolific online presence. Walcott then tapped in to complete a first-half hat-trick and Arsenal won 4-1.

That left the FA Cup Final against Tim Sherwood's Aston Villa and Arsenal were again favourites having won the league games 5-0 and 3-0. Unlike the previous year, Szczęsny benefited from Wenger's policy of playing the cup, rather than number one, goalkeeper. The selection of Walcott upfront was more of a surprise, despite the Englishman's recent goalscoring form and Giroud having one of his dry spells after being named Premier League Player of the Month for March. Despite Arsenal fans' traditional FA Cup chant of "She Wore a Yellow Ribbon," it was the only one of Wenger's eight finals where they played in their away strip.

This year, Arsenal started well and played without tension. Shay Given saved a Koscielny header, Ramsey fired over and Walcott had a close-range effort blocked. A goal was overdue and after 40 minutes, Monreal chipped to the back post, the 5'7" Sánchez climbed highest and headed back across goal, where Walcott crashed in a left-footed volley.

Early in the second half, Sánchez cut inside and unleashed a swerving and dipping 69-mile-per-hour rocket from 27 yards that flashed past Given and went in off the underside of the bar. It was a classic FA Cup Final goal and one that would be considerably more famous if the game was still the showpiece occasion that stopped the nation.

Mertesacker then got another Wembley goal when he headed/ shouldered in a corner to make it 3-0. Villa had zero shots on target and zero corners. Their only threat came after 85 minutes when Bellerín got away with pulling back Jack Grealish in the box. Three minutes into injury time,

Oxlade-Chamberlain squared for fellow substitute Giroud to net with a now-trademark near-post flick and make it a more accurate scoreline of 4-0. Villa fan Prince William handed over the trophy, which Mertesacker and Arteta lifted, and the celebrations began.

It was one of the best and most complete performances of Wenger's 13 finals, aided by a poor Villa team. Arsenal knocked it around from the start, Cazorla and Özil dictated the play as the German displayed his range of feints and clever passing, while Coquelin showed he could dribble out of tight spaces as well as break up play. Arsenal became the most successful club in the history of the competition with 12 wins, and with half of those coming under Wenger, the Frenchman joined Villa's George Ramsey as the most successful manager.

Having gone nine years without a trophy and being the only English club apart from Chelsea to win silverware in 2014/15, winning back-to-back FA Cups was a success. However, Arsenal did not push on in either the league or Europe as they again failed to strengthen the spine of the team despite spending £32m on Chambers and Welbeck – the former had only played 22 Premier League games; the latter was hard-working, strong and quick, but lacked the composure and finesse to be a prolific goalscorer. Arsenal were still crying out for a solid defensive midfielder.

They started the season poorly, not helped by having only six senior defenders nor by another spate of injuries, and were already 11 points behind Chelsea after eight games. In the last 30 games, Arsenal earnt 64 and Chelsea 65 as a new pecking order emerged with Ospina, Bellerín and the much-improved Monreal becoming first-choice goalkeeper and full-backs. Arsenal had the best record in the league against the bottom half of the table, winning 16 and drawing four.

The big revelation was Coquelin who few expected to see again after being loaned to Charlton in his seventh year at the club. The Frenchman added a tenacity and sharpness that the ageing and increasingly injured Arteta and Flamini did not have, giving much-needed protection to the back four. He formed an excellent partnership with Cazorla in centre-midfield and Arsenal's win percentage in the league with Coquelin was 73% compared with 38% without him.

However, the player of the year by far was Sánchez. The Chilean needed no bedding-in period as he carried Arsenal early in the season and never let up. Playing all across the front three, his 25 goals came in all forms – curlers, blasters, headers, scruffy tap-ins and one-on-ones. He never stopped running or pressing the opposition, and his fighting spirit set an example to, and sometimes showed up, his teammates.

Wenger's Beefs

	Arsène Wenger	versus	Alex Ferguson	
Nov 1996			"They say he's an intelligent man, right? Speaks five languages. I've got a 15-year-old boy from the Ivory Coast who speaks five languages."	
Apr 1997	"It's wrong the programme is extended so Man Utd can rest and win everything."		"He's a novice – he should keep his opinions to Japanese football."	
May 2002			"They are scrappers who rely on belligerence – we are the better team."	
May 2002	"Everyone thinks they have the prettiest wife at home."			
Oct 2004			"Arsenal got off scot-free really, they got away with murder... What Arsenal players did that day [Battle of Old Trafford the year before] was the worst thing I've seen in this sport. No wonder they were so delighted at the verdicts."	
Oct 2004	"Maybe it would be better if you have put us up against a wall and shot us all. I hope that he will calm down."			

Arsène Wenger	versus	Alex Ferguson

Jan 2005		"In the tunnel he was publicly criticising my players, calling them cheats. I was told about this when they came into the dressing-room, so I went out into the tunnel and said to him: 'You get in there and behave yourself, leave my players alone'. He came sprinting towards me with his hands raised saying: 'What do you want to do about it?' He was standing right there. To not apologise for the behaviour of the players to another manager is unthinkable. It is a disgrace. But I don't expect Wenger to ever apologise... Arsenal are the worst losers of all time."
Jan 2005	"He is going out looking for a confrontation, then asking the person he is confronting to apologise. He's pushed the cork in a bit far this time and lost a lot of credibility by saying what he said." "He doesn't interest me and doesn't matter to me at all. I will never answer to any provocation from him anymore."	
2008 and 2009	"There is a much better understanding and mutual respect now."	"We have loads of situations now where new managers come in and vanish after a couple of years. It's just the two of us and we'll probably ride out into the sunset together."
Winner	When the two sides were evenly matched during Stage One Wenger, the Frenchman refused to be intimidated by Ferguson's famous 'mind games' and his clever quips won the war of words.	

Arsène Wenger	versus	**José Mourinho**

Aug 2005
"I know we live in a world where we have only winners and losers, but once a sport encourages teams who refuse to take the initiative, the sport is in danger."

Oct 2005

"Wenger has a real problem with us and I think he is what you call in England a voyeur. He is someone who likes to watch other people. There are some guys who, when they are at home, have this big telescope to look into the homes of other people and see what is happening. Wenger must be one of them – it is a sickness."

Nov 2005
"He's out of order, disconnected with reality and disrespectful. When you give success to stupid people, it makes them more stupid sometimes and not more intelligent."

"At Stamford Bridge, we have a file of quotes from Mr Wenger about Chelsea Football Club in the last 12 months – it is not a file of five pages. It is a file of 120 pages."

Apr 2007
"If you would like to compare every manager, you give each one the same amount of resources and say: 'you have that for five years'. After five years, you see who has done the most."

Apr 2008

"The English like statistics a lot. Do they know that Arsène Wenger has only 50% of wins in the English league?"

Nov 2010
"It looks, frankly, horrible. It's a pity to see that from a big club [Real Madrid players deliberately getting booked to get suspensions out the way in the Champions League]."

"Instead of speaking about Real Madrid, Mr Wenger should speak about Arsenal and explain how he lost 2-0 against a team in the Champions League for the first time [Braga]. The history about the young kids is getting old now. Sagna, Clichy, Walcott, Fàbregas, Song, Nasri, van Persie, Arshavin are not kids. They are all top players."

Arsène Wenger	versus	José Mourinho
Feb 2014	"It is fear to fail [on rivals playing down their title chances]."	"Am I afraid of failure? He is a specialist in failure. I'm not."
Oct 2014	"What is to regret after that [pushing Mourinho on the touchline]? I wanted to go from A to B and somebody confronted me without any sign of welcome. B was get to Sánchez to see if he was injured. Was it a push? A little one. You can see when I really try to push."	
May 2015	"I believe big clubs have a responsibility to win but to win with style."	
Sept 2015		In this country only one manager is not under pressure. Every other manager is.

You know. The one who can speak about the referees before the game, after the game, can push people in the technical area, can moan, can cry in the morning, in the afternoon, and nothing happens. He cannot achieve [success] and keep his job, still be the king. I say just one." |
| **Winner** | It got personal and there was little mutual respect. Wenger surprisingly got physical by pushing Mourinho at Stamford Bridge, but Mourinho's head-to-head (won ten, lost two, drew seven) and trophy record sadly backed up his brutal critique of Wenger. | |

Honourable mentions: British Football Managers Sam Allardyce, Tony Pulis, Mark Hughes and Alan Pardew; referees and fourth officials; water bottles; and Wenger's coat zip.

2015/16
LEICESTER SHOW HOW IT'S DONE

Premier League	Second
FA Cup	Quarter-final
Champions League	Round of 16
League Cup	Fourth round
Community Shield	Winners

PREMIER LEAGUE		PL	W	D	L	GF	GA	GD	PTS
1	LEICESTER CITY	38	23	12	3	68	36	32	81
2	ARSENAL	38	20	11	7	65	36	29	71
3	TOTTENHAM	38	19	13	6	69	35	34	70
4	MAN CITY	38	19	9	10	71	41	30	66
5	MAN UTD	38	19	9	10	49	35	14	66
6	SOUTHAMPTON	38	18	9	11	59	41	18	63

Highlights: Danny Welbeck's 95th-minute winner against Leicester rocked the Emirates and set Arsenal up for a title charge; blitzing Man Utd with three in the first 20 minutes; beating Bayern Munich 2-0 at home; an unexpected St Totteringham's Day provided last-day-of-the-season fun; a must-win 3-0 victory in Olympiacos secured Champions League progression

Lowlights: Tame losses against Man Utd and Swansea were a painful comedown from the Leicester high; outplayed and outfought 4-0 at Southampton; two ten-man defeats to a struggling Chelsea; going out of FA Cup to Watford; opening day home loss to West Ham; losing leads to Liverpool, West Ham and Spurs

Player of the year: Mesut Özil had his best season at Arsenal as he created a Premier League record 144 chances, with 19 assists, for his often-misfiring teammates

Top scorers: Olivier Giroud 24 (16 in PL), Alexis Sánchez 17 (13)

Goal of the season: Giroud chested a cross and hit an acrobatic volley versus Bayern Munich, Allianz Arena, Champions League

After two FA Cup wins in a row, Arsenal had laid solid foundations to push on to the next level. They had a good squad but it was clear they needed to add quality to the spine of the team, depth for when the fixtures and injuries piled up, and more players with a winning mentality like Alexis Sánchez. The finances were in place – Arsenal director Lord Harris said, "We could go into the market and probably buy any player in the world, apart from half a dozen who are unbuyable. In the accounts, there's over £200m in the bank." However, Arsène Wenger was the only manager in Europe's leading leagues not to buy an outfield first-team player in summer 2015. When once asked by director Danny Fiszman, "What would you do if we gave you £100m to spend, Arsène?", Wenger replied, "I'd give it back to you."

He did buy 33-year-old Petr Čech from Chelsea as Wojciech Szczęsny was loaned to Roma. He gave one-year contracts to 33-year-old Mikel Arteta and 34-year-old Tomáš Rosický despite their limited game time in 2014/15, lengthy injury records and, in the case of Arteta, lack of pace. It was a reversal of his strict Stage One caution towards players once they hit 30. In Stage Three, popular players were kept on past their prime, taking up valuable squad places and first-team salaries in a club operating a self-sustaining model. With Mathieu Flamini and Santi Cazorla also in their 30s, and the former past his best, and Jack Wilshere and others suffering recurring injury problems, it

was optimistic planning to say the least. In addition, Danny Welbeck had not recovered from a knee injury sustained in April and underwent surgery just before the transfer window closed.

However, the Community Shield against Chelsea gave reason to believe as Arsenal extended their successful run at the new Wembley to six games. Alex Oxlade-Chamberlain cut inside and fired a rising left-footed shot inside the far post to make it 1-0. After 14 attempts, Wenger had finally beaten José Mourinho.

A narrow Arsenal side put in a flat performance in the league opener against West Ham. Any hopes the trophy-laden Čech would help improve Arsenal's aerial weakness were soon dispelled as they set up an abnormally high line from a free-kick and he charged out for a ball he was never going to win. Cheikhou Kouyaté easily headed in. It got worse in the second half as Arsenal lost the ball on the edge of the area and Mauro Zárate wrong-footed the goalkeeper with a shot that rolled in at the near post to give West Ham a 2-0 win. When Čech joined Arsenal, his former captain John Terry said, "He will save them 12 or 15 points a season" – Terry already needed to re-do his maths.

At Crystal Palace, Olivier Giroud opened the scoring with a brilliant scissor-kick volley. After Joel Ward equalised with a low drive, Sánchez showed typical desire to attack a Héctor Bellerín cross and head towards goal, where Damien

Delaney hacked it into his own net. A 2-1 win meant Arsenal were off the mark. On a Monday night that felt more like November than August, Arsenal and Liverpool played a frenetic match with chances at both ends, Philippe Coutinho rattling the woodwork twice and Sánchez once, Aaron Ramsey having a goal wrongly disallowed for offside and both goalkeepers making crucial saves. Despite that, it was a rare goalless draw between the two sides and Arsenal had failed to score in five of their last six home games.

At Newcastle, Aleksandar Mitrović went studs up on Francis Coquelin and was sent off after only 16 minutes. Theo Walcott shinned a rebound from Tim Krul high and wide before Arsenal finally got the breakthrough when Oxlade-Chamberlain's shot was deflected in by Fabricio Coloccini for another own-goal and a 1-0 win. Walcott was again selected to lead the line against Stoke and he used his pace to get on the end of a long ball and open the scoring. Substitute Giroud headed in a free-kick to make it 2-0 as Arsenal had 29 efforts on goal and moved up to fourth.

In mid-September, Arsenal went to Chelsea, who were already suffering from 'Mourinho third-season syndrome' with three losses in five games. The game was goalless just before half-time. As always, Diego Costa was

TYPICAL LINE-UP
(4-2-3-1)

12
Giroud
Walcott
Welbeck

17
Sànchez
Iwobi
Walcott

16
Ramsey
Campbell
Ox-Chamberlain
Walcott

11
Özil

19
Cazorla
Ramsey

34
Coquelin
Flamini
Elneny

18
Monreal
Gibbs

6
Koscielny

4
Mertesacker
Gabriel

24
Bellerín
Debuchy

33
Čech
Ospina

Players in: Petr Čech, Jeff Reine-Adélaïde, Donyell Malen, Ismaël Bennacer, *Mohamed Elneny*

Players out: Abou Diaby, Lukas Podolski, Ryo Miyaichi, Yaya Sanogo (loan), Wojciech Szczęsny (loan), Serge Gnabry (loan), *Mathieu Debuchy (loan)*

looking to stir up trouble. As they waited for a cross, Costa pushed Laurent Koscielny in the face with both hands and then swung his arm and slapped the Frenchman in the head. Costa was all over Koscielny trying to get a reaction, but the Frenchman brushed him off. Costa got up and bumped Koscielny over, prompting Gabriel Paulista to get involved. The Chelsea striker had committed two red-card and one yellow-card offences to add to his earlier unpunished dive, yet Mike Dean gave Costa and Gabriel a yellow each. Gabriel then flicked a kick at Costa, who went running to the referee and got the red card he demanded. Koscielny did well not to react, but Gabriel took the bait hook, line and sinker.

Early in the second half, Cesc Fàbregas swung in a free-kick and Kurt Zouma was left unmarked to head in. Cazorla slid in on Fàbregas to get a second yellow card and leave Arsenal with nine men for the last 15 minutes, during which Hazard's deflected shot made it 2-0. Costa got away with another dive and further altercations and Wenger rightly called out the refereeing that enabled the wind-up merchant, "In every game there's aggravation, he gets away with it because referees are weak… We are also guilty because we reacted to it, but every time somebody touches him he goes down like he has been killed." The FA subsequently banned Costa for three games and Gabriel's red card was rescinded.

In the League Cup, Arsenal faced another derby, this time at White Hart Lane. Oxlade-Chamberlain fired in a shot that Michel Vorm could not hold and Flamini smashed in the rebound. Chambers diverted a low Nacer Chadli cross past David Ospina. Late on, a clearance came out of the sky with snow on it, but Flamini kept his eyes on the ball and struck a flying volley from 20 yards to make it 2-1. The defensive midfielder was the unlikely hero with his only Arsenal double.

Arsenal then went to Leicester, the only unbeaten team in the league. It only took 13 minutes for the home side to enact their counter-attacking plan as Jamie Vardy raced on to a long ball and struck past Čech. The striker then headed against the bar and 20 seconds later Walcott sidefooted in at the other end after Arsenal had calmly played it out of defence. Then Arsenal's attack, and Sánchez in particular, clicked into gear for the first time in the season. The Chilean – who had gone eight games without a goal and looked slightly burnt out after winning the 2015 Copa América in the summer – finished a Bellerín cross, beat Kasper Schmeichel to head in a clever Mesut Özil chip and fired in a low shot from 25 yards. He became the first player to score hat-tricks in the Premier League, Serie A and La Liga. Vardy and Giroud both scored late goals and Arsenal completed an impressive 5-2 win to overtake Leicester and end September in fourth place.

In the Champions League, Wenger brought in Ospina, Mathieu Debuchy, Kieran Gibbs, Arteta and Giroud for the trip to Dinamo Zagreb. The home side was already 1-0 ahead when Giroud picked up his second unnecessary booking. Zagreb scored a second before substitute Walcott raced clear and netted an Henry Sidefoot Finish. Zagreb won 2-1, their first group stage win in 16 games.

Despite dominating Olympiacos, Arsenal fell behind from a corner. Walcott equalised, yet minutes later an unchallenged Ospina dropped a corner over the line for an own-goal. In the second half, Sánchez headed another equaliser. Yet again, Arsenal switched off and the Greek side took advantage to stun the Emirates with a 3-2 win from 30% possession.

Few teams had qualified from the group stages after losing their first two games and Arsenal's next two games were against Pep Guardiola's Bayern Munich. Wenger reversed his policy of using Ospina as the Champions League goalkeeper and selected Čech, who made crucial saves. Čech's opposite number Manuel Neuer also pulled off a brilliant stop from a Walcott header, although the Englishman should have put more on his effort. Bayern controlled the tempo yet Arsenal took the lead on 77 minutes when Neuer came out for a free-kick, missed it

completely and it went in off substitute Giroud. In injury time, Bellerín burst down the right and crossed for Özil to volley; Neuer saved but the ball was over the line and Arsenal sealed a confidence-boosting 2-0 win.

Order was restored at the Allianz Arena within ten minutes when Koscielny's replacement Gabriel left Robert Lewandowski to head in. Arsenal were injury-hit and Bayern were too good. It was 3-0 and over by half-time. Arjen Robben made it 4-0 with his first touch, 37 seconds after coming on as a substitute. Giroud chested down a pass from Sánchez with his back to goal and unleashed a brilliant volley. It finished 5-1, Arsenal's heaviest defeat in Europe. Six points behind Olympiacos with two games left, qualification was unlikely. However, Arsenal beat Zagreb 3-0 at home to give them a chance in Olympiacos where they needed to win by two goals.

It was a hostile atmosphere and a stadium where Arsenal had struggled previously, although often in dead rubbers. After half an hour, Giroud headed in at the near post to make the home side nervous. In the second half, Joel Campbell held the ball up, engaged multiple defenders and played an Özil-esque through-ball that took out the entire defence for Giroud to slot home. Arsenal got a fortunate penalty, which Giroud converted to seal his first Arsenal hat-trick and an impressive 3-0 win. Arsenal qualified in second place again and Wenger bragged, "I told you before the game it would be the greatest escape."

At the start of October, Arsenal flew out of the blocks against Louis van Gaal's one-paced Man Utd. After six minutes, Özil crossed low from the byline and Sánchez cleverly flicked in. Only 74 seconds later, Walcott teed up Özil to pass into the net. After 19 minutes, Sánchez cut in from the left and hammered into the top corner from the edge of the area to make it 3-0. The Emirates was pumped up and Arsenal could have scored more, but in the second half they were disciplined and sealed a rare win against Man Utd.

Arsenal took an hour to break down Watford at Vicarage Road before goals from Sánchez, Giroud and Ramsey gave another 3-0 win. Giroud was back in the first 11 against Everton and opened the scoring by glancing in Özil's teasing in-swinging cross. Koscielny then left Tim Howard punching fresh air as he headed in Cazorla's free-kick. Ross Barkley scored with a deflected shot and it finished 2-1 despite Romelu Lukaku, Giroud and Özil all hitting the woodwork.

A much-changed Arsenal side limped out of the League Cup, losing 3-0 at Championship side Sheffield Wednesday. It was a bad night as Oxlade-Chamberlain and his replacement Walcott both hobbled

off in the first 20 minutes to add to the lengthy injury list. Arsenal then kept Swansea at bay helped by Bellerín's incredible recovery pace. Bafetimbi Gomis rounded Čech, but the Arsenal right-back, who was now challenging Walcott as the club's fastest player, raced back and tackled. In the second half, Arsenal made it 3-0 with another Giroud header, Koscielny netting after Łukasz Fabiański made a mess of a high ball and Campbell scoring on his first Premier League start. Arsenal's fifth win in a row left them in second place behind Man City on goal difference.

In the North London derby in November, Mauricio Pochettino's Spurs were an improving side and they were quick to double up on Arsenal's main threats Özil and Sánchez. Per Mertesacker pushed up while Koscielny tried to play Harry Kane offside, leaving the Spurs striker to sidefoot in. In the second half, Özil found more space and created seven chances, including three headers for Giroud. Substitute Gibbs was the unlikely finisher as he got on the end of Özil's pass at the back post to make it 1-1.

At West Brom, Giroud headed in another Özil set-piece – the seventh game in a row that the German had assisted, a Premier League record. However, Arsenal soon shot themselves in the foot. Bellerín left James Morrison unchallenged to head the equaliser. Five minutes later, a cut back went past Čech and bounced off Arteta's knee and hand into the Arsenal goal. Arteta, who was making a rare appearance after replacing an injured Coquelin on 14 minutes, suffered a calf strain and had to come off himself after a nightmare 35 minutes.

Arsenal were well on top as West Brom only had one effort on target, but Campbell missed from four yards and Cazorla slipped and skied a late penalty over the bar. Arsenal could have gone top but the self-inflicted 2-1 loss dropped them to fourth, behind surprise leaders Leicester. At Norwich, Sánchez won the ball and played in Özil to score the opener. However, the home side equalised while Cazorla and Sánchez suffered knee and hamstring injuries, respectively – Arsenal's November curse again proved costly.

Arsenal started December better against Sunderland as Özil played a sublime ball inside the full-back for Campbell to sidefoot in. Giroud sliced in an own-goal as he tried to clear a cross with the wrong foot, but then gave Arsenal the lead with a stooping header. Ramsey sealed a 3-1 win at the end. They then won 2-0 at bottom-of-the-table Aston Villa with a penalty from Giroud and goal from Ramsey.

Arsenal faced a big test just before Christmas with the visit of Man City – second against third. Man City dominated possession with 63% of the ball but Arsenal were clinical.

AROUND THE WORLD WITH JOEL CAMPBELL

Arsenal signed Costa Rican attacker Campbell in August 2011 but soon after revealed he failed to get a work permit. He was an Arsenal player for seven years, during which time he went on six loan spells to clubs in France, Spain, Greece and Portugal before being sold to Frosinone Calcio in Italy. He saw a bit of game time for Arsenal in 2014/15 and made a mark in 2015/16, filling in well on either flank before being replaced by more established names when they returned from injury, not always on merit. He made a total of 40 appearances for the club, scoring four times.

Walcott cut inside from the left and curled brilliantly into the far corner. Man City then gave the ball away and Özil slipped in Giroud to drill between Joe Hart's legs. Arsenal defended well and held on to win 2-1 after Yaya Touré passed first-time into the top corner from the edge of the area with unerring pace and accuracy. A win against a title rival ticked a box and the Emirates fans started to believe this was the year. Arsenal had their best points tally after 17 games since 2007/08.

On Boxing Day, Arsenal had the chance to back up the Man City win and go top as Leicester had lost only their second game of the season in the early kick-off. However, Southampton's right-back Cuco Martina had other ideas as he met a weak Mertesacker header with a bending half-volley with the outside of his foot from 25 yards. The home side won all the 50-50s and overpowered Ramsey and Flamini in midfield. With the lead secured, Southampton exposed Mertesacker and Koscielny on the counter-attack time and again. On one, Shane Long tripped Koscielny off the ball to leave himself alone to finish from Sadio Mané's low cross. José Fonte was left unmarked to head in a corner and Long fired between Čech's legs to make it 4-0. Arsenal did not turn up and Koscielny seemed to have the biggest Christmas hangover as Long's constant running into the channels and harassing beat him into submission. Long was made to look a world-beater – he was not, as shown when he missed two other one-on-ones.

Two days later, a freshened Arsenal line-up was happier back at the Emirates against Bournemouth. A Gabriel header and Özil finish after a one-two with Giroud secured a 2-0 win and top place on goal difference at the end of 2015. At a wet Emirates, Koscielny poached a 72nd-minute winner against Newcastle. Arsenal's fifth win in six set them up for a 2016 title surge with Man Utd, Liverpool and Chelsea well out of the race.

In the transfer window Arsenal signed centre-midfielder Mohamed Elneny, a neat squad player but not one that raised the level of the team. Debuchy was loaned to Bordeaux. The Frenchman started his Arsenal career well, but was unlucky with injuries and then showed little fight to reclaim his place from Bellerín, with indifferent performances when he did get an opportunity.

After beating Sunderland 3-1 for the second time in the season, this time in the FA Cup, Arsenal went to ninth-place Liverpool, who were now managed by Jürgen Klopp. This fixture was often a breathless classic – aided by attacking quality against poor defending and goalkeeping – and this time was no different. After ten minutes, Čech pushed a shot out and Roberto Firmino drilled it back past him. Minutes later, Campbell played in Ramsey, who scored at the near post past Simon Mignolet. Firmino curled brilliantly into the top corner from 20 yards. With only 25 minutes gone, Giroud flicked in a corner from close range to make it 2-2. The Frenchman then failed to slide in Bellerín's low cross with the goal gaping, while Firmino grazed the crossbar.

Early in the second half, Giroud turned Kolo Touré and fired an excellent finish. As the rain lashed down, Arsenal were minutes away from an unlikely but crucial three points when they yet again conceded a late equaliser at Anfield (see also Emile Heskey in 2003, Yossi Benayoun in 2009, Martin Škrtel in 2014). It was entirely avoidable as they got deeper and deeper, and ball-watched a Hail Mary allowing Liverpool to win the first header and Joe Allen to scuff a volley that Čech could only push into the net to make it 3-3.

A goalless draw at Stoke, with both goalkeepers making key saves, sent Arsenal back to the top of the table on goal difference. The home fans again targeted Ramsey for having the temerity to have his leg broken by their player six years earlier, singing, "Aaron Ramsey, he walks with a limp."

Arsenal were back at home against Chelsea, who were down in 14th with Guus Hiddink the interim manager after Mourinho had been sacked before Christmas. It was an opportunity to get back on track. Walcott was given the captain's armband to mark his tenth anniversary at the club – a nice gesture if it had been a meaningless end-of-season run-out, but a strange move for a team going for the league and for a player that had been a passenger the week before against Stoke before being replaced by Alex Iwobi. After 18 minutes, Costa was played through, regular captain Mertesacker brought him down and was sent off. Costa scored at the near post soon after and it ended 1-0 to Chelsea – the ninth league game in a row Arsenal had failed to beat Chelsea and the sixth in which they had failed to score.

Back in the FA Cup, Coquelin and Sánchez made their first starts for two months against Championship side Burnley. Chambers curled an excellent opener with the outside of his foot. Sam Vokes headed an equaliser but Sánchez finished off a flowing move that started deep in Arsenal's half to make it 2-1. Rosický came on for his first (and last) appearance of the season after a knee injury but suffered a thigh injury within minutes. It was a sad and apt end for the talented Little Mozart, whose special moments were too few in his ten injury-hit years at the club.

The following Tuesday night, Arsenal could not get past Southampton's Fraser Forster despite Özil creating ten chances, and when Sánchez did, his shot was blocked on the line. It ended in a goalless draw, Arsenal's third league game in a row without scoring and three points from 12 dropped them to fourth, behind Spurs on goal difference.

The biggest day in the title race so far was set up after Özil and Oxlade-Chamberlain scored in the space of 88 seconds to earn a 2-0 win at Bournemouth. At midday Valentine's Day, third-place Arsenal hosted leaders Leicester looking to close a five-point gap, while Man City and Spurs played later on. Arsenal started well, but Čech had to make an excellent low save from a Vardy header.

KING OF THE ASSISTS

Özil has led the league for assists in Germany (2009/10), Spain (2011/12) and England (2015/16), the only player to do so. He has also been the assist master in the World Cup (2010), Euros (2012), Champions League (2010-11) and Europa League (2009/10). With 16 assists – perfectly-weighted through-balls, deft crosses and balls over the top of packed defences, and enticing set-pieces – in the first half of 2015/16, he was set to beat Thierry Henry's Premier League record of 20 assists in one season. However, he finished on 19 as Giroud and others fired blanks in early 2016.

Just before half-time, Vardy beat Nacho Monreal to the ball in the Arsenal area and threw himself into the full-back – this was now often seen as clever forward play and not a dive, even though the defender was not preventing the player from reaching the ball, which had gone in a very different direction to where Vardy launched himself. Either way, Monreal should have known better as it was Vardy's sixth penalty win of the season. The striker lashed the spot-kick past Čech and the Emirates fans were fuming at referee Martin Atkinson.

Ten minutes into the second half, Danny Simpson held Giroud back and Atkinson gave him his second yellow card. After 70 minutes, Giroud expertly cushioned a header into Walcott's path and the substitute sidefooted the equaliser from Arsenal's first shot on target. Arsenal threw everything at Leicester's packed defence but their 24 efforts at goal and 11 corners were undone by poor finishing and Schmeichel's saves. Vardy's pace was still a threat on the break but Chambers, who had replaced an injured Koscielny at half-time, dealt with him well.

Wenger brought on Welbeck, who had not played for over nine months. After 95 minutes, Arsenal had a free-kick and their last chance. Özil curled another cross and Welbeck soared to glance in and make it 2-1. It sparked wild celebrations from the players and the crowd as the Emirates erupted liked it had not done since Barcelona in 2011. It felt like a monumental psychological blow that would derail underdogs Leicester and propel Arsenal to the title.

In the Champions League, Arsenal were solid for a long time against holders Barcelona at the Emirates. However, they could not maintain their discipline and typically over-committed, leaving Neymar to tee up Lionel Messi in a rapid counter-attack. Mertesacker then tried to cushion a cross to

Flamini instead of clearing it and the Frenchman clattered Messi to give a penalty away 47 seconds after coming on as a substitute. Messi made it 2-0.

Arsenal then had a perfect opportunity to shake off their Old Trafford inferiority complex and lay down a title marker – van Gaal was under pressure; the home side had 14 players injured; and slow midfielders Michael Carrick and Daley Blind played centre-back, right-back Guillermo Varela only ever played three other games for the club and it was 18-year-old striker Marcus Rashford's second senior game. Two of the Man Utd back four were booked in the first 22 minutes, but Arsenal applied little pressure in an insipid display.

After 29 minutes, Gabriel's mishit clearance fell perfectly for Rashford to sidefoot in. Minutes later, Arsenal's defence again rolled out the red carpet for the youngster, leaving him unmarked to nod in a cross. Welbeck headed in an Özil free-kick similar to his Leicester winner and Arsenal had something to play for in the second half. Just after half-time, Rashford felt his hamstring and captain Koscielny obligingly kicked the ball out instead of playing on – Arsenal were an accommodating side to play against. Rashford was again given the freedom of Old Trafford and teed up Ander Herrera, whose shot deflected in off Koscielny. Özil bounced a volley into the ground and the top corner to make it 3-2 to Man Utd. Arsenal had 26 minutes to pressure the makeshift defence, which now included 18-year-old Timothy Fosu-Mensah making his debut. However, there was little increase in urgency and Man Utd coasted through the rest of the game – Arsenal had choked.

A few nights later against relegation-threatened Swansea, Sánchez lifted the ball over the defence and Campbell slid in to score. However, Čech had to pick the ball out of the net only seconds after kicking it up the other end – Özil and Ramsey lost challenges and Wayne Routledge converted. Sánchez hit the woodwork twice. Giroud rattled the bar but was now seven league games without a goal. Čech missed a free-kick and Ashley Williams scored from two yards to give the away side a 2-1 win. Arsenal were in third place, six points behind Leicester and three behind Spurs, who they faced next at White Hart Lane.

Against Spurs, Ramsey cleverly flicked in the opener against the run of play, but the game turned in the second half when Coquelin impetuously hacked down Kane to receive his second yellow card. Within seven minutes, Toby Alderweireld fired in a loose ball from a corner and Kane curled a brilliant finish out wide. Ospina, in for the injured Čech, made nine crucial saves including one that was shown by goalline technology to be 1mm from being over the line as he exhibited his strange tendency of standing behind the goalline. The ten men somehow came away with a 2-2 draw when Sánchez bobbled a shot past Hugo Lloris.

Arsenal had a third consecutive FA Cup to play for. After a goalless draw at the Emirates, they knocked out Hull for the third year running with braces from Giroud and Walcott. That set up a quarter-final against Watford at a sunny Emirates. It was a familiar story as Arsenal failed to press home their dominance and fell behind due to weak defending. Troy Deeney beat both Chambers and Mertesacker to flick on a throw-in and Odion Ighalo turned Gabriel to fire in. Adlène Guedioura hammered a rising drive into the top corner to make it 2-0.

On 88 minutes, Welbeck got one back but then clumsily failed to net with only a defender on the line after Iwobi's shot came back off the post. It was Arsenal's third consecutive loss at the Emirates and their first FA Cup defeat in three years and 16 matches.

No one expected Arsenal to turn around a 2-0 deficit in Barcelona and, although they played well enough, they lost 3-1 as the MSN attacking trio (Messi, Luis Suárez and Neymar) got one each. Elneny scored his first Arsenal goal with a fine curler from the edge of the area into the corner. Arsenal had gone out of two cups in four days.

With nine games left, there was still time for Leicester to crack, although they had reacted to their last-minute Emirates defeat like Champions.

At Everton, Sánchez played a one-two with Özil, then slipped in Welbeck to round goalkeeper Joel Robles and score. Bellerín then released Iwobi with a long ball and the lively 19-year-old drove forward and sidefooted through Robles' legs to score on his first Premier League start. A 2-0 win was Arsenal's first in four games. Iwobi scored again as Arsenal cruised to a 4-0 victory over Watford.

At West Ham, Iwobi set up both Özil and Sánchez to produce a 2-0 lead. However, just before half-time, Andy Carroll powered in a header unchallenged. Almost immediately, when West Ham returned a corner, four Arsenal players seemed to be marking each other, leaving Carroll to chest down and volley at the second attempt to make it 2-2. If there was any talk at half-time about how to stop crosses coming in and resist the Carroll battering ram, it did not work as Monreal was beaten on the right and Carroll headed in to complete a seven-minute far-post hat-trick. Koscielny hooked in a loose ball to end a pulsating 3-3 draw.

Against Crystal Palace, Welbeck cleverly scooped over the defence for Sánchez to head over Wayne Hennessey. Arsenal passed and passed but their failure to create clear-cut chances told when Yannick Bolasie exposed Čech's new-found vulnerability to shots at the near post. A 1-1 draw left Arsenal in third place and Arsenal fans supporting Leicester while fearing a Spurs title win.

Sánchez showed his class against West Brom with a clever turn and drive from 20 yards followed by a curling free-kick to give a 2-0 win. A 0-0 draw at Sunderland was notable for: (1) Wilshere's first action since the 2015 FA Cup Final 11 months previously due to breaking his fibula in pre-season; and (2) Walcott jumping out of a tackle with Younès Kaboul when Vito Mannone was out of his goal and the Englishman had a great chance to score a late winner. It said a lot about Walcott's, and Arsenal's, mentality.

A 20-pass move ended with Welbeck volleying the winner against Norwich. A protest by some fans – who held up banners calling for Wenger to leave and "Time for Change" A4 posters – was drowned out by chants of "There's only one, Arsène Wenger." The divide between fans had become increasingly toxic.

Arsenal played out an entertaining 2-2 draw at Man City, twice coming from behind. Giroud finally scored, heading his first in 16 league games. Sánchez scored an excellent strike after a one-two with Giroud. The unfortunate Welbeck, who had had a decent three months since returning from injury, suffered another serious knee injury putting him out of Euro 2016.

On the final day of the season, Arsenal faced Aston Villa while Spurs only needed a draw at relegated Newcastle to finish above Arsenal for the first time since 1995. Cazorla made his first start since November. Giroud headed the opener while Newcastle were surprisingly 2-0 up at half-time. However, Spurs got one back and Newcastle had a player sent off. As Giroud sealed a hat-trick and the win with two more, news kept coming through of Newcastle goals. It had been a long time since the Emirates fans had laughed so hard and they were united singing, "Tottenham Hotspur, It's happened again." Substitute Arteta had a nice send-off when his shot rebounded off the bar and in off goalkeeper Mark Bunn, although it was later given as an own-goal.

Arsenal won 4-0 while Spurs lost 5-1. It was Spurs' best team in decades but Arsenal finished above them in second. Rosický received a guard of honour from his teammates, who wore Rosický 7 shirts, and Flamini and a tearful Arteta also said goodbyes. No one predicted the Spaniard would return as head coach three and a half years later. Čech won the Premier League Golden Glove with 18 clean sheets and did provide more confidence at the back, but he was not the world-class goalkeeper of yesteryear and was beaten ten times from outside the area.

Finishing second, Arsenal's highest position since 2004/05, put a flattering gloss on the season aided by their now-traditional end-of-season no-pressure run-in and Spurs' capitulation. However, it was Arsenal's lowest points total for four years and their best chance to win the title in years with Man City, Man Utd, Chelsea and Liverpool all failing to challenge and replacing their manager during or after the season.

Instead, it was 5000-1 shots Leicester that seized the moment. They had a well-organised defence, a quality holding midfielder, and counter-attacking tactics that maximised the talents of Vardy and Riyad Mahrez. It was a perfect storm for Leicester as their lack of European football, early exits from both cups and clean injury record enabled them to play a settled side, while they received a Premier League record 13 penalties. Wenger's failure to sign an outfield player in summer 2015 proved costly. The likes of Leicester and Southampton showed that the talent was out there as they scouted quality players for low fees. Arsenal would have loved Schmeichel, N'Golo Kanté, Vardy and Mahrez, who Leicester signed for a total of £9m.

As expected, it was a season too far for Flamini (12 starts), Arteta (two starts) and Rosický (zero starts); while Wilshere only made one start and, most significantly, Cazorla played just 21 times. This cost Arsenal in midfield, as did the failure to recruit an elite pacey centre-forward to take the burden off Giroud. The Frenchman finished with 24 goals, but went 15 games, or 881 minutes, in early 2016 without scoring – an unbelievable run for a striker in a team that won a high proportion of matches. Giroud had always had dry spells, but this was at a different level.

Despite having plenty of possession, Arsenal's slow build-up play was often nullified, aided by Arsenal's runners Walcott and Oxlade-Chamberlain both having ineffective seasons, scoring seven goals between them in a combined 50 league games. With little width and pace, Arsenal were heavily reliant on Özil to unpick the lock, which he did consistently. Not surprisingly, they scored their lowest number of league goals since 2006/07.

However, it was not as simple as buying new players – there were no tactical changes to overcome teams with solid, deep and narrow defences apart from the Özil/Sánchez scooped pass over the top; Wenger was unable to motivate players for every game as they put in numerous listless performances, none worse than at Southampton; and every time Arsenal got themselves into a position to push for the title, they buckled. Wenger's unstinting faith in his squad and methods unsurprisingly led to yet another *Groundhog Day*.

2016/17
THE MERTESACKER FINAL

Premier League	Fifth
FA Cup	Winners
Champions League	Round of 16
League Cup	Quarter-final

PREMIER LEAGUE		PL	W	D	L	GF	GA	GD	PTS
1	CHELSEA	38	30	3	5	85	33	52	93
2	TOTTENHAM	38	26	8	4	86	26	60	86
3	MAN CITY	38	23	9	6	80	39	41	78
4	LIVERPOOL	38	22	10	6	78	42	36	76
5	ARSENAL	38	23	6	9	77	44	33	75
6	MAN UTD	38	18	15	5	54	29	25	69

Highlights: Third FA Cup in four years with an excellent final performance against Chelsea; extra-time 2-1 win against Man City in the semi-final; beating Chelsea 3-0 at the Emirates

Lowlights: 10-2 humiliation by Bayern Munich; four away losses in a row in the league culminating in a 3-0 no-show at Crystal Palace; the increasingly toxic division between fans

Player of the year: Alexis Sánchez led the way whether he played upfront or wide scoring 30 goals, including in both the FA Cup semi-final and final

Top scorers: Sánchez 30 (24 in PL), Theo Walcott 19 (10), Olivier Giroud 16 (12), Mesut Özil 12 (8)

Goal of the season: Giroud's improvised scorpion-kick volley versus Crystal Palace, the Emirates, Premier League

Unlike their previous two FA Cup Finals against Hull and Aston Villa, Arsenal went into the 2017 decider against Chelsea as firm underdogs. Chelsea had dominated the league, winning a record 30 games out of 38, while Arsenal struggled in fifth, Arsène Wenger's lowest finish since joining.

Laurent Koscielny got himself sent off and banned with a stupid foul in the last league game against Everton, Shkodran Mustafi was out with concussion and Kieran Gibbs was injured. Arsenal fans were seriously concerned – they had a back three of Per Mertesacker starting his first game of the season due to a knee injury, the inexperienced Rob Holding and left-back Nacho Monreal against Diego Costa, who bullied Arsenal defences almost as much as Didier Drogba used to. Right-winger Alex Oxlade-Chamberlain was at left wing-back.

Surprisingly, Arsenal dominated from the start with purposeful possession. After only four minutes, Alexis Sánchez showed typical perseverance to block a clearance (off his chest and arm) and calmly volleyed low with the outside of his foot past Thibaut Courtois. The linesman flagged, but after a delay, the referee gave a goal, ruling that Aaron Ramsey had been in an offside position but not interfering.

Arsenal continued to create chances as Granit Xhaka found Mesut Özil, Sánchez and Ramsey in space between the lines and Danny Welbeck stretched the Chelsea defence. Welbeck hit the post with a trademark shoulder/header and Ramsey was unable to finish the follow-up, while Gary Cahill cleared a right-footed Özil Chop off the line. Holding stood up to Costa, Mertesacker made a perfect slide tackle in the box and David Ospina saved with his face when Costa did get through. The pattern continued in the second half when Chelsea (down to ten men after Victor Moses picked up a second yellow card for diving to try and win a penalty) made Arsenal pay for their lack of clinical finishing as Costa scored with a low shot from ten yards.

Olivier Giroud was brought on and made an immediate impact – rather than hold the ball up on the left byline, he uncharacteristically turned, wrongfooting Cahill, and clipped a great ball into the box where Ramsey timed his run perfectly and headed another FA Cup winner. Arsenal should have killed the game off in one of their many counter-attacks, including Özil hitting the post when one-on-one.

But they did it – Arsenal won their 13th FA Cup and Wenger his seventh, records for both club and manager, and stopped Chelsea from winning the Double. Despite not starting a game of first-team football for 392 days, Mertesacker used his excellent positional sense and composure to make interceptions, blocks and tackles. In a performance for the ages, the BFG had a game-high 93% passing completion. The fans were united again – for one day at least – and, as in 2014, the stage was set for Wenger to leave the club on a high.

Arsenal yet again started the season unprepared, dropping five points in their first two games as Euro 2016 players were given a late summer break and Arsenal's pursuit of a forward and central defender turned into protracted sagas. With Mertesacker – who was named new club captain despite suffering a major knee injury in pre-season – and Gabriel Paulista injured, the inexperienced pairing of Holding and Calum Chambers started the opening game against Jürgen Klopp's lively Liverpool attack.

Theo Walcott missed an early penalty but drilled the opener 90 seconds later. Philippe Coutinho hit a curling free-kick from long range before Arsenal's ramshackle defence was exposed another three times in 15 minutes. Late goals from Oxlade-Chamberlain and Chambers made the score respectable, but a 4-3 loss ultimately cost a Champions League spot as Arsenal finished one point behind Liverpool.

On paper, the summer transfer business ticked all the boxes – a German World Cup-winning centre-back, a holding midfielder with a good passing range and an experienced forward coming off a 17-goal season in La Liga. They didn't come cheap – a total of £80m for Mustafi, Xhaka and

TYPICAL LINE-UP
(4-2-3-1 TO 3-4-3)

7
Sànchez
Giroud
Welbeck

17
Iwobi
Sànchez

14
Walcott
Ox-Chamberlain
Pérez

11
Özil

29
Xhaka
Ramsey
Ox-Chamberlain

34
Coquelin
Elneny
Cazorla

18
Monreal
Gibbs

6
Koscielny
Gabriel

20
Mustafi
Holding

24
Bellerín

33
Čech
Ospina

Players in: Granit Xhaka, Shkodran Mustafi, Lucas Pérez, Takuma Asano, Rob Holding

Players out: Mikel Arteta, Tomáš Rosický, Mathieu Flamini, Serge Gnabry, Wellington Silva, Wojciech Szczęsny (loan), Calum Chambers (loan), Jack Wilshere (loan)

Lucas Pérez appeased the "spend some money" brigade among Arsenal fans.

Unfortunately, the reality was different. Xhaka quickly caught the eye of referees, not because he was a physical player flying into tackles, but because he was slow, flat-footed and committed himself easily; he was thus dribbled past regularly, which he invariably followed with a crude trip or shirt pull. He did have a nice left foot and switched play well with his long passes.

Mustafi started well, getting tight to opposing forwards and nipping in ahead of them, and loved a crowd-pleasing slide tackle or last-ditch block. He did not lose his first 22 games, but the 'anti-Maldini' started to get exposed, diving into challenges, not knowing where his opposing striker was and failing to develop any chemistry with Koscielny.

After Leicester's Jamie Vardy embarrassingly turned Arsenal down, they turned to Deportivo de La Coruña's Pérez, who scored some good goals at a respectable rate. Wenger did not rate him though and started him in only two Premier League matches and nine games overall (plus 12 substitute appearances), from which he scored seven and assisted five. He was loaned back to Deportivo at the end of the season and subsequently sold to West Ham for £4m and a 75% loss. Japan forward Takuma Asano was also signed but was refused a work permit and never played for the club.

Fit-again Jack Wilshere, after only making the bench in the first few games and being omitted from the first England squad of the season, pushed for a year-long loan at promoted Bournemouth – a sad fall from grace for the former big hope of English football. 21-year-old winger Serge Gnabry refused Arsenal's last-minute contract offer after he starred at the Rio Olympics and went to Werder Bremen for only £5m. It was another Stage Three contract blunder by Arsenal and the icing on the cake for the club's worst transfer window since the system was introduced in 2002.

In Stage One, Wenger uncovered gems for low fees, often using his inside knowledge of France's golden generation, but in Stage Three every club scouted for talent all over the world. Wenger had lost a significant competitive advantage, and the inflated transfer fees and high wages spent on below-par players in summer 2016 cost Arsenal for years, both on and off the pitch. Arsenal's recruitment was poor in Stage Three and, as well as Wenger, the scouting, analytics and negotiating teams needed to take responsibility. Head of recruitment Francis Cagigao revealed in 2020 that he had identified Pérez as "a mid-table player" and on Mustafi, "The statistics made a compelling case for the player and the scouting reports were overruled."

Arsenal started to pick up points with wins against Watford, Southampton and Hull. Against Southampton, Koscielny equalised with an impressive overhead kick and substitute Giroud won a 94th-minute penalty that Santi Cazorla dispatched to give a 2-1 win. Arsenal cruised to a 4-1 win at ten-man Hull as Sánchez scored twice and had a penalty saved, while Xhaka laced a 25-yarder into the top corner.

Sánchez was now the regular starting centre-forward and his move from the left wing meant his inclination to try things and high turnover rate were less of a problem. His mobility, energy and ability to score all types of goals relegated Giroud to a regular 70th-minute substitute role (he came on 23 times compared with only 17 starts in 2016/17), which the Frenchman carried out effectively, coming on to score decisive goals numerous times. After years of telling everyone he wanted to play centrally, Walcott "said to the manager that I want to be known for playing on the right again."

Arsenal then blitzed Chelsea at the Emirates with a first-half performance of intensity, quick passing and clinical finishing. Sánchez robbed Cahill and dinked over Courtois. Minutes later, Arsenal sliced open Chelsea with one- and two-touch play and Walcott made it 2-0. Özil left N'Golo Kanté for dead with a brilliant turn, played it to

Sánchez, who chipped it back for the German to bounce a volley in. Arsenal's two marquee players always looked for each other first – recognition of each other's ability as well as their lack of faith in some teammates – and 55% of Arsenal's 121 goals in 2016/17 involved at least one of the pair. The 3-0 win was Arsenal's first victory over Chelsea in the league for five years. However, it proved a defining moment for Chelsea, not Arsenal, as Antonio Conte responded by switching formation to 3-4-3, went on a 13-game winning streak and, like Wenger, won the league in his first full season in English football.

At Burnley, Arsenal got a fortunate late winner as a corner ended up going in off Koscielny's arm. Arsenal were comfortable against Swansea after Walcott scored twice from close range, but Xhaka lost the ball on the edge of the area and Gylfi Sigurdsson curled in. Sánchez hung a ball up for Özil at the back post, who leathered a volley into the top corner rather than use his usual controlled bounce technique. Swansea made it 3-2 and the Xhaka alarm bells started to ring when he hacked down Modou Barrow on the halfway line and was sent off. Arsenal held on to win 3-2 and were second on goal difference.

Sánchez and substitute Giroud both scored twice in a 4-1 win at bottom-of-the-table Sunderland. A 1-1 draw in a low-key home derby against a Spurs team there for the taking was a wasted opportunity, followed by a fortunate draw at Old Trafford as Giroud came on to score a late bullet header from an enticing Oxlade-Chamberlain cross – Arsenal's only effort on goal in the game.

Sánchez scored twice against Bournemouth in a 3-1 win and followed it up with a 14-minute hat-trick at West Ham. The first two were low drives, the third a dink over Darren Randolph after sitting the goalkeeper on the floor with a brilliant dummy. Özil and Oxlade-Chamberlain also scored in a 5-1 win. Arsenal went behind at Stoke as Xhaka made a clumsy-looking tackle on Joe Allen and Charlie Adam dispatched the penalty. Walcott equalised before Oxlade-Chamberlain spotted Özil's run and the German scored a brilliant looping header over Lee Grant. Three consecutive wins and a 14-game unbeaten run put Arsenal in a healthy position in mid-December – second, just three points behind Chelsea.

In the Champions League, Arsenal drew twice with Unai Emery's Paris Saint-Germain. They were fortunate, especially in the away game where Edinson Cavani scored after 42 seconds, but then missed chance after chance. Sánchez equalised late on, while Giroud again made an impact as a substitute – however, this time it was by picking up two yellow cards and getting sent off along with Marco Verratti. The home tie was an entertaining 2-2 draw, with

Arsenal's goals coming from a penalty and an own-goal.

Arsenal dealt with Basel and Ludogorets, beating the latter 6-0 at home with Özil scoring his first-ever hat-trick. Sadly, though no one knew at the time, the October 2016 game was Cazorla's last for Arsenal as he underwent 11 operations on his Achilles tendon over the subsequent two years. After one, he contracted gangrene in his ankle and had to have skin removed from his tattooed arm and grafted onto his heel. The infection ate away 10cm of his Achilles tendon, which was eventually reconstructed using muscle from his hamstring. Cazorla recalled: "At night, a yellow liquid would come out. Every time they sewed me up, it split again – more liquid."

Arsenal, and Francis Coquelin in particular, badly missed Cazorla's quality in centre-midfield and ability to receive and manipulate the ball in tight spaces with quick feet. The smiley Spaniard was one of the most two-footed players of his generation. There was a happy ending for Cazorla, who had a successful comeback season at Villarreal in 2018/19 and even returned to the Spanish national team.

At Ludogorets, Arsenal were 2-0 down but goals from Xhaka and Giroud levelled the tie. In the 87th minute, Özil was played through and was the coolest person in the stadium as he lifted the ball teasingly over the goalkeeper's despairing *Platoon* dive, then dummied and dummied, leaving bodies everywhere and an empty net to score the winner. It was the German's highest-scoring season at the club with 12 goals.

Pérez's hat-trick in Basel gave a 4-1 win, the second ending a 33-pass move. Despite topping the group for the first time in five years, Arsenal were again drawn against Bayern Munich.

At Everton, Sánchez opened the scoring with a low free-kick, but the home team stepped up the intensity and got the crowd going. Séamus Coleman and Ashley Williams were left unchallenged to score headers and give Everton a 2-1 lead. Arsenal mounted a late siege that saw Monreal and Alex Iwobi efforts cleared off the line, Sánchez fouled by Kevin Mirallas but no penalty given, and Petr Čech go up for a corner and come inches from a crucial header. It led to the entertaining sight of Čech alongside Maarten Stekelenburg in the Everton goal as the defence pushed out, before the Arsenal goalkeeper rushed back onside and then back to his goal as Everton countered. It was Arsenal's first league loss since the opening day of the season.

At Pep Guardiola's Man City, Sánchez played in Walcott to score after only five minutes. Just after half-time, Arsenal's defence tried to play Leroy Sané offside but the German broke through to finish. Kevin De Bruyne volleyed

NOT GOOD ENOUGH FOR WEST BROM

When Gnabry was sold to Werder Bremen for only £5m, the deal was reported to have Bayern Munich's involvement. This was seemingly confirmed when the winger signed for Bayern after a breakout year at Bremen. He was soon winning the Bundesliga, Champions League and Bayern Player of the Season as well as being a regular goalscorer for the German national team. Arsenal's regret was only slightly eased by the sight of Gnabry smashing four goals at White Hart Lane and two at Stamford Bridge in the 2019/20 Champions League. The young speedster made some promising contributions for Arsenal in 2013/14 before a knee injury ruled him out for a year. Arsenal then inexplicably loaned him to Tony Pulis's West Brom, a manager whose style of play and "rugby" tactics Wenger regularly criticised. Gnabry played a total of 137 minutes all season as Pulis infamously said, "Serge has come here to play games but he just hasn't been for me, at the moment, at that level to play the games." After that experience and the Rio Olympics, Gnabry wanted game time.

a brilliant 50-yard pass to Raheem Sterling, who cut inside Monreal and beat Čech at the near post. The second consecutive loss after leading left Arsenal in fourth, nine points behind leaders Chelsea.

Giroud made his first league start on Boxing Day against West Brom and showed strength to score a looping header in the 86th minute for a 1-0 win. On New Year's Day against Crystal Palace, another cold and sleepy Emirates crowd was given some relief by Giroud's inspired scorpion-kick goal. It was a great piece of improvisation and the end to a rapid Wengerball move that started on the edge of the Arsenal box, saw Giroud involved with a flick in his own half, then race to the other end to volley Sánchez's cross from behind him with his heel. It flew in off the underside of the bar and topped Man Utd's Henrikh Mkhitaryan similar finish only days earlier as Giroud won the 2017 FIFA Puskás Award.

The away woes didn't get much better at Bournemouth as Arsenal started passively and cracked under a bit of home pressure to go 3-0 down. This time they came back led by Sánchez, an excellent Pérez volley and a Giroud header in the 92nd minute, which he comically celebrated by mimicking his scorpion kick from the previous week while Sánchez and others berated him to get back to his own half as there was still a game to win. Arsenal then got an away win with a 4-0 cruise at Swansea, helped by two own-goals and Giroud and Sánchez strikes.

Arsenal were on course against Burnley after Mustafi headed his first goal for the club. However, card-magnet Xhaka lost the ball in midfield and slid in two-footed on Steven Defour to again leave his team with ten men. After 92 minutes, Coquelin gave away a penalty and Andre Gray scored down the middle. A furious Wenger was sent off, and abused and pushed fourth-official Anthony Taylor to earn a four-game touchline ban. The mood in the Emirates turned from anger to joy within minutes when Koscielny won a penalty and Sánchez, who had missed his previous two Premier League spot-kicks, scored with a Panenka to make it 2-1. After the game, Wenger said about Xhaka, "He's not naturally a great tackler... He doesn't master well the technique. I would encourage him not to tackle, to stay on his feet."

On a cold Tuesday night at the Emirates, Watford went 2-0 up after 13 minutes, taking advantage of a slow start by Arsenal, something that had become increasingly common. As usual, they improved in the second half and Iwobi got one back, but Arsenal lost 2-1. Wenger said, "It was obvious we lost duels and were not sharp enough. It looked more mentally that we were not ready for the challenges."

Arsenal went to Chelsea at the start of February nine points behind and needing a win to open up the title race.

However, Chelsea were too good, with Marco Alonso heading in a rebound in a challenge that left Héctor Bellerín concussed. Eden Hazard dribbled from the halfway line, throwing off Arsenal enforcer Coquelin like a rag doll, and scored. Cesc Fàbregas returned a Čech miskick into an empty net, while Giroud made it 3-1 at the end.

In the Champions League at Bayern Munich, Arsenal invited Arjen Robben to showcase his signature move after 11 minutes – the Dutchman duly cut inside from the right wing and curled a brilliant left-foot shot into the far corner. Sánchez equalised after Manuel Neuer saved his penalty, but Arsenal capitulated in the second half after Koscielny went off injured, conceding three in ten minutes. The final score was a humiliating 5-1 as Bayern dominated with 74% possession.

In the home leg, Walcott smashed into the roof of the net before Koscielny fouled Robert Lewandowski in the area and was sent off. Arsenal again collapsed, conceding four goals in 17 minutes, and Bayern humiliated Arsenal 5-1 for the third time in 16 months. At 10-2, it was the biggest aggregate defeat ever suffered by an English team in Europe. After the first game Wenger blamed Koscielny's injury, after the second he blamed the same player's red card. However, Arsenal were outplayed and fell apart both times despite Wenger's constant references to the players' mental strength.

It was sad to see Wenger tarnish his legacy on the biggest stage. For the sixth time in eight years, Arsenal went out to Barcelona or Bayern – both top teams in Europe, but not once could Wenger engineer a tactical masterclass or motivate a fighting win. It was the seventh year running that Arsenal went out at the last 16 stage and yet again the title and Champions League were gone by early March.

Sánchez scored twice in a 2-0 win over Hull but was then benched at Liverpool after an argument in training. Arsenal lost 3-1 and the home side pushed them out of the top four. The Chilean, who, like Özil, was stalling on signing a new contract, had cut an increasingly frustrated figure during Arsenal's poor form. He was particularly animated at his teammates when they sat back while he closed down opposing defenders and Arsenal's disjointed pressing allowed an easy out ball. It was hard to discern what the team's instructions on this were.

At West Brom, Arsenal had 77% possession and made three times as many passes as Tony Pulis' side, but watched on as their centre-backs took turns to head home corners. It ended 3-1 to the home side, Arsenal's fourth loss in five league games.

With Wenger's contract ending at the end of the season, the Arsenal fans were broadly split into two camps – Arsène Knows Best and the Wenger Out Brigade. Frustration grew, protests were planned and Wenger Out banners appeared at both home and away games, but were met with chants of "There's only one, Arsène Wenger." At the Hawthorns, both sides went to the trouble of hiring a plane to fly their message over the stadium: "In Arsène We Trust, Respect AW." versus "No Contract, Wenger Out."

Arsenal fans were at different points in the grieving process for Stage One Wenger, with most in the denial or anger phases. Many wanted a change of manager as they saw that Wenger could no longer motivate the team to perform consistently, organise the defence or the team when they did not have the ball and had lost his touch in the transfer market. While others saw Arsenal were stagnating, they did not want to disrespect him or clung to hopes that he would turn it around. Opposition fans revelled in Arsenal's plight with chants of "Arsène Wenger, we want you to stay." Wenger himself was asked at almost every press conference whether he would sign the new contract he was offered earlier in the season when things were not as bad. In March, he said, "You will know very soon."

The Emirates unrest was not helped when Man City's Sané scored after five minutes. Arsenal had again started a game on the back foot, prompting Wenger to drop one of his favourite, and most frustrating, Stage Three phrases, "I feared that we could start with the handbrake on because of the pressure we are under." Arsenal equalised twice in a 2-2 draw. Three second-half goals against West Ham produced a comfortable 3-0 win.

Arsenal then barely turned up at relegation-threatened Crystal Palace. In a 3-0 loss, all three goals came after the home side had won aerial challenges as well as the second ball. Arsenal did not have an effort on target in the second half. It was the final straw for many fans who this time turned on the players, chanting "You're not fit to wear the shirt." Captain for the day Walcott said, "They wanted it more. You could sense that from the kick-off." Just as damning was Palace manager's Sam Allardyce tactical exposé: "Tactically the players were aware of how to beat Arsenal. The first thing was to defend and frustrate them, keep them playing sideways, then use the space behind the full-backs. Arsenal have been weak defensively, they leave the centre-backs exposed." Arsenal's fourth away loss in a row was their worst run in the league since 1995.

Arsenal CEO Ivan Gazidis, recognising the toxic atmosphere (or more cynically playing to the crowd), said at a fans' forum in April 2017 that the season's poor performance would be a "catalyst for change," but did anyone apart from majority-owner Stan Kroenke have the power or inclination to tap Wenger on the shoulder? Either way, it was clear the club had no succession plan.

The FA Cup provided some respite. Championship side Preston gave Arsenal a tough game, but a late Giroud goal earnt a 2-1 win. At Southampton, Welbeck produced two goals, one assist and one Salt Bae celebration in an impressive first start for nine months. Walcott scored a hat-trick against his former club to seal an emphatic 5-0 win.

Arsenal were a 'romance-of-the-cup' sideshow in the fifth round as they travelled to non-league Sutton, where 46-year-old reserve goalkeeper Wayne Shaw ate a pasty on the bench. Disappointingly, it was not a spontaneous moment of fun as a betting company was offering eight to one against him doing so, and he later resigned and was fined by the FA for breaching betting rules. Arsenal won 2-0 as Walcott became the 16th player to score 100 goals for the club. In the quarter-final, Arsenal faced another non-league team and they dealt with Lincoln comfortably, winning 5-0.

After some favourable draws, Arsenal faced a difficult semi-final against Man City. In the second half, an Arsenal attack broke down and they were inevitably punished for leaving Agüero one-on-one on the halfway line with Monreal when the Argentine dinked over a slow-advancing Čech. Ten minutes later, Oxlade-Chamberlain curled a brilliant cross to the back post where Monreal thumped a low volley in with his right foot. Agüero had a goal disallowed while both Yaya Touré and Fernandinho hit the woodwork.

In extra time, Koscielny headed a free-kick across goal, Welbeck took an air-shot and Sánchez buried it. The Chilean loved the big occasion and Wembley, scoring crucial goals in all four FA Cup semi-finals and finals he played, as well as a double for his country. A 2-1 comeback win gave Arsenal the chance to make it three FA Cups in four years. When seemingly losing the war, Wenger always managed to win a battle to fend off the mounting criticism.

Down in sixth place, Wenger then adopted the fashionable 3-4-3 formation and Arsenal won seven of their last eight league games – "Even at my age, you can change," he said. Sadly, the resurgence was not entirely the result of a tactical masterstroke (though it did suit Arsenal to have an extra defender and right wing-back seemed to make the most of Oxlade-Chamberlain's pace and direct running), but playing against teams that were 'on the beach' (Arsenal even won 4-1 at Stoke, their first win at the ground in seven years), relegated or with minds on the Europa League

(Man Utd). The win over Man Utd was Wenger's first competitive win over Mourinho at the 16th attempt.

The single loss was a convincing one at White Hart Lane to a resurgent Spurs under Mauricio Pochettino. For the first time in 22 years, Arsenal finished below Spurs and they had something to envy – an up-and-coming innovative manager, young unknown players turning into stars and a team on the rise. Arsenal's traditional end-of-season run gave them a chance of a top-four finish on the final day of the season, but despite beating Everton 3-1 with ten men, Liverpool also won.

Arsenal finished fifth and Wenger's 19 consecutive years of Champions League football was over, a run bettered only by Real Madrid.

At the FA Cup Final, majority owner Stan Kroenke made a rare appearance in a *Bugsy Malone* suit and must have seen the jubilant fans and wondered what the problem was – a couple of days later, he sidelined the Arsenal board and Gazidis, and gave Wenger a two-year contract. Unfortunately, not many believed Kroenke when he said, "Our ambition is to win the Premier League and other major trophies in Europe… Arsène is the best person to help us make that happen."

BUY HIGH, SELL LOW

In late Stage Two and Stage Three, Arsenal left an estimated £300m on the table with a string of decisions at odds with a frugal club running a self-sustainable model and that did not need hindsight to show that they would prove costly:

- Buying – Many fans implored Arsenal to "spend some money." In Stage Three, they did – often badly. No longer the masters of picking up cheap gems, Arsenal bought numerous players at well above market value (Mustafi, Xhaka, Chambers – estimated overspend £30m) and that they later sold at a substantial loss (Pérez, Asano, Mathieu Debuchy – estimated cost £20m).

- Selling – Indecisiveness, poor negotiations and high wages meant Arsenal ended up giving squad players away for low amounts, while the likes of Man Utd, Chelsea or Spurs would receive notable amounts as transfer fees spiralled (Joel Campbell, Gibbs, Wojciech Szczęsny – estimated lost revenue £10m).

- Contracts – Arsenal allowed players to run down their contracts and leave for nothing (Bacary Sagna, Wilshere, Ramsey, Welbeck – estimated lost revenue £85m) or a reduced fee (Robin van Persie, Gnabry – estimated lost revenue £20m). New contracts were given to players past their best or with long-term injury issues who thus hardly played in their final season (Abou Diaby, Tomáš Rosický, Mikel Arteta, Mertesacker – estimated cost of wages £15m).

The nadir was reached when Arsenal turned down £60m for Sánchez in summer 2017, only to double down on their mistake four months later by swapping him for an inferior player of the same age in Henrikh Mkhitaryan and giving the Armenian a big wage hike. Mkhitaryan left on a free two years later. With Özil also running down his contract, the German was given a £350,000/week deal, double the wages of the next highest-paid player. The Sánchez and Özil decisions cost Arsenal an estimated £80m in lost transfer fees and £60m in excess wages.

She Wore a Yellow Ribbon

1998

Arsenal 2
Newcastle 0

Goals:
Overmars
Anelka

Wembley,
London

2002

Arsenal 2
Chelsea 0

Goals:
Parlour
Ljungberg

Millennium
Stadium,
Cardiff

2003

Arsenal 1
Soton 0

Goals:
Pires

Millennium
Stadium,
Cardiff

2005

Arsenal 0
Man Utd 0
(Arsenal won
5-4 on pens)

Penalties:
Lauren
Ljungberg
van Persie
Cole
Vieira

Millennium
Stadium,
Cardiff

2014

Arsenal 3
Hull 2
(AET)

Goals:
Cazorla
Koscielny
Ramsey

Wembley,
London

2015

Arsenal 4
Aston Villa 0

Goals:
Walcott
Sánchez
Mertesacker
Giroud

Wembley,
London

2017

Arsenal 2
Chelsea 1

Goals:
Sánchez
Ramsey

Wembley,
London

The FA Cup Master

- Wenger had a 67% win rate (73-22-14) in FA Cup games versus 57% overall

- Wenger had an 88% win rate in FA Cup Finals (7-1) versus 0% in other finals for Arsenal (0-5)

- Wenger won the cup in three different decades at three venues (old Wembley, Cardiff, new Wembley)

Most FA Cup Wins

Arsenal	14
Man Utd	12
Chelsea	8
Spurs	8
Arsène Wenger	**7**
Liverpool	7
Aston Villa	7
Newcastle	6
Man City	6
Blackburn Rovers	6

2017/18
WENGER OUT

Premier League		Sixth
FA Cup		Third round
Europa League		Semi-final
League Cup		Final
Community Shield		Winners

PREMIER LEAGUE		PL	W	D	L	GF	GA	GD	PTS
1	MAN CITY	38	32	4	2	106	27	79	100
2	MAN UTD	38	25	6	7	68	28	40	81
3	TOTTENHAM	38	23	8	7	74	36	38	77
4	LIVERPOOL	38	21	12	5	84	38	46	75
5	CHELSEA	38	21	7	10	62	38	24	70
6	ARSENAL	38	19	6	13	74	51	23	63

Highlights: The Merci Arsène send-off and 5-0 hammering of Burnley at Arsène Wenger's last home game; beating AC Milan 2-0 in the San Siro; 2-0 win in North London derby at the Emirates

Lowlights: Going out of the Europa League in the semi-final to Atlético Madrid despite playing against ten men for most of the first leg; swatted aside 3-0 by Man City in the League Cup Final; losing to Championship team Nottingham Forest 4-2 in the FA Cup; 4-0 humbling at Anfield; seven away losses in a row in 2018

Player of the year: Nacho Monreal – the dependable left-back and sometime centre-back consistently put in solid performances and added (six) goals to his game

Top scorers: Alexandre Lacazette 17 (14 in PL), Aaron Ramsey 11 (7), Pierre-Emerick Aubameyang 10 (10), Danny Welbeck 10 (5)

Goal of the season: Ramsey's mid-air volleyed flick with the outside of his foot and over the goalkeeper versus CSKA Moscow, the Emirates, Europa League

26 February 2018, League Cup Final – Arsenal's French and German international centre-backs were marking one man, Sergio Agüero, when Man City's goalkeeper had the ball. One long ball later, Agüero was one-on-one with Arsenal goalkeeper David Ospina and scored the opening goal.

26 April 2018, Europa League semi-final first leg – Arsenal's French and German international centre-backs were marking one man, Antoine Griezmann, when Atlético Madrid's full-back had the ball. One long ball later, Griezmann was one-on-one with Arsenal goalkeeper David Ospina and scored the opening goal.

It was unbelievably bad defending rarely seen on a Sunday league pitch where most hungover centre-backs know the basic rule that one of them marks the man and challenges for the ball while the other drops off and sweeps up. It was unbelievable that such a basic error could happen once at the highest level in a big match. Unbelievable that two experienced centre-backs were so far apart, making one redundant. Unbelievable that it would happen again two months later – only for completeness, the centre-backs would swap roles of weak challenger and ball-watcher.

But it was not unbelievable because this was Arsenal defending in Stage Three Wenger – no learning from mistakes, no shape when the team did not have the ball, no urgency to get goalside or stay with runners, no pre-empting danger and covering for teammates, and no one on the pitch or the sidelines organising or berating players who did not get into position or track back.

With Arsène Wenger missing the opportunity to go out on a high after the 2017 FA Cup win, the ending seemed inevitable – the question was when. Despite chief executive Ivan Gazidis' fighting talk ("There is no complacency anywhere at this club. Our goal is to compete for and win trophies here and in Europe."), it was clear Arsenal were not going to compete for the Premier League, and it only took a couple of games to show they were also going to struggle to meet the new lower expectations of getting back into the Champions League.

Arsenal kicked off the season with their ninth consecutive success at Wembley, beating Chelsea in the Community Shield 4-1 on penalties that followed the new ABBA format. The game had finished 1-1, with new left-back Sead Kolašinac scoring a header on his debut. The league opener was a Friday night home game against Leicester and record signing Alexandre Lacazette opened his account after only 94 seconds with a smart header. Then Arsenal's poor defending came into play, with the common sequence of Granit Xhaka losing the ball and it swiftly ending up in the Arsenal net – a symptom of both his inability to play in tight spaces and his teammates being out of position high up the pitch. Leicester went 2-1 and 3-2 up before late goals from Aaron Ramsey and Olivier Giroud secured the points.

The usual defeat at Stoke followed (1-0, although Lacazette had a goal dubiously ruled out for offside) before an embarrassing day at Anfield. Wenger selected right-back Héctor Bellerín on the left, Alex Oxlade-Chamberlain at right wing-back only days after he turned down a big new contract and days before he transferred to Arsenal's opponents, and Kolašinac and Lacazette on the bench. Questions also hung over Mesut Özil and Alexis Sánchez who were refusing bumper new deals – the latter's move to Man City fell through later that week as Arsenal left it too late to negotiate a replacement. Liverpool ran riot 4-0 as Arsenal were all over the place and did not manage a single effort on target. Wenger admitted, "We were not at the level requested for such a game – not physically, not technically, not mentally." It was the manager's job to get them to that level.

Arsenal started accumulating points with comfortable home wins and clean sheets against Bournemouth, Brighton and West Brom, and had a creditable goalless draw at Stamford

TYPICAL LINE-UP (3-4-3 TO 4-2-3-1)

9 Lacazette — Aubameyang, Giroud

7 Sànchez — Iwobi, Welbeck
17 Iwobi — Walcott, Mkhitaryan

11 Özil

29 Xhaka — Elneny
8 Ramsey — Wilshere

18 Monreal — Kolašinac
6 Koscielny — Monreal, Chambers
20 Mustafi — Holding
24 Bellerín

33 Čech — Ospina

Players in: Sead Kolašinac, Alexandre Lacazette, *Henrikh Mkhitaryan*, *Pierre-Emerick Aubameyang*, *Konstantinos Mavropanos*

Players out: Yaya Sanogo, Wojciech Szczęsny, Gabriel Paulista, Kieran Gibbs, Alex Oxlade-Chamberlain, Lucas Pérez (loan), Ismaël Bennacer, Donyell Malen, Jon Toral, *Francis Coquelin*, *Theo Walcott*, *Alexis Sánchez*, *Olivier Giroud*, *Mathieu Debuchy*

Bridge. Lacazette was settling in and producing a decent goals return. Arsenal were fifth, already six points behind the leaders.

In mid-October came the first of many embarrassing away days against teams Arsenal used to deal with comfortably, often losing leads and capitulating at the sight of energetic opponents and noisy crowds. Watford drew level with a penalty won from a Richarlison dive and scored a 92nd-minute winner from midfielder Tom Cleverley as his opposite number Xhaka was caught watching on and seemingly picking his nose. The match ended an unbelievable three-year run where Arsenal's club captain did not start a Premier League game.

Watford captain Troy Deeney's words afterwards were galling because he was right: "... there's a reason they lost, and it wasn't because of one penalty... I have to watch what I say on TV, but, having a bit of cojones, I think the word is. Having a bit of nuts... Whenever I play Arsenal, I go up and I think, let me whack the first one, and let's see who wants it... And I come on today, jumped up with Mertesacker – didn't even have to jump actually – nod it down, the crowd gets up ... and they all just backed off."

Arsenal finally turned it on at Everton after Wayne Rooney scored the opener with a 20-yard curler reminiscent of the one past David Seaman that announced him to English football 15 years earlier. Helped by Idrissa

Gueye's red card in the second half, Arsenal pinged the ball around and peppered Jordan Pickford's goal with 30 shots, winning 5-2, their first away win of the season. Everton sacked manager Ronald Koeman the next day. Arsenal also fell behind to Swansea, but again came back with a goal and assist from Kolašinac to keep them in fifth place.

Arsenal had their first-ever taste of Thursday night Europa League football with non-glamour ties against FC Köln, BATE Borisov and Red Star Belgrade. The first kick-off was delayed as 20,000 fans travelled from Cologne despite an allocation of 2,900 tickets and some caused trouble trying to get into the ground. They raised the roof after ten minutes when Ospina came out of his area and miskicked, allowing Jhon Córdoba to embarrass him from 40 yards. After being booed off at half-time, Arsenal turned it around with Kolašinac cracking a volley, Sánchez curling brilliantly from the edge of the area and Bellerín netting a rebound to make it 3-1. Jack Wilshere came on for his first Arsenal action in a year.

Arsenal beat BATE Borisov 4-2 in Belarus as Walcott scored twice and Giroud converted a penalty for his 100th Arsenal goal. In Belgrade, Arsenal got their third win with a late Giroud overhead kick that finished a pinball move involving Walcott and

Wilshere – it was another showstopper for Giroud's increasingly-impressive YouTube highlights video. After two uninspiring games, Arsenal hammered BATE Borisov 6-0 with excellent strikes from Mathieu Debuchy, Wilshere and Mohamed Elneny to top the group. It was Arsenal's lowest attendance since leaving Highbury at "just under 30,000," although the official attendance was announced as 54,648.

Arsenal mostly fielded a B team, not that the one-game-a-week schedule was helping the first team in the league. One highlight was the sight of youth prospects Ainsley Maitland-Niles, Reiss Nelson, Joe Willock and Eddie Nketiah getting game time. Eddie had the crowd singing his name after coming off the bench against Norwich in the League Cup and scoring twice in a 2-1 extra-time win. Danny Welbeck scored the winner in the next round against West Ham to put Arsenal into the semi-finals.

At the start of November, Arsenal were outclassed by league leaders Man City who won 3-1. One of the best performances of the season followed in the North London derby as a soaring header by Shkodran Mustafi and close-range finish from Sánchez gave a welcome 2-0 win and boost to the fans.

A stoppage-time Sánchez penalty at Burnley and 5-0 hammering of

Huddersfield with Özil pulling the strings – Arsenal's 12th consecutive league win at home – meant another six points. At the Emirates, Laurent Koscielny and Mustafi gave the ball away in dangerous areas and Man Utd capitalised to go 2-0 up after 11 minutes. It was a frenetic game that finished 3-1 to Man Utd and featured shambolic defending, poor finishing, a late red card for Paul Pogba and 14 saves by goalkeeper David de Gea including several brilliant point-blank blocks.

Arsenal again began slowly at Southampton and Charlie Austin opened the scoring after three minutes. Giroud, who had not started a league game all season, came on and headed an 88th-minute equaliser. It was the Frenchman's 17th goal as a substitute in the Premier League – equalling Man Utd super-sub Ole Gunnar Solskjær for the most for one team. A goalless draw with West Ham was followed by a brilliant Özil volley that secured a 1-0 win against Newcastle.

Just before Christmas, Arsenal and Liverpool played out another basketball-style game heavy on goalmouth action and light on goalkeeping and defending. Xhaka decided to stop tracking Philippe Coutinho when he reached the six-yard box, allowing the Brazilian to head the opener. Mohamed Salah curled a second, but Arsenal responded immediately with three goals in five minutes – a Sánchez header, a swerving Xhaka 25-yarder and an Özil Chop – to get the Emirates rocking for one of

the rare times in the season. Petr Čech could only parry Roberto Firmino's shot into the net and a pulsating night ended in a 3-3 draw.

Sánchez scored his last two Arsenal goals in a 3-2 win at Crystal Palace. Arsenal started 2018 in fifth place and with another end-to-end thriller at the Emirates, this time against Chelsea. Wilshere smashed the opener – his first in 43 league games – but Eden Hazard scored a penalty and Marcos Alonso gave the away side the lead. Bellerín hit an excellent 92nd-minute half-volley to make it 2-2, although there was still time for Čech to save another Álvaro Morata one-on-one and Davide Zappacosta to rattle the crossbar with the rebound.

There was no FA Cup respite this year as Arsenal were humiliated 4-2 in the third round by manager-less and struggling Championship side Nottingham Forest, who had one win in seven games. Arsenal played a weakened team but there were no excuses for the tame display. Except for Alex Iwobi, who was later revealed to have been partying into the early hours before the game. More concerning was Iwobi's Gervinho-esque shooting ability – his regular failure to strike the ball cleanly was disconcerting for an attacking footballer who had been training with a professional club since the age of eight. Iwobi's quick feet and ball carrying gave Arsenal something different – it was a shame he could not match it with end-product.

There was a chance that cup redemption would come this year in the League Cup as Arsenal earnt a solid goalless draw at Chelsea in the semi-final first leg (where Iwobi started despite his weekend indiscretions, a sign of the comfortable culture at the club). In the second leg, Hazard gave Chelsea an early lead before Nacho Monreal's header was deflected in off Antonio Rüdiger's head. In the second half, Rüdiger again diverted the ball inadvertently, this time for Xhaka to poach the winner.

Arsenal's away form in the league got even worse in 2018 as they lost 2-1 to Bournemouth and 3-1 to Swansea, both games where Arsenal took the lead but Petr Čech and his defenders made bad mistakes. Wenger was at a loss trying to explain Arsenal's chaotic defence: "We were 1-0 up and suddenly we lost two goals and we don't know where they came from," and "I felt defensively we were very poor and made big mistakes. It's better not to talk about the second or third goals."

Despite several games where he bailed his teammates out, Čech was past his best when Arsenal signed him and he failed to answer the club's ten-year search for a quality goalkeeper. He led the league for individual errors leading to goals in 2017/18 at six, a stat that Arsenal dominated towards the end of Stage Three Wenger. Arsenal's ability to shoot themselves in the foot was unsurpassed as Xhaka conceded five penalties and made seven other errors that led to goals in his first three seasons in the Premier League, both unwanted league-high figures. Not far behind was Mustafi, who regularly had a solid game before an unfathomable Sunday League moment – Emmanuel Petit labelled him "the king of blunders."

The January transfer window was busy with the behind-the-scenes hires made following Gazidis' "catalyst for change" comment looking to make a mark and Arsenal needing to recoup something for Sánchez before his contract expired at the end of the season. After turning down £60m four months earlier, Arsenal accepted a £35m bid from Man City, but the deal fell through and Sánchez was swapped with Man Utd's Henrikh Mkhitaryan. Yet again Arsenal compounded a mistake with an even worse decision – taking Mkhitaryan, who had shown good moments but not set the world alight in his 18 months in the Premier League, and then not even receiving any compensation for their far-superior player.

Sánchez had experienced his worst spell at Arsenal in the previous few months, showing frustration with his teammates, trying to do too much and losing the ball regularly. The sight

of him crouching and looking around wondering where it all went wrong after another loss became increasingly regular. Defenders had also cottoned on to his cut-inside-from-the-right-and-shoot trick. However, he still scored regularly and never stopped trying, and Arsenal had again lost a quality player due to their failure to compete.

Arsenal bought goal-machine Pierre-Emerick Aubameyang from Borussia Dortmund, breaking their transfer record for the second time in six months, while Özil finally signed a three-and-a-half-year deal for a huge £350,000/week, triple that of almost all his teammates and making him one of the highest-paid players in the world. It was another huge contract blunder by a club operating a "self-sustaining business model" as such a rate was not justified by his performances and declining output and caused inevitable problems in subsequent contract negotiations, most noticeably with Ramsey. Özil was one of the most polarising players in football – a regular whipping boy for the "show some passion" British pundits who did not like his laid-back body language, but an idol for millions around the world quick to quote the World Cup winner's stellar assist stats.

The supremely-talented Özil regularly created multiple chances, especially in home games against mid- and lower-table teams, but often failed to affect big games and was not a player to carry a team on his shoulders. An attacking player of his ability should have influenced games more often and scored 12-15 goals a year, but his lack of drive to get into the box, casual finishing technique and preference to pass rather than shoot meant he hit double figures only once in seven years. In 2017/18, he only scored five goals, fewer than left-back Monreal.

Giroud and Walcott were sold to balance the books – the Frenchman needed game time before the 2018 World Cup, while Walcott needed a new challenge. Giroud won the World Cup with France despite not having a shot on target in the tournament; however, his hold-up play helped maximise the talents of his speedy and tricky teammates. He soon came back to haunt Arsenal, scoring for Chelsea in the 2018/19 Europa League Final.

The Everton game at the start of February was something of a fresh start with Aubameyang (one goal) and Mkhitaryan (three assists) making positive debuts, and Ramsey scoring a hat-trick. However, Arsenal lost 1-0 to Spurs at Wembley in front of a Premier League record crowd of 83,222 as Kane soared above Koscielny to head his usual North London derby goal. Spurs should have been out of sight, but missed chances and Čech saves kept Arsenal in it. Mkhitaryan had a nightmare, miscontrolling and shanking crosses. His replacement Lacazette had two chances to equalise at the end, but his recent poor form continued and he missed the target both times.

This was followed by the League Cup Final loss to Man City, where Arsenal gave away a terrible first goal, with Mustafi the wrong side of Agüero, and never seemed to believe they could come back. It was a 3-0 cruise for Man City and a third League Cup Final loss for Wenger. It meant he failed to join George Graham and eight other managers with the full set of domestic trophies. Even the officials were sledging Wenger now – when he complained about the lack of injury time, fourth official Graham Scott said, "Why do you want more time?"

Four nights later, the same teams lined up at the Emirates and the snow was so bad that the lines on the pitch were painted blue. The weather and Arsenal's League Cup Final performance meant there were thousands of empty seats.

Man City scored three in 33 minutes, Aubameyang had a penalty saved and it ended with the same 3-0 scoreline.

The season drifted on with a predictable pattern of comfortable home wins (Watford, Stoke, Southampton, West Ham) and insipid away losses (Brighton, Newcastle, Man Utd, Leicester), making it an embarrassing seven away defeats in a row from January to May 2018. The mocking chant "Arsène Wenger, we want you to stay" was sung with increasing regularity by opposition fans. One satisfying moment for Arsenal fans came in the 3-0 win against Watford where Čech saved 'cojones critic' Deeney's spot-kick, Čech's first Arsenal penalty save at the 16th attempt.

While any penalty save is a bonus, Čech's efforts had become the subject of mockery. He consistently made a big early dive to one corner while the taker knowingly stroked the ball down the middle into the gap left. In an age where every game and moment are available on video, it was brainless not to at least once wait for the kick to be taken and react accordingly. And another small example of the no-changing, no-improving mentality at the club. It gave Arsenal their first clean sheet in 12 games.

On 20 April 2018, Wenger announced he would step down at the end of the season. It had to happen, but it still came as a shock – after all, he had been manager for 22 years. He had to go, not because Arsenal had not won the league (neither had Liverpool for 18 years or Man Utd for five) but because they were not competing for it, they were going backwards, he could no longer motivate the players to perform week in week out (as shown by the away results) and he had not shown any willingness to change approach.

It was hard to watch an intelligent man and legendary manager doing the same thing over and over and expecting a different result. Why did he not address Arsenal's clear issues or assign someone (assistant manager Steve Bould, a tough defender who played under Graham in the Famous Back Four, for example) to drill the defence? Arsenal's goals against in Wenger's last two years soared and clean sheets were rare, putting pressure on the team to score two, three or four goals to win a game. Arsenal's goals scored tally was decent, often beating mid-table or lower teams at home comfortably. However, they struggled against tight defences due to their slow build-up, repetitive sideways passing and lack of width – most noticeably in the Europa League games against Atlético Madrid.

No manager could avoid repeating their training sessions or team talks after 22 years. Players become bored with the same routine and advice every day. Alex Ferguson showed a unique ability to reinvent his Man Utd

NO DEFENCE

Arsenal conceded 44 and 51 league goals in Wenger's last two seasons, separated only by 2011/12's 49 as his worst seasons defensively. His final season saw Arsenal's highest goals against since 1983/84. They gave away ten penalties in 2016/17, the most they have ever conceded in the Premier League, and six in 2017/18.

derided for continuing to announce high attendances, based on tickets sold, but the number of empty seats at home games was plain to see.

The season was now all about winning the Europa League, which offered the reward of a place in the Champions League and the chance for Wenger to break his European trophy drought. Arsenal beat Östersunds 3-0 on their plastic pitch in Sweden as Ospina saved a penalty, but were complacent and conceded two goals in 70 seconds at the Emirates to spark fears of an embarrassing comeback. Kolašinac volleyed in just after half-time to secure a 4-2 aggregate win, but the home fans booed at both half- and full-time.

In the next round, while AC Milan were far from the force of old, Arsenal turned around their poor away form with a strong performance and clean sheet in the first leg in the San Siro – a 2-0 win saw goals from Mkhitaryan and Ramsey. Milan took the lead at the Emirates, but Welbeck scored twice in a 3-1 win.

In the quarter-final, Arsenal again did the damage in the first leg at CSKA Moscow as Ramsey and Lacazette scored braces in a 26-minute first-half blitz. The highlight was Ramsey's brilliant volley with the outside of his foot to flick Özil's chip over the goalkeeper. There was another second-

team multiple times over his 26 years, but unlike Wenger he was willing to delegate and rotate coaches.

Arsenal had backed the manager for five years in Stage Three with hefty transfer outlays and a huge wage bill, but Wenger was no longer getting the best out of the club's resources, signing the wrong players and unable to mould them into a competitive squad.

In the end, it did not seem to be the protests, banners or YouTube rants that provoked change, but the apathy – fans just stopped turning up in large numbers (even though most had already paid for the matches through their season tickets). An ever-increasing number had moved on from the denial and anger phases of grieving for Stage One Wenger into the depression and acceptance phases. The club was

leg comeback scare when CSKA scored twice in Moscow. Arsenal did not have an effort on target for 70 minutes, but Elneny channelled his inner Fàbregas with a perfectly-weighted through-ball for Welbeck to curl in. Ramsey dinked a one-on-one late on to make it 2-2 on the night and 6-3 on aggregate.

In the semi-final, Arsenal were no match for the well-drilled Atlético Madrid, a team who knew how to get the job done. With the gift of defender Sime Vrsaljko being sent off for a second yellow card after only ten minutes in the first leg, Arsenal eventually made a breakthrough with a good Lacazette header on 60 minutes. Madrid were pinned back around their own box, but Arsenal failed to ram home the advantage – continuing to look for intricate one-twos, rarely shooting, playing narrow and when they did cross no one attacked the ball.

In the 82nd minute, Griezmann capitalised on poor positioning from Koscielny and Mustafi. Koscielny compounded the situation by, instead of hoofing the ball into row Z, trying to keep it in play with an overhead kick, but only managing to kick it into his own face and leave Griezmann in on goal. To add to the slapstick, Ospina saved the first effort and Mustafi slipped as he tried to block the follow-up. A huge away-goal blow that Arsenal never looked like reversing in the second leg (where Koscielny sadly tore his Achilles to put him out of the

2018 World Cup) as they went out with a whimper. Former Chelsea nemesis Diego Costa scored the only goal with Bellerín well out of position.

All that was left were the Merci Arsène tributes. Ferguson did a nice presentation at Old Trafford while the club, players and crowd gave Arsenal's longest-serving and most successful manager a great send-off with a 5-0 hammering of Burnley in his last home game, and he was presented with the gold Premier League trophy given to the Invincibles in 2004.

Wenger's last (and 1,235th) game came at Huddersfield, who had been partying after securing safety midweek, and Arsenal won 1-0 to avoid the ignominy of no away points in 2018. Aubameyang took his tally to an impressive ten goals in 12 starts since his January move.

Arsenal ended up sixth, 12 points off the top four and 37 points behind runaway champions Man City, Wenger's worst season by far. As well as suffering away from home, they also struggled against the rest of the top six, with just one win, three draws and six defeats placing them at the bottom of the mini-table. They went deep in the Europa League and League Cup, but neither runs were particularly inspiring and this time there was no cup win to distract from the underlying trend. The lack of players going to the World Cup was a notable reflection of the fall in status – eight versus 10-15 in the previous four competitions; Spurs had nine in the semi-finals alone.

So that was it. A low-key and sad ending for Arsenal's longest-serving and most successful manager, who was forced to leave against his wishes. 21 years and 224 days, 1,235 games (not one of which Wenger missed), 2,298 goals, a 57% win rate, three league titles, seven FA Cups, two Doubles and one Invincibles season. But no European trophy or back-to-back titles. No more clever philosophical musings or witty retorts, no more frustrating "the spirit was good" or "handbrake off" mitigations for his players, no more double-fist-pump celebrations or coat zip problems on the touchlines, no more high fives with Gunnersaurus, no more Wengerball.

NOTES & GLOSSARY

- All statistics and records are correct as of the start of the 2020/21 season.

- Arsenal players of the year are the author's view so in some years differ from the winner of the Arsenal Supporters Club or arsenal.com vote at the time.

- For Players in and Players out, those shown in italics moved during the mid-season winter transfer window or, for pre-2002/03 when the current two-window system was introduced, once the season was well underway. The others moved in the summer transfer window or pre-season. For loan deals, only long-term moves of first-team players are shown.

- Transfer fees are generally not disclosed by the clubs and therefore the figures reported in the media often vary widely, also due to the exchange rate used and the inclusion or not of performance-related add-ons (for example, Arsenal reportedly paid anywhere between £25m and £40m for Granit Xhaka). This book uses the most regularly-quoted fees where there are discrepancies and includes any add-ons subsequently paid or received.

- During the period covered, the League Cup was known as the Coca-Cola Cup, Worthington Cup, Carling Cup, Capital One Cup, EFL Cup and Carabao Cup. This book refers to it as the League Cup throughout.

- The Community Shield was called the Charity Shield until 2002. This book refers to it as the Community Shield throughout.

- St Totteringham's Day is the day when it is mathematically impossible for Spurs to catch Arsenal in the league.

- PL – Premier League; FA – FA Cup; LC – League Cup; CS – Community Shield; CL – Champions League; EL – Europa League.

- PFA – The Professional Footballers' Association.

- FWA – The Football Writers' Association.

- Vaccinate – Term used by Diego Maradona to score a goal or get the better of an opponent to a humiliating degree.

SOURCES

Books

Paolo Di Canio, *Paolo Di Canio: The Autobiography* (Willow, 2001)

Tony Adams, *Addicted* (Collins Willow, 1998)

Ashley Cole, *My Defence* (Headline, 2006)

Diego Maradona, *El Diego: The Autobiography of the World's Greatest Footballer* (Yellow Jersey, 2000)

Nicklas Bendtner, *Both Sides* (Monoray, 2020)

Jens Lehmann, *The Madness is on the Pitch* (deCoubertin Books, 2018)

TV

Keane and Vieira: Best of Enemies (ITV, 2013)

The Feud – Ferguson vs Wenger (Channel 5, 2018)

Websites

www.arseblog.com; www.arsenal.com; www.arsenalreport.com; www.arseweb.com; www.bbc.com; www.chiark.greenend.org.uk/~mikepitt/totteringham.html; www.football-lineups.com; www.guardian.co.uk; www.independent.co.uk; www.lequipe.fr; www.premierleague.com; www.thearsenalhistory.com; www.thetimes.co.uk; www.transferleague.co.uk; www.transfermarkt.com; www.whoscored.com; www.wikipedia.com; www.youtube.com

News reports

The floodlights went out and an Asian betting syndicate raked in a fortune, *The Independent* (August 2010)

I Had To Leave Gunners – Sylvinho, Sky Sports (September 2001)

Sylvinho takes the Spanish steps and makes Arsenal pay, *Daily Mail* (13 September 2009)

The inside story of Sol's move to Arsenal, arsenal.com (3 July 2018)

Ex-Arsenal star claims Invincibles were honeytrapped before Champions League tie, *Daily Mirror* (28 November 2019)

Ljungberg infected by his tattoos, *Evening Standard* (20 May 2005)

Reyes tricked into Real admission, BBC (11 February 2005)

Spain coach in mire over Henry jibe, *The Guardian* (7 October 2004)

JAMIE CARRAGHER: Luiz Suarez and Eric Cantona were both better players than Didier Drogba but..., *Daily Mail* (11 October 2014)

Kolo Touré reveals depth of feud with William Gallas at Arsenal, *The Guardian* (24 April 2010)

'Outcast' Lehmann blasts Wenger, BBC (April 2008)

'Humiliated' Lehmann blasts' dear manager' Wenger after latest snub, *Daily Mail* (24 October 2007)

Almunia comes to terms with Lehmann's 'hate', *The Guardian* (12 April 2008)

Arsenal old-boy Armand Traore: I took a KNUCKLE-DUSTER to the north London derby and ended up behind bars, Daily Mirror (14 October 2017)

Alexander Hleb reveals regret at leaving Arsène Wenger and Arsenal, *The Guardian* (13 August 2009)

Wenger: Why I snubbed Barry & Alonso, *FourFourTwo* (19 October 2009)

Bendtner off the scale in confidence test, ESPN (5 February 2011)

William Gallas feared former teammate Samir Nasri planned to have him tasered, *The Independent* (21 November 2016)

The Arsecast: Episode 570 – Cesc Fàbregas, *arseblog* (24 March 2020)

Squillaci: 'Fight for the Club', beIN Sports (14 April 2016)

Champions League key for Arsenal manager Arsène Wenger, BBC (25 October 2012)

Arsenal chief Ivan Gazidis Q&A: 'We are beginning to see the escalation in our financial firepower', *Daily Mirror* (6 June 2013)

Kim Källström – In My Own Words, arsenal.com (12 April 2020)

Kim Källström On 'The Greatest Fifteen Minutes Of My Life', *arseblog* (29 July 2016)

Moving home gives Wenger €100m to spend – if only he wanted to..., *The Irish Independent* (25 September 2007)

Former Arsenal hero slams club's new 'king of blunders', *Football365* (5 March 2019)

The making of Cagigao, the man who found Fàbregas, Martinelli and Bellerín, *The Athletic* (9 April 2020)

Transfer über Bremen: Wie Gnabry zum Super-Schnäppchen wurde, *Sport Bild* (16 October 2010)

Sport Bild: How Bayern Munich pulled a fast one on Arsenal, landing Serge Gnabry basically for free, *SB Nation* (17 October 2019)

Former Arsenal misfit Andre Santos launches blast at club's culture and lack of ambition, *Daily Mirror* (27 November 2019)

Petr Čech interview: Arsenal struggle under pressure? The bigger the occasion, the better we get!, *Evening Standard* (28 March 2019)

Juventus keeper Wojciech Szczęsny: I never improved while at Arsenal, *ESPN* (17 October 2017)

INDEX

Lightning Source UK Ltd.
Milton Keynes UK
UKHW050215180521
383875UK00003B/112